Diplomacy
for a Crowded World

ALSO BY GEORGE W. BALL

The Discipline of Power

GEORGE W. BALL

Diplomacy for a Crowded World

An American Foreign Policy

AN ATLANTIC MONTHLY PRESS BOOK
LITTLE, BROWN AND COMPANY • BOSTON • TORONTO

FIRST EDITION

T06/76

A portion of this book originally appeared in *The Atlantic Monthly*. Chapter 4 appeared in *The New York Times Magazine*, April 1, 1973, as "The Lessons of Vietnam: Have We Learned or Only Failed?" © 1973 by The New York Times Company. Reprinted by permission.

LIBRARY OF CONGRESS CATALOGING IN PUBLICATION DATA

Ball, George W
    Diplomacy for a crowded world.

    "An Atlantic Monthly Press book."
    Includes bibliographical references and index.
    1. United States — Foreign relations — 1945–
2. United States — Foreign relations administration.
I. Title.
JX1417.B34   327.73   76-6928
ISBN 0-316-07953-7

ATLANTIC-LITTLE, BROWN BOOKS
ARE PUBLISHED BY
LITTLE, BROWN AND COMPANY
IN ASSOCIATION WITH
THE ATLANTIC MONTHLY PRESS

Designed by Susan Windheim

Published simultaneously in Canada
by Little, Brown & Company (Canada) Limited

PRINTED IN THE UNITED STATES OF AMERICA

To the memory of my father, Amos Ball,
who foresaw the implications of a
crowded world long before the
rest of us

Preface

This book is divided into five parts. In Part I, I discuss the substance and practice of American foreign policy during the Nixon Administration and the months that followed when Henry Kissinger was effectively in command of American diplomacy. Those years were largely devoted to correcting aberrations in past policy, but, in the process, new aberrations developed. It is those new aberrations and their consequences that are discussed in Part II, while in Part III I suggest how we should revise our diplomatic methods, restore the effectiveness of the State Department, redesign our intelligence operations and improve the relations between Congress and the Executive Branch in foreign policy matters.

In Part IV, I try to look ahead at the shape and problems of the evolving world, taking account particularly of some of the emerging dangers from poverty, discontent, and excessive population growth. Finally, in Part V, I suggest the directions we should take to cope with the problems of a crowded world.

New York City
March 5, 1976

Acknowledgments

IT IS IMPOSSIBLE TO WRITE A BOOK OF SUSTAINED ARGUMENT while pursuing an active professional career without shamelessly imposing on one's friends.

In preparing Chapter 13, I was greatly aided by the advice and suggestions of Philander Claxton, Jr., who has done more than almost any other individual to inject a recognition of the population problem into the shaping of American foreign policy. Mrs. Anne W. Marks piloted me with subtlety and wisdom through the complexities of nuclear proliferation, which I discuss in Chapter 14. And I am greatly indebted to both Dr. Ray S. Cline and Peter Jessup for their advice and criticism with regard to Chapter 12.

Many others have helped, particularly my son Dr. Douglas B. Ball, whose comprehensive knowledge of history provided many insights and who saved me not only from long hours of research but from *gaffes* I could never have lived down. My son John C. Ball was also helpful in clarifying some aspects of the Middle East problem and assisting in organizing the book.

Professor Richard N. Gardner of Columbia University generously provided me with material on our economic relations with the Third World, and I borrowed ideas from his speeches and writings. Kermit Lansner very kindly read and criticized parts of the manuscript in its early stages.

Chapters 12, 16, and 17 bear a not coincidental resemblance to lectures I gave late last year at the University of Pittsburgh, while Chapter 8 draws heavily on the Mike Mansfield Lecture I delivered at the University of Montana. I am grateful to those distinguished institutions for condoning such flagrant acts of self-plagiarism.

I owe a special gratitude to Joseph E. Slater and the Aspen Institute for providing me the chance to clarify my turgid thoughts in the pure mountain air of Colorado.

My stern, demanding editor, Robert Manning, and his colleagues at *The Atlantic Monthly* relentlessly simplified my most elegant prose for the benefit of both clarity and brevity, while denying America some stirring homilies that would have saved no souls. For this contribution to public sanity they have my thanks.

Finally a particular word for Helen Vahey, who valiantly endured my penchant for multiple redrafting and combined forbearance and endurance in the preparation of the manuscript. Peggy Jones helped in collecting material and curbing my avidity for misquotation, while Gwendolyn Selsor, as well as Adrianne Wortzel, goodnaturedly coped with my semilegible scribblings and interlineations.

Contents

PART I

Cleaning Up Past Aberrations

CHAPTER 1

Unilateralism
and the Master Player

IN JANUARY 1961, WHEN I BECAME UNDER SECRETARY OF STATE, my chief, Dean Rusk, said to me, "You and I are going to have a miserable life. Almost everything that happens in the world touches United States interests, and, since at any moment of the day or night two-thirds of the world is awake, someone somewhere will be committing some outrage to cause you and me trouble." The Secretary was accurately predicting the problems we would face. Hardly a week went by in the next six years that one of the four telephones by my bed did not ring sometime in the night, requiring an instant response and often prompt and frequently complicated action.

Yet much of what we did was still a holding operation, for the 1960s were an ice age, with nations frozen in fixed political attitudes like an old-fashioned *tableau vivant*. Quite coincidentally — for there was no causal connection — the ice began to melt just about the time the Nixon Administration came to power.

Although during the 1960s forces of change had been at work beneath the surface, the outward signs of immobilism were almost universal. Throughout most of the decade the Soviet Union scowled and muttered at the rest of the world in almost a caricature of Slavic sullenness and bad manners. Challenging America

by threatening Berlin, a hostage deep within its grasp, it revealed
its insecurity by building a wall to encage seventeen million restless captives, tantalized by the freedom and higher living standards of the West. It sent troops and tanks into Warsaw, Budapest,
and, finally, into Prague, to maintain its hold over its Eastern European empire, while, at the same time, exploiting every chance to
extend its power and influence throughout the world.

Yet, after the Kremlin's leaders had come face-to-face —
"eyeball-to-eyeball" — with nuclear realities during the Cuban
missile crisis of October 1962, and after the boisterous Khrushchev had given way to the colorless Brezhnev and Kosygin, Soviet manners outwardly mellowed. Preoccupied with China and
urgently needing Western technology to improve its inherently
inefficient industrial machine, the Soviets sought easier relations
with the West and particularly with the United States, which
alone commanded the power they understood and respected.

Meanwhile, south of the long Siberian border, China suffered
a volcanic eruption called the Cultural Revolution and, although it
still treated other nations with that disdain for barbarians inherited from the Middle Kingdom, seismic echoes of the cata-
clysm were detected in the outside world — largely through travelers' tales and cryptic items in the regional press interpreted by
professional entrail-readers known as sinologists. Isolated since
the Korean War, it sulked offstage. Though its name appeared in
large type in the *dramatis personae* of the world drama and it was
frequently referred to by the other actors, it still hung coyly in the
wings. Yet, beginning in about 1969, the noises emanating from
Peking became increasingly less shrill and hysterical. With power
transferred through mysterious Chinese mechanisms to more moderate leaders headed by Chou En-lai and with the Soviet threat intensified by a border clash on the Ussuri River, China prepared to
make its entrance into the world arena. The gate to Peking was
unlatched, ready to be opened at a slight American push.

Japan, for quite different reasons, had survived and prospered
throughout the sixties by abjuring all political initiatives. Accepting political and military dependence on the United States, it
was able to focus on the worldwide expansion of its economic and
commercial interests. Yet, toward the end of the decade, there
were growing signs of internal restlessness at the constraints im-

posed by its American ties — particularly on its relations with Peking.

Throughout the latter sixties Western Europe had also seemed on dead center. The drive toward unity at the beginning of the decade had been abruptly halted by a domineering leader in France, while, blackballed from membership in the European club and progressively relinquishing its worldwide responsibilities, Britain withdrew to a corner of the stage. But after General de Gaulle had finally stalked to the wings in April 1969, Britain realized even more sharply that an island nation without an empire had only limited power or influence — a circumstance her continued exclusion from Europe made especially poignant.

If some areas of the world seemed immobilized by apathy, the Middle East was boiling over with conflict and hatred. With Nasser inviting a swelling number of Soviet "advisors" with tanks, planes, ships, and rockets into Egypt, Israel struck out in what she claimed to be a necessary protective action that extended her territorial hold all the way across the Sinai, over the Golan Heights, and into Old Jerusalem and the West Bank of the Jordan — where she then dug in.

Across the Atlantic, America, the only nation with the political and economic clout to take significant initiatives, was paralyzed by an irrelevant and seemingly endless war. Peking's continued supply of the North Vietnamese stifled every move toward China. Although Russia's role in Vietnam also inhibited President Johnson's efforts to improve relations with the Kremlin, he made perceptible progress until his plans to visit Moscow in the fall of 1968 were cut short by the Soviet frost that blighted the brief, sweet springtime of Prague.

Yet, although that was a serious setback, he had already taken a major action to free American policy eight months before the election of President Nixon. Johnson's announcement on March 31, 1968, that he would not run for another term, would halt the bombing north of the twentieth parallel, would send no new forces to South Vietnam, and would try to achieve a cease-fire marked the beginning of the end of the United States involvement in the Vietnam War. The 1968 elections were a vote not so much for Richard Nixon as for a leader who promised to extricate us from that beleaguered land as promptly as possible.

Taking power at the beginning of 1969, the new Administration had a golden opportunity to redefine American foreign policy — and it moved wisely in several areas. Yet its response was uneven, displaying both the short-term advantages and the long-range costs of an egocentric approach. Though it exploited some openings, it fumbled others and created unnecessary problems in several critical areas of the world. The process by which it sought to disengage the United States from Vietnam was clumsy, insensitive, excessively protracted, and exorbitantly costly. Its opening of communications with China — a long overdue move — was theatrical and gratuitously harmful to our other relationships, just as its efforts to improve the dialogue with the Soviet Union were conducted with too little attention to their effect on our fundamental alliance relations with Western Europe and Japan.

Nevertheless, the Administration deserves credit in certain key areas of policy. Although it did little to organize the collective efforts of mankind to deal with the dangers from natural forces, its performance was no worse than that of its predecessors.

If I describe its initiatives as limited, it is because they were directed almost exclusively at eliminating accumulated problems of the past. In spite of vainglorious talk, little was done to construct what was boastfully called "a structure of peace."

The major diplomatic moves of the Nixon Administration fell into three general categories.

First, it sought to correct two aberrations of existing American policy — our involvement in Vietnam and our lack of communications with China.

Second, it took advantage of the Soviet Union's tactical decision to adopt a less bellicose attitude toward the West by encouraging a mutual improvement in manners ambiguously called *détente,* which led to understandings in limited areas of direct bilateral relations.

Third, it undertook diplomatic efforts to buy time in the Middle East.

It is hard to find a single word or phrase or figure of speech to describe the Nixon Administration's diplomatic activities. They were directed largely at correcting past mistakes, sweeping up, setting things right as prelude to some more affirmative step. If one has a taste for using French words such as *détente* in a diplomatic context, one might also borrow the word *assainissement*, which comprehends many shades of meaning: the draining of a swamp, the sweetening of the soil, the reorganization of finances — in short, a cleansing operation.

But, whatever the proper word, the results were plain enough. Exploiting a conjunction of events that for the first time made action possible, the Nixon Administration swept away some of the detritus of irrelevant and obsolete policy. As in a bombed-out city, where ruined buildings once stood, empty lots bore signs announcing new construction in the indefinite future. Since plans for such new structures have not yet been disclosed — or even leaked to a vigilant press — the skeptical might reasonably question whether such announcements were more than Madison Avenue puffery.

Yet, in spite of the fact that there was no clear conception of its much talked about "structure of peace," the Nixon Administration unquestionably left its imprint on American foreign policy. As benchmarks for the changes it made, consider our relations with other nations in the decades prior to 1969 when the new President was inaugurated.

During the 1920s and 1930s our country practiced an insidious form of self-deception called "isolationism." Selfish in motivation, it was overlaid with sanctimony; for, though scornful of the cynical politics of Europe, we did not hesitate to impose our will on weak nations in the Caribbean or to use our gunboats as an instrument of policy in Asian waters. We cannot be proud of our isolationist period; it was a cheap excuse for enriching ourselves while avoiding international responsibility — a doctrine quite unworthy of a powerful, responsible nation capable of epic achievements.

Not until the Second World War had pounded home the unlearned lesson of the First, did we comprehend the predicament created by our power and interests. To stand aloof was the height of folly; for, if we continued to leave world politics to the Europeans, we would inevitably be drawn into quarrels resulting from their ambitions or ideologies or ancient rivalries. Yet, in shaping a policy for a new role in world affairs, we had only a limited range of choice.

During the brief season when we possessed a monopoly of

atomic weapons, one option — more illusory than real — was to rely unaided on our own strength, threatening the Soviet Union and any other nation that might try to extend its power by force. But, although congenial to our isolationist traditions, that was not a policy appropriate for America, and the people understood it. Thus, rather than posing as the sole protector of the West, we chose to organize defense on a collective basis, forging a treaty of alliance that evolved into an elaborate system of collective security. Although the Russians were now the adversary rather than the Nazis as in World War II, the West's imperative remained the same: to build a solid wall of strength to prevent an aggressive westward push. We were buying time, seeking to maintain a precarious power balance until time and changing circumstance could blunt the dangerous edges of the conflict with the Soviet Union.

Led by a self-confident America, the Europeans did more than merely follow. Confounding the skeptics, they created the European Economic Community, moving farther along the road to unity than most Americans thought possible, particularly in commercial and economic policy, and we wisely encouraged those efforts.

Meanwhile, since the life-force of an alliance is mutual confidence, we tried to follow consistent and predictable policies, altering course only after consulting our partners. Together we resisted Soviet pressures on Berlin and tests of strength and will in other parts of the world. Except for the Suez affair in 1956, we concerted our actions with great effectiveness until, in the middle 1960s, the conflict in Vietnam absorbed more and more attention, put everyone's nerves on edge, and alienated us from friends all over the world.

The mandate given President Nixon in 1968, to get us out of Vietnam, was thus well designed to restore and develop our alliance ties — and particularly those with Western Europe. But the new President's objectives were quite different. Neither he nor his principal advisor, Henry A. Kissinger, wished to reinstate, as central strategy, the policy of alliances that had furnished the hard substructure of our position since World War II. Instead, they chose to play a lone game, preferring to move and shake other nations by the lever of our political and economic power, while seeking to gain maximum freedom of maneuver.

The first signal of this new strategy was some muddy rhetoric the White House christened with unseemly haste the "Nixon Doctrine" to make sure that future historians would not call it something else. That pronouncement was widely advertised as a design for shrinking American commitments to dimensions more nearly in accord with our capabilities. But, as subsequent events have shown, its inarticulate purpose was quite different. Instead of limiting the worldwide range of our activities, the objective was to increase America's reach, not by consolidating our strength with that of other like-minded nations but by increasing our freedom of action through the stripping off of irksome obligations to consult and act collectively. Thereafter, the Nixon Administration pursued a strategy of maneuver and manipulation, seeking to play nations off against one another, using established alliance relationships primarily to increase United States leverage.

The concept underlying such a strategy was Ptolemaic, pre-Copernican; it perceived the United States as the center of the cosmos with other nations in orbit around it. Rejecting the fiction of equality that would require us to factor the views of our allies into common decisions, we would expect our allies to follow our lead without grumbling while we measured their value to us by the degree to which they uncritically supported our actions. We would try, in the terms of an historical parallel, to convert the Delian League into the Athenian Empire.

Thus, by deed if not by rhetoric, the Nixon Administration adopted the line of policy which America had rejected in 1945 — to keep other nations responsive to our will, to avoid the partnership implications of an alliance policy, and to maintain supremacy by setting one nation off against another. It was a policy congenial to both Nixon and Kissinger, for, though poles apart in interests and intellectual competence, they shared common tendencies of mind and temperament. Both were by nature withdrawn and secretive — essentially lone operators. Both were fascinated by the manipulation of power.

By a succession of accidents and coincidences, they found a state of affairs propitious for their line of policy, in part because the conspiratorial nature of the Communist enemy legitimized a covert American response. The taste for the clandestine had been encouraged by the furtive atmosphere of the Vietnam War; the more unpopular the war became the more the Government enveloped its sordid aspects in a cloud of secrecy intended more to conceal events from the American public than from the enemy. Exaggerated even in the narrow context of military action, the devices of concealment undermined public confidence while setting an evil pattern for successor governments. Thus, it was only natural that key figures in the Byzantine Nixon court should cite precedents from the late 1960s not only to justify their own dark practices but to distort them to the level of a pervasive obsession.

Yet it would be absurd to contend — as some academics have done — that all Kissinger and Nixon did was to carry an established trend to its logical conclusion. For a while at least, it was voguish to argue that, under the conditions of modern society, foreign policy had to be tightly controlled by the President and his White House staff — that it had to be wrapped in a thick curtain of mystery and conducted by a diplomatic Bobby Fischer, a Master Player, who could keep the world dazzled and off balance by an endless succession of unpredictable moves.

As the President's Foreign Policy Advisor, Kissinger quite easily filled the Bobby Fischer role. A man of drive, competence, and enormous energy and ambition, he would have instinctively sought to build a power base no matter what his initial assignment. I at one time thought that, had he been Secretary of State from the outset of the Nixon Administration, he might have avoided some of the anomalies and idiosyncrasies in American policy that resulted from his having to work from the side. But I now doubt that the result would have been much different, unless — and that is an interesting speculation — a strong and able competitor had been given the post of the President's National Security Advisor with an office in the White House. It is significant that when Kissinger finally moved to the State Department he insisted on retaining his White House title, freely acknowledging that, were he to let Nixon appoint even a mediocre figure as National Security Advisor, his own position would be jeopardized; within a few weeks, the President would be consulting that man rather than Kissinger simply because he was physically at hand. There is an old bureaucratic adage that "nothing propinks like propinquity" and with the Oval Office accessible only to the few, it became an iron law.

As the only President in our history who regarded the entire government as his enemy, Nixon preferred courtiers to the nobles who ran the great departments, even though he had himself conferred their titles of nobility. Later, as a result of the redoubt psychology that developed during his catastrophic second term, anyone not a member of the court came to be distrusted, while even a courtier had to keep his sword at the ready and his back to the wall. As the President so aptly put it, "Nobody is our friend."

Though Professor Kissinger clearly found such intrigue repellent for its crudeness and viciousness, he built his own defenses and made his own adjustment. As Woodrow Wilson had pointed out long before, the virulent politics of a university campus more than prepared one for the worst practices of Washington, and besides, Henry Kissinger was temperamentally equipped for the game of parry and evasion. By avoiding the terrain of other courtiers while resisting any trespass on his own, he established command of the whole domain of foreign political policy. To be sure, he was aided by the fact that Secretary of State William Rogers was an easygoing man with no knowledge of foreign policy and little taste for, or interest in, on-the-job training. Thus, in spite of the fact that Rogers and the President were old friends, it was easy for Kissinger to establish himself as the President's prime advisor, mobilizing a personal staff of articulate young experts whose brains he could pick without danger that they might gain personal influence in the shaping of policy.

The point to bear in mind is that the practices and policies of the Nixon-Kissinger era accurately reflected the instincts and habits of mind of the two men. In spite of the obvious contrast in their style and thought processes, they shared from the beginning an affinity for highly personalized diplomacy. Nixon's instincts were those of a professional politician, a political fixer, who believed that backroom deals could be made if the boys got together — or, in other words, if there were personal meetings between heads of state or chiefs of governments, in which he could be the center of world attention. He was, as Viscount Haldane once said of Lloyd George, a man who thought "in images, not in concepts." Committed to the cult of personality, he used the first person singular in speeches more often than any other President, and he had that kind of a sense of history of which Dean Acheson was particularly contemptuous. To Acheson, "a sense of history" could be "a dangerous weakness in a public man" since, as the phrase was used by Nixon, it implied that one planned his actions "in order to appear well in a great pageant of human life reaching back into the mists and moving into the clouds." In other words, wrote Acheson, a "sense of history" was all too often "a form of concern with oneself or, in the vulgarized synonym, one's image." For that Acheson borrowed a phrase from a New Yorker cartoon by Carl Rose: "I say it's spinach and I say the hell with it." [1]

Although Kissinger was quite different from Nixon, he was similarly inclined to personal diplomacy. Trained as a professor to work by himself, he felt intellectually comfortable with the role of Master Player, since he was a diplomatic Miniver Cheevy — a nineteenth-century diplomatist in a twentieth-century world.

Their shared fondness for the secret diplomacy of the Master Player was expressed in the admiration of the two men for General de Gaulle — a figure whom both hailed as the greatest contemporary statesman. Thus it was significant — though baffling to other Europeans — that, a little more than a month after his inauguration, Mr. Nixon hurried off to France to salute General de Gaulle as the towering leader of "wisdom and vision" who "sees beyond the crisis of the moment and sees the great forces at play in the world." Even more, he invited the general's judgment as to "how the United States [could] best fill its role in helping to solve [those great] problems [that divide the world]." It was an essay in masochism, since De Gaulle had done everything possible to undercut America's world role, and even as propitiation it was wildly mistimed, since two months later the disgruntled general retired to Colombey.

Still, in the years that followed, it often appeared that President Nixon and Dr. Kissinger had taken instructions from that master prestidigitator, while failing to comprehend the unsuitability of his techniques. General de Gaulle's driving ambition had been to parlay the strength of a second-rate power into a commanding world position. Though he succeeded for a time in dominating the politics of Europe, his influence was purely negative; he succeeded only in bringing progress toward unity to a grinding halt. A victim of bad timing, he had been born too late. Had his country still been the France of Louis XIV — the most powerful in the Western World — he could have dominated not merely European but world politics.

So, splendid anachronism that he was, De Gaulle taught the wrong lesson to his American admirers. His fondness for the techniques of manipulation was, though destructive, understandable in the ambitious head of a second-rate power such as France, but totally unsuited for the President of the democracy preeminent in wealth and leadership. As adapted by Nixon and Kissinger, those techniques did not enhance the power or authority of the United States but tended, instead, to erode the structure of alliances painfully built up over the years.

Though devotees of De Gaulle in the use of secrecy, surprise, and theater, Nixon and Kissinger outdid even the general in the practice of personal diplomacy. He, at least, used the well-disciplined officers of the Quai d'Orsay — led by the shrewd and articulate Maurice Couve de Murville — with cunning and effectiveness, often preferring to let them advance his own brand of French policy through normal diplomatic channels. But Nixon entrusted all operations to a Kissinger temperamentally unable to delegate any but the most routine authority, a Kissinger who told the remarkable Italian journalist, Oriana Fallaci, in a famous tape-recorded interview, that he "always acted alone." "Americans," he said, "admire that enormously. Americans admire the cowboy leading the caravan [sic] alone astride his horse, the cowboy entering a village or city alone on his horse, without even a pistol, maybe, because he doesn't go in for shooting. He acts, that's all: aiming at the right spot at the right time." [2]

Whatever its allusive origins,* his caravan betrayed a conception of the Wild West of one who grew up in Bavaria rather than Oklahoma. Still, Signora Fallaci should have understood him. His vision of the equestrian cowboy leading the caravan (of camels?) and, though "without even a pistol . . . aiming at the right spot," recalls the solecisms of the "spaghetti Westerns" filmed in Italy.

The "lonely cowboy" — the figure who, as Kissinger explained it later,[3] "symbolizes what [American society] stands for" — was a fantasy that both fitted and reinforced the shaping of the Nixon-Kissinger strategy of maneuver. That such a strategy was tailor-made for the Master Player is evident enough; indeed,

---

* It is possible that Kissinger was confused by pictures of the caravans of dromedaries imported prior to the Civil War in an abortive attempt to help the United States army with its transportation problems across the American deserts.

secret, highly personalized diplomacy is compatible *only* with a policy of maneuver. The diplomat who insists on doing everything himself, personally making all key decisions, personally conducting all major negotiations and, in effect, shaping and administering the foreign policy of a great state without engaging the resources of its foreign office can operate effectively *only* in a bilateral context with no one looking over his shoulder. And, since he can do only one thing at a time, the state cannot pursue an effective policy of alliances which, because it requires constant communication among the members at all working levels, must necessarily be institutionalized.

But if a policy of maneuver is the only game for the Master Player, is it an appropriate policy for a democracy fully in charge of itself? Just as a policy of alliances cannot be administered without diffusion of information and a delegation of authority, so a policy of maneuver cannot be institutionalized. Its administration cannot be delegated. Secrecy is essential. The Master Player must not only keep foreign nations in the dark, awaiting his surprise moves, but he must also conceal his tactics from the State Department bureaucracy,[4] the American Congress, and, of course, the American people. A democratic system will tolerate such practices for only a limited period of time. To secure the consent of the governed, major shifts and alterations of policy must be disclosed and their rationale publicly explained.

Pursued to its ultimate logic, as it has been during the past few years, a policy of maneuver risks subverting our institutions, puts a premium on furtiveness at the highest places, creates an obsession with what is banally — and for the most part improperly — called "national security," and provides a factitious justification for such trespasses on individual freedom as wiretapping and even burglary. It is a policy not for a great democratic nation, but for a weak, despotic power. It was appropriate for a Metternich seeking to shore up the deteriorating position of an authoritarian dynasty or for a Bismarck striving to unify a jerry-built nation beset by foreign and domestic enemies, but even De Gaulle, in spite of his cleverness, could not pursue it over many years without losing his legendary touch. In a democratic state such as France, the pretensions of grandeur gave way before common sense and *ennui.* A flamboyant leader can survive anything but the public's boredom; the run of even the most brilliant drama is limited.

In addition to its incompatibility with our democratic practices, personal diplomacy has made American foreign policy both jerky and two-dimensional. Refusing to delegate authority over even the most routine decisions, Henry Kissinger has been far too busy with the crisis of the month to deal with other problems that urgently needed attention.

Here, again, one should note the obvious difference between the one-man diplomacy of Henry Kissinger and the machinations of a Metternich, a Bismarck, or even a De Gaulle, all players in a less complex drama. For each of them the limits of serious concern were the politics of the continent. Neither Austria nor Prussia had interests outside the small house of Europe and, although De Gaulle claimed such interests for France, they were more in the realm of pretense than reality. His trips to Quebec and to Latin America reflected little more than his puckish delight in ephemeral mischief. His all-consuming, undeviating purpose was to establish French hegemony in Western Europe by keeping the Germans off balance and playing the Soviet Union and America against one another, and, although it was a game for high stakes, it involved a limited number of players — a game on which he could concentrate without danger of neglecting valuable French interests. Kissinger, on the other hand, is in quite a different position, for America's concerns are worldwide and acting or failing to act in almost any quarter of the globe can have widespread and long-lasting repercussions.

The government of a power with worldwide interests is like a juggler who must keep many balls in the air, but Kissinger, the virtuoso, always center-stage under the spotlight, has specialized in trying to throw one or two balls at a time to record heights, while letting the rest ricochet aimlessly around the stage. By attempting to be both foreign minister and his own diplomatic corps, he has necessarily limited the scope of his attention, and the result has been a narrowly conceived policy — a policy that ignores relations with nations that happen for the moment to be outside the spotlight, and, in the long run, encourages a practice of haphazard improvisation.

Thus, in 1971, when Kissinger was preoccupied with China, while at the same time flying back and forth to Paris in a single-handed attempt to negotiate a Vietnamese cease-fire, we drifted with a policy "tilted" toward Pakistan that assured the Soviets a long-desired foothold in the subcontinent. While Kissinger was frantically touring the Middle East, carrying the keys of his office with him, critical decisions with regard to the second phase of the SALT talks and the European Security Conference had to be postponed. Finally, when Cyprus once again burst with flames, a preoccupied Secretary of State failed to stop a Turkish invasion he might well have averted. Because he takes little advice and permits no one else to make decisions, America — as he himself admitted — long had nothing resembling a policy toward Latin America or Africa or the less developed countries. Only when a crisis occurred in one of those areas did Kissinger get in his airplane and try to do something about it.

Yet foreign policy, like Maitland's description of the common law, is a seamless web, and one cannot tinker with one part of the fabric of policy without danger of unraveling another part. When the Secretary concentrates his attention on a specific problem for resolution or negotiation, all other problems are necessarily kept waiting. Yet, unlike the patients in the office of a busy doctor, waiting their turn for the ministrations of the great man, other nations cannot be pacified with back numbers of old magazines — particularly when the doctor is three thousand miles away paying house calls on his most cantankerous patients. If the United States cannot attend to them, then *tant pis;* they will go elsewhere.

The three initiatives of the Nixon-Kissinger period * for which Mr. Nixon claimed the highest credit were the reestablishment of communications with China, the extrication of American forces from South Vietnam, and the establishment of something called *détente* with the Soviet Union. All had a major impact on American opinion but in a differentiated manner.

For many complicated reasons the reestablishment of communications with China caught the imagination of the American

---

* Though troop redeployments on the Egyptian and Syrian fronts were worked out while Nixon was still President, the Egyptian-Israeli agreement occurred during the Ford Administration.

people as few other foreign policy moves have done in recent history.

The extrication of the United States from Vietnam was greeted less with ecstasy than relief. So long as America was still engaged in Vietnam, the war was an all-consuming agony; once we had finally withdrawn, it became a national bore. Although we did not get out as quickly or as cheaply as we might, extrication was, for exhausted Americans, like Samuel Johnson's comments on a dog's walking on its hind legs: "It is not done well, but you are surprised to find it done at all." Once we were out, we were out; few cared to ask whether we could not have achieved the same results more quickly and at far less cost.

The creation of a new relation with Moscow inspired reactions of pleasure and relaxation, although in time skepticism began to qualify the initial appraisal.

In the pages that follow, both the opening to China and the extrication from Vietnam will be examined largely as case studies of what happens when the shape and methods of our foreign policy are heavily influenced by domestic politics. The President's trip to Peking illustrated the disadvantages of summitry undertaken as an exercise in domestic public relations — or "PR," as it was then reverently referred to in the White House. The Vietnam negotiations disclosed how American interests could be badly served when symbols and slogans are valued more highly than our fundamental interests. *Détente* is a mushy concept, which I shall try to reduce to realistic terms.

CHAPTER 2

Tribute to
the Middle Kingdom

NO EPISODE IN THE NIXON ADMINISTRATION HAS BEEN MORE praised or misunderstood — or, indeed, misrepresented — than the President's visit to China. Contrary to the manner in which it was presented to the American people, it was by no means an intricate diplomatic maneuver or a triumph of negotiation. The Chinese did not have to be persuaded to open their doors; they had their own strategic reasons for wishing to resume communications with the United States and they were making that point loudly and clearly.

The convergence of policies that led to an altered relation between the United States and China was a natural — though delayed — outgrowth of two developments: one was the schism between Peking and Moscow which developed in 1960; the other was the disenchantment of America with its involvement in Vietnam and its ultimate decision to withdraw.

Ideological fissures in Sino-Soviet relations first appeared when the Chinese became upset by Khrushchev's de-Stalinization moves and by the ensuing crises in Poland and Hungary. Then, in 1960, after Peking had attacked Soviet revisionism, Moscow withdrew its technicians and stopped helping China build a nuclear bomb. Thereafter, Peking and Moscow began a power struggle for control of the Communist Party structure throughout the world. Particularly after the autumn of 1968, when the Red Army entered

Prague under the self-serving mandate of the Brezhnev Doctrine, Peking began to fear a military attack. Nor were the fears all one-sided. Disturbed by rumors that China was reviving old claims to Soviet territory, Moscow began a major military buildup along the Chinese border.

With China bracketed on the north by an increasingly belli-cose Soviet Union and on the south by an India that seemed to be slipping more and more toward Moscow, Mao Tse-tung and his colleagues were encouraged to reassess their position toward the United States. Fear of America generated by our march to the Yalu in October 1950, and regenerated by our swelling deployments in Southeast Asia in the 1960s, abated once the United States began the long process of withdrawal from Vietnam. The coincidence of three events — President Johnson's speech in March 1968, halting the further extension of American bombing, the phasing down of the Cultural Revolution, and the emergence of Chou En-lai as the dominant figure in Chinese foreign policy — paved the way for China's emergence from isolation. In 1970 it established diplomatic relations with Canada even though the Canadians merely "took note" of Peking's claim to Taiwan rather than formally recognizing it. By the fall of 1971, Peking had established formal relations with about sixty nations. Since only America had the power to deter the Soviet Union from a preemptive strike at China's nuclear installations, an approach to Washington was a logical next move. Instead of encouraging the total removal of the American presence in the area, China began to see advantages in the continuance of American troop and naval deployments in Japan, Korea, and other forward positions in the Pacific. At the same time, it publicly urged NATO to stay strong and made clear its hope that America would continue to maintain its forces in Europe.

On its side, the Johnson Administration showed considerable restraint. It resisted Pentagon pressure for an outright invasion of North Vietnam, for bombing too near the Chinese border, and for attacking the dikes or mining Haiphong Harbor. President Johnson never forgot — I did not let him — that Chinese intervention in the Korean conflict had been triggered by the apparent threat to its Manchurian border when General MacArthur seized positions along the Yalu. In retrospect, his caution appears to have been wise, though perhaps for the wrong reasons. China was in such agony over the Cultural Revolution that it would probably not have responded with direct military action to an encroachment against North Vietnam, its buffer territory. In that sense our fears may have been exaggerated. But American constraint did convey to China that the United States was not a potential aggressor, thus making it easy for Chou En-lai and his moderate faction to convince other Chinese leaders that a visible relationship with the United States might be a useful warning to Moscow.

It was one of history's perverse whimsies that China began to unlock its doors to the rest of the world just when Nixon came to power, since Nixon's admiration for Communist China came late in life. As a young McCarthyite congressman, he had joined in denouncing the Truman Administration for "losing China." Even while campaigning for Vice President in 1952 he had charged that "China wouldn't have gone Communist — if the Truman Administration had backbone." Again, as recently as his 1960 campaign against John F. Kennedy, he had accused the Chinese Communists of seeking world domination.

Nevertheless, he must be given credit for conversion to a sounder view, when, in an article under his name in *Foreign Affairs* in October 1967, he observed that "any American policy toward Asia must come urgently to grips with the reality of China." [1] Thus, before he assumed office, Nixon seems to have envisaged that China might be used as a counter to the Soviet Union. On March 1, 1969, he told De Gaulle that he was determined to open a dialogue with Peking and that he foresaw the admission of Peking to the United Nations and the "normalization of relations." When De Gaulle came to Washington to attend Eisenhower's funeral, Nixon asked the general to convey the spirit of America's new policy to the Chinese — a message subsequently carried out through Etienne M. Manac'h, the French ambassador to Peking.

During 1969 the United States gave a series of small signals to China. The passports of scholars, journalists, and students were automatically validated on a reciprocal basis. United States naval patrols were suspended in the Taiwan Straits and nuclear weapons were removed from Okinawa. United States tourists were allowed to purchase up to one hundred dollars' worth of Chinese goods, which had been totally banned since 1950.

For several years the United States had been carrying on discussions with the Chinese through the ambassadors of the two countries in Warsaw, but these had been suspended in January 1968. When, in the fall of 1969, there was an indication through third nation channels that the Chinese might be interested in resuming these talks, Washington responded encouragingly. After proposing that the talks be moved to Peking, the Chinese gave positive signals to the United States, including an invitation to the American journalist Edgar Snow to stand next to Mao on China's national day.[2] While the President was sending messages to Peking indicating that he wished to know whether or not "he or his representative would be received," Snow quoted Mao as saying, in December 1970, that the Chinese "were discussing whether Nixon might be permitted to come" to China. Finally, in the spring of 1971 a message was sent through the Pakistani ambassador inviting "an American envoy" to visit Peking, suggesting either Secretary of State Rogers or Kissinger.

The President kept all of this tightly secret, which, no doubt, disappointed the Chinese, whose principal purpose in opening the door to the United States was to make it unmistakable to the Soviet Union that they had a friend in Washington. From the Chinese point of view the louder and more blatant the American show of interest, the better. Thus, it was not the inscrutable Orientals but the traditionally open Americans who insisted on smothering the whole enterprise with a Béarnaise sauce of intrigue and mystery.

Kissinger's Pakistan caper set the tone for what was to follow. Flying to Islamabad, ostensibly for discussions with President Yahya Khan, he secluded himself, on the excuse of a "slight indisposition" — translated by the American press as "Delhi belly," which did not speak tactfully for the cuisine of the subcontinent. Actually, of course, he had been whisked off to Peking.

A great nation can obviously not enlist the complicity of a poor nation in a diplomatic melodrama without paying for it, and the United States later picked up the check by siding with Pakistan against India in the Bangladesh affair. But, for the moment, the conspiratorial atmosphere of the enterprise placed the Secretary of the Pakistan Ministry of Foreign Affairs, Sultan Mohammed Khan, in an awkward position. Charged with handling the details of the trip, he had difficulty explaining to the Chinese why such clandestine arrangements were necessary. All he could think of to tell them was that the American Government was hard pressed by the "China lobby" and so did not yet dare let it be known that it was talking to Peking — a concept difficult to express in a foreign language.

To be fair, one could argue that the White House might wish to test the depth of the Chinese response before disclosing the preliminary talks. Yet that does not explain why, on Kissinger's return to Washington, the United States did not undertake full consultations with our allies, including Japan, which had the greatest interest at stake, before we announced such a flamboyant venture as the President's projected trip. In fact, we kept Tokyo in the dark until less than an hour before Nixon went on the air, when Secretary Rogers telephoned Japanese Ambassador Ushiba along with other ambassadors in Washington. The Administration's explanation, of course, was that consultation would have increased the chance of a leak. But was that important? No leak could have created anything like the breakage resulting from our neglect of consultation.

Not only was secrecy positively harmful but, for reasons I shall point out later, the President's visit itself was a mistake. The negotiation of a new relationship with China was ideally suited for emissary diplomacy, and in Henry Kissinger the President had available the ideal envoy. Not only had he thought deeply about world power relationships, but he knew the President's own thinking on foreign policy, since he was largely instrumental in shaping it.

The heart of the matter is that Nixon insisted on secrecy, neglected consultation, caught the country off balance with a surprise announcement, and cast the whole diplomatic venture in the framework of a summit visit purely for his own domestic purposes. Otherwise, there is no explanation for the Eric Ambler script or for the failure to consult — a rejection of the normal courtesy any nation would expect from its close ally. But a premature disclosure might detract from the domestic political benefit of a dramatic announcement; and he wished to milk all the emotion possible from the shock effect of what he proudly described as "the biggest surprise in history." The announcement of the President's trip and the trip itself — as distinct from the political decision to resume communications through Kissinger's visit — were a stratagem of domestic politics, and very little more than that.

That the stratagem proved effective for the intended purpose is undeniable. Without doubt it contributed heavily to Nixon's electoral victory of 1972; and in the dark summer of 1974 he constantly put it forward to offset his manifold delinquencies. But to argue, as many have, that the President had to visit China personally in order to persuade a reluctant America to accept a new China policy insults the good sense of the American people. Although there are, no doubt, situations in which diplomatic initiatives must be tailored primarily for domestic opinion, this was not one of them; nor do I believe that President Nixon thought it was. What he saw in the surprise announcement and the glamour of his visit was a chance to bedazzle and excite the country — to give the American people, in other words, the modern equivalent of a Roman circus; for, if it were no longer acceptable to feed Christians to the lions in a well-packed arena, one could still profit politically by offering color and excitement to the American voter.

As informed observers knew at the time, most of the American people had already decided that Manichaean anti-Communism no longer provided an adequate postulate on which to construct a foreign policy, nor did they believe that China was any longer an expansionist power we needed to contain. The old China lobby was dead as a mackerel. Henry Luce, its most effective supporter, was no longer around to run his magazine empire; Senators Knowland, Bricker, and Taft had either died or been defeated in the 1950s; even Congressman Walter Judd, the last of the stalwarts, had been out of the Congress for ten years. The vision of the Generalissimo's triumphant return to the Mainland, with the old guard flocking to him like Napoleon's legions after Elba, no longer evoked wishful thinking but outright laughter; it required too great a suspension of disbelief to think of the eighty-five-year-old Generalissimo as Bonnie Prince Charlie. Had not the Bay of Pigs sourly demonstrated that the invasion of a Communist state did not automatically lead the citizenry to rise *en masse*? To be sure, General MacArthur had kept his promise to return to the Philippines, but it had taken the whole of the Third, Fifth, and Seventh fleets and five million American soldiers to get him there. The same facilities were not about to be put at the Generalissimo's disposal.

Since the American people no longer took seriously the charade that had been played for so many years in Taipeh, they would have quite readily accepted our resumed communications with Peking without all the pyrotechnics. Though many applauded the television spectacular of the President's trip as a welcome change from "Gunsmoke," they would have liked it far less had they been at all aware of the breakage it entailed.

What were the dimensions and character of that breakage? Most important, our abrupt secret action shook the confidence of our allies in the steadfastness of American policy and raised questions as to how seriously Washington regarded its alliance obligations. If, without even a day's notice to our friends, we reversed a position we had held for twenty-two years, what might we do next? For two decades we had been threatening the Canadians and the Japanese with hellfire if they recognized China or voted to admit it to the United Nations, and we had squandered a fantastic amount of political muscle to deter the leaders in each of those countries from a move that would have earned them loud applause from their own people. To learn suddenly and without advance notice that a President who had emphatically discouraged America's friends from taking a particular action was now taking that action himself, was beyond the threshold of tolerance.

Though galling enough to our NATO allies, the abrupt announcement was a bombshell in Japan, where Prime Minister Sato had resisted intense internal pressure to come to terms with Peking on the ground that he did not wish to displease the American President. Quite obviously the President's trip compromised Sato's position intolerably. With the television cameras recording every banality of the Nixon visit ("That is a great wall," said the President when visiting the Great Wall), how could the Japanese people help but say to their own leader: "Why did you let him get there before you?" — with the clear implication that Sato should never have been deterred by American threats or have relied on American promises.

Other Asians were no less jaundiced, since they feared secret commitments between the President and the Chinese leaders; but, even more significantly, they equated the trip with an American humiliation. For many Chinese, the President's initiative in requesting an invitation to China stirred atavistic memories of the old tradition of the Middle Kingdom, that peoples of other countries — including rulers and their envoys — were barbarians. The Emperors of China had regarded it as an act of grace to grant any foreign visitors passage to Peking (The Heavenly City), and it was understood that they came as suppliants bearing tribute.

The governments and peoples of Asia did not view the trip as a spectacle but as a puzzling political act, and they read the meaning of that act not merely from the occurrence of the visit but the surrounding circumstances. It was here that the distinction between a Kissinger visit (emissary diplomacy) and a Presidential visit (summit diplomacy) stood out most sharply. Had the President conducted our exploratory talks with China solely through a special emissary, it would have been accepted as normal diplomatic practice, evoking worldwide interest without causing astonishment. But the Presidential visit was a drastic break with traditional procedures.

Weighed in the balance, the trip was costly, and not just in terms of taxpayers' expense (never one of Mr. Nixon's chief concerns). To be sure, the United States was subsequently able to modify to some degree its increasingly ridiculous posture of supporting Taiwan as the only legitimate government of the whole of China. But that represented a diplomatic achievement no greater than West Germany's treaty with the Soviet Union, Poland, and East Germany, a treaty which permitted West Germany to pull back from a dug-in and awkward position with regard to reunification by recognizing the existence of two Germanies. A careful search for concrete results from the whole Peking adventure reveals nothing that could not have been achieved through visits by Dr. Kissinger, who, having no State Department duties at that time, was a logical special envoy. To be sure, in exchanging musk-oxen for panda bears we clearly got the better of the bargain, but there is no reason that could not have been worked out between zoos without a Presidential visit. Nor is there any basis for believing that the ambiguous document finally extracted from the Chinese could not have been obtained without the President's journey; in spite of all the banal toast-making of a Presidential visit, the document produced by the summit's labor was clearly a mouse. All it amounted to was a *de facto* arrangement; *de jure* relations would have to wait the sorting out of the Formosan problem. Even if one concedes that the resumption of communications with China freed up our diplomacy and no doubt helped to put the Kremlin off balance, it is hard to see what the President's personal involvement added to the result. Other governments obtained just as much from Peking without all the fanfare.

It was only natural that other states should translate Washington's extraordinary deference to the Peking Government as meaning that America implicitly recognized China's dominant position throughout the whole of the Far East; that we regarded it, in fact, as the wave of Asia's future — all of which, of course, stimulated those other states to climb on the Chinese bandwagon. Certainly the President's travel schedule prompted a new respect for Peking on the part of the twenty-one million overseas Chinese who constitute a significant and troublesome minority in many Far Eastern countries.

For the Chinese leadership the symbolism and excitement of the spectacle clearly meant a Great Leap Forward in world politics. The fact that the chief of state of the world's most powerful nation came five thousand miles and was content to spend most of his visit with the second in command, Prime Minister Chou, rather than the chief of state, Chairman Mao, was an unprecedented gesture of respect, verging on subservience, which the Chinese have not seen necessary or fitting to reciprocate. By announcing his prospective China trip in July 1971, Nixon made it impossible to stop Peking from pushing into the United Nations in October, yet, forever anxious to appease the diehard right wing of his own party, he still went through the motions of opposing Chinese membership. Prodigally wasting America's shrinking political capital, he ordered a foredoomed effort to hold the troops in line against the entry of that very country of which he was about to be a self-invited guest. For many years, under the Truman, Eisenhower, Kennedy, and Johnson Administrations, our policy of trying to exclude Peking from taking over the representation of China in New York had made no sense; after the announcement of the President's China trip what had been merely fatuous became downright imbecilic. It was left for Ambassador George Bush (acting without doubt on White House instructions) to stage an emotional sham battle — probably the most futile skirmish since Britain bloodied its army against Andrew Jackson's at New Orleans more than a fortnight after peace had been signed at Ghent. It humiliated our friends — and particularly the Japanese — whom we enlisted to join us in inglorious defeat.

There is no doubt that both Kissinger and the President were enormously impressed by the Chinese leadership and especially by Chou En-lai, an astute manipulator who viewed the world through wide-angle lenses. Particularly for Henry Kissinger, life-time student of world politics, the prospect of traversing the political cosmos with Chou offered solid intellectual satisfaction. Quite unlike the Japanese, who seemed much too pragmatic for the geo-politicians in the White House (and much too preoccupied with commerce and economics, which, in Kissinger's view, were the concern of tradesmen rather than statesmen), Chou was capable of playing the "big game" in an intricate world chess match, and that was yeasty stuff. Yet it is during such games that the seductions of summitry become the most dangerous and the possibilities of mis-understanding most acute.

However pleasant the momentary good feeling, it was hazard-ous to assume that America could rely on any long-term personal understandings with Chou or any of the other Chinese leaders then in power. Even in 1972 they were an aged hierarchy whose life expectancy was sharply limited by actuarial tables (Mao was, at the time, seventy-nine and Chou seventy-four), and Nixon would have done well to recall his fawning praise of General de Gaulle just before a new leader came to power in France.

On any objective appraisal of the total situation, the Presi-dent's "triumphal visit" proved the costs and dangers of summitry. For what has happened since then to justify the hyperbole with which the trip was surrounded? Though President Nixon, con-tinually shaking his head at the sheer wonder of any event in which he personally participated, referred to his visit as "the days that changed the world," the canny and appraising Chou En-lai, speaking with the realism and maturity of a leader of a people that had survived thousands of years, limited his comments to the dry observation that, though there were "great differences of princi-ple" between the two nations, "at least a start" had been made in understanding each other's views.

Chou was, of course, quite correct, for our relations with China have remained distinctly circumscribed. We maintain a Li-aison Office in Peking but no Embassy, and while our exports to China have reached a respectable level — the U.S.A. sold her $272 million in wheat in 1973 — that could quite as well have worked out had the President remained in San Clemente or Key Biscayne or Camp David — or even Washington.

China has, of course, been opened for select and carefully controlled tourism, but the travel reports of visiting Americans should be read with a critical eye. It is instructive to recall the breathless but fatuous enthusiasm with which a whole generation of intellectuals reported on the Soviet Union during the 1920s and 1930s.[3]

Like so many of Nixon's "great initiatives," the trip to China was an overblown episode that lacked either a careful follow-up or a conceptual positioning within a coherent body of policy. Had he taken account of our larger interests, he would, of course, have kept our allies informed. Approached at the right time, the Japanese Government would have welcomed the American move, rather than regarding it as a catastrophe. Had he sent an envoy to Peking instead of going himself, the position of China would not have been distorted in the appraisal of the world, nor would America have humiliated itself in the eyes of Asian critics by sending its President to the Court of the Middle Kingdom — an act which, translated into Western terms, held some of the overtones of Canossa.

Only domestic politics were effectively served. Had the President not gone to Peking, he would have probably never received such an overwhelming vote in the 1972 election, but, in the light of all that subsequently happened, would that have been so unfortunate? In fact, should we not learn one solemn lesson from the whole Chinese adventure? To design a diplomatic initiative primarily for its impact on domestic voters is a thoroughly bad idea.

CHAPTER 3

The Anatomy of "Summitry"

THE CHINA TRIP WAS ONLY ONE EXAMPLE OF THE SUMMIT MEET-
ings that, during the Nixon Administration, characterized "The
New Diplomacy" — and were represented as essential for solving
intricate problems in the nuclear age. Yet summit meetings are, in
fact, a throwback to an earlier time, when during the palmy days
of the European dynasties, sovereigns of all titles and descriptions
made a practice of visiting one another's courts. Between jousting
and feasting and exchanging elaborate gifts, they attended to their
family affairs — arranging marriages, launching intrigues against
rivals, meddling in the management of small neighboring realms,
and discussing their financial and commercial troubles. Then
gradually, beginning in the fifteenth century, systematic machinery was established to deal with most of this business. Under
the leadership of Venice, the Italian city-states established permanent diplomatic missions in one another's capitals, and, with
Spanish and French refinements, a modern apparatus for the conduct of intergovernmental business began to emerge, complete
not only with permanent diplomatic missions but modern foreign
offices, manned by diplomats of professional competence.

Such a system was a logical by-product of political evolution.
When countries were little more than the private estates of their
absolute rulers, a king could dispose of the affairs of his kingdom

as he saw fit; but over the centuries, as Sir Harold Nicolson has pointed out, the detailed business of making and executing foreign policy shifted "from the Court to the Cabinet." [1] The result was impersonal diplomacy practiced through career ambassadors, acting on instructions from professional foreign offices — a system in keeping with the modern age.

Still, in spite of the advantages of the new system, the United States during the first term of President Nixon moved back toward the medieval dynastic practice. Even the day-to-day shaping of foreign policy was transferred from the Department of State (the Cabinet) to the White House and its staff (the Court), while the actual transaction of diplomatic business was, in increasing measure, preempted by the President (the Sovereign), acting personally or more often through his Assistant for National Security Affairs. Meanwhile, the Department of State atrophied, and ambassadors became messenger boys — a status Nixon implicitly recognized by the dubious quality of most of his appointments.

Once the President had elected to be his own ambassador as well as his own foreign office, he found himself hopping from summit to summit. Having abruptly announced that he would go to China in 1971, he felt compelled to arrange visits with Prime Minister Trudeau of Canada, President Pompidou of France, Prime Minister Heath of Great Britain, Chancellor Brandt of West Germany, Prime Minister Sato of Japan, and finally Chairman Brezhnev of the Soviet Union, in an effort to repair the damage that resulted from his failure to consult in the first place.

Summit meetings over the centuries have been a frequent source of grief. From the famous meeting at the Field of the Cloth of Gold in the sixteenth century to Woodrow Wilson's catastrophic efforts to make peace by personal diplomacy in Paris in 1919, meetings of heads of state have caused much disappointment and misunderstanding.[2] From the beginning of the Cold War, conferences between the President and the Communist leaders have been largely marked by failure. To be sure, President Eisenhower's ventures into summitry evoked momentary spasms of journalistic hyperbole with the "Spirit of Geneva" in 1955 and the "Spirit of Camp David" in 1959, just as an earlier Roosevelt-Churchill-Stalin meeting had provided the "Spirit of Yalta," a later impromptu Johnson-Kosygin meeting conjured up the "Spirit of

Glassboro" in 1967, and a Nixon-Brezhnev meeting in 1972 was to result in the "Spirit of Moscow." But where are they now? Like other spirits — whether alcoholic or ectoplasmic — they quickly evaporated in the clear dry air of reality.

The sad fact is that, since World War II, no summit meeting has ever resulted in a diplomatic breakthrough. In spite of President Nixon's assertion that, in the case of the Soviet Union and China, "which have basically one-man rule," summitry was a necessity "for major decisions," every significant gain in the whole area of East-West relations — including the Austrian State Treaty, the Limited Test Ban Treaty, the Nuclear Non-Proliferation Treaty, and the Berlin Agreement — has resulted from painstaking diplomacy pursued through traditional methods.

That is, of course, a disappointing conclusion for most Americans, because they like their Presidents to go traveling. It is only natural that people should think of their leaders as their surrogates who solve their problems for them. In medieval times disputes were often resolved through "ordeal by battle," in which, as a substitute for war, chosen heroes from each side settled international disputes by fighting to the death in full sight of the contending armies. But underlying the popularity of Presidential travel is a widespread misconception as to what foreign policy is all about. It is too often assumed that nations have no opposing interests or objectives that are fundamental and that the world's peoples could all live happily together "if only they could understand one another" — or, through some anthropomorphic transfer, "if only their leaders could talk to one another."

It says more for the vanity than the wisdom of our leaders that such a shallow idea has so often seemed valid. If it is enough that chiefs of government practice "person-to-person" diplomacy and engage in homey "heart-to-heart" talks, one does not have to worry about such squalid matters as maintaining "power balances" or "spheres of influence" or any of the other "outmoded concepts" of the "old diplomacy." It is all very easy and comforting.

Unhappily, this anodyne thesis finds no confirmation in experience. Men and women are not motivated by pure reason and, even if they were, nations do have conflicting interests that cannot be wished away. Thus there is nothing more dangerous than to rest the relations between states too heavily on the capricious interaction of diverse personalities. No one knows — least of all the experts — why individuals like or dislike one another, or why they have sudden fallings-out over seemingly inconsequential matters. What is clear is that the mysterious chemistry of human relations produces some exotic and unstable mixes.

This has been clearly apparent in our whole experience with summit diplomacy. In my own observation, Anglo-American relations were seriously impeded by the fact that President Johnson and Prime Minister Wilson were temperamentally poles apart and did not basically like one another. On the other hand, I can testify with authority (because I was present) that President Kennedy's decision to provide Britain with Polaris missiles at the ill-fated Nassau Conference in December 1962 — a decision that provided De Gaulle with an excuse to block Britain's entry into Europe — was due in large part to the fact that he *did* like Prime Minister Macmillan and was responsive to the Macedonian cry of a fellow politician in distress.

Besides giving excessive play to the element of personal compatibility in international relations, summit meetings often tend to create an illusion of understanding where none really exists. Shrewd Americans with a common heritage of ideas, language, gestures, ethics, and national experience are normally able to appraise one another with fair precision, so that understanding can often be advanced by face-to-face discussion. But when leaders have disparate backgrounds, customs, and languages and, in many cases, ethical attitudes and ideologies, summitry is more likely to produce mistaken and misleading impressions than a clear meeting of the minds.

One would do well to recall, for example, how Prime Minister Neville Chamberlain was tragically taken in by Hitler at their Munich meeting in 1938. No doubt he spoke from conviction when he told the British people on his return to London: "After my visits to Germany I realized vividly how Herr Hitler feels that he must champion other Germans. He told me privately, and last night he repeated publicly, that after the Sudeten German question is settled, that is the end of Germany's territorial claims in Europe." Thus Chamberlain had brought back, he said, "peace with honor," "peace for our time."

Why was Chamberlain so easily deceived by such a crude,

repellent liar? Not solely because he wanted to believe — though that, of course, was part of the story — but, most important, because he had had a face-to-face encounter with a man whose background and standards he could not possibly understand. Thus he had given the word of an Austrian rabble-rouser, whose character had been shaped in the jungle of the Vienna slums, the same credence he might have accorded an English friend trained at Eton. Had Chamberlain stayed in London, dealing impersonally with the crisis through his diplomatic agents, the mystique of personal contact would not have worked its malign spell, the tragic betrayal of Czechoslovakia might never have occurred, and, from what we now know about Germany's incomplete preparedness and the plotting of the German generals, the war could quite possibly have been averted.

Few myths have done more harm than the sentimental conceit that men of different countries can understand one another better through direct conversation than when their exchange of views and ideas is filtered through experts sensitive to the nuances that derive from different cultures. Such a fanciful belief becomes particularly misleading when cultural differences reflect quite different habits of thought — as, for example, between Americans and Orientals.

This is another example of where Kissinger, the diplomat, has turned his back on Kissinger, the professor, who had written in 1966, "When domestic structures — and the concept of legitimacy on which they are based — differ widely, statesmen can still meet, but their ability to persuade has been reduced because they no longer speak the same language." [3] The wisdom of these words was amply demonstrated by successive meetings between President Nixon and Prime Minister Sato of Japan, which, far from fostering harmony, led to misunderstanding, irritation, and, finally, a disastrous distrust on both sides. To understand the perennial difficulty of achieving an adequate meeting of minds between Washington and Tokyo, every President should study the catastrophic series of misunderstandings that resulted from the dialogue of the deaf in the months preceding Pearl Harbor.[4] Men of different cultures thought they were hearing one another but were instead listening only to the whispered innuendos of their own preconceptions and the exegeses of biased advisors.

Not only do summit meetings exaggerate the role of personal

chemistry and of national differences, but the sense of theater they engender cannot help but color the judgment of the participants. Thus, when the President meets with other heads of state, the occasion takes command, transforming each attending political leader into an actor on the television screens of the world, with a heavy investment in the success — or at least the appearance of success — of the meeting. It is not an atmosphere that makes for cool judgment; in fact, theater and sound policy are rarely compatible, because contrived excitement can only distract and distort diplomacy that should properly be conducted calmly and dispassionately.

To a considerable extent the misleading myths that surround "summitry" derive from the vagueness and ambiguity of the clichés with which it is generally described. The expression "summit conference" illustrates the principle that, in the process of vulgarization, neologisms lose precision and become generalized to the point of meaninglessness. Thus today the word "summitry" is used, without discrimination, to describe any occasion on which chiefs of state or heads of government get together bilaterally or in large meetings. It has, as a result, become so vague in meaning as to be not only useless but downright misleading, and if the American vocabulary is ever subjected to a long overdue culling out, that synthetic word should be among the first to go.

To approach even the beginning of a serious consideration of summitry, two broad distinctions must be made. The first is between bilateral and multilateral summit meetings, the second between substantive and ritualistic meetings. These are distinctions that the press and other media rarely point out and they suggest the urgent need for a new and more precise vocabulary.

Usually, what Sir Winston Churchill once called the "vast cumbrous array" of correspondents, commentators, and cameramen who assemble at summit meetings have little access to sources other than official briefers and leakers. Thus, they are rarely in a position to counteract the wishful tendency of their readers or listeners or viewers to believe that heads of state or chiefs of governments are endowed with skills and knowledge beyond ordinary men and that whenever their tribal leaders feed or talk together they transact serious business, not only smoking peace pipes (or, in the modern idiom, drinking fatuous toasts to mutual understanding) but actually making peace. It is a happy fantasy but far from fact. Politicians are the virtuosos of banality, and their capacity to endure boredom in one another's company is a wonder to behold. Moreover, their thresholds of tolerance for flattery and effusive nonsense far surpass those of ordinary mortals. Thus, one should take it for granted that when heads of state get together, an enormous amount of time will be wasted in what a more elegant age would have referred to as persiflage, badinage, and brummagem.

What really happens at even the most serious bilateral summit conference where there are significant issues to be discussed? It is comparable to an iceberg floating upside down; what one sees is a vast bulk; the substance is contained solely in the relatively tiny tip that is entirely submerged. Though little serious conversation takes place at the banquet table, the time consumed in eating and drinking is appalling. In the Far East it is not polite to discuss business over food, and in many countries in the Middle East no conversation at all takes place during meals. Wherever the meeting occurs, toasts are normally set speeches. When Communists are present, toasts may be useful for making diplomatic hints — particularly if the toasts are afterward handed out to the press — but by and large the time consumed in communal feeding is time wasted. Nor is anything serious likely to be said over the brandy, for, in spite of the diplomatic mystique with which tradition has surrounded this postprandial ritual, the heads of state are usually too tired to make sensible conversation, which they would probably not be able to remember with precision the next day anyway.

Beyond that there is endless time consumed in the laying of wreaths, visits to historic monuments, and the attendance at opera or ballet (where a canny head of state can at least get a quick nap since, if experienced, he will have learned to sleep with his eyes open).

Nor should one take literally reports that the President and the Soviet Chairman spent "ten hours in negotiation." Whenever a foreign head of state is unable or unwilling to transact business in English, the time permitted for the actual exchange of ideas is reduced by something more than 50 percent because, by my own observation, the process of translation more than doubles the time consumed for any exchange of ideas. Thus, in trying to measure the period permitted for a substantive exchange of views during ten hours of top-level propinquity, one should deduct at least four hours for eating and drinking, another hour or two for small talk and the normal conversational amenities, then divide the remainder by perhaps 2½ for the translation. What is left is about two to three hours in which positions are stated and ideas exchanged.

The essential question is how this relatively brief period is utilized. Each participant will have before him a large looseleaf notebook containing individual sections addressed to each agenda item and backed up by other looseleaf notebooks filled with supporting documents. Since the talk will normally cover a prearranged agenda, the book will contain an initial statement or talking paper covering each subject, outlining the position to be taken, followed by indications of the responses the other side can be expected to make and suggested answers to those responses.

It will, of course, take time for each side to state its initial position, and since, in most cases, the whole subject will have already been fully negotiated at a lower level, that exercise is likely to be largely ritualistic. Even in those instances where there may be some critical questions left undetermined, the discussion that takes place between heads of state or chiefs of government is likely to be contrapuntal to the expert discussions between the foreign ministers from each side that occur in intervals between meetings. It is in the foreign ministers' meetings that the vague and highly generalized comments of the national leaders are reduced to precise positions and their inaccuracies and inadvertent slips corrected. It is there also that variant proposals are usually tried out when an *impasse* is reached in discussions at the top level.

In any event, when the subject involves highly technical and complex questions, such as, for example, the control or reduction of nuclear weapons, neither head of state will be able to do more than make general statements. It would be absurd to expect a President to master anything other than the broad principles or high points — and certainly not the intricacies — of a nuclear agreement in a preconference weekend at Camp David or in the Florida sunshine or at a ski chalet in Vail.

Even under controlled conditions heads-of-state meetings in-

volve serious hazards. Yet those hazards can be mitigated so long
as the President relies on an alert Secretary of State and does not
feel under compulsion to pay almost any price for an agreement in
order to improve his position at home. It is when the President
decides to be his own foreign minister that the danger is the greatest. Nothing is more hazardous than for a President, in the ebul-
lience that follows a good lunch, to insist on a quiet tête-à-tête
with a foreign head of state without his Secretary of State or other
aides present.

During my tenure in the Department of State under two Presidents, my colleagues and I always felt apprehensive whenever a
foreign visitor could speak English. Aware of the easy fellowship
among politicians, we resigned ourselves to the certainty that
sometime in the course of the visit the two leaders would go off
into the Rose Garden for an intimate talk. In that event we could
never be sure that we knew just what promises might have been
made, implied, understood or misunderstood — since there were
then no microphones hidden among the rose petals.

It is fortunate that American Presidents are almost without exception monolingual. In fact, as we have lately discovered, some
scarcely even speak English. Theodore Roosevelt was the last
President who had mastered a foreign tongue, but he was too
chauvinistic to transact business in any language but English.
Since most other heads of state are unprepared, for reasons of national pride or fear of being put at a disadvantage, to discuss state
affairs in other than their native tongue — or French, which still
retains some rapidly diminishing currency as a diplomatic *lingua
franca* — an interpreter must be present. It is a long tradition in
diplomacy that a diplomat should insist on having his words translated by an interpreter of his own. But neither President Nixon
nor Secretary Kissinger always adhered to that time-honored practice. In an excessive feeling of either *camaraderie* or self-confidence (or perhaps not wishing to have his staff know what he
said or to have his remarks recorded in permanent archives), each
held conversations with heads or high representatives of foreign
governments in the presence only of an interpreter from the other
side.

The practice is lamentable on two counts. In the first place, it
makes the President or Secretary of State totally dependent on the

accuracy and honesty of the other side's interpreter. He has no
way of knowing that the words of his interlocutor are being properly translated to him and that his own comments are not being
mangled in translation either because the interpreter misunder-
stands or is afraid to offend his leader by direct blunt language —
or even has some private motive for distorting what is said.

But, beyond that, neither the President nor his staff nor the
Department of State will have a full and accurate record of the
exchange, so no one can be precisely certain just what may have
been said or understood. When an American President has his
own interpreter present, the interpreter will, immediately on the
conclusion of the discussion, dictate a full report of the exchange
from his notes. Since good professional interpreters not only have
almost total recall, but take notes in their own special kind of
shorthand, these reports will almost certainly be careful and precise. But if the American side must rely purely on the debriefing
of a harassed President, embarrassing *gaffes* can slip by unno-
ticed. Presidents — and even some self-assured Secretaries of
State — are not, as a rule, patient debriefers and even when they
can be induced to provide their staffs an account of what took
place, the result is not reliable. Not only is the memory of a
harassed President likely to be fallible, but he may well have
missed subtle implications or even substantive points because of
his necessarily spotty knowledge of the subject matter. Nor can
one be sure that words were not uttered in the exuberance of the
moment or that an inflection of voice had not conveyed an unin-
tended impression which we would only learn about later when
we would have to pick up the pieces. Then there was always the
suspicion that, recapitulating a discussion, the President might
tend to recount some comment the way he wished he had said it,
thus giving the impression the exchange had come off better than
it had, in fact. Yet when the President or Secretary of State records
nothing (as has occurred with alarming frequency during the Kissinger period), the result can be downright dangerous since there
will be no complete permanent record available in the State Department files for the benefit of successor administrations.

Secretary Kissinger is particularly addicted to dispensing with
his own interpreter. As recently as the October 23–27, 1974, Moscow visit, *The New York Times* reported that the Secretary had
spent ninety minutes alone with Leonid Brezhnev — with only an

interpreter from the Soviet side present.[5] Who will know five years from now what words passed between them? We shall have only the Soviet version.

Today's world is far too complex for two men ever again to sit on a raft in the Niemen River — or even the Kremlin or a palace in Peking — and dispose of the destinies of other nations. It would have been extremely dangerous, for example, had President Nixon on his China visit tried to concert with Chou or Mao a tactical position toward the Soviet Union, or to agree on a line of conduct toward Taiwan or on discouraging the remilitarization of Japan or promoting the reunification of Korea. Those matters might have been gingerly explored by a skilled and cautious envoy such as Mr. Kissinger, who would — had our government been functioning properly — have taken no positions except on carefully formulated instructions and who could have stalled or pondered or delayed. But when the President tries to negotiate with another head of state, he is subject to the tactical disadvantage that what he says definitively expresses what our country will do. If he ignores subtleties of policy or some relevant fact, he may well commit his government to an action he would never favor had he had the chance to study the problem with care, follow the advice of better informed assistants, factor in all relevant information, and prepare a reply in precisely written language that took into account the context of total policy.

History is replete with the mischief that has resulted from private conversations between leaders of great nations. A modern example was Prime Minister Macmillan's apparent misunderstanding as to just what President de Gaulle thought he was telling him during their Rambouillet meeting in 1962 which preceded the Nassau Conference. The two leaders conducted their tête-à-tête in French and afterwards some members of the British Foreign Office were led to speculate that the Prime Minister's mastery of that language was not so *nuancée* as he himself thought it to be. Whatever the fact, it is at least possible — though, I think, unlikely — that this misunderstanding materially altered the course of history. One can speculate that, had it not occurred, the misbegotten Nassau Conference might not have followed the course it did and De Gaulle would have had less excuse to throw his thunderbolt from Mont Elysée on the following January 14.

Again in November 1969 when Prime Minister Sato of Japan

visited Nixon at the White House, he was so overwhelmed at the President's proposal to return Okinawa to Japan that he impulsively promised to solve one of the President's own political problems by restricting textile exports to America. It was a promise he would probably never have made had he not met the President face-to-face; for, as I shall point out later, he found on returning home that he did not have the power to deliver on his commitment. Yet it was pique from feeling deceived by Sato over the textile issue that poisoned the attitude of the President and Kissinger regarding Japan and almost certainly contributed to their abrasive treatment of a major ally.

Perhaps the classical example of the mischief that can come from unchaperoned meetings of heads of state was the abortive Treaty of Björkö, in 1905, which came about when the Kaiser undertook a major diplomatic intiative of his own devising. Without telling his ministers, he invited the Czar ("Dear Nicky") to a secret rendezvous at Björkö in the Gulf of Finland. There he presented him with a draft treaty of his own devising that committed Russia and Germany to aid each other in the event of attack. As the Kaiser conceived it, the treaty was a cunning diplomatic trap, since, by signing it, Russia would be breaking her existing engagements with France, which the Kaiser regarded as the central key in a plan to encircle him.

Up to a point the Kaiser's machinations worked to perfection. With no one to hold his hand, Nicky signed on the dotted line, and the Kaiser returned to Germany in secret triumph. But he overlooked the occupational obtuseness of foreign offices. When the Kaiser and the Czar arrived in their respective capitals, each encountered the solid disapproval of his principal ministers. Von Bülow threatened to resign, while the Russian Foreign Minister, Count Lamsdorf, pointed out to the unhappy Czar that, by engaging to join Germany in a possible war, he had repudiated his military alliance with France — a detail, as one of the Kaiser's biographers explained, which "no doubt escaped His Majesty in the flood of the Emperor William's eloquence." It was not the finest hour for heads of state or other amateurs.

Among other unhappy aspects of summitry is that it obscures the concept of relations between governments as a continuing process. Since the spectators at home are bemused by pageantry and not trained to look for a coherent body of policy, most seem satisfied with a succession of unrelated vignettes. There is no better illustration of that than President Nixon's insistence on touring the Middle East in June 1974 — a visit that followed in the wake of Henry Kissinger's brilliant tour de force in arranging military disengagements, first on the Egyptian and then on the Syrian fronts. Up to that point Kissinger's exploits had occupied far too many headlines for Nixon's taste. In putting an ocean between himself and a Congress that was threatening him with impeachment, he knew the American television audience would be impressed by pictures of apparently enthusiastic crowds mobilized for him in the various Arab capitals. Thus, although eager to dissociate himself from the criminal enterprises of other White House aides, he was ready and willing to assume credit for his Secretary of State's achievements.

But the trip, far from advancing peace in the Middle East or even salvaging the Nixon Presidency, entailed a due bill whose cost strained the friendly Middle East relations Kissinger had sought to establish. Promising largesse such as nuclear power plants stirred atavistic memories of earlier potentates who had traveled the area, handing out ivory, peacocks, apes, musk, and frankincense. But, since no one had bothered to check with Congress, Nixon excited expectations he could not fulfill.

To the Arab world an American President appeared as the one national leader with the necessary clout to exact concessions from Israel, and no doubt the unusual gesture of a Presidential trip convinced many Arabs that America had finally seen the light. Nixon's visit even seemed to vindicate the oil embargo, which, as they saw it, had brought home to Washington the new realities of their strategic position. Thus they naturally assumed that the President could thereafter be counted on to assure the rectification of Arab grievances against Israel in an atmosphere of economic generosity.

Had Nixon been a student of history or even been born ten years earlier, he might have recalled the triumphal European tour of Woodrow Wilson in the latter months of 1918, just before the Versailles Conference. Then the appearance of the American President had evoked unprecedented public enthusiasm with a vast outpouring of citizens to honor the man whom Anatole France saluted as "the first citizen of the world," and Maxime Leroy hailed as "a combination Marcus Aurelius and Montesquieu ordained to restore order in the world." [6] But just six months after Wilson had been wildly cheered, the European public — and even the press — barely noted his departure for America. By then the diplomatic realities had intruded themselves and unfulfilled expectations had produced a pervasive disenchantment. Even Wilson's most prestigious booster ruefully commented that "humanity can evolve an antidote for the tyrant and the despot. It recovers hardly from the statesman who proclaims a high ideal, only to stand impotently by while it is shattered to pieces before his eyes." [7]

Richard Nixon, at the end, sought to rest much of his case for indispensability and hence survival on the claim that he was on intimate terms with General Secretary Brezhnev and with other world leaders, and that that enabled him to compose otherwise irreconcilable interests and advance America's influence in a manner denied other leaders with lesser credentials for name-dropping. Thus, toward the end of the 1973 October War, after a Soviet note suggesting possible intervention to separate the Egyptian and Israeli armies had triggered a dramatic alert to American forces around the world, Nixon asserted that he had been able to prevent a major confrontation only because he and Brezhnev knew and understood one another.

Yet all that could be carried too far. In desperately trying to capitalize on the theme that "I know Leonid Ilyich better than anyone," Nixon found himself crosswise with the Soviet propaganda line. In a toast at a state dinner on June 27, 1974, at the beginning of the Third Summit Meeting in Moscow, he boasted that past agreements between the Soviet Union and the United States "were possible because of a personal relationship that was established between the General Secretary and the President of the United States," asserting further that "because of our personal relationship there is no question about our will to keep these agreements and to make more where they are in our mutual interests." To the embarrassment of Mr. Nixon, however, the Kremlin made it clear that *détente* was founded on something other than personal acquaintance with a President whose tenure of office was precarious; thus *Pravda* omitted the word "personal" in quoting Nixon's reference to future agreements.

This action had dual significance. It meant that the Soviets definitely repudiated the "cult of personality" that had marked the Stalinist era and that they did not share the Nixonian view that personal acquaintance could act as a solvent breaking down the hard realities of interest and ideology institutionalized under the Soviet system. That old cynic N. S. Khrushchev bluntly ridiculed such a sentimental conceit in his memoirs. "Do you think," he wrote, "when two representatives holding diametrically opposing views get together to shake hands, the contradictions between our systems will simply melt away? What kind of a daydream is that?" [8]

But, in addition, the incident made clear that the Kremlin is not prepared to tie its future policy to any such ephemeral anchor as the "friendship of princes," particularly when the prince in question may not be around very long. Summit meetings, as the Soviets see them, are useful to influence public opinion in the country of the foreign prince. They provide a chance to nudge national policy in a direction compatible with Soviet interests without danger of any reciprocal effect, since with tight control over their own press they can present summit meetings any way they like to the Soviet public. Unfortunately, that is a hard point for Americans to grasp. We have heard so much of "people-to-people" relations, the "climate of *détente*," the prospect of a new "understanding between peoples," that we fail to understand that we can do little to transform the policies of a police state merely by appealing to the good will of its citizenry.

Although the wise young men who founded the United States were as conscious of their mission as were the Jacobins in France two decades later or the Leninists in Moscow in 1917, they were far less interested in preaching to the world than in providing it with a proper example. Our American forebears showed little interest in trying to spread their concepts of freedom and constitutionalism through evangelical means. Thus the idea that we might "talk over the heads of other governments directly to the people" made little impact until the end of the second decade of this century. Then Woodrow Wilson, one of America's first universalists, undertook to "penetrate the fog barrier of governments" to spread his concepts of self-determination. But he missed by months being the first exponent of that technique. The

new Soviet leaders — doctrinal universalists in accordance with
their own lay religion — had already inaugurated their version of
the "new diplomacy" at Brest-Litovsk. Trotsky and his colleagues
were pioneers in exploiting the potential of electronic communications to overleap national boundaries, transmitting their
political and ideological message by wireless, news wires, and in-
terviews with newsmen, over the heads of government to the
masses. Special editions of German-language newspapers and
leaflets were printed to win the German army away from its leadership. The Bolsheviks issued a proclamation to "the laboring
Moslems of Russia and the East" signed by Lenin and Stalin,
Commissar of Nationalities. The British ambassador wrote, "Mr.
Lenin . . . incited our Indian subjects to rebellion." [9]

What the Soviets well understood was that sealing off their
own society enabled them to infect other nations while quarantin-
ing their own people against the plague of the truth. It is an advantage they have exploited with increasing skill, as they have
gradually learned more about American tastes and susceptibilities.
Thus, after Mr. Brezhnev made his colorful visit to the United
States in June 1973, there is no doubt that many Americans felt
easier in their minds about Soviet intentions. It is hard for a free,
unindoctrinated people to focus on stern conflicts of national interest and policy when foreign leaders appear in flesh and blood or
on television screens in living color; and, since politicians make a
profession of ingratiating themselves with the people, distorted
perceptions often result.

When photographed with Roosevelt and Churchill at a succession of summit meetings, Stalin became lovable "Uncle Joe," our
crude but brave ally, in spite of the fact that he was one of the
bloodiest tyrants in history. Even that crusty Middle Westerner
Harry Truman thought Stalin an able and pleasant fellow. While
touring the United States fifteen years ago, Khrushchev appeared
as a genial and boisterous eccentric, scarcely the kind of man
one might expect to build a Berlin Wall that divided families and
encaged millions, or smuggle missiles into Cuba, or send tanks to
suppress departures from the party line, first in Poland and then
Hungary. So it was not surprising that the same magic worked for
Leonid Brezhnev; Americans quickly forgot that he had given his
name to the doctrine which sanctioned the despoiling of the brief

Prague spring in 1968. Many Americans regarded the Brezhnev visit as a great success and a demonstration of the reality of *détente*. That it accomplished nothing of substantive significance made little difference.

I do not mean to make too much of the point, but it seems clear that the presentation of the leader of the Soviet Union as a jovial and benign friend of America is a grotesque misrepresentation to which no United States President should be an eager accomplice. The only result can be to blur American understanding of the realities of Soviet-American relations, and, in the long run, discourage the exertions necessary to maintain the political will and military strength that are the essential deterrents to major conflict.

CHAPTER 4

How We Involved
Ourselves in Vietnam

IF THE OPENING TO CHINA WAS A SOUND DIPLOMATIC MOVE
flawed by President Nixon's excessive love of theatrics and desire
to impress the home folks, the withdrawal of American troops from
Vietnam, though demanded by a disenchanted country, was clum-
sily executed at excessive cost in blood and treasure. The flaw this
time was not Nixon's predisposition for pomp and circumstance
but his misconception of the nature of the conflict, his failure to
comprehend the realities of the American interest, his obsessive
desire to appease right-wing opinion, and his congenital weakness
for exaggeration.

In view of Nixon's pretentious claims regarding the so-called
"peace with honor" his administration brought about in Southeast
Asia, it is proper to ask why the extrication took so long and why it
proved so extraordinarily costly. But before we can pass judgment
on the process by which we withdrew American power from Vietnam, it is essential that we understand the process by which we
committed it in the first place and why our nation sank more and
more deeply in the morass. On that question my views reflect a
day-to-day participation in the high councils of government from
the beginning of 1961 until late 1966, the decisive years of our
Vietnam involvement, as well as my brief tour as ambassador to
the United Nations in 1968. Although I do not share Goethe's con-

viction that "you cannot understand history without having lived through history itself," I find a germ of truth in what he wrote. Contemporary books and records cannot possibly re-create the intellectual and emotional environment in which the White House was encysted, or adequately convey the play of ideas and personalities that entered into major decisions.

"History repeats itself," wrote Philip Guedalla; "historians repeat one another." And, although he was referring to the Oxford historians of his day, his epigram fits even more aptly those doctrinaire scribblers who invent fanciful explanations of the Vietnam tragedy by quoting one another's writings as though they were primary sources. We enmeshed ourselves in Vietnam, so they tell us, because our "foreign policy establishment" — whatever that banal term may mean — was coopted from too narrow a stratum of American society to reflect the wisdom of the people, or — according to others — because the "military and industrial complex" — that all-purpose bogeyman — gained the upper hand, or because the State Department was far too obsessed with Europe to understand Asia, or finally — so the Marxists solemnly assert — because the war was inevitably dictated by capitalism's contradictions.

Such pseudo-explanations should not be taken seriously; they are roughly at the intellectual level of the student who confidently assured me on a university campus some years ago, "Everybody knows why we are in Vietnam; it is because we want their tin."

The remote, and even the proximate, causes of our involvement were, in my observation, disturbingly simple.

Proceeding down quite discrete paths marked out by their individual logic and experience, two Presidents and substantially the same small group of advisors converged by unhappy destiny on a common conclusion: that a South Vietnamese defeat would endanger vital United States interests, and that we must intervene to prevent it. I contended at the time — and events have confirmed that contention — that that involved a misappraisal of the situation.

The first and most fundamental error related to the character of the conflict. For many it seemed a repetition of the Korean War, which, in the early 1960s, was still a vivid memory. On balance our role in that war was regarded as a Good Thing; we had halted a Communist invasion and thrown back the aggressor. So, during the darkest days of the Vietnam fiasco, diplomatic veterans cited cliff-hanger incidents by way of encouragement. "Don't be downhearted, we went through just as bad patches in Korea and came out all right."

Yet, unlike Korea, the struggle in Vietnam was not a classical invasion, not a simple power thrust by a neighboring country lusting to take over Vietnam. It began in the south as a revolt, though supplied and supported and — to a considerable extent — directed from the north. The revolutionary forces known as the Viet Cong were the legatees of — or, perhaps more accurately, an extension of — the Viet Minh, who had driven the French out of Vietnam and wished to complete the eradication of the white man's influence by destroying the government of the American-assisted Ngo Dinh Diem and taking over the south. Since the true nature of the war determined not only America's moral, but its juridical, position, our stubborn refusal to regard the struggle as indigenous in any respect was manifestly self-serving. By denouncing the Viet Cong as mere agents of Hanoi with no claim to southern roots, we reinforced our diagnosis of external aggression and, hence, legitimized our basis for interfering.

Yet, even apart from any conclusive showing of external direction, the then-current view of Communist tactics provided a sophisticated sanction. With a stalemate in Europe, so the experts decreed, the Communist threat was shifting from Moscow to Peking, where the Chinese masters of the agrarian revolution had devised a novel instrument of political conquest — "wars of national liberation" fought with subversion and insurgency that could be stopped only with a whole new arsenal of weapons and stratagems. Thus, in Washington a fervent cult of amateurs in the new art — or vogue — of "counterinsurgency" took Mao Tse-tung's banalities and Lin Piao's windy writings as definitive statements of the new menace — and a major challenge to the peace. For them Vietnam was a laboratory, the prototype skirmish in a series of guerrilla conflicts by which China would seek to expand its power and influence.

Beyond that there was even a further fallback; for if those fears did not prove well founded and the war were indeed primarily a local struggle to unite Vietnam — or, to put it another way, if the threat were merely Tonkinese, not Chinese, imperialism — the menace still wore a Communist face and could thus yield an increment of power for the Communist side. It mattered little that South Vietnam, or even the whole of Southeast Asia, was by itself of no more than marginal strategic interest to America; there was always the domino theory. Who could say what would happen to Laos or Cambodia, or even Thailand, if the tough Viet Cong swarmed over Saigon?

As it turned out, these arguments escaped sharp scrutiny because our intervention created its own rationale. Our initial claim that we were in Vietnam to help the South Vietnamese stop Communist aggression became submerged in an increasingly insistent contention that we must see the war through to the end because we were there. That we had no treaty obligations running directly to Saigon did not seem to matter, nor was anyone much bothered that the SEATO Treaty was never invoked until toward the middle of 1965 when external aggression had been established by the appearance in the south of main-force North Vietnamese units. The very fact that we had *begun* to involve ourselves was, it was claimed, a compelling reason why we should *continue* to do so — and, of course, we must win. We were caught up in a self-propelling, self-fulfilling process: the worse the situation became, the more we promised; the more Saigon's defeat seemed imminent, the more categorically we committed ourselves to ultimate victory.

The effect of this process clearly showed in official speeches and statements. As the threat of Chinese and Russian involvement grew less convincing, official emphasis shifted from the danger of tipping the power balance to the erosion of American prestige if we permitted a North Vietnamese takeover to occur. Thus, we transmuted our perception of the war from a conflict between North and South Vietnam into a test of our will and ability to stay the course — and, by a breathtaking leap in logic, a test of our credibility as a dependable ally anywhere in the world. We had to win because we had told the South Vietnamese we would do so, and if we did not prevail, who would trust us to defend Berlin?

Thus the war's hard-pressed apologists came to equate our efforts in the jungles and rice paddies of a small country on the edge of nowhere with our most important treaty commitments to defend our Western allies in the heart of Europe — the center of world power and hence the center of danger. Not that many literally believed this exaggerated thesis; it was more a debating point than a conviction. Yet the Bonn Government, worried but still eager to please, did play it back to us from time to time.

Nor was logic the only casualty of our failure to concede the essentially revolutionary nature of the struggle. It also led us to underestimate the staying power of the enemy. The French had made the same misjudgment some years earlier, yet few in Washington acknowledged their experience as relevant. After all, was there not a basic difference in the power of France and America — a disparity not only in sophisticated arms but also in the moral authority that flowed from the relative purity of our respective purposes?

This last point was the clincher, for Washington in the 1960s devoutly believed we were waging a selfless war to save the South Vietnamese from Communist expansionism, whereas France had merely fought a hopeless rearguard action to save its rich colonies from a worldwide anticolonial tide. It was a distinction so clear to the White House that it must be clear even to the *indigènes*.

But self-righteousness is the enemy of sound analysis and in this case it encouraged the smug assumption that the rest of the world would applaud the nobility of our motives. That, for the most part, the foreigners failed to do so was a bitter experience for a people who like to be loved. Yet our discomfiture should teach us a lesson: *before we engage our military power in a foreign land we should make quite certain that we comprehend the nature of the struggle and the play of forces it represents. Moreover, we should appraise our actions not only as we see them but also as they are likely to be viewed by other nations — and particularly our friends and allies.*

Unfortunately, we refused to acknowledge the distasteful fact that, in the eyes of mankind, our poor, wretched opponents — in spite of their barbaric cruelty — were more and more being pictured as the valiant underdog, while we were typecast as a blundering bully.

Unfair as many may regard it, such a reaction was made inevitable by the disparity of resources available to each side; in addition, it was intensified by two circumstances. The first was that our intervention involved the injection of white men into a quarrel be-

tween peoples of another race. The second — and even more important — was that, though vastly superior in absolute terms, our
power proved relatively ineffective in what the French called the
"dirty war" of the jungles and paddies against a lightly armed
enemy fewer in number yet equipped with cunning and courage
beyond normal Western experience.

That ineffectiveness — our impotence, as others saw it — was
the fatal flaw. We might have endured the temporary loss of moral
authority resulting from an intervention quickly and successfully
concluded — through, say, a land invasion of North Vietnam —
but such a course of action was quite properly ruled out, not only
because of its excessive cost in relation to our limited stake in the
outcome, but because, with the Korean War still on everyone's
mind, the specter of Chinese mass armies counseled prudence. So
Washington faced a painful dilemma. If decisive action risked
turning a small war into a large one, limited action seemed to offer
only protracted conflict. And our persistent failure to bring the
issue to a conclusion compounded the permanent damage to our
prestige ten times over.

Why did our military effort flounder so long and in-
conclusively? It is fashionable to blame the soldiers for inept military tactics and bumbling execution. Even this long after the conflict there are ten thousand Monday-morning strategists who write
books and articles and letters to the editor, and the argument may
last as long as the one that agonized the South after Appomattox.
Yet it misses the point and we would merely befuddle ourselves if
we become obsessed with it. Even had we given our military a
free hand, our effort would still have failed because *there was no
adequate indigenous political base on which our power could be
emplaced. And that provides another lesson we must learn if we
are to avoid the same mistake a second time.*

South Vietnam was never a nation but an improvisation — a
geographical designation for what General de Gaulle once described to me as a piece of "rotten country." It was an area that,
merely by a caprice of history, fell south of what the Geneva Conference designated in 1954 as a temporary demarcation line and
specifically *not* "a political or territorial boundary." Arbitrarily
carved out of what had been Cochin China and a part of the old
kingdom of Annam, South Vietnam embodied no cultural or ethnic

logic. Political power was fragmented — split among Catholics, Buddhists, Hoa Haos, Cao Dais, and Binh Xuyens, all at odds with one another, while the Montagnard tribes and the Khmer and Shan populations lived in isolation. The only effect on them of the squalid infighting in Saigon was a rotation of the Vietnamese officials who extorted taxes and exploited their labor.

That we regarded this amorphous acreage as a potential nation-state reflected a Pygmalion fantasy then common in academic circles — the fantasy of "nation-building." Our experts would draw the blueprints, train the natives to read them, and produce new democratic nations. Applied to Vietnam, this was mischievous nonsense. However impressive might be our theoretical understanding of "nation-building" as a process — and it never seemed impressive to me — it was beyond the competence of the professors to turn a poor, agrarian, Oriental society, built around the family and the village, into a modern, democratic state. We simply could not teach the natives to make institutional bricks when there was no cohesive straw and the available clay was spectacularly unsuited to the purpose. Vietnamese society possessed none of the nuclear elements from which a democratic structure could be evolved. Nor, as we have painfully learned, were there any better materials available for the creation of a traditional authoritarian regime under the likes of Diem or Thieu.

Evolving simultaneously with this intellectual preoccupation were analytical methods rooted in the operations research activities of the Second World War. Transmuted through industrial application, they inspired sophisticated disciplines, and, in an age painfully adjusting to the fearsome implications of the atom, it was inevitable that they would play a key role in strategic speculation.

Such speculation found its spiritual home among theoreticians in Harvard and MIT, as well as the think tanks of Rand and its flamboyant offspring, the Hudson Institute. It was they who invented much of the jargon and set the pattern reflected in the dialectic of the Pentagon Papers — including the application of game theory and model building to warfare, the employment of "input-output ratios" and "kill ratios," and the elaboration of doctrines of "limited war," "flexible response," and "controlled escalation." Yeasty stuff it was — full of elegant conceptions which inevitably led to an obsession with the purely operational aspects of the Vietnam struggle and the constant harping on one single

question: "By what ingenious application of our superior resources can we now achieve our purpose?" Meanwhile, the more fundamental question: "Are we not trying to do something impossible?" was necessarily rejected as denying the basic assumptions that were guiding our effort.

Thus, in the long run, what misled a group of able and dedicated men was that, in depersonalizing the war and treating it too much as an exercise in the deployment of resources, we ignored the one supreme advantage possessed by the other side: the non-material element of will, of purpose, of patience, of cruel but relentless commitment to a single objective, regardless of human cost — something that, occurring on our side, we would have called "extraordinary patriotism" but which, when displayed by the enemy, we labeled "irrationality" or "fanaticism" — a challenge to faith in quantified resources. Yet that was the secret of North Vietnamese success — a rebuke of spirit of the logic of number.

In the 1960s such skepticism was rank heresy, because it cut athwart two aspects of the American character that make life difficult for us in the cynical world of *Realpolitik* — our passionate conviction that we Americans can do anything we set our hearts on and our need that our allies be lovable. Because dynastic sovereigns of an earlier day, who were mostly all in-laws or cousins of one another, were under no illusions regarding the virtues or vices of their relatives, there was no need to view alliances in moralistic or sentimental terms; but democracies are denied a clear-eyed and cold-blooded approach. The public wants sentimental tears with its politics.

Unhappily, our indulgent conceit that Washington and the Saigon Government were "equal partners" proved a severe constraint on our freedom of maneuver. Though talking of unity in a common struggle, we had no way to compel our "ally" to follow our advice. We could preach to the clique momentarily in command in Saigon about the need for land reform; we could admonish Vietnamese leaders to broaden the base of government to include diverse elements of society; we could exhort them to try to establish their authority in the countryside as well as the cities — but when they smiled sweetly and shrugged, that was the end of it.

What few dared admit was that the government in Washington

had become the captive of its own fictions. To make the war even halfway harmonious with our own view of ourselves, our government had to portray the South Vietnamese as a democratic freedom-loving people. Meanwhile, the practical-minded juntas that succeeded one another in Saigon blithely pursued the corrupt politics that came naturally to them.

The source of their strength was their incompetence. Like heroines in eighteenth-century Richardson novels, they constantly threatened collapse if confronted with unpleasantness — a terrifying prospect that dismayed an American Government with no ready alternatives. Fear that South Vietnam was politically disintegrating was the decisive argument for initiating our ill-conceived air offensive against the north in early 1965. It led us to commit the folly of bombing while Kosygin was still in Hanoi. Finally, Saigon's fragility repeatedly blocked efforts to find a political solution, since whatever junta was then in power would howl to the heavens at the whisper of a compromise that might leave it to face Hanoi without Big Brother by its side.

The obvious lesson from all this is that America must never again commit its power and authority in defense of a country of only marginal strategic interests when that country lacks a broadly based government, or the will to create one. The political fragility of Saigon undermined our military effectiveness while destroying our freedom of choice or maneuver. We became, in all too many ways, our puppet's puppet.

The heart of the matter was the unwillingness of the American Government — and, indeed, the American people — to acknowledge, or even comprehend, the full implications of limited war. That the American interest in Vietnam was no more than marginal seemed clear even in the early 1960s when it was still widely assumed that the Viet Cong and North Vietnamese were agents of the larger Communist powers. Even then it was tacitly conceded that the control of South Vietnam was not worth a head-on clash with Peking or Moscow. Thus, the restrictions imposed by President Johnson on the conduct of the war — his reluctance to mine Haiphong Harbor or blow up the dikes or bomb the city center of Hanoi or mount a land invasion of North Vietnam — were designed to avoid too great a provocation to the major powers.

The fallacy was that, though three Presidents accepted the concept of limited war as the basis for operations, they still felt compelled to defend our intervention with total-war rhetoric. It was taken for granted that neither Congress nor the American people could be persuaded to accept even limited losses of manpower or resources unless they believed that the stakes at issue were vital to America's security.

One question raised by this experience is whether a nation, however powerful, can successfully wage a limited war against even a small nation committed to total war. Another is whether a democratic state such as America can fight a limited war that lasts any length of time and still keep it limited, since a free people will not be willing to accept sustained sacrifices unless persuaded that they are fighting for a cause which, in their view, not only justifies what they are being asked to give up but also legitimates the use of their nation's full military might. If a war for an objective so limited as to constrain the nation from utilizing its full military power should drag on to the point where the costs in blood and treasure become onerous, the President must either halt the fighting short of the goal he has set or inflate the importance of the war, and perhaps even widen its scope, so as to justify the national sacrifice. Yet the latter course will only present him with a second dilemma; for if the objectives of the war are so important as to justify a major national sacrifice, how can the President defend the continuance of constraints on the military means employed, including the use of nuclear weapons? In other words, how long will a democratic people be willing to accept massive losses in blood and treasure if they could destroy the enemy overnight by a well-placed missile or two, particularly when they have been paying heavy taxes for years to develop those missiles?

The basic dilemma facing a democracy has been stated lucidly by Colonel Edward M. Collins of the United States Air Force in his introduction to a selection of the writings of Karl von Clausewitz.[1] Since Clausewitz was born in Prussia in 1780 and lived until 1831, he witnessed in his lifetime the first emergence of the idea of the war "of whole nations." In assuming the form of an absolute struggle, war was, as he saw it, approaching more nearly "its real nature" as an act of violence limited only by the means at the disposal of the participants. Though he was not cer-

tain that absolute wars would, in fact, become the rule in the future, he considered such a development probable. Moreover, as he saw it, the tendency toward escalating violence would be directly related to the extent to which a war received mass support. This, in the words of Colonel Collins,

> would indicate that — at least in a democracy — the difficulties in "managing" a war, in the sense of keeping to proper political aims, are very great. No war can be successfully conducted without a reasonable measure of popular support, but when public opinion in a democracy becomes aroused, it diminishes the freedom of action of the leaders and increases the tendency for war to become in reality what Clausewitz conceived wars to be only in theory: "struggles of life or death, from pure hatred." [2]

In the case of our Vietnamese experience, the limited justification for fighting the war quite clearly did not support the sacrifices demanded — and the public instinctively came to recognize it. Thus, the country split into two angry camps.

One wished to treat the war not as limited but absolute, since that was implied in the terms with which two Presidents had described the implications of defeat; in other words, they wished their leaders to commit resources commensurate with their rhetoric so we could "win," which meant relaxing constraints on the means of warfare, even though that might result in widening the conflict. That simply proved, of course, what Colonel Collins's gloss on Clausewitz had predicted — that "a too greatly aroused public opinion in a democracy" would diminish the political leadership's "freedom of action" by forcing a war to be fought as a "struggle of life or death." [3] But majority opinion, as now seems clear, pursued logic in the other — and much sounder — direction. It saw the sacrifices demanded by the war as excessive in relation to its limited objectives, and thus implicitly repudiated the overblown rhetoric of the political leadership.

Unfortunately, the issues of Vietnam were never presented to the American people in realistic terms; and because our government did not ask the people to face them, it paid a high price for its false position. In exhorting the country with total-war rhetoric to fight a limited war, it undercut confidence in its own integrity.

Not merely was our rhetoric unsuited to a limited war, but so

was our military instrument. The United States ignored the time-honored practice — habitually followed by the dynastic states of Europe for which limited war was a way of life — that such contests should be fought with professional armies or hired mercenaries but never with troops raised through national conscription.

Prior to 1917, America fought five strictly limited wars: the Indian Campaigns (1789–1883), the Naval War with France (1798–1799), the Mexican War (1846–1848), the Spanish-American War (1898), and its aftermath, the Philippine Insurrection (1899–1902). In all those contests, the brunt of the fighting was borne by a small force of regulars assisted by gentlemen amateurs and volunteers. Except for the Civil War, the only conflict marked by conscription prior to 1917 was the War of 1812, when state governors drafted men into the militia to fend off a series of devastating British counterattacks in 1814.

That America had fought her wars in this manner was not surprising. English military tradition coupled with a profound distrust of standing armies, as Tocqueville shrewdly noted,[4] made a military career little esteemed. As islands isolated from the continent of Europe, England and America had encountered mass participation in war only occasionally — with British experience limited to the protracted agonies of the Wars of the Roses (1455–1485) and the English Civil Wars (1642–1661). Prior to 1916, wars for the Anglo-Saxons were (with the exception of the American Civil War) limited both in purpose and in *dramatis personae*. Yet even before 1789 continental tradition had been markedly different. The ancient Greeks and Romans had all insisted that military service was a prerequisite to citizenship, and the medieval kings paid lip service to that tradition by requiring that every male between the ages of sixteen and sixty be a member of the militia. Only when the supply of mercenaries and volunteers proved insufficient did the advent of modern weapons in the eighteenth century, coupled with the rapid growth of armies and their concomitant casualties, compel the introduction of crude conscription systems. However, the "nation-in-arms" did not emerge until the French Revolution, when, having seized the state from the dynasts, the people swarmed to its defense, with vast armies created by a *levée en masse* and driven by the ideological fervor of a fanatical nationalism.[5] Aflame with egalitarian fire, they fought truly total wars in which the whole society engaged.

It was in this spirit that the United States raised and sent its armies into the two total wars of this century, but it is a spirit that cannot be sustained in a limited war fought with limited means for limited objectives. Not many people are willing to die for a cause which most of the public regards as only marginally important. Since that view was most fiercely held by the young, who had the most to lose, it was inevitable in 1965, when we first committed forces to main-force combat, that we would set the campuses on fire. Repelled by the prospect of being dragged off to a faraway land to be wounded or killed for no clearly apparent reason, the young quite properly asked "Why?" and took to the streets when no convincing answer was forthcoming. Yet once force levels in Vietnam were shrunk to the point where draftees were no longer needed, the campuses quieted down, and opposition to the war lost much of its passion. The fact that the intensity of moral protest was directly related to the threat of compulsory involvement made nonsense of silly talk about a new saintly breed and the nobler perceptions of youth.

Still the students had reason for discontent with the contradictions of American policy. Although our government sought to fight a limited war against a North Vietnam committed to total war, while employing the total-war rhetoric and the conscription policy of a "nation-in-arms," it did not put our economy on a total-war basis through rationing, price control, or even higher taxes. Nor were these inconsistencies explained. Today we should ponder the implications of our Vietnam experience in relation to the "all-volunteer armed forces" we have created since then. Such forces will give further freedom of action to the President of the United States, whoever he may be, since they will provide him an instrument to fight limited wars with far less impact on the home front.

Still, it would be wrong to conclude that public opinion was immediately effective. Only late in the day did widespread discontent with our Vietnam involvement appreciably slow the escalation of the war; for a time, paradoxically, it dug us in even more deeply because the shrill hysteria of the public protest engendered in Washington a siege mentality. Unable to defend our effort persuasively in the traditional terms of national interest, the Johnson — and later the Nixon — Administration instinctively resorted to new extremes of overstatement to justify the mounting investment of manpower and matériel. It was a classical reaction to frustration, recalling the tourist in a foreign land who compensates for his linguistic deficiencies by shouting English words loudly. Thus, the noisier the criticism, the more apocalyptic the disaster if the United States should lose.

Mounting pressure to exaggerate the dangers of "defeat" and inflate the necessity for "victory" thus came from two different quarters: the Saigon Government, which had constantly to be propped up like a drunk by a lamppost, and the American people, who — it was thought — needed to be frightened and cajoled if they were to continue support for the war. In large part, the cajoling was ineffective, since the facts did not support the propaganda. Thus, many Americans soon perceived that, if the South Vietnamese leaders were one-quarter as dedicated, selfless, and courageous as our government represented them to be, they would have stopped their sordid politicking, pulled the nation together, and driven the enemy back across the border. On the contrary, their record was lamentable. The Saigon regime was supported by the most powerful air force in the world and assisted by an almost unlimited airlift and air support. It suffered only a fraction of the military casualties of the Viet Cong and North Vietnamese. In contrast to the formidable infiltration problems of Hanoi, its logistics were easy, and, while its cities were largely undamaged, the enemy's homeland was decimated by the air offensive. Finally, it possessed a numerical advantage that was overwhelming; it benefited from the efforts of 550,000 of America's young men, supplemented by its own army of over one million, at no time confronted by more than one-quarter of a million Viet Cong and North Vietnamese, who had no air force and no navy.

Yet the Saigon regime did everything possible to block a cease-fire in place because it lacked confidence that it could prevail in the military and political struggle without the Americans. In spite of American aid and an elaborate political apparatus that covered the country like a vast spiderweb, it showed little faith in itself, opposing any settlement that would not deliver the country on a platter.

These were the major influences that entered into our Vietnamese involvement, but, in addition, two other comments might usefully be made. One relates to the background of the responsible officials who, in February 1965, advised President Johnson to undertake the bombing of North Vietnam, and, in June 1965, to commit combat forces to that faraway land. To be sure, such recommendations were made by the military, but they were only doing their job within the framework of the directives given them. The advice that made the difference came from a handful of articulate and committed men of high intellectual attainments — all of great good will — who acted from the highest motives and were well-trained in the appropriate disciplines. Without exception, all had had experience on university and college faculties and all but one had spent the greater part of his career in academic life. I mention this not to condemn the professors who shaped our Vietnam policy, but, rather, to flash a cautionary signal at those academicians who believe that the campuses hold a patent on wisdom. The acknowledgment that the architects of our Vietnam involvement were members of their own trade union should help drain the sanctimony from the festering wound produced by the war.

Nor is that the whole story, for the policy drift which led us into the swamps and jungles in the first instance was encouraged by a dogmatic pragmatism fashionable in political science circles in the early 1960s. Expressed in slogan form, it taught that an American President should, so far as possible, "preserve his options." [6] What this most often meant in practice was an *ad hoc* approach to the individual steps in an evolving situation. It discouraged efforts to examine long-range objectives rigorously or to measure dangers and costs over the long pull or to decide how far we should pursue a given course if success did not come as hoped. I am certain that President Kennedy never believed, in the fall of 1961, that cleaning the Viet Cong out of South Vietnam would be worth the deployment of American combat forces on the Asian mainland; in fact, when I told him that this was where I thought a limited intervention would inevitably lead, he replied with an explosive denial. Yet, to my knowledge, John F. Kennedy never faced or made the explicit decision that we would *not* commit such forces, nor did he define the outside limits of our effort. Options had to be preserved; it was the received wisdom.

That it was a false wisdom has been repeatedly shown by experience; in this fast-paced modern age, time relentlessly destroys unexercised options. If a President fails or refuses to make a clear-cut decision on long-term policy, he will have less rather than more freedom to maneuver as events alter the facts and compel further action. That, in essence, was the story of Vietnam from the beginning. Successive administrations followed a Micawberish course, hoping that by abjuring long-range planning they could avoid irreversible decisions. Yet, because they failed to make the irreversible decision — or, in other words, to exercise the option to extricate America when it was easy — escape became increasingly costly.

In 1954, while briefly assisting a French Prime Minister, I encountered a competing principle that seemed more valid. "To govern is to choose," M. Mendés-France used to say — or, in other words, it is the duty of a chief of government to exercise his options while he can, not seek to preserve them. During the middle 1960s I suggested to my colleagues that the aphorism might be a sound guiding rule for an American President. After all, when Mendés-France found his country saddled with an endless struggle in Vietnam, he did not raise the ante and hope for a better hand. He liquidated the war in ninety days. For he well understood the question asked by little Peterkin in Southey's poem on the Battle of Blenheim: "But what good came of it at last?" And he remembered the old man's answer:

"Why that I cannot tell," said he,
"But 'twas a famous victory."

CHAPTER 5

The Failure to Develop a Doctrine of Extrication

ALEXIS DE TOCQUEVILLE ONCE WROTE THAT "THERE ARE TWO things which a democratic people will always find very difficult — to begin a war and to end it." [1] Judged by our experience in Vietnam, he was only half right. We found it all too easy to get involved. That, after deciding to withdraw, we took four long years to pull out our troops stemmed not so much from an inherent weakness in our democratic system as from the failure to evolve a doctrine of extrication. The Nixon Administration showed an avidity for confecting "doctrines" for other purposes — as, for example, the highly advertised "Nixon Doctrine" — and it might have borrowed a page from military learning, which is replete with doctrines to meet every situation, including retreat on the battlefield, or what the army manuals engagingly call "a retrograde movement." But it lacked strategic insight as to how a great nation could disentangle itself from an unwise political involvement without undue loss.

If our rationale for being in Vietnam was confused and shifting, Nixon had a golden chance to redefine it when he became President on January 20, 1969. The American voter had given him a mandate to extricate the United States from Vietnam, and it was left to him as to how he would accomplish it. His campaign assertion that he had a "Plan" for doing so was regarded —

and forgiven — as the gaseous stuff from which political promises are fabricated. Experienced observers wrote it off as what Wendell Willkie once called "campaign oratory," labeled "not to be taken literally." No one ever asked about the "Plan" again.

Coalescing in the President's favor were a number of factors that should have simplified his decision. Most important was the fact that he was succeeding an administration that had lost its popularity and had, by its own tacit admission, come to the dead end of a failed policy. President Lyndon Johnson had made it clear in his valedictory speech on March 31, 1968, that no further ground forces would be sent to Vietnam. Notice to the world that we were abandoning the effort to impose our will by constantly increasing the American deployment implied that a decision had been made to withdraw our troops on some unannounced timetable. Nor was there any argument as to the wisdom of what was called "Vietnamization"; the uncertainty related only to interpretation and timing. Tentative steps towards Vietnamization had begun as early as 1966, when an intensive program to train and reequip the South Vietnamese forces had been undertaken by General Creighton Abrams. By the beginning of 1969 the stage was set for progressively phasing out the American involvement.

In keeping with this, bombing had been halted in the north above the twentieth parallel. Settlement negotiations were begun in Paris, though the talks were temporarily deadlocked by a silly argument over the shape of the green baize table or tables. Even more important, the agonies and frustrations of the past years had drastically revised the American attitude toward the war. Few any longer believed that the Viet Cong and North Vietnamese were surrogates for the larger Communist nations. Since China no longer appeared as an expansionist power bent on driving its way into Southeast Asia, the relevance of the war to the containment of Peking could no longer be used to justify America's continued intervention. In other words, the war had been finally identified as a local affair, a civil war which the great powers had prolonged by outside aid, just as great powers had earlier done with the Spanish Civil War. No one in high places any longer believed that, if Saigon fell to Ho Chi Minh's legions, San Franciscans should drop everything to build bomb shelters.

Nor was there affection or respect for our ally, President

Thieu. Too many GIs had returned with lurid stories of the corruption and flaccidity of the Saigon regime at every level. Finally,
most Americans had ceased being greatly impressed by the "domino" theory. If South Vietnam collapsed, so might Cambodia and
Laos. But what difference would that make? Our only formal ally
in the area, Thailand — "the willow tree of Asia" — had shown,
over the centuries, that it could look out for itself through accommodation, or, when necessary, frontal resistance. Indonesia had effectively — even brutally — dealt with the Communists during
the abortive coup of October 1965, while Malaysia, Taiwan, Singapore, and the Philippines seemed reasonably secure by virtue of
their distance from Hanoi.

It was time for an American leader to reject the cant and hyperbole that had surrounded our feckless involvement and to ex-
ecute a skillful about-face, culling and revising the policies of his
predecessor to the relief and gratitude of most Americans. That
would, however, have required someone with wisdom, vision,
candor, integrity, independence and clarity of mind, the strength
of character to take actions that might result in a loss of votes, and
an indifference to public opinion polls. It would have required, in
other words, a President other than Richard Nixon.

What Nixon did, while talking of a "generation of peace" and
a decrease in America's overseas involvement, was to adopt, part
and parcel, the windiest clichés of the Johnson Administration and
to exaggerate them beyond even Texan dimensions. The basic
reason for this was clear enough. Though the two men differed in
skills and character — Johnson possessing a strong strain of idealism which Nixon wholly lacked — both Presidents shaped their
Vietnam policy with an alert ear for right-wing opinion. Remembering the ugly McCarthy era, Lyndon Johnson feared a savage
right-wing charge that the United States had abandoned Vietnam
to a Communist fate. More than once, he said to me: "Don't worry
about the hippies and the students and the Commies; they'll raise
a lot of hell but can't do real damage. The terrible beast we have
to fear is the right wing; if they ever get the idea I am selling out
Vietnam, they'll do horrible things to the country, and we'll be
forced to escalate the war beyond anything you've ever thought
about."

But if Lyndon Johnson was sensitive to a potential right-wing reaction because he feared it would tear the country apart, Richard Nixon, who had exploited McCarthyism for his own political advancement, played for the support of the right wing because they were his most loyal constituents. Besides, he felt at home with their concepts and attitudes, for had he not favored involving the United States in Indochina at the time of Dien Bien Phu to shore up France's colonial position in the sacred name of anti-Communism? Even Henry Kissinger, the professor undergoing a Darwinian adaptation to the Nixonian White House, justified his own hard line on Vietnam to his former academic colleagues on the ground that he was saving the country from a right-wing whiplash.

Richard Nixon added new verses to the mindless chorus that we could not disavow even the most far-out definition of our Vietnam commitment without destroying our credibility with other nations that counted on us for their security. More than that, he adopted as his own the statement that Lyndon Johnson had made with increasing frequency as our Vietnam imbroglio grew progressively more hopeless: "I'm not going to be the first American President to lose a war." It was a slogan that revealed more about the two leaders themselves than the predicament in which they were entrapped and it vividly illustrated the influence of historical myths on policy. For, was it really true that America had never lost a war? If by that one means that the United States had never lost territory as the result of war, the statement would be technically correct. Yet America had not always achieved the objectives intended when she entered a war. In the War of 1812 we set out to conquer Canada and to put a stop to foreign spoliation of our merchant marine, but, to the consternation of the War Hawks, the British gained the initiative and during 1814 took the offensive everywhere. Our seat of government was sacked and burned, Baltimore and New Orleans narrowly escaped British troops in search of "beauty and booty," and substantial portions of New York and Maine were invaded. It was only because the Duke of Wellington decided that Britain, preoccupied with the Congress of Vienna, should not commit too large a force to a far-off war that the Treaty of Ghent returned us to the *status quo ante bellum*. Fortunately for us, the duke was too wise a statesman to be influenced by empty slogans.

Since then, our interventions in the affairs of the Philippines, various Caribbean nations, and, finally, Korea, revealed limits to our power or made clear the fact that we could not escape the implacable operation of the risk-reward ratio. To be sure, we rounded up Aguinaldo and his Filipino guerrillas by 1902, and local warring factions and bandits like Charlemagne in Haiti were killed or captured. But we realized that we would have to recognize the independence of the Philippines and that, though we might keep order of a kind in Santo Domingo, Port-au-Prince, or Managua, the cost of doing so, even with a career military force, would be disproportionate to any good we might accomplish. Thus, even if it meant anarchy and brutal dictatorships, we opted to leave those nations free to create their own versions of chaos.

But those incidents were not the events country schoolbooks emphasized for young Americans growing up half a century ago. So President Johnson found other precedents for his beleaguered Vietnamese stand, missing certain distinctions in the process. It was one thing to fall, sword in hand, at the Alamo against a despot who took no prisoners or, as Lincoln did, to endure bitter personal attack in order to maintain the unity of the nation; it was quite another to flounder on endlessly in a faraway civil war, where the leaders we supported were not famous for self-improvement.

When first Lyndon Johnson, then Richard Nixon, declined to be the first President to lose a war, each was, consciously or otherwise, paraphrasing Winston Churchill's statement on November 10, 1942, that he had not become the King's First Minister in order to preside over the liquidation of the British Empire. But what they both failed to note was that, at the time Churchill uttered those brave words, the British Empire was already in the process of falling apart. Five years after Churchill's statement, the Attlee Government liquidated the Indian Empire, and, though it is true that no territories were freed during Churchill's leadership, conservative regimes that followed him gave up most of the remaining African, American, and Asian territories.

Whatever psychic fulfillment President Nixon may have received from paraphrasing Churchill's bravado, it was a poor excuse for sending fifteen thousand more young Americans to their deaths after we had already announced our intention to withdraw. For what was really meant by "not losing the war"? The meaning was, as subsequent events showed, that by taking frightful military casualties and blowing Vietnam (and thousands of its citizens) to pieces we might, by the artificial respiration of massive economic and military aid, briefly keep in place a sordid cabal of third-rate politicians, too repressive to tolerate democracy and too corrupt and incompetent to provide an efficient dictatorship.

In essence, it seems fair to say that Nixon's Vietnam policy was the extension and exaggeration of the Johnson policy. It aimed at achieving the same results but used military power more brutally and recklessly. That was, as events demonstrated, a major tragedy. What was plainly required of a new President in 1969 was not that he accept the premises of the administration he succeeded — premises which a majority of the American people had clearly rejected — but that he try by realistic analysis to put the war back into context. That meant abjuring vapid talk of "defeat" or "victory." It meant, in other words, climbing out of the pit in which the preceding administration had imprisoned itself by its own slogans.

Had he possessed the requisite qualities of character and temperament, President Nixon was in a superb position to do so, since, free from the hostages of past actions, he could forthrightly challenge the assumptions of the war — a task the Johnson Administration professors had shied away from in the 1960s. He had a chance — indeed, an obligation — to take a totally fresh look at what America was trying to achieve by its continued intervention in Vietnam. He should have analyzed the prospects of survival of each of the Indochinese states if we withdrew our forces, and — most important — he should have asked himself how much the survival of Laos, Cambodia, and South Vietnam was worth to us in lives and treasure. Did it after all make much difference for American interests whether the current regimes were perpetuated or displaced by Hanoi? To define and explain the American obligation in terms that might be accepted as both reasonable and realistic — by Americans and most friendly foreign governments — Nixon might well have restated the first principles of our relationship with Saigon along the lines established by the Eisenhower Administration, in which Nixon had served as Vice President.

The key document was President Eisenhower's letter of October 1954, to Diem, in which the late President spelled out the obligations to be met by South Vietnam.[2]

"The United States is prepared to consider the extension of aid," President Eisenhower wrote to President Diem, "provided that your Government is prepared to give assurance as to the standards of performance it would be able to obtain in the event such aid were supplied." America's purpose, the President made clear, was "to assist the Government of Vietnam in developing and maintaining a strong, viable state, capable of resisting attempted subversion or aggression through military means." However, the American Government "expects that this aid will be met by performance on the part of the Government of Vietnam in undertaking needed reforms." It "hopes that such aid, combined with your own continuing efforts, will contribute effectively to an independent Vietnam endowed with a strong government." It hoped further that such a government would "be so responsive to the nationalist aspirations of its people, so enlightened in purpose and effective in performance, that it [would] be respected both at home and abroad and discourage any who might wish to impose a foreign ideology on your free people."

The essence of what President Eisenhower stipulated, in other words, was that the United States would help the Vietnamese only if they would, and could, help themselves, with the ultimate objective of bringing about a Vietnam that could stand on its own feet. As a statement of our obligation to a small, embattled nation, his letter thus defined relations in a realistic manner. Moreover, that definition was clearly compatible not only with Nixon's concept of Vietnamization (which meant simply that we would turn the war over to the Vietnamese as soon as they were ready) but also with the spirit of the Nixon Doctrine, which stated that, while the United States might provide military and economic assistance to a nation threatened by outside aggression, "we would look to the nation directly threatened to assume the primary responsibility of providing the manpower for its defense."

Against the background of this Eisenhower letter, President Nixon, after assuming office in January 1969, was in a position to send a message to President Thieu roughly along the following lines:

"The United States has now been helping South Vietnam for

fifteen years and in the course of that time we have spent $70 billion in your defense, while thousands of our own forces have fought shoulder to shoulder with the brave men of Vietnam. We have lost over 30,000 dead and almost 100,000 wounded.[3]

"In addition, we have done everything in our power to help you build a stable government. We believe that you are well on your way to achieving the objective on which President Eisenhower and President Diem agreed fifteen years ago. That ultimate objective was, of course, to make it possible for South Vietnam to be able to stand on its own feet and to assure its own defense with its own means. It is an objective on which I know you and I are agreed, but if you are ever to achieve that desired self-reliance there must be a time of testing. We propose, therefore, that while continuing to provide your forces with intensive training and while carrying out a program that will result in the substantial upgrading of your military equipment and supplies, we will progressively withdraw American forces so that your own troops can more and more defend the front lines. We would hope to complete this withdrawal within eighteen months.

"We recognize that there are risks in this course, but I believe that the time has now come when we should move toward the objective President Eisenhower so well described. We believe that you have the ability to succeed and within the limits I have discussed we will energetically assist you."

What would have been the effect of such a message on our worldwide interests? The burden of the argument for continuing our role in the war had come to center on one contention: that if we did not stay the course and win in Vietnam it would undercut the credibility of all our other promises around the world and hence would destroy the leadership of the United States.

That contention was, as I have suggested, highly overstated, for governments necessarily interpret the worth of any commitment by its strategic importance to the country making it. Even Secretary of State John Foster Dulles, who extended America's security commitments far more widely than many thought prudent and whose activities were at the time described as "pactomania," was fond of citing the legal maxim *rebus sic stantibus*,[4] which meant that circumstances altered cases and that the force of commitments depended on the evolution of conditions.

Had President Nixon reaffirmed the Eisenhower conditions, he could have repositioned the United States so as to minimize the costs of extrication. Certainly neither the Diem Government nor any of its successors had gone far to achieve the reforms specified by President Eisenhower and had thus not satisfied the condition with regard to "the standards of performance it would be able to maintain if such aid were supplied"; nor had the Thieu regime succeeded in building an "independent Vietnam endowed with a strong Government" — a government "so responsive to the nationalist aspirations of its people, so enlightened in purpose and effective in performance" as to "be respected both at home and abroad and discourage any who might wish to impose a foreign ideology." Merely to have repeated the words would have disclosed the wide margin by which the South Vietnamese had failed to measure up to President Eisenhower's standard of performance.

For President Nixon to have pointed this out would not, of course, have improved the morale of South Vietnam nor encouraged its fighting spirit. Nor would it have goaded the Thieu Government into making the reforms Eisenhower had in mind. But it would have provided a basis understandable by other nations for the departure of our forces from Vietnam, and we would not have sent fifteen thousand more Americans to their deaths and had fifty thousand more wounded. We would have avoided such stupid blunders as the invasion of Cambodia and could have saved ourselves painful responsibility for blowing Indochina apart with massive civilian casualties. Finally, we would never have been guilty as late as 1972 of the brutal Christmas Day carpet bombing, undertaken ostensibly to improve the terms of settlement but intended also as a gesture to induce Thieu to agree to further concessions.

There were, of course, arguments against such a course of action — including the contention that great powers had an obligation to persevere in any enterprise they once undertook; if they had at one time come to the aid of a smaller nation, they could not reverse course without a loss of face that would be fatal to their interests in the Orient.

In my view, the relevance of "face" was distorted and overemphasized. I find nothing in history to indicate that America would have suffered a serious loss of face had we first demanded performance on the part of President Thieu, and then, when that was not forthcoming, staged a phased withdrawal. Quite the contrary, I suspect our firmness and judgment would have commanded increased respect, because Far Eastern leaders have never been famous for extending tolerance beyond the boundaries of reasonable cost, as is shown by an incident in Vietnamese history at about the time America was founded.

When in the year 1794 Kong-Le, the corrupt and despotic king of Tonkin, was defeated and driven from Hanoi by a member of the Ghia Long dynasty who had already established himself as a ruler of Cochin China (Saigon) and Annam (Hué), Le fled to the court of his Chinese overlord at Peking. Sympathetically answering his prayers for aid, the Manchu emperor, Ch'ien Lung, dispatched an all-volunteer expeditionary army (referred to, by an odd coincidence, as "special forces") which marched into Tonkin, captured Hanoi, and restored the deposed monarch to his throne. That, however, did not restore stability; for, when Kong-Le reverted to his old habits of debauchery, widespread guerrilla warfare broke out. After repeatedly demanding that Kong-Le reform, Emperor Ch'ien Lung withdrew his forces, which led to Kong-Le's capture and execution. Since the fault was plainly Kong-Le's, no loss of face was involved. It is an incident American Presidents would do well to study when dealing with the rulers of small countries whose interests we are defending.

I urged in a memorandum to President Johnson dated June 28, 1965, that we pursue the course of action I have outlined based on the Eisenhower letter, but at that time the Saigon political structure was in such disarray that it was feared the proposal would precipitate an immediate collapse. Later — with the advent of a Nixon Administration that did not yet carry the same baggage of grandiloquent promises as its predecessors — the time seemed propitious for a new effort. Thus I again put forward the proposal in a magazine article in December 1969,[5] which I afterward discussed with Dr. Kissinger. But what promptly became clear was that Nixon had no design for extrication other than to pound the North Vietnamese into submission — exactly the same strategic conception as that held by the Johnson Administration — except that Nixon was prepared to use more brutal means.

To anyone who had followed Nixon's career, this might, of

course, have been predicted, since he invariably viewed the world in terms of black and white. He thought in slogans, which, since they had to be pithy, were never subtle or delicately shaded. Almost without exception every speech he made from the time he was a young candidate for Congress from California had been cast in the idiom of old-time evangelism — dramatically describing his (the virtuous man's) successful struggle with temptation. Either he was denouncing an alleged enemy that was endangering the United States, or he was bravely standing against evil by rejecting alternative courses of action that he characterized as "the easy thing to do," or "cowardly," or "cheap," or "shortsighted." Often he struggled not merely with abstract choices but with anonymous advisors, asserting that "some people are urging me" or "I know that some of you may think that I should"; he then demolished such straw men with the overwhelming power of his own righteousness.

Any man who habitually saw the world in terms of a constant struggle between Ahura-Mazda and Ahriman in the Zoroastrian cosmic duality, was temperamentally incapable of conducting a limited war. Like President Johnson, President Nixon failed to recognize the contradiction implicit in defining the conflict in total war terms while still fighting it with limited means. Nevertheless, he went considerably beyond his predecessor in the application of American power. He mined Haiphong Harbor, bombed Hanoi, and multiplied the tonnage of bombs dropped on the whole of Indochina by a factor of three.[6] During the period that I served in the Government, until the late fall of 1966, every target the military selected for bombing in North Vietnam was first carefully reviewed by the State Department to make sure that civilian casualties would be kept to a minimum, then the President himself examined the target maps and frequently vetoed those where the chance of civilian casualties seemed excessive. But under President Nixon, target decisions were left to the military, while the Watergate tapes disclose his one comment on the subject: "We'll bomb them like they've never been bombed before."

Thus, though I urged my proposal for a redefinition of the conflict on Dr. Kissinger in December 1969, I did not have long to wait for an answer. Within only a few months the President had doubled the area of the theater of war by invading Cambodia, rather plaintively declaring that the United States must not act "like a pitiful, helpless giant," or "the forces of totalitarianism and anarchy will threaten free nations and free institutions throughout the world." [7] With such shrill and foolish language we dug ourselves in more deeply than ever; by a perverse confusion of geography the President had now identified not only South Vietnam but Cambodia as Armageddon.

Nixon's Cambodian adventure was, of course, anything but the prudent measure he made it out to be. While it undoubtedly discomfited the Vietnamese enemy, who lost large quantities of supplies, its effect on Cambodia was devastating. Though we might from the beginning have developed a military rationale for fighting wars in all three non-Communist states in order to coordinate their defense against Hanoi and its local allies, it was madly irresponsible to double the size of the theater to include Cambodia when we were already engaged in withdrawing from the area. All that we, in fact, accomplished was to bring destruction on a beautiful country and death and hardship for its people.

During the carnage that followed, the President rejected all sensible advice to seek a peaceful solution to the conflict on the fatuous grounds that anything less than "victory" would be another Munich — a comparison that had also been used by the Johnson Administration. He was either ignorant of, or indifferent to, the wise comment of the French writer Bernard Fall in 1966, just a year before he was killed in Vietnam, that if Munich is not a good example of how to settle the Vietnamese conflict, neither is Guernica or Sevastopol.

By outdoing even the Johnson Administration in apocalyptic rhetoric, Nixon made a total commitment to "win." Instead of insisting that the South Vietnamese stand on their own feet while we continued to supply them with matériel, he assumed the responsibility for presenting them with a cease-fire. In pursuit of that objective, America not only suffered sickening losses but resorted to an excessive use of force that shocked and dismayed even our closest friends.

Let us compare what might have happened had President Nixon at the outset of his administration undertaken a sensible repositioning of American relations with Saigon. In spite of General Creighton Abrams's intensive efforts from 1966 to 1969 to turn

Thieu's flaccid legions into an effective fighting force, I doubt that, despite their great advantage of number, they could have withstood a thrust by Hanoi's better led and more highly motivated units. Meanwhile — for under any circumstances it would have taken several months to complete an American withdrawal — we could almost certainly have negotiated an agreement that would take us permanently out of the war and, in exchange, get our prisoners returned. The South Vietnamese, who had failed to fulfill the minimum conditions of the Eisenhower letter, would have then worked out their individual formulas of self-preservation in the long-established tradition of *sauve qui peut*.

That, of course, would have entailed the disappearance of the Thieu regime, but had it earned the right to permanent survival? No doubt it would have disappointed some American bureaucrats who had devoted long months in fruitless concentration on the tour de force of keeping afloat a papier-mâché vessel in a turbulent sea. It was not their fault. They had valiantly tried to bail the ship out, had sought to discourage the corruption and authoritarian proclivities of the general and his cronies, but still — having no sanctions at their command — had been powerless to prevent the sharp practices and fraud that, in the Vietnamese elections of 1971, had converted a limited government into a despotic one. Thus they were forced to fall back on window-dressing solutions.

The actual withdrawal of American forces was not completed until March 29, 1973. During the four years that President Nixon was carrying out his "Plan" of Vietnamization, more than fifteen thousand Americans were killed and fifty-three thousand wounded in action — or half as many as had been killed and wounded during the agonizing years from 1961 through 1968.[8] Nor should the costs be measured solely in terms of American lives. During the same period of the Nixon "Plan" more than one and a half times as many bombs (4.6 million tons) were dropped on Southeast Asia as had been dropped in the aggregate prior to that time (2.8 million tons),[9] while, during the period of the so-called Nixon withdrawal, we created more than 2.5 million refugees, or roughly as many as had been created in all the long years prior to the advent of the Nixon Administration.[10]

From the time Nixon increased the weight of bombing, civilian casualties in the South went up steeply so that from the beginning of his administration through October 1972 an estimated 415,000 South Vietnamese civilians were killed and an estimated 935,000 wounded.[11] It was as though the President were saying to the people of South Vietnam: "Don't worry, we'll save you from the Communists even if we have to kill every one of you."

Viewed as a schoolbook exercise in classical diplomacy, Kissinger's negotiation of a Vietnamese settlement was a model of its kind. In theory, the essential parties to a settlement were Hanoi, Saigon, and Washington — all represented at the overt negotiations that had been pending in Paris ever since May 1968. But Kissinger recognized that a settlement might be facilitated if there were pressure from the two great Communist powers who were the source of matériel for North Vietnam. There was nothing new about this concept; efforts had been repeatedly made throughout the Johnson Administration — directly and through Eastern European governments — to persuade the Soviet Union to take a hand, and approaches had even been made to Peking at the periodic meetings of American and Chinese ambassadors in Warsaw. Meanwhile, France had been enlisted as an intermediary. For the first three years of the Nixon Administration no more progress was made than during the Johnson years, since there was little difference between the Nixon bargaining position and that insisted on during the latter months of the Johnson Administration. As a condition of settlement we demanded that there be a cease-fire "in place" throughout Indochina, linked with an agreed timetable for complete withdrawal from South Vietnam of all outside forces, American and North Vietnamese. As part of the overall settlement we also required the release of American prisoners of war and an Indochina peace conference. In other words, the Americans were insisting that the North Vietnamese withdraw across the border, even though Hanoi had never acknowledged that it had troops in South Vietnam. Hanoi, on the other hand, was asking for an American withdrawal and the removal of the Thieu regime.

The point I am making does not require a play-by-play account of the maneuvering that ensued before final agreement was reached in January, 1973. For most of that period the Nixon Administration held obdurately to the long-established — one might

even say "frozen" — American position, and no perceptible progress toward settlement was made. Though there were a number of
secret meetings between Kissinger and North Vietnamese representatives in Paris during 1971, it was not until more than twelve
months later that the administration finally offered a concession
that held serious attraction for the other side. Not until April 20,
1972, did Kissinger for the first time tell Brezhnev that the United
States would not insist on all North Vietnamese troops being withdrawn north of the DMZ but would be willing to conclude a peace
under which an estimated hundred thousand could remain in the
south. A month later Kissinger further sweetened the American
position by suggesting to the Russians that the return of all American prisoners of war was not a necessary condition precedent to
the end of the bombing of North Vietnam — though Nixon had
publicly stated just the opposite the week before. Moreover, Kissinger indicated that the United States was prepared to back a
tripartite electoral commission in South Vietnam which would include elements from the Viet Cong together with that ever-con-
venient fiction, the neutralists. The United States had hitherto
resolutely rejected a tripartite commission because of the concern
of Saigon that it could evolve into a coalition government.

The most obvious question is, of course, why Nixon chose to
wait three and a quarter years before putting forth a bargaining
position that had any hope of succeeding. By way of answer the
defenders of the policy may argue that for many months before
April 1972, Kissinger had made deliberately ambiguous noises
with reference to American insistence on North Vietnamese with-
drawals, using language that might mean one thing to Hanoi while
meaning something else to the rest of the world. However, such
diplomatic casuistry clearly did not pay off. The North Vietnamese
ignored the obligation of Orientals to be subtle by refusing to recognize the intricate shadings and implications of nineteenth-century diplomacy.

The most plausible hypothesis to explain the delay is that
Nixon and Kissinger did not want a settlement much prior to the
spring of 1972, since time was needed to improve the military balance. That involved driving the North Vietnamese out of many of
their enclaves in the south, destroying large numbers of Hanoi's
men and matériel, and further advancing a process General

Abrams had commenced at the beginning of 1966 to strengthen the ARVN to the point where they might have a chance of holding their own without the massive support of American ground forces.

During this period the evidence would suggest that Kissinger was fighting a negotiating offensive on two fronts, expending quite as much effort in trying to squeeze concessions from President Thieu in Saigon as in exacting agreement from the Hanoi politburo. It was a good apprenticeship for his later activities in the Middle East.

Still there is no doubt that the United States was almost fanatically faithful to General Thieu, far beyond — or possibly below — the call of duty. The President pursued a demonic logic which decreed that the continuance of Thieu in Saigon was worth fifteen thousand additional American dead, and the dragging on of the war for four more long years, with all the internal disruption that entailed. Moreover, the mere hope of improving certain marginal aspects of the final agreement was enough to justify the notorious Christmas bombing in 1972, despite the fact that that involved the loss of fifteen B-52s, including eighty officers and men of our air force and the death of two thousand North Vietnamese civilians.

What all this clearly proved — and proved beyond the shadow of a doubt — was that the United States — or at least the Nixon Administration, which spoke for it — was still the prisoner of President Thieu, a repressive, small-time dictator we had created and sustained.

That we let ourselves be trapped in such an ignominious position was due primarily to the lack of analysis and objectivity outlined in Chapter 4, which reduced the thinking of two successive administrations to a slavish submission to mindless slogans. Here, again, one might ask whether we might have followed a more rational policy had Kissinger from the outset of the Nixon Administration enjoyed the authority and freedom he later achieved. Would he have tried to persuade the President not to destroy our freedom of negotiation and maneuver by tying us so tightly to the Thieu regime? Though he might have had some influence on style — the rhetoric might have been less shrill — it is not clear the result would have been much different. Kissinger himself had essentially reaffirmed the essentials of the Johnson Administration position in his now much-quoted article in *Foreign Affairs* [12] in which he had asserted that "ending the war honorably is essential for the peace of the world," since "any other solution may unloose forces that would complicate prospects for international order." Thus, "a new Administration must be given the benefit of the doubt and the chance to move toward a peace which grants the people of Viet Nam what they have so long struggled to achieve: an opportunity to work out their own destiny in their own way."

That was Dr. Kissinger writing in 1969, but the most he really expected after he had been given the responsibility for negotiation was, as he made clear in many private conversations, that the Paris Accords would assure a "decent interval" after the American with-drawal before Thieu ultimately collapsed or was replaced; in fact, he never concealed his belief that Hanoi would probably prevail at the end of the road. Thus the primary object of the negotiation was to assure that, when Hanoi finally did take over, the event would be wrapped in Oriental ambiguity so that no one could say for certain just what had happened. In essence his concern was to "buy time" to provide at least a color of validation for his claimed achievement of an "honorable peace."

The problem, of course, was how long the interval had to last in order to be "decent." It did, in fact, continue from March 1973, when the last American troops were evacuated, until April 1975, when Saigon finally yielded to General Giap. But, just as the cost of prolonging the war by requiring four years to withdraw Ameri-can forces had been ghastly high in terms of American dead and wounded, the cost of extending the "decent interval" for twenty-four months amounted, merely in aid given the South Vietnamese, to well over three billion dollars — a figure higher than necessary had less been wasted through the Thieu Government's graft, indo-lence, and inefficiency. Had the laconic Thieu been a man of dry wit, he might well have amused himself with the thought that never before had so few owed so much to so many for so little in return. Yet, like most aphorisms, that would not have been quite accurate. Though he owed the American taxpayer for the vast mili-tary and economic assistance that kept him in power, his primary debt was largely to two people — Nixon and Kissinger — whose obsession with symbols made the continuance of his regime a measure of an American "victory." No doubt, of course, they were primarily responding to the pressures of the domestic right wing — Nixon because he genuinely feared and respected right-wing opinion; Kissinger because it provided the justification for the elegant diplomacy in which he delighted and excelled.

Throughout the negotiation phase, however, Nixon and Kissinger remained fiercely loyal to their Vietnamese ally. While they placed great emphasis, during the entire long negotiations, on getting our prisoners back, how can one possibly explain the delay in arriving at a treaty, unless keeping Thieu in power was their primary concern? Nor have I ever been able to understand how President Nixon could constantly harp on the theme of a "secure peace" or a "worldwide structure of peace" with reference to the "settlement" of 1973. By leaving a North Vietnamese army holding enclaves all over South Vietnam in juxtaposition with the armies of the south, he sought to freeze a situation that could not possibly lead to peace but, at the most, to a protracted struggle with an almost certain Saigon defeat at the end of the road. Would anyone argue, for example, that there would have been a "secure peace" with the Confederate States of America if a cease-fire had been arranged in the spring of 1864, leaving both sides fully armed, with elements of the Union Army occupying strong enclaves at New Orleans, Jacksonville, and other points along the coast, while Confederate guerrilla forces held considerable areas of Tennessee and Missouri — particularly if the South continued to have its arms resupplied by Great Britain?

In fact, there is evidence to suggest that the Nixon Administration never did learn the essential lesson of the tragedy — that we should stay out of the affairs of Vietnam. As late as April 1, 1974, in answer to a letter from Senator Edward Kennedy regarding our policy in that part of the world, Secretary Kissinger replied that "Hanoi's forcible conquest" of South Vietnam would have serious destabilizing effects that would not be limited to the areas under threat.[13]

There is ample reason to believe that, had Mr. Nixon not been deposed, our embroilment in South Vietnam might still be continuing at a renewed high level of intensity — unless, of course, Congress had put its foot down. At the time of the collapse of Saigon, Henry Kissinger explained that the Paris Accords he had negotiated did not work out because, among other things, of "the disintegration of, or the weakening of, executive authority in the United States for reasons unconnected with foreign policy considerations" [14] — or, in other words, because Richard Nixon was no longer President.

But suppose the Watergate relevations had been successfully suppressed and Nixon had kept his job, what would he have done when South Vietnam's military resistance started to crumble? We now know that, in order to persuade Thieu to sign the accords, Nixon had sent him two letters, one dated November 14, 1972, and the other January 5, 1973.[15] In the letter of November 14, Nixon wrote that he understood Thieu's concern about "the status of North Vietnamese forces in South Vietnam," but "far more important than what we say in the agreement on this issue is what we do in the event the enemy renews its aggression. You may be assured that if Hanoi fails to abide by the terms of this agreement it is my intention to take swift and severe retaliatory action." Nixon's second letter stated: "Should you decide, as I trust you will, to go with us, you have my assurance of continued assistance in the post-settlement period and that *we will respond with full force* should the settlement be violated by North Vietnam." What was meant by "full force"? Nuclear bombs? No one will ever know.

Thus "peace with honor" had for Richard Nixon, and presumably also for Henry Kissinger, a highly special meaning. At the time they were, in effect, saying, to quote the prophet Jeremiah, "peace, peace, when there is no peace."

According to the Senate Refugee Subcommittee,[16] the violence during the first year after the conclusion of Mr. Nixon's "peace with honor" produced 818,700 new refugees in Vietnam — second only to 1972 and 1968. During 1973, 43,166 civilian "war-related casualties" were admitted to hospitals operated by the Government of Vietnam, while the subcommittee estimated that 85,000 civilians were wounded and killed. The committee concluded that "the Vietnamese have, in short, suffered more in one year of peace with honor than America experienced during a decade of war."

Meanwhile, the United States spent more than three times more on arms for Vietnam in 1973 than the Russians and the Chinese together ($1.9 billion versus $600 million) in order to maintain 15 percent of the South Vietnamese work force in the armed services and another 4 percent in the civil service, while providing vast amounts of economic aid to bolster the desperately sagging economy. After taking account of the number of unemployed and the 150,000 still officially listed in refugee camps or temporary resettlement sites, it was estimated in mid-1974 that 68 percent of the work force was not engaged in any productive work at all.[17] Thus, what Congress did by voting $2.9 billion in 1973 and $2.2 billion in 1974 was to provide a kind of massive outdoor relief program for the 20,000,000 people of South Vietnam.

Our experience in Vietnam should provide a cautionary case study to be dissected and debated for years to come. We cannot be sure that we may not sometime again find ourselves embroiled in a situation where a strategic withdrawal is clearly indicated. Yet, to apply the lessons of Vietnam calls for a degree of self-discipline that does not easily fit the habits of politicians. It demands temperance in language and objectivity in assessing our own actions. It means that our leaders must avoid distorting the importance of a conflict. It requires that they view our allies, both actual and potential, with the same realism that marked the monarchical alliances prior to 1815. In short, we must remember that even though we try, in the phraseology of one frank New York politician, to enlist support for "our bastards," we cannot make them legitimate by rhetoric alone. It is not enough to say that an allied leader is a "great leader of men"; so were Adolf Hitler and Genghis Khan. Although it is natural that we should desire to win a victory and avoid defeat, if the conflict touches only marginal issues we should not overstretch ourselves. Finally, we should rigorously eschew such self-congratulatory slogans as "peace with honor," which, in terms of the Vietnamese struggle, conjures up unfortunate precedents.

It is a curious irony that Nixon, who repeatedly warned that a withdrawal from Vietnam would risk being another Munich, still described his ultimate achievement with the same phrase the author of the Munich Pact used to describe his own handiwork. Yet the roots of the phrase go even deeper in history, back to Disraeli, whom President Nixon openly admired, to Theobald, Count of Champagne in the twelfth century, and ultimately to antiquity. Two thousand years ago Tacitus reported the accusation of the

British general Calgacus on the battlefield of Mons Graupius that the Romans "make a desert and call it peace." Well, the Romans also spoke a great deal about honor, but most Americans have never regarded imperial Rome as a model we should uncritically follow. With the thousands of tons of bombs dropped on Indochina — more than three times the tonnage we dropped during the whole of the Second World War — the peace, to our chagrin, belongs to the other side. That we made a desert of much of the area is nothing to be proud of; in fact, in view of all the napalm and defoliants, the five million refugees and the Christmas bombing when we used mass death as an instrument of diplomacy, we should be neither surprised nor outraged if the phrase "peace with honor" now evokes derisive memories in many precincts of the world.

The exit from Vietnam as stage-managed by Richard Nixon was slow and reluctant, like an amateur theatrical with fumbled lines, much audible prompting, and extravagant curtain speeches. Even so, it provided a good time for quiet thought and a decent reticence and most Americans knew it. It was a heartening sign of our national maturity that — in spite of official cheerleading — the ending of our part in the war, though evoking relief, created no euphoria. We should continue to be careful that it does not do so — remembering the final denouement. Especially to us Americans, incorrigibly sentimental as we are, time tends to spread a softening patina over the most sordid incidents, transforming folly into epic achievement.

Still, we dare not let the revisionists distort the real meaning of our Vietnam adventure, or we shall have learned nothing. In spite of individual feats of devotion and valor — which this time were largely unsung — no one but a fanatic could regard our involvement in that war as a bright page in our history. We should, instead, pay heed to Churchill's famous comment to the House of Commons on April 4, 1940, following the evacuation of Dunkirk: "We must be careful not to assign to this deliverance the attributes of a victory." For, however one may try to justify it, it was a tragic defeat for America. Not in the military terms of the battlefield, but a defeat for our political authority and moral influence abroad and for our sense of mission and cohesion at home. A defeat not because our initial purposes were unworthy or our intentions anything less than honorable, but because — in frustration and false pride and our innocence of the art of extrication — we were forced to the employment of excessively brutal means to achieve an equivocal objective against a poor, small, backward country.

That is something the world will be slow to forgive, and we should be slow to forget.

CHAPTER 6

Détente —
A French Word for What?

OF THE FOUR DEVELOPMENTS IN WHICH HENRY KISSINGER TAKES most pride — the reopening of communications with China, the accords that for a time lowered the intensity of war in Vietnam, the development of easier relations with the Soviet Union, and the purchase of time in the Arab-Israeli struggle by the Sinai arrangements — the third item, which has come to be called *détente,* easily leads in the order of asserted importance. Yet the dimensions, qualities, and significance of our new state of grace with Moscow are so vague as sometimes to evoke a whimsical fantasy in which I think of myself as a passenger on an airplane where the captain is constantly announcing that we have just flown out of one historical era and are at the beginning of a new one. "We have passed the industrial period and are entering the postindustrial or technetronic age." "We have left the era of the superpowers and are in a multipolar world." "We have put our backs to the Cold War and are now arriving at *détente.*"

Well, since *détente* is where I plan to get off, that wakes me up. But the harsh light of early morning betrays the tawdriness of even the most elegant tags and slogans. In the quarter century since the end of the Second World War we have known a succession of phrases that have developed unpredictable authority, and then passed away, and many of these have concerned our relations with the Soviet Union. Although the fact of conflicting interests and purposes has been called the "Cold War," ever since President Eisenhower met Nikolai Bulganin and Nikita Khrushchev at Geneva in July 1955, the end of the Cold War has been periodically announced. Yet what the terminal event may have been is as fuzzy as the concept itself; some relate it to the Cuban missile crisis of October 1962; others, such as M. André Fontaine of *Le Monde*, tie it to the signature of the test-ban treaty in August 1963.[1] Whatever the preferred date — if, indeed, the end has yet occurred — the unwinding has been marked by figures of speech that display a low order of imagination. The "spirit of Geneva" produced a "thaw" resulting from an "accommodation," then a "relaxation of tensions," a "reconciliation," a "realignment," and, finally, a state of grace known as *"détente."*

It is this last term which has most bemused the West — and particularly the United States. President Nixon's repeated assurance that we must "build *détente*" with the Soviet Union injected a lamentable element of sogginess and ambiguity in discussions of American policy. Over time the "spirit of *détente*" has become such an overused phrase that the skin has worn off to disclose precisely nothing. Its constant flogging by political writers has made it as cheap and commercial as the "spirit of Christmas."

The fact that it is borrowed from the French adds to the confusion. As both the American people and American Presidents are monolingual, it would be sound practice to renounce the use of foreign words in describing foreign policy. Certainly President Ford is on solid ground in announcing that he will no longer use the word *détente*, yet his act of self-denial is probably dictated more by his belief that the public is translating the term as "appeasement" — something they do not like — than by the word's inherent ambiguity. Still, we Americans have only the vaguest idea what we intend when we use the word *détente* — or, even more important, what others intend when they use it. Before we substituted urban planning and sandal-making for the study of history, schoolboys were taught that the precision of the French tongue made it the traditional language of diplomacy, but that was French propaganda designed to give Frenchmen an advantage in negotiation. The French language is precise only to Frenchmen — and the word *détente* has no precise denotation even for them.

Mr. Nixon defined *détente* in specialized terms. It was, he repeatedly implied, a state of cordiality derived from his personal friendship with Leonid Brezhnev and the other Soviet leaders. But as we have seen, the Soviets themselves rejected that definition as too reminiscent of the cult of personality they had repudiated.

It is futile to argue whether or not we have "achieved *détente*." "*Détente*," a British general once told me, "is not something nations achieve but something they practice," and the important point is to determine what it is we and the Soviets are practicing. It is fatuous to suggest that the Soviet Union and the United States no longer have significant conflicting interests; the Soviet leaders themselves emphasize the contrary. Military expenditures continue to consume an exorbitant proportion of the total Soviet gross national product; the Kremlin has not ceased to work at cross-purposes with us in every strategic area of the world and to oppose every American initiative in international proceedings; Soviet intellectuals are still repressed; and Moscow persists in giving the phrase "Iron Curtain" practical meaning by encaging 360 million people.

I take it for granted that, in expressing those views, I condemn myself in some quarters as a "cold warrior." I had always assumed that a "cold warrior" was simply a dead hero, but I have lately learned that it is a term of opprobrium, since there is a school of thought that regards cold warriors as a threat to the peace, because they encourage the wrong Russians. The Politburo, so this thesis holds, is a wrestling arena where a constant struggle takes place between fierce militarists, such as the defense minister, Marshal Grechko, who would like to continue the Cold War, and amiable civilians led by Leonid Brezhnev, who would prefer to turn rockets into plowshares or tractors — and who sometimes succeed in turning dulcet phrases into low-priced wheat. It is argued from this that we should avoid being beastly to the Soviets or even taking too firm a line in our discussions with them, since that would strengthen the Soviet "hawks," weaken Brezhnev and thus make it harder for him to develop more friendly relations with us.

In his professorial days Dr. Kissinger expressed annoyance with such simpleminded analysis. Each period of *détente* in the past, he wrote just before joining the Nixon Administration,[2] was "hailed in the West as ushering in a new change in Soviet purposes." Yet, he insisted, "each ended abruptly with a new period of intransigence, which was generally ascribed to a victory of Soviet hard-liners, rather than to the dynamics of the system." In the years that passed since 1968 the professor's comments have not lost their cogency, and even today he often expresses the same sentiments. The mature force in Soviet politics is still "the dynamics of the system" and he does not share the oversimplified belief that we can change the Kremlin's policies by trying to encourage one faction against another. Nevertheless, the idea does not die easily, in spite of the fact that it would require us to have a clearer view of the internal politics of the Kremlin than that currently provided by our intelligence facilities. One perceptive observer of the Soviet scene has suggested a more realistic figure of speech than the wrestling arena in which everything is apparent to the spectator. The Politburo is, he suggests, a platform covered by a carpet, which is in a constant state of upheaval. It is apparent that a vigorous struggle is in progress under the carpet; grunts and cries of anger and agony are heard, but no one knows who is making the noises or who is doing what to whom.

Thus I would suggest that our knowledge of the internal politics of Soviet institutions is far too speculative for anyone to assume that we can, by modulating American policy, significantly influence an internal power struggle within the opaque walls of the Kremlin fortress. No doubt we know more about activities there now than we did during Stalin's day. Soviet policy is no longer the "riddle wrapped in a mystery inside an enigma" that Churchill described; but we certainly are in no position to predict how a particular course of American action may affect Soviet internal decisions. The suggestion that we tailor our own positions in order not to prejudice the Soviet "doves" in their struggle with Marshal Grechko seems to me fatuous. One would hardly expect Mr. Brezhnev to respond graciously if we asked him to withdraw all naval vessels from the Indian Ocean so as to diminish the political clout of our admirals who wish to enlarge the naval installation at Diego Garcia.

Professor Foy D. Kohler, a perceptive student of the Soviet Union, who served as ambassador to Moscow, has pointed out that the Kremlin has, from time to time, temporarily adopted a softer

line toward the West, particularly when its leaders were "preoccupied with domestic concerns" or were "drawing back from real
or potentially perilous international complications." [3] After Stalin's death in 1953, when a power fight was under way for the succession, Moscow cooperated in ending the Korean hostilities as
well as the French phase of the Indochinese War, and, after eight
years of negotiation, agreed to the Austrian State Treaty, which
remains, perhaps, the most important diplomatic breakthrough
with the Soviet Union in the whole long, dreary postwar period.
Again, after the Cuban missile crisis of 1962 had brought Khrushchev's aggressive diplomacy to a halt, we were able to conclude
the Partial Test Ban Treaty, negotiate a consular convention, establish a "hot line," and work out an agreement for the establishment of civil airline traffic between Moscow and New York. Once
again, with their world prestige critically impaired by the invasion
of Czechoslovakia in 1968, the Soviets sought to regain world
respectability by renewing their acceptance of America's long-
standing proposal to undertake strategic arms limitation talks
(SALT).

It is against the background of these tactical adjustments that
one must view the summit diplomacy of the last few years. Worried by their conflict with Peking and the fear of a two-front
struggle, and anxious to enlist American assistance in modernizing
and improving their creaking economy, the Soviets have once
more reshaped their policies to achieve certain immediate objectives.

It is this most recent tactical move that we call *détente* — a
word that has acquired a life of its own in Soviet-American
exchanges. Thus Brezhnev has several times threatened that a particular American action or the development of a particular kind of
situation might "menace *détente*" as though that word had any
meaning apart from the resolution of specific problems. We have
countered in the same vein. Yet it is significant that, though the
Soviets speak to the West — and particularly to the United
States — in terms of *détente*, they rarely use the term in their own
internal statements, preferring the formulation "peaceful coexistence" — an expression sanctified by having been used by Lenin.
Lately we have returned the compliment. Though for years American officials avoided the use of "peaceful coexistence," which was

regarded as describing a state of affairs advantageous to Soviet Communism and implying a continuous class struggle, the Nixon Administration embraced it explicitly in the "Basic Principles of Relations Between the United States of America and the Soviet Socialist Republics," which was signed at the Moscow Summit Conference in May 1972. In that document the two signatory powers agreed to proceed from the common determination that in the nuclear age there was no alternative to conducting their mutual relations *on the basis of peaceful coexistence.*" Moscow proclaimed this a Soviet victory, rejoicing that "for the first time in its history the United States [had] endorsed the principle of peaceful coexistence" and noting particularly that, since this was done over the signature of President Nixon, it thus carried special weight.[4]

Since the Soviet leaders equate *détente* with "peaceful coexistence by states with different social systems," or, as it is sometimes phrased, "peaceful coexistence between Communism and capitalism," it is useful to determine just what "peaceful coexistence" means in the Soviet lexicon. Immediately after the 1972 summit meeting, the Kremlin mounted a carefully orchestrated campaign to explain the significance of the meeting as a major Soviet diplomatic triumph, while avoiding so euphoric a reaction that ideological backsliding might follow. The Moscow Military District Commander said, for example:

> The soldiers of our Moscow District are well aware that the nature of imperialism has not changed and the danger of war has not disappeared and that our foreign policy is implemented under the conditions of a fierce class struggle in the international arena, and the fight between the forces of socialism and imperialism and progress and reaction.

The secretary of the USSR Writers' Union, speaking of the "triumph of Soviet foreign policy" at the summit conference, stated: "Peaceful coexistence does not mean convergence in the sphere of ideas," while the director of the Institute of the United States of America said:

> The results of the Soviet-American talks constitute the natural result of the vast efforts of our party, the Soviet state, and all Soviet people to strengthen the motherland's economic and defense might, to strengthen the ideological and political unity of our society and to

consolidate the socialist community. . . . We all know that not even
the most successful talks and the best arguments can change the unpleasant fact that a tense class struggle will continue to be waged
between the world of socialism and the world of capitalism.[5]

There are two possible interpretations of these statements.
The more straightforward is that the Soviet softer line toward
America is purely a tactical and transitory phase of Soviet policy
and that the determination to pursue the class struggle against the
capitalist nations continues undiminished. The second — more
fashionable today — is that, though the Soviet hierarchs pay lip
service to the class war, they have, in fact, largely lost interest in
ideology; the Soviet Union has, in other words, ceased to be a revolutionary power and has become a status quo power.

The truth, I suspect, lies somewhere between these two overstated positions. The Soviet Union has evolved far beyond Stalinist days, yet ideology still casts a spell over Soviet policies. So
long as the USSR remains a closed society dominated by a party
structure that draws its nourishment from an esoteric doctrine,
reversion to a harder line is possible at any moment. After all, the
leaders of the Kremlin grew up in the Communist church and
most of them are unlikely to backslide very far. For them dedication to the class struggle is a central article of faith.

At the same time there are no doubt a number of attractive
and articulate men and women in the Soviet Union who are more
interested in the peaceful development of their country as a modern industrial society than in the ultimate triumph of one system
over another.

Within the past two or three years, a small group of Soviet
spokesmen has impressed many Americans with the moderation of
their views. Several individuals come often to America and have
become well known in American business and academic circles.
They are American specialists — particularly charged with study-
ing America and making American contacts; they speak excellent
English, several have been educated in America or England, and
are sensitive to Western habits of thought and expression. It would
be as much a mistake to underestimate as to overestimate them, to
doubt the sincerity of all their expressions as to believe everything
they say. Their opinions and apparent friendliness represent an

encouraging trend rather than a controlling element in decisions of the Kremlin.

No prudent American leader dares ignore the Kremlin's constant admonitions to the Soviet people that easier relations with the West do not in any way indicate abandonment of the struggle "between the world of socialism and the world of capitalism." That struggle continues, though the means are changing. Though peaceful coexistence, as the Soviet leaders define it, is made possible by the increased "power and might" of the Soviet Union, it still requires constant "vigilance" at home. After a period of "coexistence" will come "the triumph of the great ideas of Communism." [6]

What distinguishes the present policy line from that followed in the earlier days of the Cold War is that the Soviets have come face-to-face with the reality of nuclear warfare. Recognizing that it could mean their own destruction, they no longer regard a great war between the competing systems as "fatalistically inevitable." Thus, they find peaceful coexistence a useful cover phrase for a relationship enabling them to obtain what they need from the West — and particularly the United States — while still reassuring the faithful that they have not ceased to struggle against the capitalist evil.

It seems reasonable to assume that, to a considerable extent, some elements of the Soviet leadership have lost their fierce ideological drive and are thinking less in terms of world revolution than of pushing the Soviet Union into world recognition as a superpower, matching in might and resources its archrival, the United States, whose wealth and strength they both envy and respect. Yet it is by no means assured that the pull of nationalism will always prevail over the doctrinal push toward world revolution if opportunities for spreading the true faith should present themselves; the policies of the Kremlin will continue to be schizophrenic.

One should not overlook the fact that the bland and conciliatory talk Soviet officials indulge in with Americans frequently contrasts with the hard line taken by the Communist leaders in their own publications and in speeches to the Soviet people and Soviet allies. For example, on his visit to the United States in 1973, Brezhnev was the essence of warmth and geniality. He seemed, in

a slightly dated idiom, "a regular guy." Yet immediately on returning to the Soviet Union he said to a visiting North Vietnamese delegation that, when the Soviets proposed relations with the capitalist countries on the basis of "peaceful coexistence," "[we] never
waived our class principles or the interests of the revolutionary
forces that wage struggles for national and social liberation." *Kom-
munist*, the theoretical journal of the Party, emphasized the same
point in commenting that "as historical experience has shown,
under peaceful coexistence more favorable opportunities are
created for socialist and Communist building and for the struggle
of the working class in the Communist countries, and the struggle
of the forces of the national liberation movement is facilitated." [7]

Thus we should, to paraphrase the notorious phrase of Nixon's
attorney general, "watch what they do and not what they say" or
we shall find ourselves on the short end of some dubious bargains.
We saw a practical illustration of the Soviet interpretation of
"peaceful coexistence" in the Middle East War of October 1973,
when the Soviet Union sent massive arms shipments to Egypt and
Syria. Although Moscow knew in advance that hostilities were
about to break out, it did not advise or consult with Washington.[8]
Once hostilities began, it encouraged the Arabs to use their
weapon of an oil embargo. Yet, when the Arab drive slowed and
the Egyptian Third Army was encircled, the Soviet leaders — invoking the "spirit of *détente*" — summoned the American Secretary of State to Moscow and demanded cooperation in securing an
immediate cease-fire. When Israeli forces once again began to
move, the Soviet Union, on October 24, threatened to intervene
unilaterally and — although that provoked a United States military
alert — the Soviet ploy still achieved its objective; another cease-
fire was called for by the Security Council, and this time the
United States made sure it was observed.

One can mention other incidents where, in spite of their constant references to *détente*, the Soviet leaders have continued to
do what comes naturally, which is to try to frustrate American policy. The practice has been so consistent — in the Egyptian and
Syrian disengagement negotiations, in the Cyprus crisis, in the
Indian-Pakistani War, in the Angolan Civil War — that it is not
possible to name a recent situation where the Soviet Union has
lived up to anything approaching the "spirit of *détente*."

One reason the concept of *détente* comes easily to Soviet ideologues is that they regard war and diplomacy as different facets of the same endeavor — the effort to advance their interests at the expense of the interests of others. In commenting on the Clausewitz dictum that war is politics by other means, Lenin noted that "rightly, the Marxists have always considered this axiom as the theoretical foundation for their understanding of the meaning of every war." [9] Yet, as a scholarly air force officer has suggested, just as Marx turned Hegel on his head, so Lenin turned Clausewitz on his head by interpreting his famous aphorism to mean that politics is war by other means.[10]

As an expression of the Communist doctrine of continuous conflict with the non-Communist world, that view casts considerable light on the meaning of "peaceful coexistence" — or, if you will, on the meaning of *détente*. Mao was even more explicit when he said that "politics is war without bloodshed, and war is politics with bloodshed." Thus *détente*, in the Communist view, is war by other means, which suggests that the phrase "Cold War" may be a more accurate description of the state of East-West relations today than in Stalin's time.

Although the priesthood that applies its exegesis to every shard turned up from the Moscow kitchen midden is in marginal disagreement as to precisely how and why Soviet policy began to sound a softer tone, the broad lines of evolution seem indisputable. One must start with Nikita Khrushchev, who in his de-Stalinization drive measurably liberalized life for the Soviet people, decentralized the management of the economy, and opened channels of communication with the West. But, although his limited internal reforms did not go far enough to solve the pressing problems of the Soviet system, they so outraged Stalinist authoritarians that many of them were reversed or restricted soon after his dismissal.

Brezhnev and Kosygin, less flamboyant and more bureaucratic, steered a wavering course between the pro-Stalin factions who wanted to move backward and the moderates who still wanted "Khrushchevism" without Khrushchev. Beginning in the spring of 1965, the new, insecure leaders began the rehabilitation of Stalin, increased the defense budget, and took harsh measures to repress the liberal intellectuals. Strict censorship was reinstituted; intellectuals such as Solzhenitsyn were put under severe pressure; progress toward economic decentralization was reversed; the Army resumed its central importance; and Russian nationalism was once again emphasized.[11]

But this time the hard line was limited to the domestic front. In dealing with the West, including the United States, the Kremlin tempered its hostility with a more engaging diplomatic demeanor. To understand the reasons for these improved manners, one must bear clearly in mind two dominant but related objectives that clearly emerge from current Soviet literature, writings, and speeches. One driving ambition is for the nation to emerge from the continental chrysalis in which it has languished throughout the centuries and spread its wings as the foremost European power. The other — largely an extension of the same objective — is for the Soviet Union to achieve world recognition as a power of equal status with the United States. That these ambitions are reinforced by the deep ideological conviction that the Communist system will ultimately prevail goes without saying. But added to that is something peculiarly Slavic — or, more precisely, peculiarly Russian — in its nationalist and imperialist overtones: the desire to become more than the last great relic of Byzantium, a nation on the wrong side of the cultural tracks, looked down on by the West as poor and backward. It is, in other words, a deep-seated wish that Russia — the Soviet Union — should take its place as coequal with the greatest power in the world. It is an ambition with temporal, ideological, and deeply nationalistic roots.

The investment of enormous resources in the development of nuclear capability and a wide-ranging navy was prompted by this insistent urge to graduate from continental status. The commitment of resources to a space program that had little practical utility was clearly the action of an *arriviste* power prepared to squander its limited scientific and technological assets to make a display of spatial fireworks that would impress the world and hearten the Soviet people because its economy could show so few tangible achievements. The drive to acquire nuclear weapons was not merely defensive — the acquisition of a threat that could deter the United States from interfering in Eastern Europe — it was motivated even more by the wish to extend the Soviets' military reach beyond the continental land mass that it occupied. That was only a first step in a longer-term process. Building a navy for all the seven seas was another manifestation of the same ambition.

Today the Soviet Union no longer thinks exclusively in terms of its own defense. No longer does it concentrate all its military effort to prevent a tidal engulfment by Eastern hordes that in the past swept across the flat steppes from Mongolia, or to block the invasion of its homeland from the West, as occurred in the days of Charles XII, Napoleon, and, finally, Hitler. It now feels the power and the national ambition (reinforced by ideological zeal) to stand at the center of the world stage on the basis of equal billing with America.

There is an American school of thought that tends to make light of that Soviet ambition. It is, so the argument goes, merely a mark of adolescence — the instinct of a nation for the first time feeling its own strength but failing to recognize that its ambition is essentially outmoded. World power, this scornful argument holds, is no longer a rational objective; the Soviet Union is trying to acquire the clothes that today's academic couturiers regard as last year's style, and the fact that it seeks such obsolete glory through the obsolete means of expanded naval power discloses the pathetic absurdity of its ambition. So why worry? Instead of fretting about what the Russians are doing, the United States should be curtailing its own far-flung efforts, should leave other nations and groups of nations to develop their own regional power structures, should turn its attention progressively inward toward its own pressing domestic problems.

Plausible though it may seem on the surface, I find this thesis quite unsupportable. If some American academics regard the Soviets' ambition as musty and shopworn, the extension of wide-ranging Soviet military power still poses a problem the United States cannot ignore. It is quite wrong to assume that because America has, for the most part, tried to utilize its power with a benign intention — if not always with wisdom — the Soviet Union will show anything like the same benignity. The fact is that Soviet temporal ambitions are still at the service of an ideological commitment.

The territorial limits of the Soviet sphere of influence were established in the years after the war, with the outer periphery finally fixed in 1948 by the Communist takeover of Czechoslovakia.

But the fact that the lines have been stable ever since does not mean that the Soviets have not tried to expand their empire. One need only recall, for example, the Korean War, the efforts to establish beachheads in the Third World and on the southern littoral of the Mediterranean through the acquisition of naval or air bases in Egypt, Iraq, and Somalia, the persistent attempts to absorb Berlin and to use it as a hostage to wring concessions from the West, and, finally, the introduction of missiles into Cuba, which triggered a confrontation that sharply underlined the superiority of the American nuclear arsenal.

It was the Cuban crisis of October 1962 and Russia's withdrawal that led the Soviet leadership not merely to get rid of Khrushchev, who had launched the abortive effort, but also to face up to the humiliating realities of their position. The Kremlin finally recognized that, if the Soviet Union were to hold its own as a superpower, it had not only to catch up with America in nuclear might but also to expand its industrial base and try to raise its economy to a new level of efficiency.

That the Soviet Union lagged far behind was easily documented. Indeed, Japan, a nation of only one hundred million people with almost no indigenous raw material resources, was then rapidly approaching the aggregate figures of Soviet production, and threatening to overtake them. Compared with the growth rate of Japan — and, indeed, with that of most Western European countries — Soviet growth was disturbingly slow. As an expert in Soviet affairs, Professor Wolfgang Leonhard, summed it up in 1973:

> At the end of the 1960s the United States produced nine times more petroleum, three times more natural gas, four times more trucks, forty-five times more passenger cars and seven times as many paper–wood pulp products as the USSR. In 1970, the Soviet Union produced as many refrigerators as the United States had in 1950.
>
> Where Khrushchev's program of 1961 had foreseen a 250% increase in agricultural production in the decade 1960–70, an increase of only 50% was achieved. Soviet production of key agricultural products is not only two to three times less than that of the United States, but is smaller than that of a middle-sized European country. As a whole, Soviet agricultural workers are only one-sixth as productive as American farmers.

Some of the increase in industrial productivity fell short of expectations; although it had risen by an average of 7% in the 1950s, it fell to 5% between 1961 and 1965, and to 4.5% between 1969 and 1970. Stagnation was especially serious in exactly those branches of industry which are decisive for a scientific technological revolution: electronics, computers, petrochemicals and the production of consumer goods.[12]

What the Soviet leaders could not admit, even to themselves, was that a command economic system, the cornerstone of their theology, was quite incapable of producing efficiently or of generating an adequate flow of innovations and improvements in production processes. After fifty years of socialism, the Soviet Union was still a less developed country. Though the United States is endowed with more arable land, a better mix of raw materials, and a more temperate climate, that could not possibly account for the fact that a Russian farmer produces only 5.3 metric tons of grain while his American counterpart produces 50.8 metric tons, or almost 9.6 times as much. The 37 million people in Soviet agriculture in such poor crop years as 1972 were unable to produce enough wheat to feed 250 million Soviet citizens, requiring the Kremlin to spend its precious foreign exchange in the purchase of wheat produced by the 4.3 million farmers of America, who were able not only to feed 220 million Americans but to export 42 percent of their wheat crop.

That the Soviet system is inherently inefficient strikes even the most casual visitor. The amount of concealed unemployment is horrendous, with countless man-hours devoted to filling out chits that leave the bureaucracy hip-deep in useless pieces of paper. Lacking the automatic regulator of the market, the Soviet industrial machine continues to produce shoddy goods, out of phase with demand or geographical need, thus creating distortions as surpluses pile up in one part of the country while shortages bring factories to a halt in others. Since such obvious inefficiency could not be forever ignored by intelligent Russians, particularly as more information trickled in regarding Western industrial achievements, there have been some advocates of a modified market mechanism and of decentralization. But such heterodoxy not only challenged the infallibility of Marxism; even worse, it threatened the power of the Party hierarchs themselves — the spiritual heirs of that small, conspiratorial minority which seized power in 1917. Though managerial logic desperately called for decentralization, the Party chieftains, insecure as such a minority must inevitably be, did not dare let effective economic power pass to local non-Party managers. To them the centralization of economic control was imperative to make certain that central political control was not threatened or disturbed.

Agriculture, of course, remained even more vulnerable than industry, so that the preoccupation with improved farm production gave special meaning to the tractor as the symbol of modernity. Still, tractors were not enough, for the system simply would not use them properly. I recall five years ago, on a two-hundred-mile drive from Orel to Kiev, counting seventeen tractors standing idle and unattended in the fields because they lacked spare parts or because the drivers were soldiering on the job. But if the command system did not — and inherently could not — work efficiently, and it remained impossible for ideological or power reasons to create a modified Socialist market mechanism or make the system more responsive through decentralization, what could be done? The only possibility was to try to speed the pace of development by obtaining ready-made from the West the technology the Soviet system proved unable to generate. Committed ideologues could never concede that the failure of the command system to work efficiently was due to an inherent flaw in the system itself; they had to insist that the concept had been improperly or inadequately applied — that planning was inadequate or that plans were not being properly followed. Thus they wishfully decided that these deficiencies could be rectified by the importation of sophisticated computer and other technology. That this decision was the triumph of dialectics over experience seems clear enough. To believe that the built-in dislocations of a command economy could be overcome by elegant computer systems and the other apparatus of modern industrial society was to display more faith than logic; the argument was accepted only because more rational explanations bordered on heresy. So a nation, rejecting the market principle, decided that it should acquire the tools developed by a market economy to "improve" the functionings of a command economy.

Oddly, it had all happened before. There was nothing at all

new in coupling a quest for Western technology with a disdain for almost all other aspects of Western civilization. Though Russia, as the cultural legatee of Byzantium, had for centuries regarded itself as a beleaguered bastion of orthodoxy constantly threatened by rival creeds, it had often sought help from its potential adversaries. The specter of foreign invasion inspired gingerly approaches to England during the reign of Elizabeth I and Ivan the Terrible. Fear of Sweden sent Peter the Great on his celebrated Western trips in search of allies and shipbuilding know-how, as well as German administrators, mercenaries, and technocrats to help modernize the machinery of his government. One can discern the ambiguous nineteenth-century reactions to such imported technicians in Mussorgsky's operas, *Boris Godunov* and *Khovanshchina*, in which the imported German supporters of Boris and Peter are both praised and execrated by the Russian bassos. Nor should we forget the comment attributed to Peter the Great on his return from the West: "For a few score more years only shall we need Europe. Then we shall be able to turn our backs on her." [13] Later, between 1763 and 1917, France replaced Germany as Russia's source of technology and culture and — most important — of investment capital.

After 1917, the Communists did not hesitate to follow the Czarist precedent. Lenin employed the very archetypes of capitalism — Ford, Du Pont, and General Motors — to provide machinery and teach Russian workers how to make trucks and tractors, heavy chemicals and radios. Until about 1937, hundreds of American engineers and technicians worked in the Soviet Union. Stalin himself told Eric Johnston, president of the U.S. Chamber of Commerce, that "the Soviet Union is indebted to Mr. Ford. He helped build our tractor and automobile industries." In fact, Johnston reported Stalin as saying in June 1944 that about two-thirds of all the large industrial enterprises in the Soviet Union had been built with American material aid or technical assistance. Later, in the 1950s, the Kremlin reached again for Western processes to produce fertilizers and synthetic fibers.

Each time the Kremlin sought help from the West, however, it adjusted its manner to the objective, for the West was not prepared to let its brains and pockets be picked by a nation quite noisily hostile. Thus the Soviets were repeatedly compelled to turn to seduction and flattery as a substitute for the habitual rudeness that had marked both Czarist and Soviet diplomacy.[14] One approach was to cultivate businessmen from Detroit, Cleveland, Memphis, or Santa Monica, since, in Soviet mythology, Washington was subservient to Wall Street and big business. The aphorism attributed to Lenin that "when the time comes to hang the capitalist regimes, they will compete with each other to sell us the rope" had become an article of Soviet faith. Thus Nikita Khrushchev, on his initial visit to the United States in 1959, insisted, as first priority, on meeting the American business elite, whom he regarded as the soft underbelly of the American body politic.

The pressures on the Soviet hierarchy to increase industrial output converged from several sectors. Not only had the Soviet leaders committed their nation to a faster pace in the arms competition, but they needed more consumer goods. The riots in Warsaw in 1956 had made them aware that even a thoroughly indoctrinated proletariat could also become outraged customers. The Soviet people were more and more questioning whether a one-room apartment with a communal kitchen was sufficient reward for a half-century of glorious socialism. Besides, incentives were needed to entice the peasants to raise Soviet agriculture to even a modest level of efficiency. Why should they work if there was nothing to buy?

Yet providing consumer goods presented hazards. Soviet leaders understood that the automobile was a revolution on four wheels. Peasants with cars would be mobile, more able to assert their individualism, and hence less easy to control; automobiles would lead to huge expenditures on roads, overnight inns, and even filling stations. The last was mind-boggling. How long could Soviet Communism survive if the peasantry ever came to demand clean rest rooms?

If Soviet leaders found it essential to seek technological help from the West, and particularly from the United States, Americans were by no means sure how to respond. On the one hand a diminishing tribe of conservative Americans still spoke of the Soviets as "godless Communists" as though it were one word, like damyankees. They would not sup with the devil, no matter how long the spoon, and, in fact, the American Congress had long refused to extend Most Favored Nation treatment to the Soviets, largely on the ground that any form of trade might strengthen the Soviet military machine. Much of this conservative opposition reflected the naïve belief that every item manufactured contributed to a nation's war-making power. Producers of every kind of gadget derived comfort from the conviction that their products were essential to the survival of the nation. When I served as a director of the United States Strategic Bombing Survey toward the end of the European phase of the Second World War, I was constantly assured by technical advisors from branch after branch of American industry that we could have brought the German war effort to an abrupt halt by bombing mills and factories producing their particular specialty. Of course, they underestimated their own capacities for improvisation; had they been put to the test, they would have found substitute materials and processes to keep production going, as the German factory managers had almost invariably done.

That attempts to deny goods to the Soviet Union did not always serve a useful purpose was shown by a minor episode in which I was involved during the early 1960s. At that time the United States Government was concerned lest, as Western Europe turned from coal to oil as a principal source of energy, it might grow increasingly dependent on Soviet oil supplies and, hence, vulnerable to a Soviet oil embargo. Since the Soviets were planning the Friendship Oil Pipeline to the West, we decided to block their procurement of wide-diameter pipe, which they could not produce themselves. Because orders for the pipe had already been placed with German mills, it required us to exert considerable pressure on the German Government to secure the cancellation of those orders.

Although OPEC oil producers have since demonstrated that an oil embargo can be effectively used as a political weapon, our effort to block the Freedom Pipe Line was still of dubious wisdom. The end result was to force the Soviets to build their own pipe facilities, thus gaining their independence of the West with regard to a significant product — an outcome for which the Soviet ambassador satirically thanked me.

Still, we must avoid creating patterns of production and commerce that would make us inordinately dependent on Soviet supplies — particularly with relation to energy, as our recent experiences with Middle Eastern oil producers should have taught. Today the Soviet Union is preoccupied with developing its own energy resources. Although, for the time being, it is the largest world oil producer and a net oil exporter (the first nine months of oil exports following the fourfold price increase in January 1974 yielded it three billion dollars), some of its oil fields have peaked earlier than predicted, thus threatening a shortfall in meeting future requirements. Its long-range reliance, however, is on vast potential resources in basins in the northeast and Arctic regions of the country, where geography, climate, and the thinness of population make exploitation possible only with the expenditure of immense capital and the development of highly specialized technology.

A recent memorandum by Academician N. N. Nekrasov [15] envisages a joint East-West effort for the realization of huge projects, including the creation of an all-European electrical grid. The West would provide capital and technology to develop Siberian oil, gas, coal, and other raw materials, as well as facilities to produce liquefied gas and methanol, and would establish a regular cargo navigation service from northern ports.

What makes such Soviet plans particularly revealing is that they contemplate the construction of industrial complexes surrounding sources of energy and raw materials. The Soviet Union would control the production of energy, raw materials, and basic production, while the West would provide the capital, special machinery, and technology. In strategic terms, the Soviet Union would thus gain a strong advantage: by threatening to cut off the flow of materials and supplies to the West, it could exert significant leverage.

No doubt these Soviet dreams will never be realized in the terms in which they are now being put forward. Nor do I believe that the United States capital market will ever provide the vast funds required for the exploitation of the Arctic resources of Siberia. Still, having grown used to international dealings in the postwar period, American businessmen are, for the most part, ready and eager to exploit the Soviet market. Not only have they seen their European competitors do well at it, but some have uncritically and unconsciously embraced a theory known as the Manchester Creed, which flourished in business and intellectual circles during the nineteenth century. The essence of that creed was that the peace could best be promoted by encouraging the worldwide exchange of goods and commodities. The free flow of goods across national boundaries would, it was contended, erase misunderstandings and differences of opinion among the world's peoples. Trade would break down national barriers, because merchants carried in their packs fresh ideas and new visions.[16]

Yet even in the nineteenth century proponents found it difficult to explain civil wars, such as the American "War of Rebellion," in terms of the Manchester Creed, since there was obviously no lack of trade or even any major cultural differences between the contending parties. Even more embarrassing was the First World War, which could not be reconciled with any theory that international commerce assured the peace. The extensive trade that flourished in pre-1914 Europe had in no way deterred the march of armies in the fatal August of that year. Professor Gregory Grossman, in a statement before the Joint Economic Committee in 1973, emphasized the point as applied to the Soviet Union: "History provides little reassurance that trade insures peace, and Russia's own history least of all. Germany was her largest trading partner just before each of the two world wars, while China was her largest trading partner (and Russia, China's) before the break between Moscow and Peking around 1960." [17] During the "debunking" days of the 1920s and the early 1930s, the creed was, in fact, turned upside down. Not only did trade not prevent wars, but a new theory emerged that wars were caused by international cartels, the munitions makers, the "merchants of death" who produced and peddled arms and thus profited from conflict. It appealed to my generation of iconoclastic innocents, and enjoyed a brief vogue during the 1934–1935 hearings of the Nye Committee. But it, too, was washed away by the brutal realities of World War II.

In encouraging trade with the Soviet Union the Nixon Administration seemed influenced by three considerations.

One was the conviction that the Soviet Union desperately wanted American technology and would pay for it by concessions in other fields — a manifestation of the "linkage" theory that will be discussed in the next chapter.

The second was the belief that involving the Soviet Union in world trade would tend to open the doors and windows to the West and give the Soviet Union a stake in Western prosperity.

Finally, there was the administration's promotion of the mystique of *détente*, a mystique it had itself largely generated.

The belief that the reduction of trade barriers could be used as a bargaining counter was by no means new; what was new was that it had now attained some validity. During the arguments over East-West trade legislation in the 1960s, conservative Congressmen wildly overestimated the Kremlin's desire to trade with the United States. As an official of the Department of State during the Kennedy and Johnson Administrations I was constantly admonished by members of Congress to insist on quite extreme concessions from Russia before selling them such commodities as wheat. What would have puzzled Karl Marx was that some of the Congressmen who flatly opposed selling wheat under any circumstances came from the wheat-producing areas that would directly gain from the sales; the Good Book was stronger than the pocketbook. But at that time, the Kremlin showed little interest in expanding trade with America; since the Soviets were not prepared to make even such a minor concession as settling their Lend-Lease accounts, the only argument for East-West trade was that it would be mutually beneficial — a "two-way street," as the prevailing cliché described it. Most of what the Russians needed they could then procure from European and Japanese industry; they had not yet reached the painful conclusion that American help was required to build an efficient industrial economy.

Today all that has changed. That the Soviet Union urgently wants American trade is obvious; that fact has already made a bulge in commercial statistics. Why, therefore, should the United States not utilize its leverage to require substantial concessions from the Soviet side — enlisting their acquiescence, if not outright help, in solving local quarrels and mobilizing the effort and resources acquired to meet emergent world requirements? Should we be put off by the Soviet insistence that they should make no extraordinary concessions for dealing with the United States since trade is a matter of mutual benefit? That depends on the type and composition of trade and the long-term intentions of the trading partners. The Russians have tended historically to seek self-sufficiency rather than expanding world trade for its own sake.

Today their interest in developing their industrial economy with Western help is likely to be directed less at establishing permanent trade links than at promoting their own autarky. Probably more than any other country, the Soviet Union is capable of developing a relatively high standard of living without participating in the world division of labor.*

It is important that we carefully consider this point if we are to evolve a sensible policy toward East-West trade; so far it has been largely ignored in discussions of the subject. Is it in America's interest to turn over the fruits of our vast investment in technical progress, our most highly sophisticated machinery, for the Soviets to copy, and our capital and know-how to help them develop their natural resources, if their ultimate purpose is merely to increase their own national power? Should we help them modernize their economy if they continue to play a spoilers' role in our efforts to mobilize the support of the competent nations for an attack on emergent world problems? The subject obviously requires a far more rigorous scrutiny than has so far been given it.

The Soviet desire for American capital and technology, though important, was still not the only motive of the Kremlin for seeking *détente* with the United States. Fully as important was its worry about China. China posed a two-pronged menace. As a military power capable of deploying an almost infinitely expandable mass army, it threatened the integrity of the Soviets' vast territories in Asia, although the menace was probably more apparent than real in view of the limitations of transport and the difficulties of civil and military food production and supply. As the schismatic Eastern capital of the Communist church, China posed a canonical — or, more properly, an ideological — threat to Moscow's authority over the Communist Party structure around the world. No wonder the Kremlin's constant preoccupation with an emerging China encouraged it to reassess its relations with the West, for the potential of trouble on two fronts was disturbing to a nation with territories spreading one-third of the way around the globe.

A desire for American capital and technology, and a need to

---

* I use the phrase as Adam Smith used it; to the Communists, "division of labor" denotes not the allocation of tasks resulting from the operation of a market system but an allocation achieved through agreement among nations and carried out through governmental decisions and commands.

assure security in the West in order to cope with the menace of China on the east and south — these were compelling arguments for the Kremlin to try to reduce tension with Western Europe and the United States. But in addition there was another, perhaps even more compelling, reason: a continued posture of hostility toward America and the West was defeating its ultimate objectives. The Russians had had a succession of disappointments. Their attempt to take the leadership of the emerging Third World had been rebuffed. In spite of their substantial investments in Ghana, Indonesia, Egypt, Syria, and India, little return was forthcoming, while they watched the countries of South Asia grow increasingly aloof and unfriendly. Even in Europe the Soviets had not been able to build a belt of neutrals, except the "People's Republics" of their Eastern European empire, and even among the "People's Republics" there had been trouble. The effort to unite all the world Communist parties under the Soviet banner had been blocked by controversy, forcing abandonment of the project for a new world — or even European — Communist Party Conference.

Still, the Kremlin could never give up the central promise of Marxist theology that Communism would, in the long run, triumph. So, if the political means utilized had not succeeded, a change in tactics was obviously needed. If a hard line only strengthened the West by providing it with an essential unifying element — the specter of a common enemy — a softer line might undermine the West's concerted resistance to Soviet ideas and Soviet influence. With the prevailing mood one of relaxation, the nations of Western Europe might drift apart; both they and the United States might well reduce their defense efforts and America might be induced to withdraw its forces from Europe.

That argument gained increased urgency from the fact that, though the Kremlin's Western antagonists had so far maintained a considerable unity of purpose, the Soviets' own empire was showing symptoms of weakness and decay. Less than six months before President Nixon's inauguration, the frightened men in the Kremlin had felt compelled to try to cure, by tanks and troops, a Czechoslovakian fever of freedom that threatened to infect the whole body politic of Eastern Europe. It had been a painful time for Brezhnev and his colleagues. Their agonizing decision to intervene in Prague played havoc with the Kremlin's authority over the

Communist Party structure in many nations, while the Brezhnev Doctrine (the so-called "doctrine of limited sovereignty"), invoked to justify that intervention, sent chills of apprehension throughout the whole Communist world — and particularly Roumania, Yugoslavia, and China. I was acutely aware of their apprehensions, since, as ambassador to the United Nations at the time, I spent long hours with the Yugoslavs and with the Roumanian Foreign Minister. It gave them little comfort to reflect that Soviet intervention would be undertaken in that same spirit of "fraternal solicitude" Moscow had shown other socialist republics. They knew only too well the meaning of that term: it was the same kind of fraternal solicitude Cain had shown his brother, Abel.

CHAPTER 7

Détente
and Henry Kissinger

JUST AS POWER IN PEKING WAS SHIFTING INTO MORE MODERATE hands that made possible new communications with the United States, Brezhnev was — at the time the Nixon Administration took office — emerging as more equal than his equals. He was given the title of General Secretary of the Party in April 1966, a distinction not awarded since Stalin's day. Though he apparently favored a more open foreign policy, he and the other Soviet leaders faced a dilemma. How could they adopt a friendly posture toward the West without unleashing internal forces that might disrupt the Kremlin's hold over its citizens and lead to disorder and defection among the Eastern European nations?

It was a difficult problem to resolve, especially since there is evidence of some confusion of counsel. Though we know relatively little of what goes on behind the high Kremlin walls, it is a fair assumption that a compromise was struck to please competing schools of opinion. In return for flexibility to pursue a policy of "peaceful coexistence" Brezhnev promised to give the military larger defense budgets as well as complete control of the Defense Ministry; he agreed also to protect purity of thought on the home front by a return to more repressive policies — thus positioning internal policy halfway between Stalinist tyranny and the relative liberalism of Khrushchev.

This was the evolving state of affairs when President Nixon came to power. The assumption that he opened a new chapter of East-West relations by unprecedented initiatives that produced a wholly new set of Soviet-American relations substantially distorts the record. Ever since the Second World War the West had repeatedly tried to achieve better relations with Moscow. Secretary Marshall's famous Harvard speech offering aid for the rebuilding of Europe had been directed to the Soviet Union as well as the West. Even before that, General de Gaulle had visited Moscow in December 1944, to discuss a new Franco-Russian alliance, but Stalin had rejected the idea out of hand. Conscious of the realities of comparative strength, he would not respond to a Western leader whose world position seemed as evanescent as the *grandeur* to which he aspired. Ten years later, Chancellor Adenauer, on his own pilgrimage to Moscow, also proposed a *modus vivendi* with the Kremlin — only to have his efforts abruptly terminated by the bloody events in Budapest in 1956, followed six years later by Khrushchev's erection of the Berlin Wall and the resulting Berlin crisis.

During his second incarnation as the leader of France, Charles de Gaulle once again explored a possible arrangement with the Soviet Union. When, on a special mission for President Johnson, I met with him in September 1965, he informed me in detail of his intention to withdraw French forces from NATO. Although I did not realize it at the time, that disclosure was a carefully planned step in preparation for his forthcoming trip to Moscow in March 1966; in fact, the actual withdrawal of French forces in March was staged to take place just before that visit. Underlying this artful timing was the general's penchant for playing both sides against the middle — the desire to exploit the rivalry of the "two great hegemonies," the United States and the Soviet Union. So, faintly — for our ears were not yet well-tuned — we once more heard the old, old music of the Entente Cordiale and the showy but ineffectual Franco-Russian Pacts of 1892, 1935, and 1944 — though this time in a distinctly minor key.

What now seems clear is that France's flirtation with the Soviet Union and her withdrawal from NATO profoundly shocked the Federal Republic, and, with America increasingly obsessed with Vietnam, the Germans grew lonely and ill at ease. By the time Erhard departed as chancellor and the Grand Coalition took over in 1966, the Germans were already beginning to push aside the rigid pro-Western, anti-Soviet policies of Adenauer, while there was increasing talk of an *Ostpolitik* — the policy that became the focus of German attention in the autumn of 1969, when Willy Brandt became chancellor. The main thrust of the resulting treaties — with the Soviet Union in August 1970, and with Poland in November 1970 — was to recognize the status quo resulting from the war, to acknowledge the Oder-Neisse line, as well as the boundary between East and West Germany — steps that finally led to the recognition of East Germany as a sovereign state.

Though, in a sense, the *Ostpolitik* was a foreshadowing of later bilateral diplomacy between the Nixon Administration and the Kremlin, a limited view of *détente*, it disenchanted Washington at the time. Both Nixon and Kissinger apparently felt, as I did myself, that excessive preoccupation with the *Ostpolitik* was leading some Germans to believe that the Cold War was over, and I feared it might revive an atavistic ambivalence — particularly among the younger generation of Germans, who had never experienced the hot war. Running through German history was a thread of uncertainty as to Germany's most advantageous positioning between East and West; one could still find traces of two schools of thought — one favoring Eastern ties and the other Western. It was the "Easterners" who had, more often than not, won those intramural debates. From General Yorck's Convention of Tauroggen in 1812 to the Drei Kaiser Bund to the Chicherin-Rathenau Agreement at Rapallo and the Molotov-Ribbentrop Pact of 1939, German foreign policy had faced eastward for security and "compensation." Thus I could not forget that Adenauer's policy of "the Western link" was a radical break in the continuity of German diplomacy, that it was not the norm but something quite new in the world.

Though there was no doubt that Willy Brandt was a man of the West, some later chancellor might not be so firmly committed, and it was with this in mind that, in December of 1970, I wrote an article for an Italian foreign affairs quarterly expressing worry as to where *Ostpolitik* might lead.[1] Later, when that article was picked up by the German press, I found my views quoted — and misquoted — in a manner I neither intended nor enjoyed. Fortunately, German parliamentary processes consume many months, and by the time the treaties with Warsaw and Moscow were finally ratified, the mood of euphoria had been replaced by greater realism.

Still, the treaties that resulted were anything but a victory for the West. On the whole, the *Ostpolitik* was primarily of value to the Soviet Union, since it legitimized the status quo resulting from the Second World War. The total effect was to lay to rest the last vestiges of the Hallstein Doctrine and to write off the idea of reunification except in the tenuous theory of "two German states in one nation." [2] In practice, the arrangements to assure the German people easy passage between East and West Germany proved disappointing. All that saved the *Ostpolitik* from being a wholly one-sided bargain was the fact that an Allied agreement on access to Berlin, finally concluded in September 1971, was made a precondition to the signing of the basic treaty on December 22, 1972. In that way the Federal Republic's *Ostpolitik* provided a lever for clearing away — at least temporarily — an area of contention between the United States and Moscow, and thus created sufficient confidence to encourage President Nixon to go ahead with his summit diplomacy.

Nixon's moves toward Moscow had their roots not only in the efforts of Western European leaders but in earlier American initiatives. During the period in which both France and Germany were probing the fruitfulness of bilateral relations with the Soviet Union, the United States had not sat idly by. As early as June 1963, in a speech at the American University in Washington, President Kennedy had tried to sound the Soviets out on a "relaxation of tensions" aimed primarily at developing a common Soviet-American position against Communist China.[3] Though the Soviet response was not notably enthusiastic, Kennedy was able to achieve limited progress with Moscow. His administration successfully negotiated the test-ban treaty of July 1963, and made the first wheat sale to the Soviet Union. The latter was a transaction for which I had key negotiating responsibility and, though Richard Nixon denounced it at the time as harmful to the "cause of freedom," it is worth noting that we were not discussing a Soviet wheat purchase at a subsidized price, such as occurred on July 8, 1972.

When Kennedy's search for *détente* was tragically stopped by a bullet in Dallas, Texas, Lyndon Johnson sought to maintain the momentum. In 1964, he announced in a speech in Lexington, Kentucky, that the United States would "continue to build bridges across the gulf which has divided us from Eastern Europe. They will be bridges of increased trade, of ideas, of visitors and of humanitarian aid." The following year he established a committee under the chairmanship of an industrialist, J. Irwin Miller, to study the whole problem of East-West trade, including the extension of Most Favored Nation treatment to the Communist countries; and in 1966 he sent an East-West Trade Bill to Congress.

Although so long as the Vietnam War was the center of attention such legislation could not flourish, President Johnson did not give up hope of improving East-West relations, and shortly after the Glassboro meeting with Kosygin on July 23 to 25, 1967, he persuaded the Soviets to agree to serious talks on the control of nuclear weapons. On July 1, 1968, the Kremlin announced that the two governments would, in the near future, undertake discussions to limit and reduce offensive strategic nuclear weapon systems, as well as defensive systems. On August 19, the Soviets accepted the American proposal for a summit meeting in Moscow.

Once again the Kremlin's compulsive need to keep an iron grip on its Eastern European empire got in the way of serious talks. The night before the planned release of an agreed announcement that President Johnson was to visit Moscow in the first days of October 1968, word reached Washington that Red Army tanks were moving into Prague. I shall never forget Lyndon Johnson's somber mood when I met with him on the morning the trip was to be made public, for he had envisaged his Moscow visit as the crowning event of a presidency then in its waning months. Later, after the November elections, he proposed to President-elect Nixon that they go together to a summit meeting, but Nixon flatly refused, and soon thereafter the Soviets turned cool about a visit from President Johnson. It left Johnson with the "strong feeling that they were encouraged in that view by people who were very close to the Nixon camp." [4] As history now makes clear, his suspicions were correct.

It is clear from this recital that efforts to achieve a *détente*, a *rapprochement*, or — to put it in English — some easier working arrangement with the Soviet Union, had been underway well before the Nixon Administration came to power. But even in 1968 the results of such efforts could not be accurately foretold. In a chapter written for a Brookings Institution publication called *Agenda for the Nation,* designed to suggest a course of policy for the Government about to take power, Professor Kissinger had expressed major reservations regarding any bilateral approach, commenting with less than total approval on the French and German ventures earlier described. "During periods of *détente,*" he wrote, "each ally makes his own approach to Eastern Europe or the USSR without attempting to further a coherent Western enterprise." [5]

Thus it is hardly surprising that Kissinger did not press immediately for a Washington-Moscow dialogue. Once the Nixon Administration had taken over, the Soviet Union continued to express interest in nuclear weapons negotiations, but, instead of accepting that opportunity promptly, the administration — quite likely on Kissinger's urging — held off for almost a year, until November 1969. Meanwhile, the arms race continued. Whether or not the protracted delay prejudiced the ultimate success of the discussions is a matter for debate; Lyndon Johnson thought it did, and so, apparently, did the Secretary of State, Mr. Rogers, who seemed anxious to get started. Several members of the Senate Foreign Relations Committee suspected that the administration was deliberately stalling in order to gain time to launch new weapons programs and particularly antiballistic missiles (ABMs) — a program, Nixon insisted, that was needed as a protection "against any attack by the Chinese communists," as a safeguard for our long-range missile sites, and, finally, as a safety element against any "irrational or accidental attack."

Whether the delay was dictated by the President's desire to gain a "bargaining chip" or by Kissinger's desire to elaborate a large-scale strategy based on "linkage," or for some other reason, may never be definitely known; what is clear is that there were strong pressures and cross-pressures within administration circles. The military wished to expand their strategic weapon arsenal in order to regain American "superiority." Elements of the Senate and some experts within the administration wanted a prompt negotiation so as to halt new programs for more sophisticated weapons before they could create a fresh imbalance that would require the other side to catch up.

In any event, during the period of foot-dragging, not only did the United States embark on an ABM program but also a substantial augmentation of the number of warheads. The President no doubt saw the combination of those two new programs as providing him additional bargaining chips, but they changed the balance between the Soviet Union and the United States so decisively as to put pressure on the Russians to complete new programs of their own before any agreed equilibrium could be achieved.

One reason for Kissinger's wish to delay negotiations was that he was dissatisfied with the adequacy of the preparatory work inherited from the Johnson Administration, as he emphatically told me at the time. To rectify this, he established several task forces that produced a number of huge and impressive volumes. Though those studies were described as providing the "building blocks" for an ultimate structure of controls of nuclear weapons, their practical value has not yet been proven by results. Many experts thought them too metaphysical to be of much use in the give-and-take of negotiations. Some regarded their preparation primarily as a filibuster to enable Kissinger to gain time while more bargaining chips were acquired. Others emphasized Kissinger's understandable desire to satisfy his academic curiosity. What sublime luxury for a professor to be able to deploy the total resources of the Government on studies that had long interested him! [6]

Still, such a jaundiced view probably reflected little more than the envious reactions of specialists who spun their own theories and resented it when one of their fellow theoreticians became famous; for, of all issues in international politics, none is more abstruse and arcane than the limitation and control of arms. Because there is no solid experience to supply a precedent, professional disarmers are thrown back on intricate and often convoluted logic and, since the problem also inspires the experts with urgency and passion, objectivity is hard to maintain. The most esoteric technical arguments develop theological ferocity, and the lines between heresy and the true faith are drawn at different points by different prophets.

Since disarmament arguments tend to focus on highly tech-

nical speculations, the *aficionados* find it hard to regard the problem as only one element in a larger political context. Thus, it is
not surprising that, as a group, they showed little enthusiasm for
the Kissinger concept of "linkage," a noisily advertised part of the
doctrinal baggage he had brought with him.

That concessions in one area might be conditioned on progress in others was scarcely a new thought; only the terminology
was new. Throughout the whole history of Soviet-American relations, each side had recognized that the success of any particular
initiative depended in part on the atmosphere of confidence and
approval that existed at the time; when the Soviet Union wanted
something from the West, it had regularly tried to create a climate
that would promote its objective. What the United States set out to
do, according to Secretary Kissinger's testimony before the Senate
Foreign Relations Committee on September 19, 1974, was to "capitalize on the tentative beginnings made in the sixties by taking
advantage of the compelling new positions of the 1970s." In other
words, we were "to provide as many incentives as possible for
those actions by the Soviet Union most conducive to peace and individual well-being . . ." and "when Soviet policy moves toward
conciliation . . . to turn what may have started as a tactical maneuver into a durable pattern of conduct." A basic assumption of
the approach was that, "in moving forward across a wide spectrum
of negotiations, progress in one area adds momentum to progress
in other areas," and that, if American diplomacy succeeded, no
agreement would "stand alone as an isolated accomplishment vulnerable to the next crisis." [7]

Secretary Kissinger has been careful to point out that the
Nixon Administration "did not invent the relationship between
issues expressed in the so-called linkage concept; it was a reality
because of the range of problems and areas in which the interests
of the United States and the Soviet Union depend on each other."
The underlying hope of the policies, he stated, was that, "by acquiring a stake in this network of relationships with the West, the
Soviet Union may become more conscious of what it would lose
by a return to confrontation."

That the Soviet Union has been prepared to make some token
accommodations in the interests of preserving public confidence
in *détente* is undoubtedly true. The pertinent question, however,

is whether the United States in its desire to sustain a public belief in the reality of *détente* (in part because of its domestic political value) may not have made concessions more far-reaching than any it has obtained. When any administration sets such a high value on an attractive abstraction, there is a reluctance to utilize it for fear it will vanish. The American people regarded President Eisenhower's enormous world "prestige" as a national asset, yet he often seemed more anxious to preserve that prestige than to risk it for useful objectives.

The same criticism can be made of Secretary Kissinger. Though there has been some progress in involving the Soviet Union in a "network of relationships with the West" — which is the basis for what is called *"détente"* — Kissinger has been unwilling to test the leverage implied in *détente* for the advancement of significant United States interests. Thus, our experience so far has tended to demonstrate the limited practical value of the concept of linkage — if, indeed, it should be dignified as a concept.

Still, no one could quarrel with the desirability of an East-West strategy designed to settle as many divisive problems as possible. And, though each side had its own priorities, the tactic of insisting on interlinked movement on several fronts made at least superficial sense. It was a logic that seemed irresistible to an administration eager to involve the Soviet Union in securing a settlement of Vietnam, and there are grounds for suspicion that Kissinger held off nuclear arms negotiations primarily in an effort to push the Soviets into service on the Vietnamese peace front.

What has been the cumulative result of the negotiations America has conducted with the Soviet Union in the highly advertised "spirit of *détente*"? That wise European, Jean Monnet, with whom I worked for many years, invariably approached difficult problems of judgment with the admonition: "Add up the advantages and disadvantages, the successes and the failures; make a *bilan*, a balance sheet." A balance sheet of our negotiations with the Soviet Union shows entries in both the asset and liability columns. Most important of the entries is SALT. Not only would a limitation on nuclear weapons development tend to dampen down the frenzy of competition between the two superpowers, it would halt — or at least slow — an escalation of what, in economic terms, was pure waste. Without some such agreement, each nation, in order to keep pace with the other, might feel compelled to devote an increasing share of its national income to the development and production of more and more sophisticated — and, in military terms, quite useless — weapons, until the two exhausted superpowers lost the economic race to other contestants, such as Japan, that did not carry such heavy baggage. But, though each nation had a clear motive for wishing to stabilize the nuclear balance, such stability was possible only if something approaching parity were achieved.

Having been forced into a humiliating recognition of its nuclear inferiority at the time of the Cuban missile crisis, the Soviet Union had, by frenetic efforts, achieved a balanced second-strike force. Now the Soviets had political reasons for wishing to preserve the parity they had achieved. For one thing, the recognition of parity would advance their ambition to be regarded as the equal of the United States, capable of dealing with America on a self-respecting basis. For another, the Soviets believed — and in subsequent experience have put this belief to test — that with America's acknowledgment of Soviet strategic parity they could pursue a more adventurous diplomacy. Thus SALT, according to one expert, was, like the Congress of Vienna, "a political negotiation concerned with finding an equilibrium in which the Great Powers could feel secure." [8]

SALT I dealt in quantitative terms, leaving questions of qualitative competition for later resolution. Agreement was reached to restrict the numbers of ABM installations. In addition, we conceded the Soviet Union superiority of about 40 percent in the number of offensive nuclear missile launchers during the five years of the freeze, although we were partially compensated by the possession of many more bombers and more than twice as many warheads. Our acceptance of the disparities was based on the optimistic assumption that SALT II would soon establish throw-weight limitations and a rough equivalency for the two strategic arsenals.

Unhappily, at the summit meeting in July 1974, the White House and the Kremlin remained far apart. The United States sought equality both in the number of launchers and the throw-weight of MIRVed missiles. The Soviets insisted on retaining their superiority in the number of launchers, while denying the United States claim for an offsetting advantage in MIRV and heavy bomber capabilities. In view of the gap between the two sides, no permanent agreement was possible, but, since a frantic Nixon was anxious that the conference not be regarded as a failure, an attempt was made to paper over divergent views by postponing any effort to reach such an agreement until later discussions could be held in Geneva.

Henry Kissinger testified during the hearings on his nomination for Secretary of State before the Senate Foreign Relations Committee that if SALT II should fail, a "spiraling of the arms race" was "inevitable" and that the Soviet Union "could wind up with both more warheads and more destructive warheads than we will possess by the end of the present decade." [9] In other words, SALT I was accepted on the gamble that SALT II would succeed.

SALT I — as its title, "Interim Agreement," implies — was essentially a holding action that authorized a further buildup of strategic weapons to levels already planned. Aside from limiting the ABMs in a separate treaty, there were to be no cutbacks except for obsolete equipment. Although the agreement permitted both sides to continue to stockpile more, and more sophisticated, weapons, Kissinger justified the misnomer — "Arms Limitation Accord" — by explaining that the Russians would have built even more in the absence of an agreement, while the United States would have remained at the same levels. As a matter of fact, under the agreement, the Russians were permitted more land-based and more sea-based launchers than was the United States. It was not until November 24, 1974, at Vladivostok, that the Soviet Union agreed to what is known in the trade as "equal aggregates" — permitting each side an equal number of strategic launchers of any mix it might choose.

The total number of 2,400 "offensive strategic delivery vehicles," of which 1,320 could carry multiple warheads, was, however, attacked as being far too high, even by such defense-minded critics as Senator Henry M. Jackson. Only four months before, Nixon had proposed a limit of 600 to 700 MIRVs for another type of agreement of shorter duration than the ten-year term for the proposed SALT II accord. No sooner had the ceiling been set than the United States (in September 1975) was proposing to add a new category, above and beyond the 2,400, to accommodate a new weapon, the cruise missile. The Russians quite understandably responded that, if each new weapons development were to bring a demand for a higher ceiling, there would be no sense in concluding any arms control agreements. The new American proposal, the Russians said, would be tantamount to a call for the renegotiation of Vladivostok.

Once again, the administration argued that the ceilings set at Vladivostok were not high when measured against the fact that the Soviet Union could deploy 40 percent more if there were no accord. Speaking of Vladivostok, Kissinger declared, with characteristic understatement: "This can be justly described as a major breakthrough . . . and its significance becomes all the more clear if one compares the numbers not with some hypothetical model that one might have in mind, but what would have happened in the absence of this agreement." [10]

Dr. George B. Kistiakowsky of Harvard, who was chief of the explosives division at the Los Alamos laboratory and was subsequently President Eisenhower's special assistant for science and technology, described the Vladivostok agreement in quite different terms as "one that protects the arms race for the next ten years from interference by the arms controllers." [11] At the time this is written there seems a reasonable prospect of concluding a SALT II agreement at ceilings somewhat lower than those established at Vladivostok. That agreement would still permit advancement in weapons technology, as for example the cruise missile and the Soviet Backfire bomber. Nor would it require either side to make significant reductions in its strategic arsenal — a development that would presumably have to wait for SALT III.

Although SALT is the central exhibit in Kissinger's museum of *détente*, it was clearly of interest to both sides and should therefore not have required us to provide other quite extraneous incentives. Still, to give some shadow of verisimilitude to the concept, a handful of lesser agreements — largely of a technical nature — were negotiated at a lower level. These included, among others, arrangements for some exchange of information and effort in the field of cancer research, as well as some coordination of studies on methods to protect the environment. There were also understandings in connection with the use of the oceans' resources and the application of atomic energy for peaceful purposes. Joint studies were contemplated regarding methods to conserve energy, construction techniques for regions subject to earthquakes, and new transportation methods. The list also includes agreements regarding the prevention of incidents at sea and the exchange of information and research methods in agriculture.

Few concrete results have flowed from any of these agreements, and for American participants the total program has been disappointing. Of far greater intrinsic significance has been America's attempt to secure an arrangement for a mutual and balanced reduction of forces. Yet, though long meetings have been held in Vienna, there has been little tangible progress, and, since the Soviet Union has already rejected the idea of a balanced withdrawal, it seems unlikely that any agreement acceptable to the West can be reached. Nevertheless, one should note in at least a footnote on the credit side that the pendency of these negotiations has helped deter the United States Congress from rashly removing American forces from Europe.

In addition to this whole bundle of agreements, the "spirit of *détente*" has been expressed in elegant declarations. Thus, at the May 1972 summit conference, the two governments issued a "Statement of Principles" to govern relations between the United States and the Soviet Union. Later, on the occasion of General Secretary Brezhnev's visit to the United States in 1973, he and President Nixon signed an "Agreement for the Prevention of Nuclear War," which affirmed that the objective of each nation was to remove the danger of nuclear conflict and the use of nuclear weapons. As Secretary Kissinger explained it, that agreement "presupposed the renunciation of any war or threat of war not only by the two nuclear superpowers against each other, but also against allies or third countries." In other words, the principle of restraint was not confined to relations between the signatories; it was explicitly extended to include all countries.

Of the two documents, the "Statement of Principles" was clearly the more far-reaching. Its provisions were, in the words of the then Assistant Secretary of State for Near Eastern and South Asian Affairs, Joseph J. Sisco, specifically aimed at the Middle East and were understood to mean that the Middle East "should not be an area over which there should be confrontation between us." [12] Yet, rather than trying to resolve the prickly problems of the Middle East by enlisting Soviet support, we have, as I shall point out later, consistently tried to exclude the Soviets from our peace-making efforts. This, of course, is the implicit — and fallacious — assumption underlying *détente* as it has so far been interpreted in practice: that if we and the Soviets sort out our bilateral relations we can avoid a disastrous conflict. But that flies in the face of all experience. A direct and deliberate confrontation is not the central danger. So long as we maintain an adequate military posture, the Soviet Union will not deliberately direct its nuclear weapons against America — or even Western Europe. The Soviets, after all, are as aware as we of the "balance of terror" and they have no taste for suicide. The prime deterrent to such an attack is not *détente* but the Kremlin's continued awareness that each of the superpowers is a hostage of the other.

The most serious danger faced by the two nations is that they may be propelled into a confrontation neither desires by their involvement in the affairs of third countries. So, rather than drawing up rules to govern our relations with one another, we should use the leverage of *détente* to persuade the Soviet leaders to work with us in resolving local conflicts where we are now supporting opposing sides.

History has proved *ad nauseam* that governments are by no means masters of their own fate. In her remarkable study *The Guns of August*, Barbara Tuchman vividly showed how alignments with small nations embroiled in local conflicts led the great powers of Europe to mutual destruction in 1914. We Americans did not deliberately attack China in 1950; it was the fact that we and the Chinese were on opposite sides of the Korean War which led to that conflict. Nor, as I have pointed out in Chapter 4, did we consciously commit ourselves to a protracted land war in Southeast Asia; we were pushed into ever deeper engagement by our commitment to South Vietnam.

In spite of the fact that, ever since Mr. Nixon's trip to the Soviet Union in 1972, many Western Europeans have worried about what they call a Soviet-American "condominium," no anxiety could be more misdirected; rather than collaborating to impose on other nations arbitrary peace settlements, the superpowers have continued to wage proxy wars. Not only did Moscow and Washington support opposing sides in the Vietnam War, but, even after the Paris cease-fire of January 1973, the Soviet Union continued to pour arms into North Vietnam, while America continued to arm the south. At the time this is written (March 1976), the Kremlin is seeking to establish its influence in Angola by arming one faction, while, until prohibited by Congress, our government undertook to arm other tribal factions, which were the ones China and South Africa also favored.

It is, of course, the Arab-Israeli conflict that poses the gravest danger; for the United States is committing itself to a massive supply of arms to Israel, which will no doubt impel the Soviet Union to provide equally sophisticated weapons to Iraq and Syria. Yet, as we shall see, by failing even to touch the substantive issues of the Arab-Israeli quarrel yet weakening the drive for an overall settlement, the partial Sinai withdrawal is laying the basis for future war. It leaves the Palestinian, Golan Heights, and Jersualem issues to fester with increasing virulence, while the oil-rich Arab nations and the Soviet Union provide increasing resources to arm the frontline states.

Let us suppose that, within a year or two, the Israelis should feel compelled by the specter of overflowing Arab arsenals to launch a preemptive attack against Syria. Could one rule out the possibility that the threatened fall of Damascus might lead the Soviets to drop a paratroop division or two on the battlefield? And what would be the United States response? To intervene would place our armed forces in direct opposition to the Red Army. To stand down might assure the destruction of Israel.

In view of this danger of confrontation, why has the United States not interpreted *détente* to require common action to resolve dangerous conflicts in sensitive parts of the world?

The answer to this baffling question can be found in the implicit contradiction between Secretary Kissinger's desire to preserve *détente* as a monument to his diplomacy and that irremediable addiction to unilateralism which lies at the heart of his entire policy. He is first and last a unilateralist, firmly committed to a policy of maneuver in which the United States reserves full freedom of action to make decisions and play a lone hand, while it utilizes friends and allies only as instruments for its own tactical purposes. Thus, in spite of all his encomiums to *détente*, he avoids drawing on it for the collective action that might qualify his flexibility of maneuver or detract from the effectiveness of his solo performances.

But if Henry Kissinger is by character and preference a unilateralist, so are the strategists in the Kremlin. Regarding Moscow as the center of the world and relating all strategic moves to the advancement of Soviet interests, either in terms of national power or doctrinal supremacy, the Soviets seem as addicted to playing a lone role of maneuver as is the Secretary.

Still, we do not know the limits of that addiction, since we have never tested them. To be sure, the Soviet leaders talk as though they would cooperate, but the time is long past when we should probe their flexibility and good will, invoking the presumed benefits of *détente* as reasons for changing the reflexes that now set the superpowers at cross purposes. At the least, we might establish the emptiness of the concept, which would be a contribution to realism.

A second — and equally important — area in which *détente* has not been tested relates to the common dangers that civilization faces unless the developed nations mobilize a vast common effort. Without such an effort we can never master the problems created by the play of forces affecting the relations of man to nature in areas such as population, food, raw materials, and ecology.

If, therefore, there is any substantial leverage in *détente,* we would be foolish not to insist, as a condition to our continuing to act out the charade, that the Soviets cease undercutting American initiatives designed to deal with urgent world problems. If they are not willing to do so, we should rigorously reexamine all aspects of Soviet-American relations. Why should we help the Soviet Union improve its absurdly inefficient economy with our capital and technology, why should we sell grain to meet the food deficits created by its ridiculous agriculture system, and why should we collaborate to give it world recognition as a superpower, so long as it perversely frustrates every sensible initiative to deal with world problems that are as dangerous to the Soviet Union as to ourselves? Have we grown so accustomed to its mulish opposition that we have lost our capacity for outrage and with it our sense of perspective? Why should we sit calmly by when Soviet spokesmen proclaim that the danger of overpopulation is an imperialist bogeyman and that, but for capitalist greed, there would be ample food for everyone, no matter how rapidly the world population might continue to grow — chutzpah of epic dimensions from a richly endowed nation that can no longer even feed itself because its agricultural system is a dismal fiasco.

Only by dispersing the fog of wishful thinking and self-deception created by mindless chatter of *détente* can we even begin to comprehend the fundamental question, much less the answer that should shape our own policy: can we, by pumping technology and capital into the lagging Soviet economy, feeding the Soviet people, and building up the Soviet state as equal to America in the eyes of the world, effectively transform a revolutionary power into a legitimate status quo power?

That is a question on which Henry Kissinger in his professorial days expressed firm views. Legitimate powers, as he saw it, were nations that accepted the established international order, while revolutionary powers were those that regarded it as unacceptable. As between legitimate powers, diplomacy could play an effective role of adjusting differences. But, in dealing with a revolutionary power, any adjustments achieved through diplomacy were only tactical concessions preliminary to an inevitable showdown.[13]

Appeasement of a revolutionary power was, in the view of Professor Kissinger, a futility. Diplomacy, which sought agreements to limit the exercise of power, was wasted effort. Conferences would be sterile because the participants would lack a common basis of understanding as to what constituted reason, good faith, and accommodation. Instead, the revolutionary power would make charges calculated to thrust the responsibility for hostilities onto the other side while appealing over its shoulder to uncommitted potential allies. Moreover, wrote Professor Kissinger, since those who deal with a revolutionary power are usually reluctant to accept the fact that its leaders mean precisely what they say, they change their assessments far too late — only when confronted with overwhelming evidence of the revolutionary power's true intentions. Status quo powers must learn — all too often by costly experience — the ultimate objectives of a revolutionary power. But legitimate powers greatly wish to believe that, if only they are sufficiently reasonable, the revolutionary power will become part of the system. A shrewd revolutionary power will encourage that idea until it can safely cease its dissembling.

Professor Kissinger's description of a revolutionary power accurately fitted not only Nazi Germany but also Stalin's Soviet Union. Although born of revolution, dedicated to the class struggle, and committed to the ultimate triumph of the Communist system, has Brezhnev's Soviet Union become, in fact, a status quo power?

That it is in the process of doing so or, at least, may be induced to do so is the unstated premise of Secretary of State Kissinger's diplomacy. He has concentrated on trying to develop areas of mutual accommodation with the Kremlin; but that could be fruitful or even prudent only if — contrary to the implied views of the pre-1969 authority, Professor Kissinger — the Soviet Union is renouncing its revolutionary past and beginning to accept the existing system. Has American recognition of Soviet equality helped transform the USSR from a revolutionary to a legitimate power? That young skeptic, Professor Kissinger, would have thought the idea quite foolish.

There are today certain primary reference points by which we can judge Soviet actions and perhaps determine whether or not *détente* is more than the rhetoric of politicians.

So far excessive emphasis has been placed on various aspects of the direct relations between Washington and Moscow. Of these clearly the most important is the extent to which the Soviet Union proves willing to accept reasonable restraints on its nuclear arms buildup; a second aspect concerns the evolution of Soviet-American trade. Yet it would be a mistake to read too large a meaning into the developments in either of these areas. Certainly the Soviet Union has an obvious interest in stopping the diversion of scarce resources into the production of weapons that are relevant only in the context of mutual suicide; in fact, it presumably needs a SALT agreement more desperately than the United States, since its resources are more restricted, so why such a mutually beneficial endeavor should require us to provide any extraneous incentive is by no means clear.

Such an asymmetry of benefit is even more evident with regard to trade, for the Soviet Union is today suffering from economic pellagra — an acute deficiency of technology and capital it can obtain only from America and the West, while the trade we may generate with Russia could provide only marginal benefit to our overall prosperity.

Thus, the Kremlin's softer attitude toward its bilateral relationships with the United States is not the acid test of *détente;* it has nothing to lose and much to gain from our eagerness to reach agreement in that narrow context. The critical question is the Kremlin's position with regard to third-party struggles, and the most urgent test today is the Middle East. Will Moscow be prepared to cooperate in resolving the Arab-Israeli conflict, which is today the most dangerous potential source of confrontation? As will be pointed out in the following chapter, we have so far avoided the question.

Equally important is the Soviet Government's willingness to stop playing cheap politics with the formidable problems we now face in mankind's relations with nature (such as population, food, raw materials, and ecology).

Finally, East-West relations may face a fourth test if continued inflation, depression, and unemployment should result in serious damage to the capitalist world's financial and economic structure. If serious depression in the West were to lead to the fragmentation of Western unity, to the sealing off of markets and restraints on the movements of goods and capital, to a competitive dog-eat-dog spirit among Western nations, and, finally, to the collapse of weak governments and the growing ascendancy of Communist influence in certain key Western countries, would the Kremlin resist the temptation to exploit the situation to its own ideological advantage?

As one might expect, Soviet professional spokesmen insist in private conversations that the Soviet Union now has a major stake in Western prosperity and that the Kremlin would be dismayed to find the Western economy disintegrating. Yet the ultimate failure of capitalism through its internal contradictions is a prime article of Marxist faith. If the West were faced with a catastrophic crisis in its financial and economic life, with all that implied in terms of political instability, would the Soviet leaders desist from actions that might help vindicate the writings in their holy books and the predictions of their prophets?

Certainly the Kremlin leaders are aware of that possibility. In September 1974, when Western economies were beginning to feel the destructive pressures of the oil price increase, Leonid Brezh-nev diagnosed the "symptoms of the disease of capitalism of our time" — inflation, economic crisis, falling production, and rising unemployment. He contended that those developments were "speeding up the disintegration of the political machinery of capitalist rule," since capitalism was proving unable to answer today's requirements. This, asserted Brezhnev, was "unavoidable" since it stemmed from the "very nature of capitalism." [14]

That Brezhnev should be constrained to reaffirm such a famous and fundamental doctrine of Comrades Marx and Engels was hardly surprising. What rendered it of special significance, however, was that such reaffirmation was not left to classical ideologues of the Politiburo such as Mikhail Suslov or Boris Ponomarov, but was put forward by the very Brezhnev who had invested immense political capital in *détente*.

Evidence that the Kremlin may have altered its tactics during 1975 rests largely on two documents. The first was an article in February by A. E. Sobolev, entitled "Questions of Strategy and Tactics of Class Struggle at the Present State of the Central Crisis of Capitalism." The general theme of the Sobolev article was that, with capitalism in an advanced state of crisis, peaceful coexistence (in other words, *détente*) was working effectively to advance the position of the world Communist revolution. Sobolev thus favored the continuance of efforts to extend Communist power through quiet political action and temporary coalitions between Western Communist Parties and other left-of-center and center groupings. In fact, he saw *détente* giving Communist Parties respectability and thus undermining resistance to their assumption of power.

Immediately following the Helsinki conference, however, the line seems to have changed, for on August sixth, just a week after the signing of the Helsinki resolutions, an article was published in *Pravda* by a man named Konstantin Zaradov, the editor of a magazine known in its English edition as the *World Marxist Review*, which is a channel of communication between Moscow and the Communist Parties around the world that owe it allegiance. That article was given particular authority by the fact that in the following month, on September 17, Brezhnev, in spite of his apparent illness, gave a highly advertised audience to Mr. Zaradov, publicly expressing his "high approval" of Zaradov's magazine.

The Zaradov article could be read as a signal to the Commu-

nist Parties of Western Europe — particularly France and Italy —
that Moscow is undergoing one of those sudden shifts in policy
that have marked its history ever since the 1917 Revolution, for
the essence of Zaradov's message, in direct contradiction of the
views of Sobolev, was that Communist Parties should *not* "dis-
solve" themselves "in an ideologically amorphous organization or
any alliance set up according to the formula 'unity for unity's
sake,' " which he condemned as a "Menshevik" concept. The true
course was to establish the hegemony of the proletariat, and Communist Parties should not seek to come to power through a kind of
"nationwide referendum." Though Lenin relied on the popular
majority, the majority was not, as Lenin conceived it, "an arithme-
tical concept but a political one."

Reading through all the Communist jargon, one can only interpret Zaradov as saying to the Communist Parties around the
world that they should not seek, as the French and Italian Communist Parties were seeking, to gain power through coalitions
with other left-of-center parties, but should remember that they
were, after all, parties of the Revolution. Since then, other Soviet
Communist spokesmen have been reiterating the belief that the
Western World's economic problems create opportunities Communist Parties should exploit.

I had suggested in an article in *Newsweek* in August 1975 that
the Helsinki conference might well mark the beginning of a
harder Soviet line; because Brezhnev would have obtained a
Western benediction on the Soviets' hold over Eastern Europe, he
might consider that he had gained all he needed from *"détente."*
Evidence is now accumulating to support this hypothesis. The
Kremlin leaders inevitably view the West's economic troubles in
terms of the fantasies of their own prophets, while their desire to
exploit Western weakness has presumably been encouraged by
the flabbiness of governments not only in Europe but also in the
United States. Meanwhile, with continuing uncertainty as to the
consequences of the changing of the guard in Peking, no one can
rule out some new effort of rapprochement between the two Communist capitals.

Soviet aggressiveness in Angola bears out the prediction of a
more activist Soviet policy, while there seems little question that
the Peking leaders made clear to Ford and Kissinger their doubts

that the United States had either the will or cohesion to continue its role of effective balance between the two great Communist powers. What this may mean in the longer term is by no means clear.

PART II

Breakage and
Unfinished
Business

CHAPTER 8

Shuttle Diplomacy — The Preference for Tactics over Strategy

IF THE FOREIGN POLICY ACTIVITIES OF THE NIXON ADMINISTRA-
tion were primarily directed at sweeping up some of the errors
and distortions of past policies, Henry Kissinger's preoccupation
during the interregnum and the early months of the Ford Administration was largely with developments in the Middle East. I use
the term "interregnum" to refer to the last, rapidly darkening,
period that began in the summer of 1973 as the clouds circling the
White House crept relentlessly lower and ended on that climactic
morning of August 9, 1974, when the principal occupant caught
Air Force One's last flight to San Clemente.

During those extraordinary months, Henry Kissinger enjoyed
a unique role in American history as a foreign minister responsible to no one but himself. To be sure, Nixon was nominally still
President, but he played almost no part in the shaping or direction
of policy. Distracted by the lowering clouds, he either barricaded
himself in a White House that had become a redoubt, flitted mind-
lessly between his two pleasure palaces on opposite coasts, or
toured foreign capitals in a vain effort to demonstrate that the
peace could not prosper without his friendship for foreign princes.
Although his effort to take credit for his Secretary of State's activities unquestionably galled Henry Kissinger, the Secretary was in a
tactically secure position, with untrammeled authority beyond his

wildest dreams; if his initiatives went well, he was clearly the author of events; if they went badly, he could — as he now often
does in moments of reminiscence — blame his failure on the
breakdown of executive authority.

Fortunately for Kissinger's reputation, the vacuum of Presidential power coincided with a further outbreak of Arab-Israeli
war in October 1973. It enabled him, without having to share the
stage, to engage in the kind of virtuoso diplomacy for which he
was remarkably gifted and which fulfilled his elemental need for
power and glory.

Ever since the recognition of the state of Israel in 1948, the
Arab-Israeli conflict had been an intermittent concern of American
diplomats. John Foster Dulles's sanctimonious action in repudiat-
ing the inept efforts of the French and British to seize the Suez
Canal in 1956 had left America as the only Western power with influence in the area, although another result of Suez was to permit
the Soviets to establish a Middle East beachhead. Inhibited by our
special attachment to Israel, the Arabs' common enemy, as well as by
our economic interest in oil concessions, we Americans could not
maintain the Middle East as an exclusive sphere of influence, as Britain had done in an earlier day — even had we wished to do so.

The awkwardness of the American position was made worse
by the decisiveness of Israel's victory in the Six-Day War of June
1967, which humiliated and demoralized the whole of Araby. Disturbed that the Israelis had struck without advance notice, much
less consultation, the Johnson Administration tried to initiate at
least the beginning of a solution. After intense haggling, the
United States Security Council, in November 1967, finally approved Resolution 242, based on a British initiative, which established the broad framework for a settlement. That resolution
provided for "withdrawal of Israeli armed forces from territories
occupied in recent conflict." It also provided for the "termination
of all claims of states of belligerency and respect for and acknowledgment of the sovereignty, territorial integrity and political independence of every State in the area and their right to live in
peace within secure and recognized boundaries free from threats
or acts of force."

But Resolution 242 remained a bare framework, never a completed edifice. Although endless conversations took place be-

tween the State Department, on the one hand, and Israeli and Arab leaders, on the other, the situation settled into stalemate. Weakened by its Vietnam embroilment and deterred by the heightened effectiveness of pro-Israeli sentiment in an election year, the Johnson Administration eschewed the tough initiatives required for progress. Thus, the absence of heroic action added one more missed opportunity to the dismal Middle East chronicle. By the end of 1967 the Arabs, frustrated and unhappy, had issued an extravagantly hard-line declaration at a conference at Khartoum, while the Israelis, increasingly convinced that time was working on their side, had persuaded themselves that, if they only continued long enough to occupy — and develop — the territories they had taken in 1967, the world would accept the new boundaries as a *fait accompli.*

I was made vividly aware of this latter attitude when, as United States Ambassador to the United Nations, I flew over Israel in 1968 with the Minister of Defense, General Dayan. Looking through the helicopter windows at the verdant land below, I remarked on Israel's extraordinary achievement in making the desert blossom like a rose. "But," I said, "when I look out over the sands of the Sinai, I wonder how long you can sit on all that real estate and still have any security."

"Security?" he replied, "Why do you talk about security? Never have we had such security. For the first time, we have defense in depth, we have the possibility of an early air alert, we have boundaries with the Arab world only half as long as they were before. Why do you speak to me of security?"

"All right," I said, "let me rephrase the question: How long do you think you can sit on all that real estate?"

"How long has it been since 1948?" he replied.

Though the incident is of no historical importance, Dayan's reaction reflected the belief then widely held by many — though by no means all — Israeli leaders that the Arabs were too divided and incompetent to regain the occupied lands by their own efforts and that no other nation would intervene to help them.

But five years later the war of October 1973 shattered Israeli complacency. Not only did the Arabs succeed during the first days of fighting beyond anyone's expectations — including their own — but Israelis began to ask whether time was still working on their side, if, indeed, it had ever been. No one could any longer take it for granted that 3.5 million Israelis would be able forever to stand off a hundred million hostile Arabs — particularly after the February 1974 increase in oil prices assured the Arab world of unlimited funds to buy armaments. Thus, some Israeli sentiment developed for a political settlement, while the Arabs, with their pride restored, also adopted a more flexible stance.

Once a ceasefire had become effective (under pressure from the Soviet Union) on October 24, 1973, America had no option but to arrange for the separation of the hostile forces on the Egyptian and Syrian fronts. Not only was this essential to avoid a resumption of the shooting but it was also a necessary condition to the lifting of an oil embargo that Europeans tended to blame on America's pro-Israeli policies.

Although it was a task unsuited to routine diplomacy — particularly since we then had no formal relations with Egypt — there were ample precedents for the President or Secretary of State to dispatch a special emissary to try to work out a settlement. Ambassador Ellsworth Bunker, for example, had spent a patient but exhausting year in the Dominican Republic, resolving the tangled politics of that tortured island on behalf of President Johnson, while Ralph Bunche had arranged the Arab-Israeli armistices in 1949 through a rudimentary form of shuttle diplomacy under the aegis of the United Nations. But the seductions of virtuoso diplomacy were too great and, in spite of the fact that newly installed Secretary Kissinger was promising to "institutionalize" our foreign policy, he could not resist the temptation to play the emissary role himself.

One can argue that the success of his effort vindicated the Secretary's personal involvement, yet it established a clumsy pattern. Not only did it keep the Secretary of State away from Washington for an average of one out of every six weeks during 1974 and 1975, but his involvement impaired the usefulness of less newsworthy emissaries. Thus no one should have been surprised that Kuwait refused to accept a visit from the able and respected Joseph J. Sisco, then Assistant Secretary of State for Near Eastern Affairs, insisting that it would be *infra dig.* to receive anyone other than Mr. Kissinger.

But, more important than these immediate effects, shuttle diplomacy had major political implications, since, by dramatizing our preemption of the negotiations, it notified the world that the United States would go it alone. Not only did we rigorously exclude the Soviet Union from any part in the negotiations, but we reduced Moscow to so humiliating a position that the Soviet Foreign Minister, Mr. Gromyko, felt compelled to fly repeatedly to Damascus to see President Assad of Syria, each time arriving after Kissinger had left town — resembling, as one wit put it, the assiduous lover of a traveling salesman's wife.

If the initial round of shuttle negotiations could be justified as a limited diplomatic operation to achieve battlefield redeployments, the search for a substantive settlement involved political commitments far more complex and important than the mere movement of armies. Yet the time was propitious as never before for a concentrated drive for such a settlement, since, by a fortunate coincidence, there were relatively moderate leaders in all the relevant capitals.

Although President Assad of Syria was not totally a free agent, since there were hardliners in his own government, he would have preferred an overall settlement that would enable him to concentrate on the peaceful development of his country rather than accept increasing Soviet domination as the price of keeping pace with Israeli armaments. Even the chance for rational Palestinian leadership seemed brighter in the early months of 1975 than at any time since that explosive weekend in Rabat the preceding October, when Arab leaders had pushed the PLO forward to negotiate the Palestinian issue and administer whatever Palestinian state might emerge. The swaggering appearance of the PLO leader, Arafat, before the United Nations General Assembly on November 13, 1974, had been largely forgotten. Lacking a clear political base, the PLO had tended to recede into the impenetrable fog of Arab politics, while by his courage, persistence, and skillful diplomacy, the moderate King Hussein had gradually worked his way back into Arab respect.

In Israel, also, a fresh appraisal was in progress. The bloodletting of the 1973 October War had injected a new realism into popular attitudes, particularly since increased oil wealth had added a new potential to Arab military power. Thus many Israelis turned, with a new sense of hope and yearning, toward the practical possibilities of a lasting settlement with their neighbors that would provide them the opportunity to develop their country in peace.

Finally, now that Nasser, with his dreams of a pan-Arab empire, had been succeeded by Anwar Sadat, Egypt was led by a reasonable man who saw his country's future in strictly national terms. Sadat, moreover, needed peace — needed it desperately — if for no other reason than to keep pace with the pressures engendered by Egyptian fecundity. The population was growing at the rate of 2.7 percent, doubling between 1947 and 1975 and threatening to double again within twenty-five years. Already the benefits of the Aswan Dam, in terms of increased agricultural production, had been more than offset by the 14.6 million people added to the Egyptian population since the dam was begun in 1956.

Egypt was, and still is, in desperate economic and financial shape, with 30 percent unemployment, and the Egyptians could not face the expense of another war — at least unless somebody else paid for it. But Moscow was not prepared to pour money endlessly into a nation capable of launching hazardous military adventures on little advance notice that were not only expensive in material terms but might lead to a Soviet-American confrontation. Yet if the Russians were unhappy with the Egyptians, the Egyptians had even greater cause for discontent. Not only were the Soviet military representatives contemptuous of Egyptian competence, but their refusal to give the Egyptians full custody of sophisticated equipment meant Soviet control over Egyptian policy.

With the evolving mood of the area creating favorable conditions for a major American effort to bring about peace, Kissinger had available at least two possible approaches. He could continue to pursue shuttle diplomacy between Israel and Egypt in the hope of arranging a truce on the western front that would buy time or he could try to engineer a comprehensive agreement that would dispose of the fundamental issues of the Golan Heights, the Palestinians, and Jerusalem, and thus bring about a permanent settlement.

A bilateral deal between Israel and Egypt offered the seductive attraction of speedy results, for, apart from the Abu Rudeis oil fields, the arid desert of the Sinai had only military significance. Moreover, to an inveterate tactician such as Kissinger, there was classical beauty in the prospect of dividing the Arab world by neutralizing Egypt, which contains one-third of all the Arabs and has historically been Israel's principal military threat. The approach promised at least the illusion of progress with little pain, for it would enable the United States to avoid the hard, substantive problems, such as the Golan Heights or Jerusalem or the Palestinians, which engaged deep emotional reactions — resulting from long-held grievances or from religious passions or fear. And, finally, even though Henry Kissinger was publicly committed to the rhetoric of *détente,* he saw advantages in excluding the Soviet Union from participation, thus preventing Moscow from gaining a solider foothold in the area — even though, as he conceded, the Soviets would have to be brought in at some point before a final settlement could be achieved.

Those were the points Kissinger's staff emphasized to all who might give them currency. But they did not tell the whole story. Above and beyond those reasons — or, perhaps, to a considerable extent overriding them — was the fact that further shuttle diplomacy would keep Henry Kissinger in exclusive control of the negotiating process, would place him squarely in the spotlight of world attention, would, if successful, contribute further to his legend and would help President Ford in the 1976 election.

The arguments for continuing bilateral diplomacy were, in my view, far from persuasive. In fact, I felt deep regret as I watched the United States turn its back on a serious effort to solve the overall problem in favor of a tactical maneuver that bought time at the expense of ultimate peace. To exploit Sadat's strong desire for peace merely to separate Egypt from the rest of the Arab world was the profligate waste of an invaluable asset, since it removed the strongest and most moderate voice from Arab councils. By engineering Sadat's defection from the broader Arab cause, yet leaving the basic issues and grievances untouched, we appeared in the eyes of many Arabs to be supporting Israeli ambitions to consolidate their hold over the territories seized by force in 1967. Thus, with Egypt alienated from the more radical Arab states, and with those states increasingly embittered by a growing sense of isolation and betrayal, a separate Egyptian truce assured the continued division of the Middle East into armed camps, with each side building toward an even more explosive war.

My concern with the Arab-Israeli struggle was by no means new. Not only had I dealt with various aspects of the problem during my years in the State Department, but as early as 1969 I had set forth, in an article in *Foreign Affairs*,[1] my fundamental conviction that a permanent peace was possible only by common action of the United States and the Soviet Union. The immediate parties to the conflict were, in my view, too consumed by suspicion, fear, and passion and too imprisoned by history to be able, by themselves, ever to reach an enduring settlement.

Thus, with the Secretary of State pondering his next move, in January 1975, I published a magazine article [2] outlining the basic approach that was needed, elaborating it further in a newspaper piece in May of the same year.[3] The essential first step, as I saw it, was for the United States to establish its own independent position. To that end, I proposed that the President announce a set of principles which should, in the United States view, govern a final settlement. Such a statement of principles, designed to amplify the provisions of Resolution 242 that the United Nations Security Council had adopted following the 1967 War, would set forth certain propositions:

• The United States would continue to give its full, unremitting support to the secure existence of Israel.

• This did not mean, however, that we envisaged Israel's retention of the territories taken by force in 1967. A final settlement, as we saw it, must involve the withdrawal by Israel to substantially the borders existing prior to the 1967 War, subject to such minor boundary rectifications as might be achieved through negotiation. For this purpose, we would support the principle of direct negotiation between the parties.

• A final settlement must provide for full, nondiscriminatory treatment of Israel by the other states in the area. That should include *de jure* diplomatic recognition, the cessation of hostile propaganda, provision for the free movement of peoples, the right of Israeli ships, as well as cargoes, to pass through the Suez Canal, and so on.

• The issue of the Golan Heights should be settled by demilitarization and the maintenance in the area of a United Nations presence that could not be withdrawn by either party. The West Bank should also be demilitarized and treated as belonging to the Palestinian people, leaving it to the Arab states and the Palestinians, with the help of the United Nations, to decide by some process of self-determination of their own choosing how and by whom the area should be governed. The issue of Jerusalem should be settled by some form of international arrangement for which a number of formulas have been devised.

In making this statement, the United States, by interpreting and amplifying Resolutions 242 and 338, would insulate itself against the pressures of those who still held larger territorial ambitions for Israel. Since the statement would accord with established international law and with the United Nations Charter, it would provide the United States with a morally unassailable position — unbiased in favor of either side — thus enabling it to play an effective role as impartial peacemaker. To establish America's freedom of action, it was essential for the President to assert these principles promptly and publicly, because, in spite of Kissinger's desire not to be hobbled in his diplomacy, Israel was insisting that the United States take no positions not approved in Jerusalem.

Once the President had made a public statement along this line, we should, I proposed, promptly ask not only the nations of Western Europe but the Soviet Union to join with us in seeking a final settlement on the basis of these principles. I even suggested that the United States make Soviet agreement to such common action a condition to the President's attending the summit conference at Helsinki in the summer of 1975 to sign the declarations developed by the European Security Conference. But the time is now past when that might have been done.

Since we, together with the Soviet Union, Britain, and France, constitute four of the five permanent members of the United Nations Security Council, we should then be able to obtain a Security Council Resolution setting forth the terms of a final settlement on the basis of these principles. Such terms would necessarily include ample provision for buffer zones and for the insertion of United Nations forces in buffer zones. Nor should we foreclose the possibility that the United States and the Soviet Union might jointly guarantee the final boundaries and that we might both supply elements for the United Nations peace-keeping forces, just as American and Soviet forces had jointly patrolled Vienna in the days before the Austrian State Treaty. Finally, we should seek with the Soviet Union and the Western European arms-producing countries an agreement to limit the flow of weapons and military equipment into the area.

Although I discussed this approach with Secretary Kissinger, it was not the course he adopted. Instead of announcing a statement of principles, he and the President used the threat of such an announcement to bring pressure on Israel to make concessions for a bilateral truce with Egypt.

There is no need to recount the events that marked the diplomatic activity following the breakdown of negotiations on March 22, 1975, or the impact of those events on American domestic politics. On a preliminary shuttle reconnaissance in February of that year, Kissinger had gained the impression that, when he began his second round of talks on March 8, the Israelis would move beyond the position they had taken earlier and agree to a Sinai withdrawal without insisting that the Egyptians make a full declaration of nonbelligerency. When such movement was not forthcoming and the talks broke down, the Secretary gave signals of an intention to slow down delivery of advanced arms and in other ways indicated Washington's displeasure with what Kissinger tended to regard as Israel's duplicity. But his efforts to press Israel for a more conciliatory line were largely offset by a letter signed by seventy-six Senators that, in effect, urged that Israel be given what it wanted.

Here, then, in the spring of 1975 was another moment when America had the chance to alter course and launch a drive to settle the underlying causes of Middle Eastern turmoil. But Egypt was eager for quick action that would bring a period of respite, and Israel saw a bilateral deal with Cairo as preferable — at least in the short term — to a United States statement of principles that might require it to yield the occupied territories. Thus, both governments encouraged Kissinger's natural inclination to try to vindicate his earlier, abortive effort by once more seeking an Egyptian-Israeli truce in exchange for a limited Israeli withdrawal in the Sinai.

Unhappily, the enterprise lacked the useful element of symmetry, since both Henry Kissinger and Anwar Sadat wanted a partial settlement far more than Yitzhak Rabin and the Israelis did.

Kissinger did not conceal his desire to buy time. With Egypt neutralized, it would take months for the more radical Arab states to get ready for war, and that should assure a period of relative quiet lasting beyond the 1976 American elections. Meanwhile, Kissinger would enjoy applause for a major diplomatic coup.

Sadat desperately needed a truce in order to prevent the total disintegration of an already rapidly crumbling economy. He was gambling on the chance that, if granted two or three years of peace, he could halt the rot and get Egyptian industry and agriculture moving.

Israel's problems were more complex. In principle, a separate truce with Egypt was the lesser of two unattractive possibilities, while to resist all movement would hazardously strain Israel's vital relations with Washington. Egypt had always been Israel's major military threat and, if the Egyptians were eliminated from the leadership of the Arab side, Israelis could once again begin to hope that Israel might hold on permanently to the West Bank, the Gaza Strip, the Golan Heights, and Jerusalem. Yet, when they faced the issue in concrete terms, the proposed arrangement seemed illusory. To relinquish the Sinai oil fields was a significant hardship for a country that had few other indigenous oil sources; moreover, even though the oil fields might be passing the peak of production (the reports are not clear on this), the cost of importing oil would be a further foreign exchange drain on Israel's already depleted reserves. To hand over both the Gidi and Mitla passes also posed grave problems — both military and emotional — for did Israel dare yield a position of strategic advantage without being sure its security would be adequately underwritten through other means? Here was a major sticking point, because Sadat at his most forthcoming could not be expected to offer a permanent state of nonbelligerency so long as large areas of Egyptian territory remained in Israeli hands; to move any distance at all toward a separate truce would risk infuriating the rest of the Arab world, including the Saudis and Kuwaitis on whom he must count for enormous subsidies if his leaking economic boat were to have even half a chance of staying above water.

To overcome these grave Israeli misgivings Kissinger felt compelled to employ elaborate means of persuasion. Yet, the letter of the seventy-six Senators on May 21, 1975, severely limited his leverage, since the Israelis felt — and did not hesitate to tell him — that they had the political clout in Congress to override any sanction he might threaten. What they failed to remember, of course, is that the interests of nations are often worse served by their friends than by their enemies. The Senators' letter was not in Israel's long-range interests; by making it possible for the signers to display their allegiance to Israel under conditions that cost them nothing, it freed them to argue later, when the Senate would consider specific measures, that, since they had already expressed their support and sympathy, they could now take a more balanced position.

But, for the time being, the letter did circumscribe Kissinger's means of persuasion. Because it ruled out the use of the stick, he must provide carrots in abundance. Thus, to secure the partial settlement he devoutly wanted, he had to promise to tie America's diplomacy and military support far more closely to Israel than was good for either country.

Had the Egyptian-Israeli agreement really been, as many thought, a first step toward a final settlement, much could have been said for it. But, unfortunately, Kissinger's tactical objective of "buying time" was not in the interests of peace. Since Sadat no longer had to worry about Israel for the next three years, the transaction deprived Egypt of the incentive to participate in further diplomatic effort. Instead, in order to try to mollify other Arab states that would inevitably accuse him of defection, he had to take an extremely hard line regarding any settlement — as he did when he visited Washington in October 1975. Moreover, by putting the Sinai issue to rest for the foreseeable future, the agreement removed from the bargaining table a whole geographical area wherein trade-offs could be envisaged. Had the agreement not been reached, withdrawal from the Sinai could, for example, have been exchanged for concessions on obdurate issues elsewhere.

Far from easing the road to final settlement, the tactic of trying to split the Arab world may well have created an insuperable impediment to a settlement. By promoting a separate arrangement with Egypt, the United States discredited Egypt's moderating influence on the other Arabs, leaving negotiations to the more radical states so directly affected by the Palestinian issue as to be incapable of diplomatic flexibility. Geographically separated from the critical area, Egypt could take a relatively relaxed view of the Palestinian problem, but the Arab nations at the eastern end of the Mediterranean were under much sterner constraints.

If the agreement deprived Egypt of both the incentive and authority to bargain further, it rendered Israel equally rigid. Having made a national decision of the most agonizing kind in agreeing to a partial Sinai withdrawal, the Israelis were in no mood for additional concessions. They felt that if they had achieved anything, they had bought peace on the Egyptian front for at least three years. They had been promised by the United States enormous supplies of military equipment as well as an underwriting of their oil requirements. Still, many Israelis feared that they had been bludgeoned into making concessions against their interests in return for Egyptian promises of dubious validity. What it all added up to was that so much persuasion had been exerted to secure the Sinai withdrawal, so much division and resentment had been stirred up, that the Israel Government became, for the time being, disabled from making further concessions. In our efforts to achieve a transaction that settled very little, we exhausted the Israeli tolerance for further compromise.

Even more than that, the temporizing nature of the arrangement revived the hope that the Israelis might retain most of the territories taken in the 1967 War. Thus — perhaps without meaning to — we reinforced the long-standing tendency of many Israelis to equate territory with security. It is an understandable reflex for the people of a small country who, as shown by General Dayan's comments to me in 1968, put great weight on the indispensability of defense in depth and an early air alert. Yet it is a view subject to progressive obsolescence, since forecasts of renewed Middle East fighting more and more emphasize the importance of surface-to-surface missiles and other weapons of long-distance destructive power.

But, even more fundamental, the Israeli hope of maintaining present borders is based on an illusion, because, in the long run, the effort to keep possession of the occupied territories is more likely to undermine than assist Israeli security. History has repeatedly shown that there is no more potent generator of conflict than irredentism, that fierce amalgam of frustration, homesickness, and bitterness that follows the displacement of men and women from the lands they tilled and on which they have lived and brought up children — emotions which grow more rancid and irrational with the passage of time. They are emotions deeply felt even by Palestinians who have never seen the occupied territories but who have been indoctrinated in refugee camps with a profound sense of grievance. Moreover, the issue of Jerusalem — related more to religion than homesickness — will not remain quiescent, so long as the holy places of Islam remain in Israeli hands.

Today, of course, Israel is militarily stronger than her neighbors and we have promised to keep her so, yet some cold-bloodedly realistic Israelis view with fear future projections of Arab military potential. Even in the absence of Egypt, the three states on Israel's northern front — Syria, Iraq, and Jordan — have an aggregate population three times that of Israel, while the funds that the oil-rich Arab states can potentially afford to provide for arms and equipment will, in the long run, far exceed anything Israel can solidly count on from the United States. Nor can Israel indefinitely sustain the financial cost of its inordinately large military establishment.

Yet, Israel will be compelled to remain a garrison state so long as she continues to be an occupying power. Until a final settlement is reached, the prospect of renewed war must dominate almost every aspect of Israeli life. For, can anyone seriously believe that the million and a half to three million Palestinians — nobody knows exactly how many — scattered over the Arab world will be content forever to accept Israeli occupation of the West Bank? The Palestinians are not, as many Americans assume, merely wretched refugees without political clout. They are a gifted people, and there is hardly an Arab capital in which some Palestinians do not hold influential posts at a level at least as high as the second echelon of government. Moreover, what they regard as Egypt's defection is already driving them toward more extreme leaders and positions.

Nor can anyone be sure that Syria and Iraq will always remain semihostile to one another. The continued Israeli occupation of Arab lands could well drive those two states not only to increase their dependence on the Soviets as their principal supplier of arms, but to close ranks and join forces.

All this is, of course, complicated by recent events in Lebanon, where, at the time this is being written (March 1976), Syria seems to have gained a large measure of control. Should that continue, the PLO may acquire the political base they have so far lacked, but it seems unlikely they will be willing to sublimate their yearning to recover the West Bank to the effort to play a useful role in a Syria-dominated Lebanon. They are much more likely to consider Lebanon as a staging area for another assault on Israel in some future shooting phase of the Arab-Israeli struggle. Thus the collapse of the moderate Maronite-Arab state may well complete the encirclement of Israel's northern flank by activist Arab regimes. Finally, so long as the key bitter issues remain unsettled, the major oil-supplying states — such as Saudi Arabia and Kuwait — will feel under irresistible pressure to commit more and more of their oil wealth to the rearmament of Syria, Iraq, and even Jordan; in fact, Saudi Arabia may someday feel required to play a direct military role against Israel.

To assess the future realistically, one must also ask how enduring is Egypt's commitment not to use military force. It is a question that darkens much Israeli thinking. Does the Sinai agreement represent a solemn pledge of the Egyptian people, or merely the promise of Anwar Sadat? Having had two heart attacks, he is anything but a healthy man, nor is his tenure in office assured for a long term. His very anxiety to achieve a period of tranquillity attests to the fragility of his situation, since he knows he must get capital and technology for Egypt's economy and weapons for its soldiers if his regime is to survive.

It seems likely he has aroused expectations he can never fulfill. I have been told by a well-informed Egyptian, for example, that Sadat has promised the commanding officers of the Egyptian armed forces that, as a result of the Sinai agreement, they will receive arms and equipment in magnitudes and sophistication comparable to those America is now giving to Israel. But, if my informant is correct, disillusion is just around the corner. If the United States Congress were even to permit the sale to Egypt of any military equipment at all — which seems doubtful — it would be limited in amount and purely defensive in character. How long will the Egyptian army sit still once it has grasped that realization?

Nor will Sadat be able to buy elsewhere the arms he needs to satisfy his own commanders. Having turned its back on the more radical Arab states, Egypt can expect only limited financial help from the oil-rich nations with excess revenues, Saudi Arabia and Kuwait. As a feudal kingdom in a sea of progressive Arab states, Saudi Arabia depends for its legitimacy on taking a strongly pan-Arab line, sending most of its assistance to the front-line Arab states rather than Egypt, the defector. With a relatively small population (probably less than eight million, although no one can be sure), it simply does not dare get crosswise with the better armed and more radical Arab nations. Nor does tiny Kuwait have any military defense whatever against its activist neighbors.

Yet financing is by no means Sadat's whole problem. Even if current (March 1976) rumors are true that Saudi Arabia has promised Egypt one billion dollars for arms, there is little chance that the Congress will permit him to buy them in the United States over Israeli objections — particularly not in an election year. Yet he will scarcely be able to rebuild a decent military competence — or even keep his military commanders happy — merely by purchasing bits and pieces of equipment from France, Britain, and Germany for an army and air force still subsisting on the remnants of their Soviet arsenal.

Moreover, if the oil-rich states are unlikely to provide Egypt all the means Sadat needs to keep his generals and colonels under control, there seems little chance that they will supply anything like the funds Egypt requires to finance, for instance, the $2 billion of infrastructure projects in housing, roads, transportation, and refuse disposal needed just to keep Cairo in livable condition. Though Saudi Arabia has apparently promised an initial soft loan of $300 million and there are indications of collective help from other Arab states, it is not likely to prove adequate, particularly in view of the $4 billion of debts Egypt must repay to the Soviet Union.

The Egyptian predicament is, thus, acute, since, if it has by its separate truce largely turned down the spigot of Arab assistance, it has no chance whatever to fulfill its requirements from America. All that the administration has asked Congress to provide to Egypt is seven hundred fifty million dollars, which is a drop in the bucket compared with what Egypt urgently needs for its industry and agriculture.

If President Sadat has been led to develop exorbitant expectations regarding aid from America's public sector, his hopes also seem excessive for the injection of private investment by American business. Here the major — but probably unmanageable — obstacle is the overblown Egyptian bureaucracy, which now smothers investment projects in huge wrappings of red tape — and effectively discourages the inflow of capital. Anyone who has seen that bureaucracy in action — or inaction — stands in awe of the monumental task Sadat faces.

Realistically, we can expect the American Government to take no serious initiatives regarding the Middle East until after the Presidential election in 1976 and the installation of the newly elected President in January, 1977. Whether Sadat will be able to survive during the intervening months — inevitably a time of disillusion for the Egyptian people and their armed forces — seems doubtful. What is almost certain, however, is that, if he does not survive, his successor will be more demagogic, bellicose, and adventurous and much more likely to lead the Egyptian people back toward Moscow. After all, there is a perceptible rhythm in Egyptian affairs — a tendency to play first with one great power and then another — and the resumption of an even closer Moscow-Cairo relation than we have seen in the past is by no means to be excluded unless America moves with determination to try to bring about a final settlement.

Yet, today we should not minimize the difficulty of that task. Now that we have neutralized the most powerful Arab voice for moderation, it will be extremely hard sledding to make progress in resolving the substantive issues. To think that we can go farther with bilateral diplomacy is quite absurd. The Sinai pattern simply does not apply to the Golan Heights. The Heights now contain Israeli settlements, they are too small to permit the Israelis to yield significant acreage, and their strategic high ground is considered vital to Israeli security. Even less can the Jerusalem and Palestinian issues be settled by bilateral negotiation, for they involve the interests of all the Arab states.

So far, Secretary Kissinger has pursued a practice that most medical doctors would deplore; he has sewn up part of the wound, leaving a raging infection inside. But since no one can make time run backward, we must treat the patient as best we can. What, then, should be the next American move? I return to the fundamental proposition I have urged all along: that, if negotiations are to make real progress, the United States must focus the discussion on a specific settlement proposal we ourselves put forward. Moreover, particularly since the Secretary of State has now publicly agreed that no final settlement is possible without Soviet concurrence, we should try, at an early point, to gain Soviet, as well as British and French, agreement to support — or, at least, not oppose — that proposed settlement before convening any formal or informal meeting of the parties.

Nor should we disparage the utility of obtaining United Nations Security Council approval of a settlement plan once the Soviets have expressed agreement. I am not suggesting that the Security Council, led by the United States and the Soviet Union, should behave toward the nations of the Middle East as the Concert of Europe behaved in 1897, when the then great powers abruptly halted a threatened war between Greece and Turkey over Crete by sending a fleet, landing an army, and decreeing the terms of settlement. But, at the same time, I do not believe the world should be condemned to helplessness — watching with impotent dismay while the temperature of a whole strategic area of the world moves nearer the flash point. Thus, once the Security Council has laid out the terms of settlement, every effort short of military force should, I think, be employed to bring about acceptance.

To utilize the Security Council thus, as it was intended, would, it seems to me, accomplish several objectives. It would, first of all, test the real meaning of *détente*. It might enable the Soviets and ourselves to limit the arms flow into the Middle East rather than accelerate it through a mindless competition. If the Soviets agreed to join with us in a serious effort to establish an enduring peace in the Middle East, it would mean that *détente* extended beyond the mere improvement in Soviet manners and the development of East-West trade and other strictly bilateral problems. More than that, it would offer some promise that we might, after three decades, begin to make the peace-making machinery of the United Nations function in the manner its designers intended. Too often it is forgotten that the original concept of the Security Council was that the great powers would, through its procedures, agree on measures to keep and secure the peace.[4]

Thus, with Soviet assent to a plan for a Middle East settlement, we might work our way toward a more rational world order in which — over the years ahead — the Cold War could recede into the mists of history. It may be too much to expect, but the experiment is worth trying.

That this line of action will be more difficult than had we undertaken it before the Sinai agreement is unfortunately true. Not only have we lost influence with the Syrians and other front-line states, but we have made commitments to Israel that could seriously limit our negotiating hand. However Washington may interpret the whole basket of agreements and understandings exchanged in connection with the Sinai truce, there is no doubt that the government in Jerusalem believes — and with good reason — that we have, at least implicitly, promised not to pursue any line of negotiation without prior consultation, if not Israel's prior approval. In addition, the Israelis made it clear throughout the fall of 1975 that they would bitterly oppose any American declaration of principles that might — as it must, if it is to mean anything — envisage an Israeli withdrawal from the occupied territories.

Still, we have few options now open. It is clear that we will get nowhere by gnawing at further bits and pieces of the problem. If the Palestinians and front-line Arab states finally lose hope of a settlement, we shall, sooner or later, face an explosion far more costly and dangerous than any previous Arab-Israeli conflict. Both sides either have or are now procuring weapons of high sophistication, including not only the most advanced supersonic aircraft and laser-guided bombs, but surface-to-surface missiles that will inevitably menace the civilian population on both sides.

Meanwhile, by agreeing to assign two hundred technicians to man the early warning system in the buffer area, we have more deeply engaged American interests. Not only is there a danger that terrorists might kill or injure one or more of our personnel, which would create a strong emotional reaction in America, but our men might be caught in a cross fire if one side or the other decided to launch a quick strike. In addition, the mere fact of an American presence creates a psychological impression that we are more willing than in the past to commit military forces if the fighting should resume. Call it what one likes — a "trip wire" or an implied guarantee — it gives visual reinforcement to written commitments we have made to each side that, in the event of a violation of the agreement, we will consult with the aggrieved side "as to the significance of the violation and possible remedial action by the United States Government." Moreover, we have also agreed that, in the event a "world power" (for which read "the Soviet Union") should take military action in the region, the United States will view that action "with particular gravity" and, "in the event of such a threat, consult promptly with the Government of Israel with respect to what support, diplomatic or otherwise, or assistance it can lend to Israel in accordance" with United States Constitutional practices.

The ultimate meaning of all this is that the United States has — although in ambiguous language — committed its undefined support primarily to Israel — but, under some circumstances, to both sides — in a situation seething with turmoil.

Viewed in retrospect, the Sinai agreement clearly bears the unique Kissinger imprimatur. Like the Paris Accords that ended the Vietnam War, it is a product of personal diplomacy — highly complex and reinforced by secret commitments. Like those accords, it was primarily intended to buy time — a "decent interval" in the case of Vietnam and, with luck, three or more years in the case of the Middle East. Like those accords, the Sinai agreement, by avoiding the tough issues, has created a situation of inherent instability. Just as the Paris agreements left armed elements of North Vietnamese fighting forces scattered throughout South Vietnam, the Sinai accords have left Israel in control of the territories it occupied in 1967. Thus it has assured a brief season of relief, followed — unless we pursue a more active diplomacy than I think likely — by a fearful catastrophe. It is the work of a tactician when the times call for a strategist.

CHAPTER 9

Western Europe
in Disarray

TO THOSE WHO DELIGHT IN POLITICS ON THE GRAND SCALE, conversations between the world's two superpowers are inevitably exciting. Snobbery plays its role. Why should the United States bother to deal with any power but the strongest? Why should Americans worry about the opinions of Western European nations which, though formerly great, now dine out on the vestiges of their power and history, evoking images of expatriate nobility, with sad, fading remnants of grandeur and the servants long since departed? Stripped of their colonial possessions and confronting a world with expanded requirements of scope and scale, the former stars of empire are now disqualified for the world stage. Lacking the will to unify, they cannot regain their prior status; so what difference does it make what they say or think?

Vague thoughts of that kind lie just beneath the surface of consciousness of many Americans, yet they do not reflect realism, as some would like to think, but impatience with a world structure too complex to be easily comprehended. What does it mean to have the nations of Western Europe free and allied with us? In quantitative terms the answer is easy, for Western Europe is an area with a combined industrial production far superior to that of the Soviet Union. It is, moreover, the source of much of the world's scientific discovery and modern technology. Yet, for me, the irrefutable basis for our continued preoccupation with our European partners does not depend solely — or even principally — on the imperatives of defense or economics but on the fact that there are concepts and values that transcend political allegiance. Thus our society cannot be adequately defined by the archaic and accidental limits of national boundaries, because the most important values and purposes of Western Europeans are shared by Americans — the very elements that give meaning to our own national life. Although Europe has not developed the unity enabling it to play a world role commensurate with its physical, moral, intellectual, and human resources, we still depend on the Old Continent for the good health and continued enrichment of our common civilization. No society can flourish in isolation; it needs sustenance from many quarters.

To be sure, much that gives color and quality to America today has not come from Western Europe; it has either been generated here or imported from other continents. But it is from Western Europe that we have derived the solid bone structure of our law and institutions, our basic concepts of social, moral, and political legitimacy in relations between individuals, social classes, and political regimes — and it is precisely the lack of such shared concepts with Moscow that makes the inescapable difference. European civilization originated, or at least transmitted, many, if not most, of our guides and our goals, and that continued cross-fertilization makes Western Europe vital to us today.

Were significant portions of Western Europe to fall under the dominion of Moscow, Americans would feel both menaced and lonely. Not only would we become introspective and preoccupied with our own affairs, but many would experience remorse that we had let such an unhappy event occur. Deprived of the stimulus of thought and ideas from the Old Continent, we would, in spite of the size and resources of North America, become an insular people.

Since Western Europe lies in the middle between the two superpowers, the ancient states of the European peninsula form not only the geographical but also the ideological divide between West and East, between the cultural legatees of Rome and of Byzantium. With its industrial might, its wealth, its culture, and its gifted population, Western Europe is situated at the center of power; and, as has so often occurred in history, the center of power is the center of danger. One should never forget that the two great wars of the twentieth century have been fought in Western Europe and that the United States, inevitably but reluctantly, has been drawn into both of them. Thus, it is hardly surprising that, for twenty-five years following World War II, the central aim of American policy was to assure close collaboration with the Western European nations — ranging from military defense to economic cooperation to mutual diplomatic reinforcement in major international disputes.

From the end of the Second World War to the middle 1960s, Europe was animated by a clearly defined purpose. Working closely with the United States to rebuild an economic and financial structure in a manner that brought prosperity to all, collaborating with America in creating the institutions and material means for a common defense, consulting with America about problems all over the globe, the Europeans felt challenged and *engagé*. Not only were they achieving a prosperity beyond anything they had ever known, but they were casting off the heavy burden of old rivalries in an adventurous attempt to forge the institutions of unity. Yet, unhappily, early in the 1960s, those efforts were abruptly halted by a willful French general with anachronistic dreams of French hegemony. Within months after De Gaulle had blocked Britain's accession to the Rome Treaty, Europe's spirit of common purpose began to wane, just at the time when America began to divert its attention to Vietnam.

It was an ironic conjunction of events. Frustrated by the general's atavistic passion for *la gloire*, Europeans felt deserted by Americans, who had so long been their prop and encouragement, and disenchanted by our faulty judgment; for in committing massive forces to Vietnam, America seemed bent on repeating the worst mistakes of the Fourth Republic in the days of *la guerre sale*.

Nevertheless, the situation was far from irretrievable, had the Nixon Administration's concentration on wooing the Communist leaders not created a new source of suspicion. There was exaggerated talk of a condominium of the superpowers, while secret meetings in the Kremlin, attended by Nixon and Kissinger — or sometimes merely Kissinger — conjured up the haunting memory of Napoleon and Alexander on a raft at Tilsit.

Added to this was the fact that our highly personalized diplomacy necessarily inhibited easy transatlantic understanding. While Henry Kissinger was preoccupied with Vietnam, and thereafter with China, the Soviet Union, and the Middle East, our day-to-day relations with the Europeans fell into desuetude, resulting in a series of quite unnecessary misunderstandings. We took Europe off guard by precipitate announcements of Presidential visits to Peking and Moscow. We shook Europeans even more drastically by our abrupt economic actions of August 15, 1972, which directly and heavily touched their interests. As the world learned to its amazement, the Secretary of the Treasury, John Connally, seemed obsessed with the idea that our trade negotiators had not been good Yankee — or, as he saw it, good Texas — traders. The United States, he maintained, had been taken in by other, more selfish, nations; now, since America had the resources to be top dog and the financial power to impose its will, we should make the others fall in line. It was a tearjerking account of American innocence betrayed, but few cried visibly, although other expressions of emotion were widespread. Language of such arrogance had not been used by an American cabinet minister since Secretary of State Olney in the Cleveland Administration had sent a note to the British Government in a dispute over Venezuela, pronouncing the United States "sovereign" in the whole Western Hemisphere and insisting that "its fiat is law upon the subjects to which it confines its interposition" because "its infinite resources . . . render it master of the situation and practically invulnerable as against any or all other powers." Unhappily, Nixon chose to play Cleveland to Connally's Olney, reinforcing the Texan's self-righteousness with similar statements of his own.[1]

The bizarre Connally interlude was an unhappy time for Henry Kissinger. Having renounced all interest or involvement in economic and financial policy, he watched from the sidelines as Connally swaggered across the international stage like the two-gun badman in a Western saloon. Only after the Treasury Secretary's continued bad manners threatened to undermine the authority of the United States did Kissinger join with the governor of the Federal Reserve Board and a few other sensible individuals to persuade the President to corral his rambunctious Secretary of the Treasury.

Yet our monetary vagaries were not the only source of

Europe's discontent; its growing sense of alienation was intensified by President Nixon's compulsive soliloquies on the shape and character of a *Realpolitik*. For whatever reasons — and I shall leave primal causes to psychologists and the authors of learned footnotes — Nixon became intoxicated with the vision of a world of five equal powers — the United States, the Soviet Union, China, Western Europe, and Japan — each orbiting in a state of celestial suspension, each balancing the other and thus assuring peace.[2]

In retrospect, we may dismiss such Presidential fantasizing with an indolent shrug, but that was not the reaction of many Europeans, who perceived Nixon's vision as an American wish to break with the policy grounded on the Western alliance. Fascinated by Peking and Moscow, Washington appeared to be paying more respect and attention to the Communist powers than to its old friends — which was obviously disquieting.

It was in delayed recognition of such disquiet that the White House let it be known that 1973 would be the "year of Europe." A remarkably gauche formulation, the slogan implied to Europeans that the United States leaders had been so busy with the superpowers they had been unable to pay attention to Europe's trifling affairs. Only now were they able to fit them into their schedule. Kissinger heightened the disenchantment, when, on April 23, 1973, he called on the Atlantic powers, in a spirit of renewal, to develop a new Atlantic Charter that would "create for the Atlantic nations a new relationship." [3] As he had earlier expressed it, it would "constitute a new act of creation equal to that undertaken by the postwar generation of leaders of Europe and America."

In a sense the proposal was only one more example of a tendency to substitute rhetoric for action, one more effort to conceal a fundamental change in policy by a high-sounding affirmation that there had been no change at all. But, as things worked out, the project furnished a test of the Nixon Administration's commitment to the idea of European unity which America had been persistently encouraging ever since General Eisenhower had urged the creation of "a workable European federation" in his seminal Guild Hall speech on July 3, 1951. Since both Nixon and Kissinger had not only reaffirmed the hope that Europeans would unite but had echoed Kennedy's phraseology of an "Atlantic partnership," none could have foreseen the intensity of Kissinger's angry reaction when the nine members of the European Economic Community postponed bilateral discussions of a "new Atlantic Charter" until a common European answer could be prepared.

What Kissinger had failed to consider was that the Europeans would behave in a manner Americans had long encouraged: they would try to provide a "European" response by "speaking with one voice" — or, at least, answering with one document. He had taken it for granted that he could exploit his talent for bilateral manipulation, negotiating separately with nine different foreign ministers on the basis of an American draft, playing one off against the other until a final document evolved. He was, therefore, outraged to receive a "European" draft from the Danish Foreign Minister, who was at the time president of the Council of Ministers of the European Economic Community but who was in no position to negotiate revisions.

What the Europeans wanted, of course, was nothing like a "new Atlantic Charter," but rather, a pattern of conduct that would demonstrate America's willingness to regard Europe as something more than an accessory to its own policies. Kissinger's reaction to Europe's community approach only confirmed what they already strongly suspected: that the United States proposed to conduct diplomacy not as the leader of an alliance but as an independent superpower for whom the alliance was merely an aid and convenience.

But all this was nothing compared with the divisive issue of oil. Ever since John Foster Dulles had forced Britain and France to withdraw from Suez in 1956, America had preempted the West's relations with the Middle East. Yet — much to the discomfiture of the Europeans — Washington's favoritism toward Israel inhibited friendship with the Arab nations, while adding to Europe's sense of vulnerability was the fact that American oil companies largely dominated the oil supplies that were its lifeblood.

Under the circumstances, a more sensitive Secretary of State would have anticipated a negative reply when he requested the European governments to grant landing rights for an airlift of military supplies to Israel soon after the outbreak of the war in October 1973. In view of their almost total dependence on Arab oil, they could not possibly collaborate in speeding weapons to Israel for use against Arab armies in the middle of a war, and there was no rational basis for Kissinger's ill-concealed tantrum at their refusal. As it was, the Secretary's widely quoted expletives created deep resentment. It was a resentment that turned to panic when Arab nations, on October 17, 1973, announced an oil embargo that imperiled the industrial life of not only Western Europe but Japan. The statistics were implacable: Europe relied on Arab oil-producing countries for 72 percent of its oil and 47 percent of its total energy requirements. America, on the other hand, depended on the same sources for only 19 percent of its oil and 2 percent of its energy requirements.

What was clearly indicated was for us Americans to offer to share our oil with our European allies, as we had done in 1956 and again in 1967, when the West had been threatened with earlier embargoes. But this time all the President did was to announce that America would become self-sufficient in energy; he said not a word about the urgent plight of our friends. Only after we had finally convened an energy conference, four months after the embargo had begun, did the Secretary of State even suggest the possibility of sharing, by which time it was too late to redress the loss of leadership we had suffered. Nor could this failure to act be excused as an inadvertence. When, on November 30, 1973, I had published an article in *The New York Times*, calling for a program of sharing, Secretary Kissinger had replied that my proposal was "impossible" for reasons of domestic politics — which meant either that the President was unwilling to exert leadership, or Kissinger would not ask him to.

Although at the time he showed little sympathy for Europe's desperate predicament, Kissinger denounced European efforts to help themselves. When the nine members of the European Economic Community proposed to meet with the Arab oil-producing nations, the Secretary cried "foul." With a presumptuous *démarche* that undercut the whole concept of a political Europe, he demanded that, prior to reaching any common view within their own European councils, the governments of Europe should first make sure that Washington approved.[4]

It was a strange demand from one whose indifference to the practices of consultation had marred European-American relations ever since 1969. What he requested was that Washington have a voice in the internal councils of Europe without offering any reciprocal privileges in return. For many Frenchmen, this *démarche* only confirmed what General de Gaulle had always told them: that America never wanted a united Europe except as an instrument of its own policy.

The American response to the oil embargo was a murky chapter in the postwar history of European-American relations. Nor was the situation improved when Europeans were told on October 25, 1973, only after the fact, that America had put its forces on worldwide alert because Moscow had threatened to intervene unilaterally to enforce the Egyptian-Israeli cease-fire. It was a shock for European governments to hear from President Nixon on television that, without their knowing it, we Americans had just passed through the "most difficult crisis we have had since the Cuban missile crisis of 1962," [5] since such a crisis would involve Europe's fate along with ours.

That the nations of Europe have often had their interests ignored, that they have been excluded from participation in the councils of the superpowers but expected to comply with American policies and actions with which they might or might not agree, and, finally, that they have been explicitly relegated by Secretary Kissinger to a regional role — all of that has tended to force Europeans in on themselves.

For the time being, Europe's predicament demands special patience, since Europe is as yet not a political unit, nor is it fully integrated economically. It is at that awkward stage in early adolescence when it is neither one thing nor the other. It is understandable that America should find it exasperating to try to conduct business with the European Economic Community. Even in commercial matters, where the Community purports to act as a collectivity, decisions are delayed and diluted by the need to engage in complex intramural negotiations.

As a result, an increasing number of Americans, both in and out of government, dismiss the Community as little more than a mechanism through which self-centered European nations concert policies that damage the interests of the United States. Obviously, that is a reflection of reality in a badly warped mirror; yet there is enough vocal anti-Americanism in Europe to give it a measure of credibility.

An old adage of political philosophy holds that in order for a group of nations to achieve unity, there must be a unifying state — either the dominant member of a group, such as Prussia within the Germanic Confederation, or a common enemy that compels unity by posing a common threat. But anti-Americanism is no substitute for common purpose; a sense of outrage at America will not move Europe to unite. No matter how stridently anti-American sentiments may echo through Europe, the United States can never play a constructive role as a common enemy. Though it may annoy, it will never terrify. Because resentment of the United States arises from pique at American neglect rather than fear of American aggression, the alienation of the United States from Europe or of Europe from the United States would be far more likely to lead Europe to fragment than to unify, to revert in its *ennui* and waning hope to ancient habits of division and rivalry.

To the credit of both the Nixon and Ford Administrations, they have steadfastly resisted efforts to whittle down or withdraw our troops deployed in Germany. Although, with the prevailing concern at events in Portugal, Spain, and other states along the northern Mediterranean, the pressure for such withdrawal is temporarily abated, it is bound to mount again — particularly if our relations with the Soviet Union should enjoy a period without serious crises. Yet *détente* has made our ultimate withdrawal not less but more dangerous. In today's uneasy climate, the withdrawal of our troops would set in motion a series of reactions that could lead to a critical weakening of the West. It would not only undermine European faith in our nuclear deterrent, but individual European countries would be likely to respond to the new American unilateralism with a unilateralism of their own. Thus, a number of European governments might be tempted to make their own pilgrimages to Moscow to negotiate special arrangements from positions of relative weakness.

At an earlier time, European-American relations could have survived a protracted period of neglect without permanent damage. But during the past few years Europe has been suffering from a protracted recession different in character from any since the Second World War. In the past, while there have been periods when certain countries experienced economic problems, others were spurting forward toward increased growth, but recently the curves have almost all moved in one direction, which has not only deepened the recession but made its reversal more complicated. Thus an already serious stagflation has been aggravated by the vaulting rise in oil prices that has imposed an additional push to inflationary forces, while draining the capital that might otherwise have gone into savings and investment.

At the same time, the new respectability given the Communists by our constant talk of *détente* and the to-ing and fro-ing of American and Soviet leaders between Moscow and Washington has given new impetus to efforts to include the Communists in the governments of several European countries. Finally, there has been a diminution of confidence in the European ideal, although the current interest in proposals for the direct election of delegates to the European parliament renews hope for progress.

Still, it was hardly surprising that, in March 1975, a study group under the leadership of Robert Marjolin, a brilliant French economist who was for years Vice Chairman of the European Economic Community, was set up. In laying to rest the initiative to achieve economic and monetary union, it called into question the whole thesis of the last twenty years, that a united Europe might come about through small steps. Further progress toward European integration, in the opinion of the group, "required the manifestation of a political will. This will is today uncertain and needs to show itself and to fortify itself by action."

That the economic and monetary union has failed and efforts to achieve economic integration have reached an *impasse* is both a reflection and a cause of the divergent courses now being pursued by individual European countries. No longer are they all bent, as seemed to be the case in the first two decades following the war, on emulating America's success in building sophisticated industrial societies that could provide a limitless flow of material goods by responding to the dictates of the marketplace and exploiting the economies of scale. That Europeans saw their future in roughly the same terms made possible the Treaty of Paris and the Treaty of Rome — courageous initiatives to create a continental European market comparable in scope to that of the United States and, through that process, to achieve a unity enabling Europe to deal with America on something approaching an equal basis. Both treaties included antitrust measures to give market forces greater freedom.

But, with the faltering of the European idea, each European country is now pursuing a separate course, responding to an internal play of forces that is accentuating the differences in national policies. With few exceptions each is moving at a different rate of speed toward some national variant of either state capitalism (corporatism) or socialism. Under corporatism, ownership is left to the private sector while government controls many of the major decisions of enterprises; under socialism government assumes both ownership and control. In either event, the marketplace yields much of its power and function to the bureaucrat.

Though the nations are pursuing separate paths, they exhibit a broad common tendency that puts them sadly out of phase with an America which is developing differently. The most conspicuous feature of European economic life today is the fading strength of the entrepreneurial class and the rising power of labor and bureaucracy. It would be little exaggeration to say that in most of the major Western European countries there are only two effective political forces: the trade unions and the bureaucrats.

One sees this clearly in Great Britain, where a vocal minority in the trade union hierarchy no longer wishes to work within the system but seems intent on its destruction. Even though that motive is not shared by the great bulk of union membership, the union leaders still give preference to garnering a larger piece of existing national wealth rather than seeking a larger share of an expanding national income. Without effective countervailing pressure from the entrepreneurial class, who have too often seemed oblivious of the need to participate in the political process, Britain seems incapable of economic growth and far from assured of sustaining her present level of production.

Nor is fragmentation limited to the conflict between economic groups; it expresses itself also in Scottish, and even Welsh, separatism. Here, again, oil is playing a divisive and corrupting role; Scots are clamoring for a separate state that would enjoy the revenues from the oil lying off its coasts without having to share with the English.

Great Britain today seems bent on giving an ambiguous answer to the famous prophecy of Professor Joseph Schumpeter [6] that the supplanting of an ownership class by professional managers who constitute a private bureaucracy (with the concomitant diffusion and "depersonalization" of ownership within an amorphous mass of stockholders) would pave the way for the ultimate triumph of socialism. Made secure by pensions and retirement rights, and lacking the zeal of owners defending their own property, managers would prefer compromise to warfare when trade unions and the government encroached on the interests of their enterprises. Thus, over a period of time, they would yield the field.

Scandinavia, as well as the Netherlands, is apparently moving in roughly the same direction. Sweden has shifted even farther toward its own version of socialism without yet suffering the same reduction in growth.

What is happening in Britain is still not entirely clear. In spite of the fact that the government has had to bail out enterprises in order to keep them alive and prevent further unemployment, the controlling personalities in the Labour Government have lost much of their zeal for nationalization. In fact, one of the most important ministers told me recently, "The public sector is expanding only very slowly, and I am opposed to further expansion." What seems to be emerging instead is a kind of corporatism in which the government encourages key industries to consolidate through mergers and takeovers, while "cooperation" is substituted for competition. The apparent objective is to create a managed society, with the role of the market greatly diminished. Thus the government encourages a compact between labor and management, while it increases its active intervention in major sectors of private economic activity.

Within recent months one can see evidence of a new spirit of realism pervading all sectors of British society, but for a time it appeared that the recession and the stagflation it brought with it might lead Britain toward economic chaos. With inflation apparently out of control, the leaders of the trade unions seemed at once too rigid to compromise in the interests of labor peace and too weak to impose discipline on their own troops. Thus headstrong shop stewards caused continual work stoppages in key industries by wildcat strikes that stemmed from the most trivial complaints.

It is too early to predict whether the industrial collaboration sponsored by the new corporatism will provide a long-term answer or simply be a way station on the road to socialism. If labor proves too impatient to accept the discipline of voluntary arrangements, the government, whether Labour or Conservative, may feel compelled to move toward state control of labor markets, with increased government intervention to control strikes. In any event, given a widespread commitment to welfare, as opposed to personal economic success, the transition from corporatism to an ultimate socialist state is not to be ruled out.

But whether the corporatism toward which Britain is presently moving provides an enduring answer or Britain moves farther toward socialism, nationalism is likely to dominate government policy. Not only is the appeal to cooperation based on the improvement of Britain's national economic position (for the British are almost morbidly concerned with their poor comparative showing in terms of economic growth, per capita income, investment, inflation, balance of payments), but the effort to improve that comparative position will almost certainly take protectionist forms. Thus, one may expect a further public sector absorption of companies in trouble, stronger governmental opposition to American takeovers of British companies, efforts to obtain exceptions to Common Market rules to permit special defensive arrangements, pressure for a greater concentration of industry, and a relaxed attitude toward cartel arrangements and other devices to stabilize prices, divide markets, and reduce competition, whether internally or through agreement with continental European enterprises.

If Britain is moving toward corporatism, Germany has developed its own form of modified capitalism. Almost alone among the major European countries, it seems to be clinging tenaciously to the traditions of liberal capitalism that contributed so hugely to its rapid economic growth during the postwar years. Yet, though the state has abjured the direct ownership of German industry, that ownership has, to a remarkable degree, fallen under the control of the major German banks. At the same time, German labor has seemed less interested in the redistribution of wealth than in gaining a role in corporate management through the extension of "codetermination." In spite of the fact that labor has shown greater discipline and restraint than elsewhere in Europe, it has succeeded in increasing its share of a national income that continues to grow.

What most sharply distinguishes France and Italy from Great

Britain and Germany is the existence of large Communist Parties. In France, not only does the Communist Party dominate a large part of the trade union hierarchy, but it regularly commands the vote of roughly 20 percent of the population. In fact, in the last presidential election, in May 1974, the Communists, in coalition with the parties of the Left, brought Mitterand 49.19 percent of the national vote against Giscard d'Estaing's 50.81 percent. But, apart from the fact that both countries have to cope with large Communist parties, France and Italy bear little resemblance in their political and economic structures.

One great asset of the French people is the existence of bureaucratic elites (the Inspection des Finances, the Conseil d'Etat, the Court des Comptes, etc.), which played a quiet but essential role in giving continuity and stability to French politics during the years of the Fourth Republic, when governments changed with monotonous regularity. Because of their discipline and competence, members of these groups (and, particularly, the Inspection des Finances) have acquired an extraordinary leverage over the French economy, exercising particularly tight control over sources of credit, not only through their top positions in the management of the state-owned banks but also the various government special credit agencies, such as the Caisse Nationale d'Epargne et de Prévoyance, the Caisse de Dépôts et Consignations, the Crédit Agricole, and so on. In addition, many members of the Inspection des Finances have retired into major positions in French private finance, thus constituting an "Old Boy" network constantly in touch with the French Treasury and the Bank of France.

If France has failed to achieve the same degree of income leveling as now appears in Britain, it is primarily because the French Left has never harnessed — or even fully comprehended — the devastating effect of taxation as an engine of change. As a result, although France appears to be evolving a Gallic socialism, the transfer of wealth is proceeding at a sluggish rate as compared with Britain. Even today rich Frenchmen enjoy a vast opportunity for the avoidance and evasion of taxes.

Italy is today the sick man of Europe. Because it possesses few indigenous natural resources, its remarkable economic progress since the Second World War has depended heavily on the importation of raw materials and their transformation by relatively low-paid labor. The concentration of industry in the north resulted in the migration of vast numbers from the poorer regions of the south, the so-called Mezzogiorno, to Milan and Turin in the northern industrial area (a migration roughly comparable to the migration of our Blacks from the South to the northern cities during the 1930s and 1940s), where many of them, no longer subject to the tutelage of priest or family, fell prey to local Communist recruiters.

With a substantial slowing down of economic activity in its principal Western European markets, the weak Italian economy has been unable to withstand a series of misfortunes, including the impact of increased oil prices; while its export of workers to the burgeoning industrial cities of northern Europe, which provided substantial remittance income, has not only diminished, but the advent of unemployment throughout Europe has meant the return of many of those workers to swell the unemployment rolls of the Italian cities. The result has been not only a marked slowing down of the Italian economy, but massive balance-of-payments deficits and a quiet capital flight.

Since the response of the government to labor discontent has been to make it increasingly difficult for companies to close plants and to promise labor such protection as three-year unemployment benefits at a level of 80 percent of normal compensation, this has inevitably resulted in a drying up of investment. For a substantial period during the early part of 1974, Italy exhibited the odd spectacle of a country showing all the signs of a boom while its economy rapidly fell apart. But, with the passage of time, the impact of hard times was felt throughout Italian society. As might be expected, this has meant a substantial increase in the Communist vote until, in regional elections in June 1975, the Communist Party was able to achieve 33.4 percent of the vote, or only 2 percent less than the Christian Democratic Party.

One result of the developments I have described is that the Western European nations seem to be moving in different directions and at a different pace, which obviously complicates the problems of economic integration and the development of close cooperative measures. The continuance of these separate national trends cannot help but impose severe strains on the fabric of European unity.

In addition, the differing pace and direction as between

Europe and the United States is steadily diminishing the areas of common purpose, or even common conversation, across the Atlantic. Less and less do Europeans and Americans think along the same lines or share the same preoccupations; they are taking diverging paths. That does not mean, however, that American society is immune from all the pressures now being felt by European societies. But America benefits from the happy circumstance that its politicians are not, as in some European societies, doctrinally committed to the point where compromise becomes virtually impossible, although increased polarization could well take place if the two-party system should continue to decline. America's principal advantage is that it has never been burdened with a rigid class structure such as Great Britain retained for far too long into the twentieth century. Social mobility has absorbed the shocks of change. In addition, more than most European countries other than the United Kingdom and Sweden, America has a well-developed tax system; taxes are faithfully paid and have been widely employed in the aid of social objectives.

Perhaps what most distinguishes America from the major European countries is that our trade unions, unburdened by the doctrinal baggage of the class struggle, have chosen to rely more heavily on their strong leverage in collective bargaining than on seeking to advance their interests through legislation. Far from being Communist, as in France, or even having Communist fringes, as in Britain, the top union leadership remains the most rigidly anti-Communist element in American society. Thus, although the trade unions constitute a strong political force, they are, for the most part, committed to the status quo, while a more vigorous impulse for change comes from a burgeoning bureaucracy, sustained by a diverse range of special-interest groups. These groups, representing management, labor, what is vaguely defined as "the public interest," and minority claimants, including women (a "minority" of 51 percent), promote transfer payments from public tax revenues to one sector or another or seek special protection or advantage through government interference with market forces and intrusion into what have traditionally been areas of private decision.

The emergence of the bureaucracy as a major force in American society and economic life dates primarily from President Roosevelt's New Deal, when Americans first grew accustomed to employing the instruments of government for the rectification of social and economic evils. The question now is whether the increasing power of "invisible" government — the commissions, agencies, and departments only indirectly responsible to the public will — may not too severely interfere with freedom of decision, particularly if they are increasingly charged with establishing equality of "condition" or "result" or "entitlements," rather than concentrating on preserving equality of opportunity and equality before the law — the fundamental rights recognized by the American constitution.[7]

Tocqueville, who lived at a time when — particularly in France — the dominant passion of the day was for equality of condition, was convinced that in a democratic society the pressures were bound to be stronger for equality of condition than for freedom.[8] Yet the endeavor to achieve equality of condition — an objective that reflects the thinking of Jean-Jacques Rousseau and such modern egalitarians as John Rawls rather than of the Founding Fathers — can be accomplished only by creating an ever larger bureaucracy, at increasing cost in the shrinking of individual liberties.[9]

That the expansion of the bureaucracy in both America and Europe — and the expansion of the public sector in several Western European countries to include increasing areas of economic activity — constitutes a trend toward "convergence" with the systems of Eastern Europe seems obvious. Instead of dictation by a party, there is danger of dictation by a bureaucracy that tends to become both self-perpetuating and doctrinaire. In Europe, although not in America, that trend may be accelerated if national Communist Parties join governments and take increasing political power and responsibility.

In some European countries, the trend to the egalitarian bureaucratic state seems well established. In America, there has even been a tendency in certain intellectual circles to toll the bell for democracy,[10] yet the pessimism intellectuals express may, in fact, prove to be the essential first step in sounding the necessary alarm. Today elements of resistance are beginning to consolidate; the problem is whether that resistance can find a respectable focus so as to appear as something other than the reflex of big business or racism or the opponents of minority rights.

If the United States should manage to slow down the current

trend toward egalitarianism, the transatlantic dialogue might become even more strained. As some Western European states tend toward a greater "convergence" with Eastern Europe in their increasing adoption of the bureaucratic state, they may diverge increasingly from America. Moreover, if, at the same time, Europe shifts with increasing speed away from a qualified capitalism toward variegated forms of corporatism or socialism or semisocialism, in which the market mechanism plays a diminishing role, the problems of reconciling American and European economic, as well as political, policies will become increasingly difficult. Thus, Americans dare not assume that European governments will patiently await without cavil the next American initiative, or even caprice.

If the great nations of northern Europe move toward variant systems increasingly less compatible with ours, we may have even greater difficulties with the nations of southern Europe that belong less to the European than the Mediterranean traditions.

Italy, in many ways, poses the most acute problems. The critical issue in the months ahead is the so-called historic compromise proposed by the Secretary General of the Communist Party, Enrico Berlinguer. It contemplates that the Communists would form a coalition, not with their natural allies, the Socialists and left-wing Catholics, but with the whole of the Christian Democratic Party, in the pattern of the "Grand Coalition" between the Social Democrats and the Christian Democratic Union in Germany. It would thus differ from the Popular Front in France or from the present Union of the Left, through which left-of-center French parties formed a voting cartel with the Communists in the last presidential election.

Since it would avoid the polarization that would otherwise result from a purely leftist coalition and the consequent creation of a solid opposition, it has tactical appeal to the Communists. At the same time, weary of the impuissance and demoralization of the Christian Democrats, many middle-of-the-road Italians hope that Communist participation in government might provide increased stability. There is a widely held belief — or superstition — based largely on the record of Communist mayors in towns and cities throughout Italy that the Communists would know how to run the government tightly and efficiently. Already the Communists control or participate in local governments in five of Italy's twenty regions, one-third of its ninety-four provinces and, except for Rome, every major city from Naples north.

The attitude of many Italians seems colored by a combination of unreality and wishful thinking. For some time now the Communists have been giving tacit support to the Christian Democrats, while avoiding the painful issue of actual participation in the government. This has been possible because the Italian Communist Party has shown considerable independence, both of the Kremlin's dogma and its authority. The Party has, for example, supported continued Italian membership in the European Economic Community, as well as NATO. And, unlike the leadership of the French Communist Party, the Italian leaders have long been willing to criticize the Kremlin. Still, a "Grand Coalition" that included the Communists would create major problems, not only for the Italians but also for other Europeans. With a substantial part of Italian industry already under at least indirect government control through huge government holding-company conglomerates, such as I.R.I., or E.N.I., Communists in key portfolios might have exceptional opportunities to spread the tentacles of party influence. There would undoubtedly be a stepped-up capital flight, which would furnish an excuse for even more stringent controls. There is a good chance that it would mean the end of democratic government in Italy. The political structure and the democratic tradition may both be too weak to withstand the machinations of a disciplined party, committed not to the system that has put it in power, but to a system inherently repressive that, if given the chance, would severely constrict Italian freedoms.

The impact on the rest of Western Europe would be mixed. It would create immense problems for the European Economic Community, and even greater problems for NATO, where embarrassment would result from the presence of Italian military representatives on certain key committees — particularly those having to do with nuclear defense. Nor can the hard questions be answered categorically, including the most difficult of all: once installed in office, would the party cede power if defeated at the polls? One fact alone provides a measure of reassurance. Unlike situations involving nations of Eastern Europe, the Red Army is not now on the doorstep, and that, in the showdown, could well make the difference.

Once participating in the government, the Italian Communists would be likely, for a time, to maintain exemplary discipline. One might expect them to suppress labor disputes and demonstrate an ability to govern responsibly and efficiently. The fact that they would presumably withhold major political action until they had consolidated their hold on the levers of power would only increase the danger that the infection would spread to other countries. Certainly the creation of an Italian government with Communist elements could constitute for France a critical test case. Within recent months French Communist leaders have been actively positioning themselves. Georges Marchais, the head of the French Communist Party, has now not only publicly criticized Soviet repressive measures but has renounced the dictatorship of the proletariat. In November 1975 he issued a joint statement with Berlinguer, of the Italian party, in which they committed themselves to political pluralism, the rights of oppositions, and "the free formation of majorities and the possibility of their alternating democratically." This appeared to represent an attempt by the French and Italian Parties to coordinate policies in advance of the European Communist Party Congress, in order to resist the Kremlin's possible new line as suggested by the Zaradov incident I described in Chapter 7.

According to the Spanish Communist Party leader, Santiago Carillo,[11] the specter haunting Moscow is that the assumption of political power by Communist Parties in France and Italy might lead to the formation of a "bloc of European socialist countries," which could form another schism in the Communist church, competing both with Moscow and Peking. Thus it is possible that historians may someday look upon the Marchais-Berlinguer compact as a document of considerable importance.

But if Communist participation in governments in France or Italy would create problems for European cooperation, even greater problems would develop in transatlantic relations for the very reasons I have mentioned — that there is already substantial divergence in thinking between the two sides of the Atlantic. From the point of view of American opinion generally, little purpose would be served in pointing out that the Communists in Italy or France, or whatever Western European country might be affected, did not hold key portfolios. The fact that they were in the government at all would be sufficient. Just as Europeans would seek to move capital out of Europe, American multinational corporations would be under pressure to repatriate their European investments, while there would undoubtedly be insistent voices in the Congress and the public for American troops to be brought home and for the United States to reduce its commitments within the NATO system.

I do not write this in any alarmist mood; yet I do feel that many Europeans underestimate the likely consequences of having Communists in their governments. For, even though Western European Communist Parties are no longer subservient to Moscow, they would clearly use their influence to move Europe down an economic course even more rapidly diverging from that of America. And when the chips were down, they would be likely to stand together with the Communist Parties of Eastern Europe to frustrate much that the West was trying to do.

In three other countries of southern Europe, crises or the threat of crises result from the fact that old dictators have either passed from the scene or are about to pass — all within a short time span. Thus America has watched with intense concern the attempt of a small minority (not more than 12½ percent in the last election) to take control of the Portuguese state by conspiratorial means — by Lenin's "political majority" rather than the "numerical majority" recognized in democratic societies. Using disenchanted, naïve military officers as his instruments and with his funds supplied from Moscow, a Soviet-trained party leader, Alvaro Cunhal, has sought to reenact the drama of Petrograd in 1917, but, at the time this is written, still without success. With the public denied political participation for a half-century, the body politic of Portugal has developed no antibodies — no well-established structure of groups and institutions experienced in political action. But, even so, the yearning of the people for democracy has come through loud and clear — and, so far, effectively.

In Spain, also, the agonies of transition from dictatorship to some form of democratic system promise both problems and hazards. The desire of the Spanish people to regain a place in Europe, and even to join the European community, may well spur the process of liberalization.

Fully as significant as these situations will be the events that may follow the disappearance of a third old dictator — Marshal Tito in Yugoslavia. As with most strong men, Tito has permitted no obvious successor to grow up in his shadow, and there is a question whether anyone now on the scene will be able to repeat his tour de force of holding together disparate peoples with bitter and ancient enmities. Within the past two or three years there has been increasing restlessness in Croatia, aggravated by a well-financed assist from the KGB and other Eastern European operatives working to promote the Croats' ancient feud with the Serbs. In addition, Albania, which asserts a claim to portions of Yugoslavia, keeps tribal emotions aroused with inflammatory radio broadcasts. Nor should one forget that some of the Hungarians in the Voivodina across from Belgrade would prefer to be part of Hungary, while the Macedonians have for years nurtured secessionist ambitions through terrorist organizations Sofia has been only too happy to support.

Given the intense interplay of these forces, there is always the possibility that a civil war, inaugurated perhaps by Croatian separatist leaders, could provide a pretext for the Soviet Union — or, at least, its Bulgarian or Hungarian allies — to recapitulate the role the Red Army played in Prague.

Even though Mr. Brezhnev may resent our meddling in the affairs of a country just outside Moscow's sphere of influence, the President and Kissinger should still make clear to the Soviets that any effort to exploit confusion in a post-Tito Yugoslavia would critically undercut United States–Soviet relations and mean the end of *détente*. In fact, they should imply that, since Yugoslavia is not a member of the Warsaw Pact, the United States would not feel constrained to withhold its intervention as it did in the case of Hungary or Czechoslovakia. It is a point that should be made — at least ambiguously.

CHAPTER 10

Japan — The High Cost of Insensitivity

IF OUR RELATIONS WITH EUROPE HAVE SUFFERED FROM NEGLECT and presumptuousness, interspersed with occasional pettiness — as, for example, in the Kissinger-Jobert feud — the Nixon Administration was reckless to the point of irresponsibility when it weakened the alliance ties that bound Japan to the West.

The primal cause of the deterioration of relations was a tradesman's argument over the export of Japanese textiles to the United States. The fact that textiles were involved was not surprising; for they are the prototype of light labor-intensive manufacture that causes the most headaches in international commercial relations. In classical theory, nations would, as they move up the technological ladder, progressively shift toward increasingly sophisticated and capital-intensive types of manufacture, leaving to less developed countries the simpler labor-intensive operations where a low wage scale offers the only comparative advantage. But ours is not by any means a perfect world, and textile producers in the industrialized nations have been naturally reluctant to yield their domestic markets to the products of foreigners. Perhaps because the textile industry is less concentrated than many other sectors of production, it has shown less tendency to develop on a multinational basis, but instead has fought to defend its domestic market from outside encroachment. Until recent years the United States textile industry principally consisted of relatively small units yet employed a very large labor force. It was thus able, in collaboration with the craft unions, to command a broad built-in political constituency widely distributed throughout the country. As a result, it became customary for American Presidents to promise the industry special protection, and, in his frantic drive for southern votes during the 1968 Presidential campaign, President Nixon went all out to assure the textile companies and textile unions he was on their side and would deliver for them.

That was the state of affairs when Prime Minister Sato came to Washington in November 1969. He, too, was a politician under pressure, since the Japanese public was demanding that he gain some concessions from the new Nixon Administration with regard to the status of Okinawa, which had become a brooding political issue in Japanese politics. Quite wisely, President Nixon agreed that he would help a fellow politician in distress by agreeing to the reversion of Okinawa under certain conditions. In gratitude, Prime Minister Sato promised Nixon to assist him to meet his own political problem by taking steps to assure restraints on textile exports.

What is clear in retrospect is that the Prime Minister greatly underestimated the domestic opposition of which his own textile industry was capable. Sato did not have authority under Japanese law to act without the approval of parliament, and the Japanese textile industry was capable of exerting as great pressure on the Japanese Government as our domestic industry was on the White House. The earliest large-scale manufacturing industry in Japan, it had remained highly fragmented, with more than 85,900 plants, 92 percent of which had fewer than ten employees. The fact that it was labor-intensive, employing a total of 815,000 people who were widely dispersed throughout the Japanese islands, gave it formidable political muscle. As a result, when Sato returned to Japan he found, to his dismay, that he could not deliver on his political promise.

That failure might have been forgiven, however, if Prime Minister Sato had not, on a second visit to Washington in January 1972, spontaneously asserted that he would keep his promise on the textile issue. When Sato's weak government tried again and he failed for the second time to deliver on his promise, the President

went into a furious rage. Though the incident was obviously an-
noying — and may have caused the President embarrassment with
his benefactors in the textile industry — the overreaction of both
Nixon and Kissinger poisonously distorted the relations between
the two great nations. As Nixon and Kissinger brooded on this development together, the interaction of their piques and prejudices
generated a resentment against the Japanese leadership that inflated a mere commercial incident to a dimension that seriously
impaired America's relations with one of its principal allies. Just
as genetic inbreeding may give dominance to congenital weaknesses, the inbred nature of a foreign policy secretly shaped by
two men without benefit of a foreign office produced a misshapen
American policy toward the Far East.

Thus the White House nurtured an attitude of vindictiveness
toward the government in Tokyo. Still obsessed with proving himself to his textile friends, the President sent a series of heavy-
handed, inexperienced messengers to Japan to cajole and
threaten. Among them was Maurice W. Stans, the Secretary of
Commerce, majordomo of Republican fund raisers, whose approach
to the Japanese Government displayed roughly the same subtlety
he later used in extracting campaign contributions from intimi-
dated corporate executives. Finally, the President compelled Japanese compliance by employing a threat to embargo Japanese textile imports under the Trading with the Enemy Act — the modern
version of sending gunboats. It was an extraordinary way to treat
one of America's principal allies, and the implications of the action were not lost on the Japanese.

America's treatment of the textile issue was by no means an
isolated episode; it reflected the general level of disdain the
Nixon Administration systematically displayed toward Japan. That
disdain was first revealed with the surprise announcement on July
15, 1971, of the President's projected trip to China, when the Japanese Government was given less than an hour's advance notice
that the President was about to reverse America's long-standing
China policy. That was, however, only the first of the Nixon
"shokku," which many informed Japanese regarded as a systematic campaign to free the United States from its commitments to
Japan and, in effect, to condemn the Japanese to second-rate
status.

On August 15, 1971, one month after the jolt of the China announcement, the President compounded the damage by abruptly proclaiming a new economic policy designed quite explicitly to reduce Japan's trading advantage. Finally, after the China visit had come and gone, Tokyo was enlisted in a kamikaze effort to block China's entry into the United Nations, an effort which the President had doomed to defeat the moment he announced his projected visit to Peking.

Against this background, it is easy to understand why many Japanese were deeply suspicious of the President's formal talks with Mao and Chou En-lai, and the much longer conversations Henry Kissinger had with Chou on his two earlier trips. They feared that the Americans had reached understandings with the Chinese that could threaten their interests, for they found it absurd to think that the President would fly five thousand miles to China and stay eight days merely to move the ambassadorial talks from Warsaw to Paris, make arrangements for tourists to visit the Great Wall, and trade musk-oxen for pandas.

The first reaction in Tokyo was a strong push toward its own reconciliation with Peking, for reasons compounded of more than geography and history. Though the old comparison of Japan as the Rome to China's Greece is far from the mark, the Japanese still feel a sober respect for the depth and richness of China's civilization. Today one even detects a certain pride in the achievements of the People's Republic in turning vast, sprawling China into an orderly, if regimented, nation-state. Added to this is a pervasive guilt. Beginning toward the end of the last century, Japan participated in the cynical rape of China by the great powers; from the invasion of Manchuria in 1931 through the Second World War, Japan was responsible for perhaps as many as fifteen million Chinese deaths.

Yet pride and guilt do not tell the whole story. It is fashionable in some sophisticated Japanese circles to express regret that Japan betrayed her Asian heritage when she opted a century ago to follow Western patterns in her economic and political development. As a result, some Japanese intellectuals now suggest that, if their nation's modern industrial society seems empty and insipid, it is because Japan turned her back on the cultural riches of her spiritual fatherland without receiving enough of value from the

West. Even at this late date, should not the Japanese again try to tap the abundant wellsprings of Chinese culture and wisdom? [1]

Unaffected by this strange amalgam of history and nostalgia, the more materialistic elements in Japanese society see definite advantages in a tie with the Chinese. Most Japanese businessmen today regard China as a source of needed raw materials and a potential market of almost unlimited magnitude as the masses of Chinese people gradually achieve incomes above the subsistence level.

It is too early to know what these shifting forces may mean for the higher geometry of Far Eastern *Realpolitik*. Japanese history has never been charted by the same kind of wavering curve that has marked the progress of other countries; instead, it resembles more a succession of straight lines, broken periodically by sharp angles, as the whole nation, moving at full speed, has suddenly wheeled like a well-drilled army corps to follow a new course. There is nothing in all human experience to match it. From the seventh to the ninth centuries, Japan borrowed and assimilated the culture and administrative apparatus of China, creating an eclectic but distinctive civilization of her own; then in 1638, fearing the infection of Western ideas, she abruptly seceded from the world, sealing herself off in almost total isolation for more than two hundred years. Not until a hundred years ago did the Japanese once again sharply alter direction as a new generation perceived that, to cope with the Western barbarians at the gates, they must absorb not only the barbarians' technology — which they rapidly mastered — but political institutions alien to their traditions, which they only partially understood. In retrospect, it was a fateful decision. To acquire Western weapons while retaining a warrior tradition sent Japan down a dark, imperialist road — a road that led to Korea, Port Arthur, Manchuria, Pearl Harbor, and Hiroshima, until final and total surrender on the battleship *Missouri*.

Once humiliating defeat had been followed by occupation, there came still another sharp twist of the rudder. Bereft of faith in her prewar institutions and blocked off from China by Mao Tse-tung's takeover, Japan turned for guidance to the America that had defeated her, sublimating her power drive in a spectacular industrial achievement. Nor has Japan wavered during the past two decades. As a rising industrial nation, she has fixed her eyes steadily on the West, stubbornly repressing the atavistic pull of the mainland.

Yet for many Japanese it has been a strangely unsatisfying time. Although Japan has more than proved her superb competence in the commercial and industrial arena, she is only gradually feeling at home in that sterile environment. To use an obnoxious cliché where it has real meaning, Japan is a nation in search of an identity.

These considerations have particular relevance as a new world emerges in which more and more countries will acquire nuclear capabilities. India has set the pace already — a desperately poor country squandering its meager resources to seek illusory status as a so-called nuclear power. Soon we shall see a whole succession of countries enroll — Brazil, Argentina, Iran, Israel (if it does not already have a nuclear device) — until the nuclear club loses its exclusive cachet, becoming less like the Royal Yacht Club and more like the National Geographic Society. Even though sentiment against becoming a nuclear power is still a strong force in Japanese public opinion, no one can be as certain as was once possible that Japan may not sometime in the future endure the national agony of revising her constitution so as to go down the nuclear road.

There will be pressures and counterpressures, but the desire for bombs of its own may take a great leap forward once China develops ICBMs capable of reaching North American targets. For many Japanese, that may cast doubt on the validity of the American guarantee. "Who can believe that America would jeopardize her homeland by firing nuclear weapons in Japan's defense?" the skeptics will ask. It is De Gaulle's old question, but it may find a special echo in Japan.

Yet the greatest pressure on Japan to become a nuclear power is less likely to stem from anxieties over security than from a desire for political status. Observant Japanese are impressed by the fact that, with the admission of Peking to the United Nations, the five permanent members of the Security Council are precisely those powers that have nuclear weapons, and they noted the implications of President Nixon's statement that his China trip was necessary because of the "great danger of the most populous nation in the world becoming a major nuclear power" fifteen or twenty years from now.

Clearly, there is no problem of capability. Apart from the social and political upheaval that might be involved in opting to be a nuclear power, Japan unquestionably has the scientific competence and industrial might to build a modest nuclear arsenal within a remarkably short time. The working principle is generally recognized as "N minus 2," which means that she will keep her technology constantly up to date so as to be able to produce operational nuclear weapons within two years after a decision to proceed.

Such a working principle is, of course, welcomed by some Japanese businessmen who believe that nuclear weapons technology would offer valuable spin-offs to private industry. As one might expect in the highly involuted algebra that shapes Japanese policy, the managers of heavy industry provide a key element of pressure for remilitarization — and we strengthen their hand when we continue to push Japan to increase expenditures for her military establishment, as seems compulsive with American Secretaries of Defense. From our own experience, we can hardly expect that a highly industrialized nation such as Japan will long continue to buy from us the military hardware her own enterprises can produce quite as well or more cheaply. And we should never lose sight of the fact that the uniquely intimate structure of Japanese business and government relationships is tailor-made for a "military-industrial complex."

If the Japanese were to decide to become a nuclear power, what of it? On the face of it, the answer might be that it would not matter much — which is a view that may well prevail in the top reaches of the United States Administration. Why should we worry if there is one more nation with a nuclear arsenal? After all, there are four and a fraction already, and the nuclear stalemate still seems to hold.

Like other issues in international politics, however, the question will not be posed as a sterile academic problem but in a context providing special color and meaning. A decision by Japan to go nuclear would be as significant for the change of Japan's state of mind as for the problems it directly creates. The Japanese will go down the nuclear road only if they feel alienated from the West and strongly nationalistic — and these are the very conditions that might render Japan's nuclear power disruptive and dangerous.

It is this possibility that made the Nixon-Kissinger disregard for Japanese interests and sensitivities particularly reckless. It is one thing to envisage a nuclearized Japan tied closely to the West, and quite another to have to cope with an alienated nationalistic Japan armed with nuclear weapons. A great nation such as Japan, rootless and turned in on itself, could be an unpredictable force in world politics, threatening the stability of the Far East like a loose cannon on a ship in a high sea.

For this reason, among others, I have long felt that Japan must be brought into helpful collaboration, not merely with the United States but with Western Europe. In the early sixties I initiated the move for Japanese admission to membership in the Organization for Economic Cooperation and Development (OECD). But it has not been easy. Until recently the nations of Western Europe tended to regard Japan as a special preoccupation of America. For Europe Japan was primarily a dangerous commercial rival, and Europeans feared the disruptive effect of Japanese exports even more than America.

Even so, we have now gone far to break down the barriers to communication with a nation that was for so many centuries closed to the world. The result has been a healthy cross-fertilization of ideas. Today Japanese intellectuals and businessmen are constantly meeting in seminars and conferences with their opposite numbers not merely from the United States but also from Europe; no longer are they politely silent, but participate with vigor and enthusiasm in the exchange of ideas and opinions. A number of useful private-sector organizations have helped speed this process, of which perhaps the most important is the Trilateral Commission, created with the help of David Rockefeller.

Action in the public sector, however, has displayed little sense of direction; it has all too often been uninformed by any coherent policy. Under pressure of the individual complaints of particular industries, we have resorted to restrictionist improvisations imposed through bilateral discussions, often ignoring the special history, structure and relationships of Japanese industry. We have not always fully comprehended the intricate task of bringing Japan into a trading system constructed largely in response to Western institutions and habits of thought — a task that cannot be accomplished by America alone, but only by a common effort of all the industrial trading nations.

Though preoccupation with Japan as an industrial competitor has led us to overlook her political significance, that only partially explains our obtuse performance during the Nixon years. Fully as important was the lack of professionalism that increasingly marred the execution of policy after the White House had opted to become its own foreign office — or, more accurately, sought to get along without one.

Troublesome as this problem was for our relations with other parts of the world, with respect to Japan it got completely out of hand. It is significant that during the time Mr. Kissinger was the President's special assistant for national security affairs and before he became Secretary of State there was not one Japanese expert among the 165 members of his staff.

Still, it would be oversimplifying the problem to attribute Japan's threatened estrangement merely to the carelessness of a President and the distractions of a Secretary of State too egocentric to delegate; the Nixon Administration consciously decided to regard the reactions of Japan as of only secondary importance.

The Japanese found President Nixon's image of five balancing powers particularly disturbing. They saw in that figure of speech a key to the game the White House seemed to be playing — to deal bilaterally with Moscow and Peking, trying to play off one against the other, while letting America's allies — particularly Japan — shift for themselves. Though with Europe the damage was not unmanageable, it was different with Japan. Ties across the Pacific are dangerously fragile, because there is no common heritage of history or language or culture, and we face an enormous problem in trying to understand one another. Experience provides only bewildering indicators as to the direction Japan might take if alienated from America and left to her own devices. Europeans retain the constructive alternative of unification, but the Japanese have nothing comparable; their most likely alternative would be aggressive nationalism.

Let me suggest again that, instead of continuing to play a lone-wolf role of maneuver and manipulation, America should seek, as first priority, to create a working coalition of the major non-Communist industrialized nations. An initial step on the Japanese front might well be to turn the United States–Japanese Mutual Security Treaty into a mature coalition, while, at the same time, seeking to incorporate that relationship in an expanded partnership, to include the Atlantic powers and Japan. Just as it seems inevitable that Europe will slowly expand its political horizons to resume an interest in Far Eastern affairs, so Japan will, in support of its global industrial role, extend its political interests worldwide. Thus, by bringing Japan into active participation in existing Atlantic economic institutions and by expanding Western political institutions to include the Far East, we should, in the long run, be able to build a broad and solid base from which a better *modus vivendi* could gradually be worked out, with both the Soviet Union and China.

Within recent years, the obsessive emphasis on our relations with China and the neglect of our relations with Japan have reflected a lamentable lack of balance and perception — a failure to look hard and realistically at the configuration of forces in the Far East, or, indeed, at the pattern of world politics generally. In part this results from the predilection of diplomats to treat commercial nations as second-class powers. Although in the history books commercial Carthage has suffered in comparison with expansionist Rome, it was a power of great importance; its destruction had a disastrous effect on Mediterranean trade for centuries and even contributed to the economic decline of its victorious rival. Yet, unlike Carthage, Japan has historically been a warrior nation, and the mere fact that it has renounced its military traditions is no reason for treating it as relatively less important than China. On the contrary. China is, in economic terms, far less powerful than Japan, but just how great the disparity may be is hard to determine. The Chinese reject bourgeois national accounting concepts; since their ideology regards the provision of services as "unproductive," normal statistical measures are hard to apply. Thus, estimates of China's gross national product range anywhere from $112 billion to $223 billion, which means that her output is either at about the level of Italy's or substantially more than Great Britain's. Nor is there agreement as to China's annual economic growth rate, since estimates range all the way from 5 percent to 10 percent. One ironic tendency I have noted is that experts on China, whether American or Asian, estimate China's economic potantial in far more expansive terms than do experts on Japan.

In view of recent world attention to raw materials, and particularly to energy, sinologists have written a number of papers on China's resource potential. Here, again, China specialists put great weight on China's potential as an oil producer, seeing it not only as a source of foreign exchange earnings, but as increasing China's political leverage with other Asian countries, and particularly with Japan. No doubt this is a factor to be taken into account; yet experienced oil men are skeptical at overebullient estimates of Chinese potential oil production. They are particularly skeptical as to the time span necessary for China to become a significant oil exporter. Thus, while it is an intriguing thought that China might use its production of energy and raw materials, as well as its capacity as a market for imported manufactures, to gain a political hold over Japan, I doubt events will work out that way. Much of China's oil lies offshore. The speed at which the Chinese can exploit it will depend largely on the extent to which Peking accepts joint ventures with other nations and private interests. Official Chinese rhetoric would seem to preclude such collaboration with barbarians, though it is quite possible that, particularly after the departure of Chairman Mao, dogmatic insistence on "self-reliance" will give way to the imperatives of more rapid progress.

No doubt China will one day become a major factor in world economics; it may even, as some have estimated, take its place among the top five economies by the year 2000. Still, it has a long way to go. At present, its contribution to world trade is 1 percent or less of the total. Nor is it clear that the Chinese will be able or even willing to establish economies of scale rapidly enough to supply a population that may reach a billion by 1980, yet still have a surplus for world markets.

Though there is no doubt that the Chinese are an extraordinarily gifted people, their technical education is weak. Unless they are prepared to emulate their Japanese neighbors and purchase foreign technology on a vast scale, they may be doomed to develop their economy at a far slower pace than many are predicting. Still, we may feel the brunt of Chinese commercial progress earlier than most. It requires little effort to imagine our relations with China taking an abrasive turn — just as occurred with Japan twenty years ago — if the Chinese were to flood world markets with cheap textiles, radios, and other light labor-intensive manufactures. The prospect of a billion Chinese working at what a less sensitive America used to refer to as "coolie wages" and flooding the American market with cheap merchandise could well elicit a noisy cry of alarm from American demagogues.

Nevertheless, China's potential as a trading nation is not the principal basis for China's world importance. Prestige remains China's most valuable trump card, a prestige solidly grounded in history, culture, and population. One can never ignore the Chinese; there are simply too many of them.[2] This adds a measure of importance to whatever China says or does. China holds a special fascination — the magnetic attraction of mass — and, in view of the industry, discipline, and undeniable intellectual capacity of her people, the great teeming nation is bound to cast its spell, particularly among the poor nations of Asia. China is itself a poor land with whom other poor nations quite naturally feel kinship and to whom they are likely to look for leadership. The Chinese leaders constantly exploit this advantage by sanctimoniously proclaiming that "China will never be a superpower."

Moreover, China is no longer the sick man of Asia. No matter how much one may deplore the authoritarian character of the Peking regime, it has unquestionably succeeded in replacing a corrupt and antiquated social and economic structure with a structure that appears to work. Finally, in assessing the power position of China, one cannot overlook her leadership of a schismatic Communist faction, which — combined with her military threat to the Soviet's Asian territories — gives her special importance as a constraint on Moscow's freedom of action.

Some years ago, China's principal claim to attention depended on her presumed capacity for mischief as the principal source of support and encouragement for "wars of national liberation." But the fear of such insurgencies is no longer in vogue. Now China has substantial status in Asia because, through her capacity to keep the Soviets off balance, she has become a significant factor in determining the power equilibrium. That such a role greatly improves her bargaining position with the West was dramatically shown by the fact that both Presidents Nixon and Ford have visited Peking, while Kissinger has been there nine times, with no reciprocal visits from high Chinese dignitaries.

The political drama in Asia during the next few years is likely to be dominated by the competition between China and the Soviet

Union for hegemony in Southeast Asia. That competition, set in motion by the collapse of South Vietnam, may assure a stronger position for the United States in the area than would otherwise have been the case, since the Chinese are primarily interested in avoiding encirclement, and no longer view America as a menace. That is not so with the Soviet Union, which, in Chinese perspective, currently threatens them on the north, and they will no doubt go to great lengths to prevent Soviet expansion elsewhere in Asia. Thus they will watch with particular care the development of Soviet-Indian relations, and they would be enormously concerned at any signs of friendship or collaboration between Moscow and Tokyo.

That, however, seems unlikely to occur, in spite of the fact that the Soviet Union, as a move in the game of power politics, has made friendly approaches to Japan. Though some Japanese political strategists are attracted by the potential of improved Soviet-Japanese relations as a counterbalance to China, a warning to Washington, and a hedge against the loss of American support, there are solid inhibiting factors. If Japan approaches closely to China, she cannot help but gain the Kremlin's distrust; nor do the Japanese either like or trust the Russians. Not only is there an unpleasant lingering argument over the three lower Kurile Islands, but the Russo-Japanese War at the turn of the century left a bitter memory of diplomatic frustration. Finally, the Japanese do not forget that forty years later the Russians stabbed them in the back at Yalta, tearing up their treaty of neutrality in a sordid rush to grab a share of the spoils.

But, if Japan mistrusts the Russians, how will her relations evolve with China? Though acknowledging that any speculation will probably be far from the mark, I would suggest that neither of the present superpowers is likely to dominate the theater of Asian politics; instead, I would foresee expanding roles for both Japan and China — possibly leading, in the long run, to an abrasive rivalry. Japan has vast industrial capacity but a future labor shortage and almost no indigenous raw materials; while China, with unlimited manpower and an untold wealth of unexploited natural resources, remains a basically agrarian economy. Yet, though the vision that the two might make common cause, that there might be a powerful intermeshing of machines, manpower, and materials awes some and terrifies others, I doubt that a marriage would be possible or, if achieved, have much survival value. Instead, it seems probable that the inherent contradictions between a "backward" China and an industrially advanced Japan are more likely to lead to a rivalry that would pit the magnetic pull of China's vast population against Japan's increasing economic leverage over the whole of Asia.

The inevitable competition of two such proud and regionally dominant nations seems almost certain to result in strained political relations. Already one can foresee a struggle for raw materials — oil under the China Sea, off Vietnam, perhaps Korea, for example — that must inevitably lead to dissension.

Of all the great powers of the area I would expect the Japanese to achieve the greatest power and leverage, not only in Southeast Asia but in the whole Asian theater. Whatever may be the efficacy of securing political power through other means, Japan's overpowering economic position in many of the smaller nations of Asia is a fact that no one can effectively challenge. One would not overstate the matter to suggest that, in economic terms, Japan's position in East Asia may come to resemble the United States role in Latin America — creating all the same disenchantment and complexity. Already there is evidence of resentment among the smaller Asian nations — a resentment exacerbated by the fact that almost all of them bear the scars of brutal Japanese occupation policies during the Second World War.

At the moment, Japan is going through one of its recurrent periods of self-examination, disturbed by evidence that the basic assumptions on which it founded its spectacular growth may no longer be valid. It can no longer count on cheap energy. Other raw materials may also suffer severe price increases, since there is clearly a new militancy among raw-material-producing countries, inspired by the spectacular success of OPEC. Particularly aggravating to the Japanese is the impact of high food costs on their balance of payments, made worse because, during recent prosperous years, they have shifted the emphasis of their diet from direct cereal consumption to imported proteins. Finally, rapid wage increases have deprived Japan of the comparative advantage derived from low per-unit labor costs, while the adjustment in currency parities has denied her the great benefits of an undervalued yen.

The result of all these developments is not only an interruption in Japan's spectacular growth rate, but an uneasy period not only for Japanese intellectuals but for the more thoughtful members of the Japanese managerial class in both the public and private sector. Has Japan not put too much emphasis on a growth rate that cannot be permanently maintained? On an increase in material wealth that has brought less than total happiness to the Japanese people? Aggravating the malaise have been unsettling developments not unlike those experienced by the United States. A soaring inflation and the Tanaka and Lockheed scandals at the top reaches of government have been as disturbing for the Japanese people as Watergate and recession have been for America. Not only is there grave disquiet within the ranks of the Liberal Democratic Party (LDP), which has administered Japan's destiny ever since 1945, but one can no longer be certain as to the LDP's long-range continuance in power.

In spite of these troubles, Japanese resilience remains its invaluable national asset. In a sense, the existence of Japan's problems is easing her tensions with the rest of Asia, for there is now a realization that the Japanese are not imperialistic supermen but subject to the same misfortunes and maladies as other peoples. Given their national will and discipline, there seems little doubt that they will find their way back to a new level of prosperity within a relatively short time, though not necessarily tied to the same abnormally high growth rate. What Japan possesses beyond any other large nation except China is national discipline — and the discipline of the Japanese is more impressive than that of their Chinese neighbors because it is not imposed by force but operates within the framework of a democratic society. The ability to concentrate the efforts of a whole great people on precise targets is a formidable asset — never to be underrated.

PART III

Revising Our Institutions

CHAPTER 11

Overhauling Our
Foreign Policy Machinery

WHEN JUSTICE OLIVER WENDELL HOLMES OBSERVED THAT "THE substance of the law is secreted in the interstices of procedures," he might quite as well have been referring to foreign policy, where procedures and policy are intertwined to the point of being indistinguishable. A policy of maneuver contains its own built-in precondition — the concentration of power and authority within a narrow group — just as a policy of leadership requires that authority be delegated to make possible collaboration with other nations at every level.

But if it is true that the nature of policy determines the diplomatic procedures required, the choice of policy is likely to reflect the personality and inclinations of the Secretary of State — or the President, if he has strong views about our international relations. General Marshall, a very competent Secretary of State, would have been totally incapable of devising and carrying out a policy of maneuver. Accustomed to a military system in which delegation was a central feature, he adapted that practice to the shaping and administering of an active but balanced and truly global policy during the months that followed the Second World War. By contrast, Henry Kissinger's insistence on personally working all the levers of policy has produced an episodic and asymmetrical policy by narrowing our diplomatic attention to one or two problems — and, hence, one or two foreign countries — at a time.

A wistful hope that has shown remarkable survival value is that we could improve the quality of our diplomacy by "restructuring our foreign policy machinery" — which usually means, in practice, reshuffling and renaming the little boxes on the State Department organization chart. Over the past three or four decades, at least a baker's dozen of committees, study groups, task forces, and commissions have undertaken this task. Hundreds of man-hours (or, to appease the new vogue, I should say "person-hours") have been devoted to the drafting of reports which have been judiciously composed, nicely bound, and systematically filed. I do not know of a single study that has had serious effect on the way we have designed or administered our relations with other nations.

The ineffectiveness of these exercises has resulted, in large part, from the fact that they have been addressed to the wrong question. The problem is not how to organize the Department of State as an abstract study in public management or political science, but how to organize it to carry out a particular kind of foreign policy. Secretaries of State such as George Marshall or Dean Acheson required a department that could maintain relations at multiple levels with all countries with which we had relations, with the Assistant Secretaries actually conducting American foreign policy in their areas of responsibility. Only major issues and the overall strategy of the department were reserved for decision by the Secretary (or the Under Secretary) and the President. But under Kissinger's regime the Assistant Secretaries (or even the Deputy Secretary, as he is now called, and the Under Secretaries) have little more than administrative authority. The department itself has become, in essence, a collection of desk officers who answer the mail, compose and receive telegrams, and carry on relations with foreign governments at the level of the routine and pedestrian. A policy of maneuver that confines key decisions, and even communications, to the Secretary and his personal staff, limiting significant contacts with governments to personal meetings between the Secretary and foreign dignitaries, leaves the department as an institution lamentably underutilized.

Marshall and Kissinger represent the extreme opposite ends of the spectrum. The most effective of our Secretaries of State — such as, for example, Dean Acheson — dominated the intellectual exercise of shaping policy, while still respecting, and drawing on, the judgment of experts, subjecting their own views to an adversary process, and fully utilizing the resources of the department. That does not mean, of course, that the institution has not had to evolve to meet the requirements of a changing world, or that considerations of taste and style have not entered into its structure. Of course, there are certain problems every Secretary of State has to decide in accord with his own prejudices. For many years the heart of the department has been the geographic bureaus, yet in a day when economic relations and scientific developments have an increasing impact on policy, there is an expanding role for the functional bureaus which exist alongside — the Bureau of Economic and Business Affairs, the Bureau of International Organization Affairs, the Bureau of Oceans and International Environmental Affairs, the Bureau of Intelligence and Research, and so on. Just how their work should mesh with that of the regional bureaus is a matter of endless argument. Should each regional bureau have its own economists, and how many? Or should economic problems be left to the Bureau of Economic and Business Affairs? The problem is not confined to the Department of State. Every multinational company faces it; some resolve it one way and some another.

Any Secretary of State with the will to do so can make the department work to suit his own style of operation without having to adjust the machinery much. Nor is there any optimum formula for relating the work of the department to the rest of the government. The solution largely depends on the President, the State Department's top management, and the personality and standing of the Assistant to the President for National Security Affairs, or whomever else the President particularly depends on for foreign policy advice and guidance.

There is also a special interplay between the Secretary of State and the Secretary of Defense and between the Secretaries of State and the Treasury, where the controlling influence on particular policies may well be determined by the relative interest, aggressiveness, and competence of the individuals concerned.

From the earliest emergence of the nation-state, foreign policy has depended heavily on the condition of a nation's finances and its military power. As a result, there has frequently been pulling and hauling between foreign secretaries and finance and defense ministers. Since the advent of nuclear power, the central problems of diplomacy have seemed to call increasingly for expert knowledge and opinion, and some political scientists have concluded that, at the top of the United States Government — but short of the President — there should be an official competent to draw all the skeins of policy into a manageable ball. Some have conceived this as the responsibility of the Assistant to the President for National Security Affairs; others have suggested the creation of a Presidential Deputy, or Deputy President, who, as a kind of superminister, would rank higher in the bureaucratic hierarchy than any other cabinet officer — and would, subject to the final decision of the President, exercise the ultimate authority on the design and administration of foreign policy.[1] A proposal of that kind was, for example, put forward to President Eisenhower in 1952 by a commission that included his brother Milton and Nelson Rockefeller.

In practical effect, we had such a superminister until November 1975, since the Secretary of State was also Assistant to the President for National Security Affairs. The Murphy Commission — latest of the study groups to recommend how the State Department should be reorganized — tactfully suggested in its report in June 1975 that this combination of functions might be all right so long as Mr. Kissinger was in office, in view of his "extraordinary abilities," but that, in the future, the two jobs should be separated.[2] Tactful, but in my view, they got it backward. The consolidation of the two jobs in a single individual would, it seems to me, be a sound idea only if the Secretary were prepared to perform his State Department tasks in the manner, for example, of Secretary Acheson, delegating authority and utilizing the Department of State as an institution. It is not a sound idea when the two jobs are held by a man who insists on playing every position on the team — pitching, catching, covering all three bases as well as center field, and acting as umpire — all by himself.

That the Secretary of State is, at the same time, the President's principal advisor on foreign policy and the head of a large foreign office presents difficult problems of emphasis. Mr. Dulles is reported, when he was first appointed Secretary of State, to have considered establishing himself in an office in the Executive Office Building, next door to the President but away from the State Department, so that he could concentrate his attention primarily on the first aspect of his job.[3] But that, of course, would have led to the same infirmity that now afflicts our foreign policy — a Secretary unwilling or unable to utilize the resources of his own department.

To interpose a super-Secretary next to the President would only perpetuate the Dulles mistake which Mr. Kissinger has repeated with flourishes. Not only would it cause confusion within the United States Government, but it would create great embarrassment in our relations with foreign governments. The pattern for nations all over the world is to entrust foreign policy primarily to a foreign minister, who is constantly in touch with his opposite numbers in other capitals. But if there were a superminister in the United States Government, foreign ministers would insist on dealing with him rather than with the Secretary of State, who would be only the third man in the American foreign policy hierarchy — or, alternatively, there might be an inflation of titles all over the world.

Within the American Government, that inflation has been going on for some time; it has become, in fact, a seemingly incurable disease of the bureaucracy. Until 1919, the officer next in line to the Secretary of State was an Assistant Secretary. Then additional Assistant Secretaries were created and an Under Secretary was interposed between them and the Secretary. When, during the first years of the 1960s, I served as the Under Secretary of State, there was already a second Under Secretary, who, under the terms of the law, could be designated either as Under Secretary for Political Affairs or Under Secretary for Economic Affairs. Now there are three Under Secretaries, while the occupant of my old post is known as the Deputy Secretary of State.

This process of inflating — or, more accurately, debasing — titles has gained its own momentum because, when once a title is inflated in one department of the Government, other departments must follow suit. Thus, if the second officer in command of the State Department is known as an Under Secretary, the second official in other departments must be an Under Secretary in order to be able to deal with him on a basis of relative equality, while, if other departments create a number of Under Secretaries, the State

Department must follow suit or find their agents outranked and outnumbered in interdepartmental meetings. It is, therefore, no accident that there are in the Department of State today as many Assistant Secretaries as there are Vice Presidents of a medium-sized suburban bank. Where will the inflationary process end?

The view of some political theorists that the Assistant to the President for National Security Affairs should be given substantive responsibilities and thus have a major voice in policy equal to that of the Secretary of State — or, for that matter, the Secretary of Defense — reflects a widespread misunderstanding regarding the operation and capability of the National Security Council, which he heads. One of the illusions encouraged by the way Presidential press officers announce the news is that decisions are reached and policies are made through the formal mechanism of the National Security Council.

That, of course, confuses our Presidential system with the cabinet governments that prevail in democracies with a parliamentary system. Unlike a parliamentary cabinet which does determine policy, the National Security Council never takes a vote, because, under the American Constitution, only the President makes the large, final decisions for the Executive Branch, and he normally makes them alone or in discussions with a handful of trusted aides.

Accustomed to the military tradition, General Eisenhower liked the tidiness of the National Security Council and established a superstructure of formal coordinating committees in connection with it. But he did not regard the Council as a place to make policy any more than he considered the Assistant for National Security Affairs as a man of substantive responsibilities. He left large areas of decision to Secretary Dulles, who, strong-willed and intolerant of bureaucratic interference, personally dominated not only the shaping but the execution of policy, so that, while the Council met formally, decisions were largely codifications of Dulles's own views.

When President Kennedy came to power, one of his first acts was to sweep away Eisenhower's superstructure of committees. Instead, he entrusted to Mr. McGeorge Bundy, as his Assistant for National Security Affairs, a considerable substantive influence on policy. Still, the National Security Council, as an institution, remained merely a formal mechanism. Decisions on major foreign policy problems were made by the President, usually in consultation with the Secretary of State, the Secretary of Defense, and the National Security Advisor. When military matters were involved — as was increasingly the case after Vietnam came to dominate policy — the Secretary of State and the Secretary of Defense coordinated their views or discussed them with the President and his National Security Advisor and often one or two others — the Chairman of the Joint Chiefs, the Under Secretary of State, or the Deputy Secretary of Defense. Only after a matter had been fully discussed within this small group was a meeting of the National Security Council ever called. There the President often asked such members of the cabinet as the Secretary of the Treasury or the Permanent Representative to the United Nations to express their views — particularly if the problem had a financial or United Nations aspect — but I recall few situations under either Presidents Kennedy or Johnson where the President had not already made his decision before calling a meeting of the Council. Thus the meeting had only two objectives: to inform the other members of what the President had already decided so they would not deviate from the line, and to give them at least the illusion of participation. This is as it should be. Foreign policy matters cannot be intelligently decided in a large general meeting.

In the final analysis, the relationship between the President and his Secretary of State has little to do with how the boxes are arranged on an organization chart. As the President's primary advisor on foreign policy and as the senior member of the cabinet, the Secretary of State should play the major role in melding military and intelligence policy into an integrated whole; and, if designating him also as the President's Assistant on National Security Policy would help him to carry out that role, considerations of organizational neatness should not stand in the way. Our military establishment, after all, is merely a tool at the service of the foreign policy of a great nation; it should not lead a life of its own in a democracy any more than should an intelligence service. If our foreign policy is to be coherent both in conception and execution, our military capabilities and actions must be factored into it. Thus, in advising the President where and for what purpose to apply our military power, the Secretary of State should have the loudest voice — although obviously coordinating policy in close consultation with the Secretary of Defense.

At the moment, the Department of State is in a sad state of disrepair. The origins of its malaise date back to 1953, when the guerrilla tactics of Joseph McCarthy went unchallenged by Secretary of State Dulles, and when Mr. Dulles tried — as Henry Kissinger was to do later — to operate as a one-man foreign office. A decade later, under Presidents Johnson and Nixon, the department again suffered a grievous blow when the rest of the world was neglected while American diplomacy was narrowly concentrated on Vietnam.

The only way to restore an atrophied muscle is by exercise and the only way to restore an atrophied institution is to give it a job to do and support its activities. Having spent fruitful years in the department, I respect the talents that can be mobilized within that currently muscle-bound institution. It contains a substantial but depleting reservoir of currently unused competence: specialists whose knowledge of Cyprus or India, the dynamics of the Middle East or the problems and potential of Japan, the implications for both Africa and Europe of a revolution in Portugal, the policies of oil and energy and raw materials, food shortages and demography — to offer only a random list — could have been drawn on to America's great advantage within recent years, had the Secretary of State only chosen to do so.

But today the ablest and most imaginative career officers are discouraged. Many have never met the Secretary of State, are never consulted even when their own special areas of experience and expertise are involved in crises. They watch uninformed, insensitive actions of their own government with understandable dismay. They feel futile when their advice is unheard and disregarded. It has taken a generation to build up this resource of talent and dedication; it would be reckless to let it decay much longer.

The bad name the State Department has acquired in many quarters results, in part, from the fact that it has long been the scapegoat for every foreign policy failure, while Presidents have systematically claimed the successes. It is traditional for the White House to announce all happy foreign policy events, leaving the State Department to put out the bad tidings. In addition, the department suffers from a common American disability: it is inarticulate. Sensible advice based on solid experience gets so deeply buried in a blancmange of clichés and bureaucratic jargon that it suffers by comparison with the glib views of less experienced academics.[4] As a result, all too many career officers have developed an overly cautious reticence, fearing the disdain of the Secretary if their ideas do not happen to coincide with his preconceptions or meet his stylistic standards.

These are only the superficial aspects of an even more profound distemper. During the fifties many career officers were so unfairly persecuted for alleged mistakes — which were, in many cases, perceptions in advance of their time — that a whole generation of officers developed excessive prudence. But it is different for younger officers, whose careers span a more salubrious era. Today there are plenty of bright ideas floating around Foggy Bottom — floating aimlessly because they are insulated from the Seventh Floor, where the Secretary is secluded in his office, surrounded — one might even say insulated — by a small personal staff that is able and dedicated but limited both in experience and breadth of knowledge.

A Secretary of State prepared to share decisions and responsibilities is in position to command the finest talents in America from all relevant sectors — the universities, the law, the sciences, industry, and labor, as well as the career experts and diplomats. So it is extraordinary that the personal staff through which Secretary Kissinger conducts almost all his operations consists, with almost no exceptions, of young foreign service officers with brief and limited experience. In spite of his outspoken scorn for professional bureaucrats, Kissinger has — in sharp contrast to the practice of the Kennedy Administration — enlisted almost no new blood from the universities. Presumably because of his disdain for other intellects, none of his old academic colleagues has been brought to Washington. This is unfortunate; we badly need to tap our nation's variegated riches of learning and experience, for, in the long run, an effective foreign policy for a democratic society must rest on a wide national consensus.

To achieve that consensus will require more than the rehabilitation of the Department of State; it will mean also the development of effective working relations with the legislative branch of the government. Otherwise, we shall have to endure — as was increasingly the case during 1975 — a petulant and self-defeating exercise in mutual frustration. The current lack of trust between Congress and the Administration over foreign policy is not — as is sometimes alleged — merely a problem of discordant personalities, although that is part of it. But more important is the fact that a policy of maneuver pursued in an atmosphere of intense secrecy is quite incompatible with our government of coordinate branches. For all too long the executive branch has preempted foreign policy while the Congress has stood idly by.

This point was vividly illustrated by the Moscow summit conference of 1974 — which will no doubt be remembered, if at all, as Richard Nixon's "last hurrah." In an interview four years earlier, the President had sought to justify the need for him to deal personally with Brezhnev on the ground that as the Soviet Union had "basically one-man rule" and thus he made the key decisions. But what happened at the 1974 conference? Immediately after the President arrived in Moscow on July 1, 1974, Brezhnev felt obliged to call a protracted meeting of the Politburo to discuss the nuclear weapons proposal the President had brought with him. Because the Politburo finally decided to reject the American proposals, the negotiations came to a dead end. That night Kissinger cleared with Nixon on the telephone an improvised proposal designed to save face for a President who frantically wished his trip to show progress. The following day, while Nixon was paying a visit to Minsk, Kissinger handed that proposal to Gromyko, who responded that it was "at least worth another Politburo meeting." It was only after the Politburo had again reviewed the matter fully on July 2 that Brezhnev felt authorized to go forward along the line Kissinger had suggested.[5]

It is not hard to determine from this incident which of the two leaders exercises unchecked and arbitrary powers. It is the Soviet leader, not the American President, who must negotiate *ad referendum* to higher authority. In earlier situations Brezhnev had even withdrawn positions he had accepted or put forward on the ground that the Politburo had not concurred.[6] After his own insistence on long, full discussions with the Politburo, Brezhnev must certainly have been impressed with the freedom of action of democratic leaders — the fact that Kissinger could counter a negotiating breakdown by a proposal he had hatched up on the spur of the moment, discussed with the President briefly on the telephone, and disclosed neither to key members of the Congress, nor — so it seems — even to the Government's own experts.

The 1974 incident is significant for more than one reason. Not only did it disclose the transparency of Nixon's justification for summit conferences and demonstrate the autonomy exercised by Nixon and Kissinger, but it showed how deeply ingrained was their disregard for Congress. If Nixon really had to go to Moscow at all, he could easily have taken two or three members of Congress with him; instead, he did not even tell them in advance the line of policy he intended to pursue, nor did Congress challenge his improvised compromise when he returned. The Congress was, alas, far less vigilant in its role than the Politburo.

Only now, after years of quiescence to the point of paralysis, Congressmen are beginning to ask hard questions and to assert their responsibilities. To understand the nature of those responsibilities and, thus, the meaning of the pendulum swing, one must, of course, begin with the American Constitution; yet it contains no clear answer. Instead of delegating exclusive authority over foreign policy to the President or the Congress, the drafters gave certain powers to the President, while assigning others to the whole Congress, and specific duties to the Senate.

Exactly how the two branches would adjust and accommodate their respective roles was largely left to Providence, whose good intentions the delegates to the Convention took for granted but could neither foretell nor greatly influence.

During the years that followed the Second World War, when first General George Marshall and then Dean Acheson were Secretaries of State, executive relations with key leaders of Congress were relatively relaxed. The leaders knew how the government intended to proceed, and Senators Connally and Vandenberg, who were Chairmen of the Senate Foreign Relations Committee, actively involved themselves in the formulation and direction of policy.

But today relations between the Executive and Congress are increasingly strained and abrasive. For a long period under weak leadership, Congress subsided into apathy and shirked an active role in foreign policy; recently, impatient at being kept in the dark and presented with *faits accomplis*, it is trying to force the Executive to redress the balance. As might be expected, since the legislative power is a blunt instrument, the result has so far been a series of uncoordinated actions that annoyed the Secretary of State more than they advanced a coherent policy — actions such as insisting that the President enforce the conditions under which we provided military assistance to Turkey, requiring that Export-Import Bank credits and tariff policy be conditioned on a liberalized Soviet emigration policy, denying trade preferences to OPEC countries in language that sloppily included Venezuela, Ecuador, Indonesia, and Nigeria, none of which took part in the oil embargo, and cutting off military supplies to favored tribal factions in Angola.

It was clear that such actions resulted from the Senate's justifiable impatience with an arrogant American policy. They constituted a warning that, if the Administration persisted in acting secretly on its own, the Congress would paralyze it. No matter how haphazardly manifested and destructive in its immediate effects, the instinct of Congress to reassert its role in American foreign policy was both normal and healthy — an overdue effort to redress a balance that had got badly askew.

It would have been well had both the President and Secretary of State recalled the poignant experience of Woodrow Wilson in 1919 after his protracted experiment in summit diplomacy. Although his visit to Europe had begun as a triumphal tour, he found, on returning to Washington, a mounting opposition in the Senate to the Versailles Treaty, including the Covenant of the League of Nations he foresaw as his prime contribution to an enduring peace.

In repeated postmortems since that day, critics have blamed Wilson's failure on his own self-centered obstinacy. He should not have gone personally to Versailles. At the very least, he should have made advance arrangements for Congressional support and approval, which would at least have meant taking some recently victorious Republican leaders with him to the conference. But Wilson was both egocentric and self-righteous, contemptuous of the mental capability and moral purposes of lesser men; he alone, as he saw it, possessed the vision and competence to translate his ideas into action. As Secretary of State Kissinger has shown us, it is an attitude not uncommon among intellectuals exposed to the temptations of official power.

Though an aggressive public figure such as a Wilson or Kissinger may, for a limited period, capture the imagination of the public and thus immunize himself from responsible criticism, he cannot sustain that role very long, for American opinion is volatile and the American attention span limited. Although members of Congress sensitive to the public mood may refrain for a time from challenging a transient hero, eventually the pendulum will swing; Congress will become ashamed of its supineness, Americans will recapture their native skepticism, and grow weary of a diplomatic "miracle worker" whose miracles tend to come unstuck.

On those occasions in the past when easy working relations prevailed between the State Department and Congress, there was fruitful accomplishment. Secretaries of State John Hay and Elihu Root, for example, made it a practice to confer with leading Senators in advance of treaty negotiations, and, for a period following America's participation in the Second World War, cooperation between the two coordinate branches worked quite well. Franklin D. Roosevelt was too shrewd and experienced a politician not to learn from Wilson's devastating defeat, and, when the United Nations Charter was first contemplated, Secretary Hull carefully solicited the views and interests of the Congress, keeping closely in touch with leaders of both Houses. As a result, during the summer recess of 1945, ten Congressional teams, each consisting of a member of the Senate and House, toured the country to drum up support for the United Nations and both the House and Senate passed favorable resolutions. Finally, immediately following the Moscow Conference, where agreement was formally obtained for a new adventure in universalism, the Secretary of State for the first time in history addressed the two Houses in joint session.

During the actual drafting of the United Nations Charter, four Democratic and four Republican members, representing both Houses, met with the Secretary about once every ten days to discuss the drafts as they progressed, and Senators Vandenberg and Connally were appointed as delegates to the San Francisco Conference which prepared the final text.

Thereafter the practice of close collaboration with the Congress made possible such measures as Greek-Turkish aid, the

Marshall Plan legislation, and NATO. During the Berlin crisis in 1948 and 1949 the Secretary of State consulted with the leaders of the Senate and House Foreign Affairs Committees, informed them of the line the United States proposed to take, and thus assured their support.

On foreign economic policy the same kind of collaboration was carried out. The ranking members from both parties of the Banking and Currency Committees were present at the Bretton Woods Conference and participated in the development of the organic documents which created the World Bank and the International Monetary Fund.

All this from the annals of our history is known even to Americans who are not professors of government. (It is amazing that none of these lessons has recently been applied in practice.) Yet, during a period when summit diplomacy has become commonplace to the point of tedium, neither President Nixon nor President Ford nor Henry Kissinger has ever taken leaders of the Senate or House on important diplomatic travels in faraway countries. Instead, they have committed the United States without advance consultation with the legislative branch, expecting Congress — like an indulgent father — to sign the checks. They have taken Congressional leaders by surprise with unexpected announcements of decisions already made or actions already taken.

The new assertiveness of Congress is, therefore, a warning signal that the patience of Congress is wearing thin and that such practices will no longer be tolerated. It is also an indication of increasing distrust, stemming from the growing conviction that, even though the Executive does possess the advantage of receiving a steady flow of information, it is quite capable of distorting, concealing, misrepresenting, and misinterpreting facts for its own purposes.

There was a breakthrough, I suspect, when Congress undertook to review the commitments made by Secretary Kissinger in order to secure the Sinai truce. Although the only question formally presented for Congressional action at the time was the narrow issue of authorizing our commitment of two hundred technicians to man the early warning system in the buffer zone between Israel and Egypt, the Senate Foreign Relations Committee and the House International Relations Committee were not content, as they had been on similar occasions in the past, merely with a secret briefing from the Secretary of State. Instead, they not only insisted on extracting from him all the secret commitments he had made and, against his strong objections, chose to make them public, but they even held open hearings with skeptical witnesses to discuss those commitments. Moreover, they required the State Department to advise them which commitments were regarded as binding on the United States and which merely represented pious statements of intent that would have only a moral effect on a succeeding President.

Clearly the Senate Foreign Relations Committee had, at long last, begun to take its responsibilities seriously. Many Senators deeply regretted the cavalier way they had given President Johnson a blank check to wage all-out war by approving the Tonkin Gulf Resolution. Then had come the shock of learning from a South Vietnamese source more than two years after the fact that, to induce President Thieu to sign the Paris Accords, President Nixon had written the letters of November 14, 1972, and January 5, 1973, promising to "take swift and severe retaliatory action" and "respond with full force" in case the North Vietnamese violated those accords.[7]

In reviewing the Sinai arrangements, the Congress had good reason to fear that commitments might have been made to both Egypt and Israel, but most probably to Israel, that could create major problems at a later time. As I have suggested, some of the promises, made or implied, in the agreements are, indeed, extremely troubling. Though its Sinai inquiry was informative for Congress, it left a brooding question in the minds of some members of both Houses: considering the scope of the secret promises Secretary Kissinger proposed to make to Israel and Egypt, what might be the secret commitments given to other governments in the past, during quiet tête-à-têtes between Kissinger or Nixon and foreign chiefs of government, or in secret letters? It will be a miracle if some expressed or implied commitments are not discovered in some government archives or disclosed by some foreign government to embarrass America at some future moment of crisis.

One of the most troubling developments brought into sharp relief by the Foreign Relations Committee hearings was the extent to which executive agreements have now largely displaced treaties as the instruments for registering United States commitments to foreign governments. In 1930, the United States concluded 25 treaties and only 9 executive agreements; in 1968, the United States concluded 16 treaties and 266 executive agreements; and by January 1, 1972, the United States was signatory to 947 treaties and 4,359 executive agreements, in force and outstanding.[8]

Against this overwhelming trend toward nullifying the treaty powers delegated to it by Section 2, Article II, of the Constitution, the Senate has so far made only token resistance. In 1969, it agreed to the National Commitments Resolution (S. Res. 85, April 16, 1969), which warned that the Senate intended to exercise its constitutional role and reserved the right to decline to implement Presidential commitments. Three years later, in 1972, it agreed to Senate Resolution 214, expressing its sense that a 1971 Presidential agreement, which provided for the use of military facilities in Bahrein, should be submitted to the Senate as a treaty.

The most far-reaching effort to reclaim its authority was in 1973, when Congress passed the War Powers Resolution, which prohibited the Executive from inferring from any treaty the authority to introduce armed forces into hostilities unless that treaty was implemented by legislation specifically authorizing such action. In addition, Congress, by the Case Act,[9] passed in 1972, provided that all international agreements must be reported to the Congress within sixty days after taking effect. But that was purely to assure disclosure; it did not give Congress any power to approve or disapprove such agreements and it provided that memoranda which the President classified as secret would be transmitted only to the House International Relations Committee and the Senate Foreign Relations Committee. When Senator Ervin introduced a bill to authorize Congress to veto executive agreements, nothing came of it.

One could hope that the experience with the 1975 Sinai Agreement would stimulate the Congress, and particularly the Senate Foreign Relations Committee, to reexamine the whole issue of executive agreements. In the opinion of some respected experts, such agreements, except when made pursuant to statutory authority (as are, for example, reciprocal trade agreements) or under a treaty or a delegation from the Senate, are unconstitutional, even though they may give rise to commitments regarded as binding in international law. If the Senate is to regain anything like the role intended by the Constitution, it must act decisively to rectify this executive usurpation of power.

The hearings also made clear what had already been widely suspected, that Secretary of State Kissinger does not regard commitments, even in written form, as very important; particularly if they are so loosely drafted that, even though the other signatory government might interpret them as satisfying its requirements, the United States could always avoid responsibility by giving them a broader, or different, interpretation. There is no doubt that the agreements made in connection with the Sinai truce are so imprecise that they can be construed in more than one way, but it is not clear whether that resulted from careless drafting or design. In either event, the practice of equivocal exchanges is extremely hazardous.

Although nineteenth-century diplomats often took pride in contrived ambiguity, it is not a practice to be indulged in by a democratic power such as the United States. Admittedly, it may ease the task of an American Secretary of State to be able to assure Congress in secret that the agreements do not mean what they might be interpreted to mean, but there will almost certainly be serious misunderstanding and trouble in the future if a contrary interpretation is being placed on them by the government of the other signatory. In fact, it is well to remember that treaty ambiguities have on past occasions led to war, as was the case with equivocal language in the Treaty of Uccialli in 1889, which resulted in war between Italy and Ethiopia and the bloody Italian defeat at Adowa in 1896.[10]

The usurpation of the Senate's authority over the making of commitments to other governments is, of course, only one aspect of Executive-Congressional relations in the field of foreign policy that urgently needs overhauling. In the final analysis, whether Congress's resurgence of interest in foreign policy is channeled along useful or destructive lines will depend, more than anything else, on the willingness of the President and, particularly, the Secretary of State to adapt their attitudes and procedures to the requirements of a democracy and the spirit of our Constitution. So long as a Secretary of State or a President practices a personalized policy of maneuver that depends on his ability to decide major issues without consulting with Congress, give broad commitments without review, and present Congress with *faits accomplis,* as was the case with the Sinai Agreement, there will be deepening hostility between the two coordinate branches in the area of foreign policy.

Unfortunately, the Congress has so far sought to assert itself only on the periphery of policy without seriously attacking the procedures that lie at the heart of the problem. Except in the case of the War Powers Act, it has concentrated primarily on individual substantive matters. Although I sympathized with the Congressional desire to make its will felt in those instances, it was still the wrong way to go about it. If Congress wants to take back the powers it has allowed the Executive to preempt, it must face that problem frontally by sharply restricting the area of executive agreements and requiring the Executive to submit treaties and substantive agreements it considers binding.

The effect of such Congressional action would, in my judgment, be profound. Indeed, it would seriously discourage the personalized, secret diplomacy of the kind for which Mr. Kissinger has become famous. That would be a major step in restoring to the United States a foreign policy suitable for a democratic society.

CHAPTER 12

The Right of
Privacy of Nations

DURING THE LATTER PART OF 1975 A NOISOME GEYSER OF NEWS reports about the excesses of the CIA offended American nostrils. Not everyone recognized the outpouring for what it was, the concentrated effluent from the self-cleansing mechanism built into the American system. Operating on Justice Brandeis's principle that sunlight is the best disinfectant, that mechanism, though indispensable, is often costly to operate. It makes us Americans appear to the peoples of other nations as masochists — the word used by one chief of government in describing his impressions to me — or exhibitionists who insist on publicly washing our dirty linen. But what foreigners fail to understand is that, in an open society dependent on the consent of the governed, there is no substitute for such a corrective process.

The excesses of the CIA in the last decades occurred precisely because that institution, by the nature of its function, was not exposed to the sunlight. Sealed off from the public view, it became, in effect, a closed society operating within the framework of an open one. Once that seal was broken, evidences of disease were apparent.

It was not a corruption, sickness, or impairment of integrity that derived from evil motives. By and large, its practitioners were faithful to the code of their calling, which, in many cases, involved subjecting themselves to considerable danger — for there are acts of high valor recorded in the secret archives of the CIA. The problem was that the encysted microcosm of the CIA had acquired an independent will of its own, no longer fully attuned to the requirements of the time or the mood of the nation. Reflecting a nostalgia for the wartime OSS, its code had evolved in the chilliest days of Stalin's Cold War, when we faced what many envisaged — and with reason — as a vast conspiracy aimed at democracy and American power. It was a code for fighting conspiracy with the weapons of the conspirators — and its first rule of order was to preserve the secrets of the secret society even from the prying curiosity of Congressmen.

During the wintry nights of Stalinist depravity, most Americans accepted without question the need for such activities. Living themselves in the open sunlight, they drew reassurance from the thought that there was a closed society operating on their behalf — a band of devoted men and women capable of countering, and coping with, a conspiratorial government in Moscow that deployed its agents throughout the world. At least until recently, most Americans did not wish to know what the CIA was doing; they were content to believe that it was at least as pervasive and efficient as the KGB — with agents quite as adept at overturning hostile governments and subverting foreign agents as those in the pages of Ian Fleming or Eric Ambler. Many of those who now make clucking sounds of outrage at the revelation of CIA antics were, until recently, quite content to keep quiet about the agency's activities and even to cooperate with it.

What finally undid the CIA was the growing suspicion of the American people that they could no longer trust their own government. Two administrations had kept the country so long in the dark regarding the costly, brutal, and destructive Vietnamese war that the delayed exposé of lurid events stirred ugly feelings of betrayal, while the relentless unfolding of the Watergate scandal left no doubt as to shabby goings-on even within the White House. The public lost trust in leaders who, illegally as well as officially, sanctioned covert activities. They insisted on knowing the facts, even though their revelation might temporarily impair our intelligence capability — a reaction no doubt intensified by a heightened taste for the journalism of exposure.

The prime responsibility of the CIA is obviously to collect and analyze intelligence and to conduct counterintelligence. In addition, as director of Central Intelligence, the head of the CIA has special responsibility for coordinating the intelligence activities of other agencies. The agency's most controverted activities, its covert operations, depend for their legality solely on a brief clause authorizing the agency "to perform such other functions and duties . . . as the National Security Council may from time to time direct." Exercising that authority, the National Security Council has from time to time directed the CIA to undertake certain clandestine operations under the council's general direction. It has also mandated the agency to organize and operate para-military forces through what is known as its Special Operations branch, of which examples are the unfortunate recruits shipped to the Bay of Pigs and the Meo tribesmen organized to fight in Indochina. There is no need to comment on these paramilitary activities other than to make the obvious point that large operations of that kind can never be hidden and should not be attached to an intelligence agency. In fact, they were placed under CIA direction only because that was the easiest way to arrange secret funding. To the extent that, barring a war, they may be needed at all (which seems doubtful), such operations should be entrusted to the Marines, or some other branch of the official armed services.

The overt collecting and analyzing of intelligence raises few questions. To dismantle unilaterally our intelligence service would be quite as foolish and hazardous as to disarm our military forces unilaterally. The days are long since past when we Americans could dare to shut up our cryptographic shop, as Secretary of State Henry Stimson insisted on doing in 1929, with the alleged comment that "gentlemen do not read one another's mail." It is a measure of America's innocence during that period that Stimson, who on many occasions showed great wisdom, should not have known that the club of nations includes thugs as well as gentlemen; there is no blackball procedure to exclude the undesirables. Nor should we regard intelligence gathering, by whatever means, as merely an effort to intrude on the privacy of other countries. With the prospect of further nuclear proliferation, covert intelligence gathering may become more necessary than ever if we are to know the state of development programs in potential nuclear powers. In addition, we need effective intelligence so that we can make agreements with thugs and be reasonably certain they are lived up to. Only by spying on others can our nation, with its open society and free institutions, assure itself that closed societies with tightly controlled institutions are doing what they have promised to do.

So far, the Soviet regime has, for example, opposed on-the-spot inspections of its nuclear installations and, since furtiveness is a central principle of its conspiratorial tradition, it is unlikely to relax that opposition in the future. Yet the Kremlin's phobia for secrecy becomes less important as we develop satellite photography and electronic detection devices that enable us to survey from afar what is going on inside the whole vast Soviet Union. Thus, we owe to our intelligence operations the conditions that make *détente* more than a wishful figure of speech. Progress toward the beginnings of arms control — for example the limited test ban agreement and SALT — is possible only because, primarily through the initiative of the CIA, the scientific community has been mobilized to devise the highly complex detection devices that are making secrecy a wasting asset.

By and large, the utility of covert intelligence operations of the type celebrated in espionage novels is far more limited than is generally suspected. Apart from the curious episode of Colonel Penkovsky, a Soviet recruited by British intelligence, who, until caught and killed, provided a vast volume of useful information, our experience with traditional espionage in the Soviet Union has yielded little of value. We gain windfalls of information from occasional defectors, but during my tenure in the State Department, I was continually astonished at how little we knew on a current basis regarding the inner workings of the Politburo. And, of course, we knew even less about the government in Peking, as recent surprises have shown.

Except for occasional excesses in our practice of traditional espionage, the most critical doubts regarding the CIA have been generated by its clandestine operations through which we have sought to influence and, in some instances, to overthrow governments. On a balancing of costs and benefits, some serious critics have suggested that we totally abolish the operational capability of the United States Government in this area.

Since Americans do almost everything on an ample scale, our clandestine operators have become the Paul Bunyans of the trade, the heroes of topical mythology, universally regarded as both iniquitous and ubiquitous. If a government falls anywhere in the world, the Communists proclaim we have brought it down; if a revolution breaks out in any backwater country, demagogues denounce the CIA. The mere fact we have any capability in the field is enough to create suspicion of our motives and our institutions, undermine our moral authority, and call into question the sincerity of our friendships. After all, it is the means a nation employs and the practices it follows, rather than the rhetoric of its statesmen, that weigh most heavily in the appraisal of its qualities. The world pays more attention to what nations do than what they say.

Thus, a plausible argument can be made that the CIA's operations do us more harm than good and that, so long as we even maintain the capability for operations, no one will believe we do not engage in them.[1] Yet that is a conclusion we should not accept without careful scrutiny. Not all operations are of the same kind, and before passing any broad judgment, it might be well to examine the several varieties of operations in an ascending order of offensiveness.

It is an elementary rule that an embassy accredited to the government of a country must refrain from interference in the internal politics of that country. In nations where the government is authoritarian, or even mildly intolerant of opposition, that is normally interpreted as meaning that the embassy cannot maintain overt communications with opposition leaders without risking offense to the government.

In such countries, it is customary for the principal embassy officers to deal only with the representatives of governments in power, leaving it to employees of the CIA, frequently with embassy cover, to maintain contacts with opposition leaders. Such contacts are beneficial in several ways. They add to our collection of intelligence. They enable the American Government to keep in touch with the views and evolving plans of an opposition and be in position to conduct business on a friendly and understanding basis if its leaders should ever come to power — whether by peaceful or forcible means. I doubt that many will deny the utility of such arrangements, particularly since even intolerant governments, although suspicious of such activities, have been inclined to accept them in a realistic manner.

Problems of judgment and propriety arise, however, when the opposition leaders turn to their CIA friends for help. Let us assume a situation in which a government rules in total disregard of freedom and democracy, while a beleaguered opposition, forced to operate secretly, does its best to keep alive the spirit of liberty. The opposition leaders tell their American CIA contact that they can continue their lonely fight against the government only if they obtain funds to print opposition newspapers — perhaps clandestinely — publish literature, travel throughout the country, and conduct the activities essential to opposition movements. Should we provide those funds? Should we secretly subsidize newspapers? Should we pay money to bribe corrupt members of the government to ease the harassment of the opposition? Should we let CIA representatives furnish secret subsidies to émigré groups who may be working for the downfall of the repressive government?

In terms of strict diplomatic principles, one could easily give a negative answer to all those questions. No matter how noble the cause may be, to pay political leaders or subsidize newspapers in a foreign country is to interfere in its internal politics. Recall the justified revulsion of many Americans at the corruption of the press in Paris during the decadent latter days of the Third Republic, when great French newspapers such as *Le Temps, Le Figaro, Le Matin,* and *La Liberté* all received monies from dark sources that included the Nazis. It was a not inconsiderable factor in undermining the moral texture of the French nation and preparing the way for Hitler's triumph during the ghastly June of 1940. So, some contend, it is not a practice in which the United States should indulge.

Yet, in the light of reality, is it not better to help those fighting for freedom through clandestine financial, or even military, assistance than to let a repressive government fasten itself on an unhappy nation? How, after all, can America live with itself if it does not come to the aid of men and women fighting to be free? If, for example, a free press is being suppressed by a deliberately contrived economic squeeze, why should not the United States help keep it alive? During the recent junta in Greece, should not America have been quietly, yet tangibly, helping the opposition with money or arms, particularly since we were blamed, anyway, for allegedly supporting the colonels?

Those are intricate questions that cannot be answered categorically or dismissed with broad generalizations. We must thread our way with great sensitivity. It is not easy to supply oxygen to the flames of liberty without leading other governments to suspect that, even though the United States maintains formal friendly relations with them, we may still be working with their opposition against their interests. Nor can one easily draw a line between liberal and conservative answers; I cannot help but recall that some of my liberal friends, who today fume with outrage at all CIA activities, were at one time or another vigorously promoting quiet help to opposition elements in several countries — as, for example, funds to encourage the opening to the Left in Italy.

I encountered such a contradiction ten years ago in connection with American relations with our NATO ally, Portugal, then enduring the seemingly endless stultification of the Salazar era. At that time, certain key officers in the Bureau of African Affairs of the Department of State were urging American assistance to such revolutionary groups as Holden Roberto's FLNA, fighting to break the metropole's hold on Angola. Devoted to liberty and fiercely anticolonialist, these officers personally knew the African revolutionary leaders, saw them quietly, and were in touch with their plans. Yet, though they were high-minded men, they did not hesitate to recommend that, if Prime Minister Salazar should accuse the United States of assisting the revolutionaries, we should categorically deny it. The argument by which they reconciled what we said and what our government did was, to my mind, casuistical. America was not, they insisted, helping the revolutionary activities of the dissident groups, but simply providing educational and medical facilities and other similar aid to their camps along the borders of Angola, from which they launched their raids. That aid was not of great dimensions — no more than a few hundred thousand dollars a year — but the amount is not the point.

A more difficult case is presented when a CIA employee in a country ruled by a repressive government is told by a high-minded opposition leader that a coup is being planned at a specified time and place through specified means. That is obviously useful information for Washington, since it enables our government to make plans to deal with the evolving situation, but is the United States justified in withholding that information from the head of the government with which it has official, and ostensibly friendly, relations? Can the ambassador, in other words, deal in good faith with the prime minister of a country when he knows that next Thursday that same prime minister is to be displaced by the opposition, and perhaps even shot? Or, let us go a step farther and suppose that the opposition has not merely informed the CIA employee of its planned coup, but requests arms or the money to procure them. As our diplomatic experts see it, United States interests would be admirably served if the coup were to take place and succeed, but should we in any way assist it? From the point of view of Anglo-American law, an individual is an accessory to a crime whether he actually participates in it or merely fails to disclose it to authorities when he learns about it in advance. Should that same principle be applied to relations between states?

To answer these questions in the abstract is clearly not possible, since every situation involves variations, nuances, and imponderables. America's efforts to redesign foreign governments in its own image, or shift the balance of influence of one group or another within a foreign country raise issues of international politics and pragmatism more than legality or ethics. To interfere at all, whether openly or covertly, in the political affairs of a foreign country is obviously illegal under the laws of that country. Moreover, since it violates principles of sovereignty, it flies in the face of normal rules of conduct among nations.

Solutions to the problem of covert interference depend on one's assessment of policy. If one sees little difference between the strategy and intentions of the Kremlin of today and in the time of Josef Stalin, then he must conclude that we are still everywhere engaged in a fight for survival, a fight in which anything goes. If one believes, on the other hand, that the Soviet Union is no longer concentrating its energies on the international triumph of Communism, that ideology no longer fuels the engines of the Soviet system, one might well conclude that America should have few worries about what happens in peripheral areas of the world. Say that small, poor countries on remote continents do adopt revolutionary forms of government: are they not most likely to be home-grown variations on Communism, unresponsive to the Kremlin's control?

If, as I suspect, most Americans are not totally persuaded of either extreme position, but believe that the Soviet Union and Peking will aggressively exploit situations of opportunity to try to expand their influence against American interests, the answers become less categorical.

The proponents of what is called the "just war" theory purport to offer certain guidelines, but those guidelines provide little comfort to anyone faced with concrete decisions.[2] The three criteria put forward to justify interference in the affairs of other countries are: (1) that the objective of the action must be just; (2) that the means employed must be both just and appropriate; and (3) that the action must have a reasonable chance of success. Under these criteria, one would certainly reject the carpet bombing of Hanoi in Christmas of 1972, intended merely to gain a slight diplomatic improvement in the terms of a political settlement with North Vietnam as a classical example of excessive means. Although it has been argued that the Bay of Pigs adventure was undertaken for the just objectives of providing the beleaguered Cubans an alternative to dictatorship, and of eliminating a potential threat to American security from Soviet aggression, the invasion would fall short under the second criterion, since the means were inappropriate because inadequate, and under the third because the action, as conceived, did not have a reasonable chance of success. But that is mere logic-chopping; at the end of the day, one has to fall back on a commonsense judgment.

For better or worse, the nation-state is still the dominant form through which men and women organize their affairs and carry out their political business. And, although sovereignty is a mushy concept, qualified in a thousand ways by the realities of interdependence, sovereign nations should assure themselves a decent degree of privacy and freedom to go about their business without dictation or interference from others. Yet, in the absence of some overriding supranational political authority, governments must also, in their own protection, insist that other governments follow acceptable patterns of conduct. Each government must decide largely for itself whether it dares risk letting threatening forces in another nation build up to the point where that nation becomes its enemy.

By almost any standard, the Soviet Union still remains a "revolutionary power" in its rejection of fair play in international conduct. There is solid substance in the theme that runs through the writings of all the dissident Soviet intellectuals today — from Almarik to Solzhenitsyn to Sakharov — that the Soviet Union can never be trusted to behave with decency and restraint in its relations with other nations so long as it remains a closed, repressive society. Today the KGB is both a symbol and instrument of Soviet policy and we cannot assume that it will refrain from meddling in the politics of any nations where it sees a chance to advance Soviet influence.

For many years I have abhorred the whole idea of the United States covertly interfering in the politics of other countries. I wish we could safely dismantle the operational apparatus of the CIA. Once we had done so — and other nations came to believe it — we would, I think, have regained some of the confidence in our "exceptionalism," which is, as I shall point out later in this book, one of our major resources. But there is still no international police force to deal with thugs, and until we develop one, if we ever do, great nations must retain a capability to intervene in situations that endanger their security. Thus we should continue to provide limited help to local patriots who are seeking to resist the subversion or conspiratorial seizure of their governments by either Moscow or Peking, as well as to liberal elements in nations of major strategic importance where dictators — either of the left or right — are trying to steal, or maintain themselves in, power against the will of the people.

Before any American becomes excessively self-righteous about the iniquity of our government passing money or weapons to dissident elements in friendly foreign countries, he should be asked to answer the following question: "Would it be right for a major power to secretly provide arms to a revolutionary group in a country with which that power maintains friendly diplomatic relations in order to assist the revolutionary group to overthrow the government?"

If the answer is an indignant negative — as it may very well be — it should be pointed out that the question accurately described military aid which France secretly provided to Britain's disaffected American colonists beginning even prior to the Declaration of Independence. Moreover, the question is a particularly relevant one in this Bicentennial year, since that secret aid was indispensable in bringing into being the United States of America.

To ask the question is a useful exercise because the answer is likely to illustrate two points. The first is the fact that Americans for the most part, and particularly those who have done their undergraduate work since the Second World War, are lamentably ignorant of their own history; and the second is that a knowledge of history is the best antidote to self-righteousness.

The CIA-type operation by which the American revolutionaries were financed began when Arthur Lee, the colonial agent for the province of Massachusetts in London, approached Caron de Beaumarchais (best known as the author of *The Barber of Seville* and *The Marriage of Figaro*). Beaumarchais arranged with Louis XVI to smuggle into the colonies one million livres' (about two hundred thousand dollars') worth of arms to the disaffected colonists in America. The arms were provided by the king's royal arsenals and many bore the king's monogram. The operation was carried out in the approved CIA pattern through a fictitious trading enterprise named Rodérique Hortalez et Compagnie, which Beaumarchais created for the purpose. Thereafter Charles III of Spain added another million livres to the same fund.

The importance of this operation for the future of America can hardly be overemphasized. As one leading American diplomatic historian has written: "Agricultural America, with its critical lack of military equipment, simply could not have carried on without this aid. Ninety percent of the powder used by the colonials during the first two and one half years of the war came from Europe. Most of it was supplied by Hortalez et Compagnie, which at one time was operating fourteen ships." [3]

As we celebrate the Bicentennial, we should bear in mind, therefore, that had pious elements at Versailles persuaded Louis XVI that covert aid to dissident British citizens in revolt against the crown was not a proper practice for a self-respecting monarchy such as France, the United States might never have come into being. Today disenchanted Americans might be writing letters to *The Times* and protesting to the House of Commons rather than marching up and down in front of the White House. Such historical precedents may be useful in purging the public discussion of some of the cant and sanctimony, misapprehension and deliberate distortion by which it is currently afflicted. No one mentions the fact that some of those now expressing great outrage at the CIA would favor our providing money to liberal elements in South Africa that might be seeking to overthrow an *apartheid* government, and regret we did not help liberals in Greece when the junta was in command.

The central question we face is the nature of the constraints we should impose on all of our covert operations. A first step might be to shrink the apparatus we maintain for this purpose, greatly reduce available funds, and abstain from operations where there is no overwhelming justification in terms of our own security. In principle, we should, for example, refrain from interfering in situations where Communist elements seem likely to take power through reasonably fair and free elections, even though a Communist electoral victory might encourage others elsewhere.

Here, again, broad generalizations do little to illuminate the problem. In Chile, for example, the Allende Government came to power through established processes in accordance with the Chilean Constitution, though the party received only 36.4 percent of the popular vote. But, once in power, there is evidence that it employed a variety of illegal and coercive means to neutralize the legislature, the Supreme Court, the opposition parties, and news media. In Portugal, of course, the Communists are distinctly a minority — they received only 12.5 percent of the vote in the election of April 25, 1975 — and their efforts to take power with the help of leftist elements of the army resemble the conspiratorial practices of Lenin in 1917 far more than American democracy. The argument of those who would have us conspire to block Communist electoral victories is that, once Communists are in power, they systematically destroy democratic processes, while the apparatus fastens its hold firmly on the country. It is not an argument to be dismissed lightly.

The principal vice of our covert operations during the past few years is that we have, far too often, sought to interfere in situations that only marginally concerned our interests. In my observation, that has happened most often when events in a far-off colorful country have, for one reason or another, caught the imagination of a President. Thus, a great deal of time, money, and effort — including a substantial amount of President Kennedy's own time — was expended in 1962 in trying to keep Mr. Cheddi Jagan from coming to power in Guyana (then British Guiana), although most Americans could not find the country on the map; while our intense preoccupation with Patrice Lumumba and the tribal wars in the Congo in 1961 appears, at least in retrospect, to have bordered on the obsessive. When in the Department of State, I once scrawled across a memorandum in which one of my colleagues recommended urgent American counteraction because of the appearance in Zanzibar of an ominous number of Communists: "It is my impression that God watches every sparrow that may fall; I do not see why we should compete in that league." Although the sentiment was not well received by the State Department officers absorbed with the problem, it may not be a bad guideline to follow.

Before any President involves the CIA in elaborate covert operations, he would, I think, do well to recall Talleyrand's famous advice to young diplomats: *"Et surtout pas trop de zèle."* Certainly we should avoid the imperialist presumption implicit in President Nixon's repeated comments to European statesmen after the Allende election: *"We* have lost Chile."

The exercise of greater constraint in our covert interventions is essential, not only because such activities contravene basic American principles but also because we pay an exorbitant price for indiscriminate interference. Our activities in Chile, for example, gave left-wing demagogues and revisionist historians a propaganda theme they will exploit to our eternal disadvantage; the Allende Government, they contend, was installed by the free expression of the Chilean people and overthrown only because the United States, through the CIA, treated Chile as a vassal state. Moreover, they insist, the United States was acting primarily to defend American commercial interests — which, of course, is nonsense.

The warfare in Angola clearly illustrated a now familiar pattern. What was basically a conflict among three tribal elements for control of the country after the departure of the Portuguese soon became a proxy contest between the United States and the Soviet Union — another skirmish in the Cold War. When Moscow supplied the MPLA with several thousand Cuban mercenaries and a substantial quantity of sophisticated weapons, the efforts of the Ford Administration to counter with increased supplies for the

FNLA and UNITA were frustrated by a reluctant Congress, sensitive to any move that might even faintly suggest a repetition of the Vietnamese experience. In this case, the traditional rationale for using covert channels — that disclosure would embarrass United States interests or help the Soviets — quickly ceased to apply, since aid of such magnitude could not be kept secret — nor was it. The African leaders, as well as Moscow, knew what we were doing. Thus, the only reasons for continuing to treat this as a covert operation were the fact that use of the CIA greatly facilitated funding, fear that Congress might not approve the venture, and concern that the overt supplying of arms might increase America's commitment in the event our client tribes should be defeated.

But the central question was not what mechanisms were most appropriate for intervention, but whether America should have intervened at all. Four lessons from our Vietnam experience, pointed out in Chapter 5, could have provided illumination on this point.

The first was that the United States should never intervene without fully comprehending the nature of the struggle and the play of forces involved. Thus, in Angola, we should rightly have viewed the situation as creating an African rather than a Cold War issue. By automatically assuming that this was just like all other struggles that had regularly followed the withdrawal of colonial power, we ignored the realities of African politics. Largely in response to the fact that the Soviets were supporting elements of the Mbundu people in a tribal struggle for power, we acted, by conditioned reflex, to prop up the Owambundus (UNITA) and Bakongo (FNLA). The alternative was, of course, to insist from the outset that the Africans must settle their own problems, to make clear that we were staying out of the local power fight, and to demand that other foreign powers — including South Africa — stay out. Then, if the Soviets insisted on continuing their intervention, they could hardly avoid the appearance of great power interlopers — or "imperialists," to use the customary jargon.

A second lesson was that we should consider not only how our actions might appear to us, but how they were likely to be viewed by other nations. It is enough to note that for us to assist the same factions as South Africa invited immediate and automatic opprobrium.

A third lesson was that the United States should refrain from involvement in areas only marginally involving its strategic interests. Exaggerated claims as to the strategic value of Angola rested heavily on the contention that Soviet possession of an Angolan naval base would enable it to interdict tanker shipping lanes from the Persian Gulf to Europe. It was a contention reminiscent of Admiral Mahan.

Finally, we should have learned from the Vietnam debacle never to tie our prestige to political factions that lacked a broad and solid political base. As so often, we took on all the wrong clients. The MPLA, supported by Moscow, which draws heavily from the urban population of Luanda, includes a high percentage of the nation's educated elite — elements best equipped to build a durable Angolan Government. The Bakongo people, who are the core of the FLNA, are, as we should have learned from our Congo experience a decade ago, not notable for their fighting qualities.

That we ignored these lessons suggests an uncomfortable parallel to Talleyrand's comment on the Bourbons, that they learned nothing and forgot nothing. There was certainly no assurance that, even if the Mbundus should triumph with Moscow's help, the Soviets would gain a permanent advantage. The Kremlin's ineptitude in dealing with Africans is notorious. A decade before, after they had poured millions of aid into Ghana, their arrogance and ill-concealed racism led to their expulsion. There was no reason to think they would be more skillful or sensitive in Angola.

Why, then, was the Ford Administration so anxious to play power politics in that marginal area? A large part of the answer can probably be found in the coldness shown by the Chinese leaders during President Ford's trip to Peking in December 1975. With new Chinese personalities challenging the reliability of America as a bulwark against Russia, the Administration felt compelled to prove its virility in Angola, no matter what the consequences for our African policy.

Although the Angolan incident raises broad questions as to the wisdom of America's involvement in proxy wars, it does not go to the heart of the CIA problem. To put the whole of our intelligence activities back into proper focus, we must reshape the institutions that are the instruments of policy. Despite the fact that the great bulk of its professional employees are serious and responsible scholars dedicated to objective and perceptive analysis, a few practitioners of the intelligence arts still need to be disabused of the idea that they are an elite corps with special immunity from the normal rules of our society. Over the years, as it has developed in secrecy, the CIA has appeared to at least a handful of its professional employees — and to some young recruits — as a combination of a secret fraternity, a dedicated body of knights from the age of chivalry, and a club entitling its members to picaresque adventures. Yet, what many CIA recruits looked forward to as experiences in the pattern of James Bond turned out, on a number of occasions, to be dubious escapades cooked up by a bureaucracy out of touch with the real world, recalling the writings of John Le Carré.

That, of course, is a flaw in the system: the free indulgence of fantasy has made it possible for employees of the CIA to operate outside the law, to commit reprehensible acts in the name of high principle. That, as an intelligence-gathering and analytical organization, the CIA has displayed great competence I can testify from my own experience, but its less than perfect record in operations was vividly demonstrated by the fantastic debacle of the Bay of Pigs, which was not scripted by Ian Fleming but by Evelyn Waugh. Yet we must be careful to put the blame where it properly belongs. In the confused public discussion of our intelligence excesses, there has been a tendency to treat the CIA as though it is the whole of our intelligence apparatus — or at least that it is, in fact, the "central" and commanding agency in the intelligence field — the authority at the hierarchical pinnacle from which all other government intelligence agencies take directives. But, in fact, although the director of the CIA has some centralizing responsibility in his capacity as director of Central Intelligence, his authority is severely limited, since he has no control over the overall intelligence budget. Today the CIA spends only 15 percent of that budget; almost 80 percent of the total budget of four billion dollars is spent by the Pentagon.[4] No wonder that many of the actions which the ordinary citizen automatically attributes to the CIA are, in fact, actions of some other agency.

There are a number of techniques by which this diffuse machinery might be brought under firm control; in fact, proposals for the reform of our intelligence structure are now being put forward not only by the President but by several committees of the Congress, and by the time this book is published the problem could well have become moot. Nevertheless, it may be useful to make certain suggestions for illustrative purposes, although I am fully aware that any structural or procedural arrangements will be no more effective than the personalities charged with developing and applying them.

In order to bring the current diffuse machinery under control, it would seem logical to create a new post of Director General (or, if preferred, he could be given a more grandiloquent title). Since the central element in bureaucratic muscle is control of funds, he should be entrusted not merely with general authority over what is known in the jargon as the whole "intelligence community"; he should have responsibility for allocating funds among the various intelligence agencies — not only the CIA but the National Security Agency (NSA), the Defense Intelligence Agency (DIA), the Bureau of Intelligence and Research of the Department of State (INR), and so on. Although those who know nothing about the practical operations of government cherish the illusion that one can enhance the status of a government official by dubbing him with the mystical accolade of "cabinet rank," I can think of nothing more useless. The United States constitutional system provides no significant functions for the cabinet, and membership in that shadowy body is an empty distinction.

I am fully aware that to endow the Director General with the powers I recommend would stir up a fearful bureaucratic row, leading to the mobilization of vehement opposition in the Congress. Still, it might help expose the avidity of vested interests and educate the people in the realities of the bureaucratic jungle. Thus I would suggest that the Director General have somewhat the same relationship to the various intelligence agencies as that which now exists between the Secretary of Defense and the service secretaries. It would be his task to supply intelligence to the President and the National Security Council, eliminate duplication in intelligence activities, and establish overall intelligence policy.

Although the President must necessarily have the final responsibility for our intelligence operations, as he has for every other activity of the executive branch, it is essential that the

Congress exercise effective and continuing oversight. The command of a vast intelligence machine — whether it operates domestically as does the FBI or abroad as does the CIA — presents an enormous temptation to Presidents. Since they are conditioned to living in the public domain, they feel exposed to their enemies on all sides; thus, they tend to have more than the normal curiosity not only about what is happening in the world but about who is making it happen and why. It is not surprising, therefore, that, as recent disclosures have shown, Presidents have sometimes displayed an unrestrained avidity when confronted with the almost unlimited potential of our intelligence machinery for catching their enemies off base and discovering who really loves them. The air in the Oval Office is far too yeasty to leave even a President in command of a vast intelligence apparatus without selected members of the legislative branch looking over his shoulder.

That point has been thoroughly documented by the various investigations of the CIA, for what comes through with crystal clarity is that dubious covert operations or activities were more often ordered from on top than initiated at the working level. Yet it is not easy to devise the machinery for effective Congressional scrutiny. By and large, Congress does not like joint committees; the occasional splashy investigations from which committee chairmen can make political capital are obviously more attractive than the hard, anonymous work of running a continuing committee of oversight that has taken a vow of silence. Still, the Joint Committee on Atomic Energy has worked with exceptional effectiveness and has kept its secrets well; it obviously provides the proper pattern for a similar joint committee to oversee all our intelligence operations. That would provide a clear and constant line of communication between the Director General and the Congress. It should exercise an unspoken restraint even on overcurious Presidents.

One of the first tasks of the new Director General should be to separate and redistribute the present functions of the CIA so as to reduce the sense of power and eliteness that has resulted from its size and institutional identity. At the same time, procedures should be devised to make our intelligence managers effectively accountable not merely to the Executive but to the Congress.

This is not the place to lay out in detail how the various functions of the CIA might be reassigned; by the time this book is published, Congress may already have completed that task. By way of illustrating a general approach, however, I would suggest that the intelligence analysis and overt collection functions might be returned to the Department of State, in which case it would be necessary to allocate ample funds to the department from the intelligence budget to enable it to perform its task properly. This latter point cannot be overemphasized. Although the State Department is currently charged under NSC directives with responsibility for economic reporting, it lacks the resources. The CIA, however, has 240 economists. Alternatively, as suggested by Dr. Ray S. Cline, who has had experience both as deputy director of the CIA and head of the State Department's Bureau of Intelligence and Research, we might establish something on the order of what he calls an "Institute of Foreign Affairs Research" which would exercise operational and budgetary control over the analytical elements of all intelligence agencies, whether located in the State or Defense Departments or elsewhere. That institute would, as Dr. Cline envisages it, prepare current intelligence reports and strategic estimates, not only for the executive branch but for the Joint Congressional Committee of Oversight and, so far as possible, make public its findings. The institute would also have responsibility for establishing requirements for intelligence collecting by other agencies.

Clandestine collection activities should, Dr. Cline suggests, be placed under the operational control of a small professional staff in the White House that would conduct its activities in response to requirements and priorities established by the Institute of Foreign Affairs Research. As he sees it, no permanent organization for covert operations should be maintained, but occasional programs of support for moderate elements in foreign countries might be carried out covertly on an *ad hoc* basis, under the formal order of the President, using whatever personnel might be required.

There has been general agreement among those experienced with the problem that the present Forty Committee is inadequate and that it should be replaced by a statutory body with a fulltime Chairman and a fulltime staff. Congressman Les Aspin has proposed that each member of that body be required to write and

sign an individual analysis of each proposed clandestine operation in order to make certain that the committee is not bypassed.[5]
Professor Arthur M. Schlesinger, Jr., has suggested that it might be
made a criminal offense for any official to authorize clandestine
operations in violation of these clearance procedures.[6] While the
oversight committee would be informed, it would probably not be
wise to give Congress the power to veto such operations.

Yet structural changes, the reassignment of responsibilities,
the drawing of new boxes on organization charts — these technical
devices will never solve the problem of an effective, yet responsible, intelligence arm of our government unless those charged
with the conduct of the business are explicitly instructed as to
what they are to do and not to do. That is not a matter of drawing
broad guidelines which, in any event, will never fit the unique
facts of every evolving situation. People are too devilishly ingenious, the world too full of surprises, for us to foresee every con-
tingency. So policies must be made as we go along, but within the
broad framework of an overall political and diplomatic strategy,
and to design that strategy we must answer certain key questions.
What kind of a world are we hoping to achieve and what kind of a
nation do we wish to be? We do not have the answers yet.

PART IV

New and
Old Dangers

CHAPTER 13

The Danger from Mankind's Second Enemy

UP TO THIS POINT, THE DISCUSSION HAS CENTERED PRIMARILY ON how to reconcile conflicting interests among nations so as to keep men from killing one another. But that is only one of the problems mankind now faces. Equally important is the need for nations to work together to meet common problems arising from natural phenomena that have once again become man's second enemy.

By interfering with the intricate checks and balances evolved over the millennia, man has exposed himself to undefined but very real dangers. The heart of the problem is the vaulting pace of growth of the world population that will create unmanageable problems unless we act promptly and wisely before demographic momentum carries mankind past the point of no return. Excessive population growth rate is by no means the sole new problem that beclouds the future, but it intensifies both the causes and effects of all the rest. At current high rates of consumption, and with an increasing world population, we are depleting natural resources at an alarming pace. Our industrial processes and the careless and wasteful habits of too many consumers poison the environment, pollute the water supply, despoil the air, and contaminate the seas. And there is always the danger that our scientific discoveries may get out of hand; in our strenuous efforts to meet the world's burgeoning energy requirements, we may, for example, raise the world's temperature to a point beyond human tolerance.[1]

These new problems could, in time, dwarf many of our familiar anxieties. No longer dare we focus our attention solely on preventing men from destroying one another through wars. We now know that we may invite ultimate disaster by letting our affairs get out of joint with natural forces.

Our predicament recalls the anecdote in vogue some years ago of the airline pilot who announced to his passengers that he had both good news and bad. The good news was that, with the aid of a powerful tailwind, the plane was flying faster than any other plane in history; the bad news was that the navigational system had failed, so no one knew where the plane was going. Today the speed at which the world is moving and changing is clearly breaking all records. Yet, hobbled by the imperfections of our habits and institutions, we may be unleashing natural forces beyond our capacity to resolve or control.

Fear of nature as an implacable enemy is as old as time. Running throughout Greek and Roman thought was the sense of unknown and incalculable powers lying just beyond an undefined threshold of knowledge — powers that might destroy man if he pressed the outer limits of inquiry too far. Aeneas, so Virgil suggests, would never have been subjected to the hazards of the high seas had man not discovered the art of navigation. Daedalus defied the air by inventing wings, with which his son, Icarus, flew too near the sun and was destroyed. Insisting on opening the box she had brought from Mount Olympus, Pandora released evils on the world, while, in the Hebrew myth, Adam ate of the Tree of Knowledge and was ejected from Eden.

In the classical credo, Fate kept mankind in its place; to expect earthly improvement was to rattle the bars separating the human from the divine. Although men of the Middle Ages used a different vocabulary, they held a similarly dour conviction: man's original sin destroyed hope for his moral improvement. With no prospect of improving his human lot, he could rely only on a happier afterlife.

Not till late in the Renaissance did the idea of progress begin to emerge. It was that extraordinary frontalist, Francis Bacon, who first suggested that, rather than fearing nature, man could, by increasing his knowledge, ameliorate its hazards and increase his prospects for happiness. The role of science was to endow human life with new "inventions and riches" or, to put it another way, to establish the reign of man over nature. "It was wrong to assume," wrote Bacon, "that men of antiquity had any monopoly of wisdom." Since knowledge was cumulative, each succeeding age had good reason to achieve even greater things than its predecessors. In other words, as Leibniz later put it, "the present is pregnant with the future."

Thus, the concept of progress slowly unfolded.[2] Descartes sharpened the argument by insisting that the laws of nature were invariable. What gave the theory of progress its value was, as Fontanelle pointed out, the postulate of an indefinite future. Since progress depended on invariable laws, it was, he contended, both necessary and certain, while, implied in the concept of progress was the obligation of men and women not merely to themselves and their contemporaries, but also to posterity — to generations yet to be born.

With the popularization of Darwin's concept of evolution in the latter part of the nineteenth century, optimism became the order of the day. Renan saw mankind perpetually achieving a more perfect state through the growing domination of reason. Herbert Spencer, interpreting Darwin, envisaged humankind undergoing an evolutionary adaptation to the point where "the ultimate development of the ideal man is logically certain."

Thus, at the close of the nineteenth century, with the prospect of man's perfectibility, the human race seemed assured not only that it was here to stay but also that it had a noble future. Nature was to be mastered rather than feared. Even the German pessimist, Professor Rudolf Hermann Lotze, though unpersuaded that human nature was capable of improvement, could still argue that "as far as men may judge, it seems that in our days there are greater safeguards than there were in antiquity against unjustifiable excesses and against the external forces which might endanger the continued existence of civilization."

It is remarkable that such an optimistic idea could survive the convulsions of two brutal world wars. Yet, though doomsayers, such as Spengler, conjured up apocalyptic visions, it was not until the development of nuclear weapons that many men turned toward a new skepticism. The advent of the nuclear bomb marked the end of Western, and particularly of American, innocence; it inspired long thoughts about last things and a renewal of the ancient anxiety that the world might someday — even soon — destroy itself. When, after the Cuban missile crisis, the Kremlin made at least a tactical decision to reduce its bellicosity, the leaders of the West felt they had been given a reprieve. It even seemed possible that the United States and the Soviet Union could gradually agree on arrangements to check the endless escalation of nuclear armaments.

Yet optimism enjoyed only a brief Indian summer. Inquisitive men and women began to extrapolate trends, putting together bits and pieces of evidence that challenged the basic assumptions on which Western civilization had long proceeded. The nuclear weapon had been only a warning of even more subtle dangers that were not easy to comprehend, nor did the doctors agree on the diagnosis — much less the cure. Permeating these doubts and fears was one increasingly compelling idea. The worst threat to man's well-being was not, as Marx had insisted, the overproduction of goods but the excessive production of people. Unless that process could be slowed down, there would be no way to cope with other problems.

An English parson named Thomas Malthus had sounded that alarm a century and a half ago when the population of Europe first began to grow at a faster pace. Projecting population increase at a geometric rate and expansion of world food supplies at only an arithmetic rate, he foresaw starvation on a vast scale. What damaged Malthus's reputation as a scientist and prophet was that, largely through the introduction of fertilizer, man tripled the food yield per acre. Although fortunate for the human race, this development led scientists to treat Malthus's theories with disdain to the point where, as late as 1938, respected intellectuals such as Dr. Gunnar Myrdal were dolefully predicting the collapse of the West because of its declining birthrate.[3] But that concern was abruptly ended by the baby boom following the Second World War, and, beginning in the 1950s, American intellectuals turned their attention toward a new phenomenon — the arresting spectacle of nearly a third of the world's population essaying the perilous passage from colonialism to juridical independence and, in the process, creating almost one hundred new nations.

Relieved of the humiliations of colonialism but no longer able to depend on their colonial masters for subsidies and protection, many of these new countries became world charges. America was quick to respond. Exhilarated by the success of the Marshall Plan that had helped the nations of Europe rebuild their war-shattered economies, President Truman, in his State of the Union message in 1949, promised his Point Four Program, by which the United States would furnish modest technical assistance to poor countries. Then American experts shifted the emphasis to the transfer of real resources and the financing of national development plans they had themselves largely put together. By the beginning of the Kennedy Administration in 1961, droves of development economists, nutritionists, medical doctors, agronomists, veterinarians, and experts in chicken diseases saw their future in terms of progressively expanding foreign-aid programs. In the exuberance that survived for at least a brief season, the faculties of many universities were depleted, with their members busy expanding the gross national product of dozens of new nations to whom America was providing foreign assistance. I recall a chance encounter with an old acquaintance who solemnly told me that he was occupying the Pan American Chair at MIT.

"What," I asked, "is that?"

"It's a first-class airplane seat to anywhere in the world."

Unfortunately, few, if any, of these practitioners of the new art gave enough thought to the fact that, by reducing infant mortality so that more females survived to childbearing age, they were ballooning the birthrate and thus largely neutralizing their own efforts to raise living standards. I am reminded of a suggestion someone has made that parallel to the Law of the Conservation of Matter is the Law of the Conservation of Trouble. It holds that problems are never solved but, just as a liquid may be transformed into a gas, problems are merely transformed into other problems. Although our doctors helped eliminate diseases, our engineers drained swamps, our PL-480 programs distributed food, we hastened the danger of a Malthusian debacle by ignoring the total equation. Yet it was by no means all the fault of our foreign aid administrators; our own social taboos got in the way. Even after our aid experts had begun to recognize the need to limit the rate of population increase in the countries we were helping, religious groups imposed obstacles to effective action.

Just how fast the world population will increase over the next fifty to a hundred years no one can say with assurance — although many try and arrive at widely differing answers. But short-term estimates are easier to make, and certain basic calculations are not in dispute.[4] Thus a continuation of the current population growth rate with the current mortality rate would bring the present four billion population of the world close to seven billion by the year 2000, eleven billion in the 2040s, and twenty-eight billion in the 2070s. In fact, if the fertility rate should remain constant but the mortality rate continue to decline, as it has been doing, the population of the world could be 7.4 billion in 2000 and close to thirty billion by 2050.[5]

The effects of this immense growth in population would be far from evenly felt. In the developed countries, an increasing number of people are producing small families and living to see their grandchildren grow up, so that the rate of natural increase has been slowing, especially during the last decades, to the point where it is now well under 1 percent a year. But in developing countries as a whole (excluding China) it is currently estimated to run at an average of 2.6 percent per year, and in many countries it is even higher. If their fertility rate should not decline, the developing countries would almost double their present total population by 2000 and would keep on doubling every twenty-seven years. But such astronomical numbers can never be realized, if for no other reason than that they would outpace the increase in the earth's carrying power and invite massive famines and epidemics.

Whatever action may now be taken, immense future growth is assured by the built-in "momentum" in the populations of most developing countries. Improved health and sanitation programs have led to the survival of hundreds of millions of children who, if born a decade or two earlier, would have died, so that most underdeveloped countries now have very "young" age structures. In other words, a large proportion of their populations are children and adolescents — perhaps 45 percent to 50 percent under fifteen years of age, so that the number that will enter the childbearing age each year will greatly exceed the number of older people that will move beyond the reproductive age. Thus there necessarily will be an annual increase in the number of potential parents.

This means that for most developing countries even a rapid reduction in birthrates would still not prevent a massive increase in population. Even if those countries could — which seems impossible — reduce their fertility by 1980–1985 to the "replacement" level (the two-child family average now characteristic of developed countries), the population of the developing world (excluding the People's Republic of China) would nonetheless continue to grow for five or six decades and level off at almost twice its present number. If, as still seems quite optimistic compared with past experience, they were not to attain that "replacement" level (two-child family average) until the years 2000 to 2005, the population increase in the developing countries in the following five or six decades would total nearly 4 billion above present levels, instead of the 2.2 billion that would result from achieving a replacement level twenty years earlier. If the two-child family average were not attained until 2050, the populations of the developing countries would continue to grow until about 2100 and level off at about 4.5 times today's size.

No one can be certain which of these theoretical projections may be nearer the mark. That considered by many demographers to be most reasonable is the United Nations "medium projection." In its 1973 revised form, it projects a total world population of 6.25 billion by the year 2000, 11.2 billion by 2050, and over 13 billion in the latter half of the twenty-first century. Because of the food import requirements such numbers would create, the populous countries of Asia and the Pacific have set as a desirable goal the attainment of a two-child family average by 2000. It is an ambitious objective.

Two conclusions can be drawn from all this. The first is that no matter what we do, the world will, by the end of the century, have a total population from two billion to more than three billion higher than at present, with the probability of substantial additional increases next century — and it will make a great difference for the future of the world whether the total is closer to two than three billion. The second is that rapid action can make a difference of several hundred million in the world's population at the year 2000; in fact, whether developing countries achieve a fertility decline to the "replacement" level by the end of the twentieth century is likely to determine whether a number of critical world problems will either be manageable with difficulty or totally unmanageable.[6]

The most immediate question raised by these figures is, of

course, whether the world will be able to feed and sustain such huge populations in the decades ahead. On one side are the alarmists; on the other, the Marxists and those who blandly assert that "science will provide all the answers." [7] The alarmists overestimate the problem by extrapolating curves without adjustment for intervention, either by nature or man. The skeptics, reacting negatively to the alarmists, display excessive optimism. Yet it is not necessary to side with the doomsayers to be gravely concerned; even if one goes fairly far down the line with the anti-Malthusians, the problems still loom hugely through the fog — dark and impenetrable.

William and Paul Paddock first predicted in 1967 in a book entitled *Famine — 1975!* that, since finite food supplies would not be enough to go around, mankind would sooner or later face a hard decision as to who should be fed and who should starve.[8] To describe the predicament, they borrowed the word "triage" — from the French verb, *trier*, to sort — which came into usage during the massive slaughter that accompanied trench warfare in World War I. Triage was the system for separating the wounded into three groups — those likely to die no matter what was done, those who would probably recover even if untreated, and those who could survive only if cared for immediately. Because of limitations on supplies and manpower, attention was given to the third group alone. It was the Paddocks' proposal that, where the population growth trend had already passed the agricultural potential, it would be "throwing sand in the ocean" to try to provide food. The country they foresaw as most likely to suffer this tragic crisis was India.

The Paddock book was written during a drought in Bihar province in India, where famine was averted only because President Johnson ordered the shipment of one-fifth of the entire American grain crop. Thereafter, the authors suffered somewhat the same fate as Malthus, because the "Green Revolution," with its miracle rice and miracle wheat, promised almost limitless expansion of world food production. Yet, the argument was kept alive by the publication in 1968 of Paul Ehrlich's *The Population Bomb* and by the appearance of an article by a distinguished University of California ecologist-biologist, Garrett Hardin, "The Tragedy of the Commons," in the magazine *Science*. The figure of speech this time was a commons, or common land, which would inevitably become overgrazed, since it was in each user's interest to put as many cattle on it as he could. Dr. Hardin concluded that although, when the planet was sparsely populated, human beings might appropriately have felt free to have as many children as they wanted, compulsory birth control was now imperative.

Dr. Hardin, in subsequent writings, devised another figure of speech to illuminate the "triage" dilemma. He spoke of "lifeboat ethics." The rich nations, as he saw it, are adrift in lifeboats, while those with high growth rates are swimming outside. To take everyone aboard would sink the lifeboats. Thus, Dr. Hardin argued, since we may already have exceeded the carrying capacity of our land, we should apply the realistic "ethics of a lifeboat." In other words, we should, as someone has put it, be cruelly kind instead of kindly cruel.

As might be expected, concepts as shocking as "triage" or "the commons" or "the lifeboat ethic" have been subjected to a strong counteroffensive. By far the most formidable attack has been mounted by experts who contend that there will — or, at least, that there could — be enough food to go around. What is required, they argue, is a massive effort to develop food production in the less developed countries, some modification of highly wasteful consumption practices in the advanced countries, and a vigorous population control effort to assure that the demographic curve will flatten out. Dr. Alan Berg, a food and nutrition expert on the staff of the World Bank, points out, for example, that India "has nearly as much good agricultural soil as the United States but produces only half as much food." [9] He suggests that, if the groundwater under the Gangetic Plain — perhaps the greatest reservoir of untapped water in the world — were exploited, every irrigated acre could be planted with a high-yielding variety of seed that could increase production by as much as 400 percent. The construction of massive barrages and dams in Bangladesh could channel flood waters to irrigate as much as ten million acres, while cultivable land could also be expanded. Less than 8 percent of Brazil's land is now being cropped, and, with massive investments, the country could produce an additional forty-five million tons of food, while "even heavily populated countries like Indonesia and the Philippines have good land for expanding production, provided people can be persuaded to move from the densely populated major islands to the thinly populated outer islands." Finally, Berg reports, "the opportunities offered by the new seed varieties are great." Asian and African countries now produce only one-fourth to one-fifth the grain per acre of North America, and one-half the countries of the world produce one-fourth as much corn per acre as the United States or one-fifth as much as New Zealand. Rice is a particularly important element of the diet where population pressures are the greatest, and it is here, too, Dr. Berg suggests, that "existing seeds and cultivation methods can multiply yields — a typical Japanese farmer produces five times as much rice on an acre as a typical farmer from Bangladesh — and new and better varieties appear to be on their way."

Unfortunately, these sanguine predictions depend on assumptions that experience calls into question.[10]

The first — and perhaps the most doubtful — assumption is that the United States and the other advanced countries will be willing to finance vast projects of dams and irrigation and essential fertilizer production.

A second is that those projects could be completed in time to meet the growing emergency and would not create environmental damage that would more than offset their value. There is reason to be skeptical. By the time the Aswan Dam was in operation, for example, the increased demand generated by the increment in population during the construction period more than offset the expanded food production contributed by the project. Moreover, by preventing the annual flooding of the Nile that enriched the farmland, the dam is now resulting in progressive depletion of the soil, while schistosomiasis with its debilitating effects has spread to a larger segment of the population. Too little is known about tropical and subtropical agriculture to be confident of the results that may flow from applying fertilizer and pesticides lavishly to relatively untested soils and ecosystems; while, in several areas of the world, salinization produced by extensive irrigation projects has disastrously reduced the fertility of the land.

Dr. Berg's third assumption is that those who work the lands could be induced — or that their governments would have the will and efficiency to induce them — to make the changes in agricultural methods required by irrigation, fertilizer, and new seed varieties; that the developing countries would, or could, restructure their food distribution systems to eliminate graft and waste and incompetence; that food costs would be subsidized for the poor; and that the developing countries would adopt all the other measures we take for granted. No doubt a typical Japanese farmer produces five times as much rice per acre as a typical farmer from Bangladesh, but what basis is there for thinking that, even if the Bangladesh farmer were given both new seeds and instruction in new cultivation methods, he would come within miles of matching the performance of his Japanese counterpart? What are involved are not merely new techniques but the alteration of whole cultures and attitudes toward life — a process begun in Japan many decades ago.

A fourth assumption is that developing countries will take the heroic measures needed to turn down the population curve and that the economically advanced nations will assist them with the resources and technical help required. If population were to increase even for two decades at the current rate while mortality were to continue at its present reduced level, the situation would get irretrievably out of hand. Few besides the most dogmatic Marxists contend that world resources of food and other essential raw materials are infinite. Out there somewhere is a terminal limit to the earth's carrying capacity. The question is: does the West, and that means primarily the United States, as the leader of the West, have the political will to make the vast effort of assistance for food production, the control of population growth, and social and economic adjustment and development that are required if we are to avoid such repulsive choices as those implied by triage or the lifeboat ethic?

Finally, if the United States and other advanced nations do make the effort, will they be frustrated by the developing countries, all too many of whom seem unwilling to subordinate ideology to the realistic requirements of progress? One of the major reasons for the current disenchantment with foreign aid programs is the widespread feeling of the advanced countries that they have too often been pushing uphill the bicycles of cantankerous adolescents who take perverse delight in backpedaling.

Yet, as the demographic statistics make clear, time is of the essence. If matters remain long in the present state of doctrinaire contention and inadequate action, the prophets of disaster — the inventors of figures of speech such as triage or the commons or the lifeboat ethic — may well be vindicated at the end of the day.

Someone has suggested that the succinct formulation of the problem we face is how to keep the rich from consuming too much and the poor from having too many babies. But that does no more than sum up the contrasting attitudes of the two sides. The Indians and other poor countries object to the West's "limitless consumerism." What they seem to be saying is: "Don't eat your food; give it to us." The argument put forward by the Communists and by the socialist countries of the Third World, that there are enough riches to go around if they were only leveled off on a basis of equality, totally ignores the effect of population increases, which, the Communists say, do not matter. Yet, if the pie is not increased in size, dividing it and redividing it with populations increasing in the poor countries at a breakneck speed would result only in smaller and smaller portions. "The sole purpose of human experience," as Dr. Philip Handler, the president of the National Academy of Sciences, has pointed out, "is not to establish experimentally how large the sum of human misery may be." [11]

Nothing could be more harmful to the peoples of Third World countries than to provide them with food on a continuing basis without insisting that their governments take effective measures to expand indigenous food production and bring population into balance with it. Sooner or later, the leaders of the productive part of the world — which means, in food terms, largely the United States and Canada — would almost certainly tire of the process. They would recognize that the consequence of trying to keep people alive on a permanent food dole would be the expansion of population to the point of ultimate catastrophe.

Yet it will not be easy for the United States to mobilize a common effort of the Western nations to take the measures necessary to assure the expansion of agricultural production in the poor countries while, at the same time, helping the peoples of those countries reduce the rate of population growth. That will require not only a high degree of political will on the part of the American people but also a clear common understanding among the experts as to what is required if we are to get a firm hold on the total problem. There is still a residual feeling among many economists, even in the government, that if we only concentrate on developing industry in the poor countries, the population problem will solve itself. They rely heavily on trends apparent in Europe during the eighteenth and nineteenth centuries, when birthrates went down as the Industrial Revolution spread across the continent, contending that economic development and industrialization in the less developed countries today will inevitably bring down the birthrates and slow their population growth. Unhappily, arguments based on the European experience should not be taken at face value.

Although the rates of population growth in Europe were at the time only a fraction of the increases that prevail in some Third World countries today, they still brought about a doubling of the European population during the nineteenth century, and the pressure this generated, combined with some agricultural and economic reverses, set in motion a European migration that swelled into a vast stream flowing to all parts of the world. Only after many decades, one hundred to one hundred and fifty years — in matters of this kind time spans are critically significant — did birthrates decline to their modern levels and with low death rates complete the "demographic transition" from high to low birth and death rates. Why this drop in birthrates occurred is by no means clear, although the learned doctors have put forward a dozen competing theories to explain it. Three facts, however, are indisputable: population growth rates in most countries in most years were under 1 percent; when this growth could not be absorbed, tens of millions could, and did, emigrate to the New World; and it took one hundred to one hundred fifty years to make the transition from high birthrates to low birthrates.

In today's Third World countries, the average population growth rate (about 2.6 percent) is still more than three times the average in most countries of Europe during that period. Although it is impossible for the Third World countries to provide employment for populations growing at that rate, there is now no New World haven for the men and women who cannot find employment. Finally, if the developing countries are to avoid catastrophe, they simply cannot wait the one hundred and fifty years of the European demographic transition to bring birthrates down to the low levels to which death rates have already been brought.

Some of the economists who maintain that industrialization can solve all problems point also to the success of a group of countries — South Korea, Taiwan, Hong Kong, and Singapore — that have attained rapid economic growth in reducing their rates of population increase from the traditional 2.5 percent or 3 percent a year to 1.5 percent or less. Yet too much should not be made of those precedents either. Hong Kong and Singapore are not really countries but small city-states, while South Korea and Taiwan received very large infusions of capital from the United States that helped them reach their phenomenally high rates of economic growth. Moreover, all these nations are dominated by Sinic culture, with its Confucian traditions of social discipline, all have strong governments, and all have been efficiently carrying out comprehensive programs of family planning.

The optimists who insist that the world can accommodate an almost unlimited number of people if we only develop and mobilize all available resources and cut down the consumption of the rich tend to ignore the central question: even if we can, by enormous effort, provide for the physical needs of a swollen and continually swelling population, what will life be like in an overcrowded world? Only some of the consequences of excessive population can be solved by producing a new miracle of manna from the skies or, in this case, from the soil; overcrowding can still have disastrous effects on the social and political structures man has painfully erected over the centuries.

We live in what — on an analogy from the physical sciences — might well be termed a political and economic "ecosystem" in which no significant trend, action, or event can take place without repercussions elsewhere. As late as 1930, the world, with no more than two billion people, was relatively sparsely populated, and, since industry was simpler than today, national economies impinged on one another to only a limited extent. But, with the world's current population of four billion and with highly sophisticated industrial processes, the reality of interdependence obtrudes at almost every level of human activity.

Thus, the shrinking of living space, and the effects of population densities outpacing increases in the provision of social services will, without question, produce profound social, economic, and political repercussions. It will mean herding together vast numbers of wretchedly poor human beings and transforming many capitals into vast cesspools like Calcutta. Nations with swollen populations are destined to become, in General de Gaulle's graphic phrase, "a mere dust of peoples."

The current complex interlocking of systems leads to only one conclusion: we cannot add to the number of individuals on earth without each of us interfering more and more with the well-being of others, or, in turn, becoming more and more interfered with by — and dependent on — the actions of others. That means that we shall have to endure increasingly elaborate rules and regulations and that each will have to accept greater constraints on his own behavior to avoid conflict. Unquestionably, overcrowding will have noticeable political consequences. Professor Henry Steele Commager has pointed out that the spread of nationalism in Europe after the French Revolution coincided with the first great population explosion in modern history. Already, in some of the overcrowded nations of the Third World, an intensifying nationalism borders on xenophobia. The ethologists Konrad Lorenz and Robert Ardrey have supplied us with evidence as to the effect of overcrowding on the development of aggressive tendencies among animals.[12] The violence of American youth in the 1960s took place when the children of the postwar baby boom entered college and were crowded into institutions accustomed to smaller numbers. The overcrowding of the black population in northern cities has created situations of social turbulence.

Although scholarly efforts have been made to determine the exact relation between overcrowding and violence, the results are far from conclusive. Yet one does not need a computer to predict that poor, heavily populated countries will become unmanageable when governments are unable to supply the needs of overgrown populations for essential goods and services. Bangladesh, which one high State Department official is reported to have referred to as "a basket case, but not our basket case," illustrates the problem. Its present rate of growth would, if continued, mean a doubling of its present population of 75 million or so in twenty-three years, so that it would exceed 170 million by the year 2000. But, because Bangladesh will never be able to earn the foreign exchange to finance the mounting level of food imports required, it must remain an increasingly desperate object of charity. With the population increase forcing people off the land and into the cities, the Bangladesh Government concedes that unemployment is running at at least 30 percent. Crime is widespread as the landless unemployed, equipped with arms left over from the India-Pakistan War, form gangs for murder and armed robbery. Such chaos cannot be contained by national boundaries. Already, Bangladesh refugees are illegally crossing into India and Burma, and there is always the possibility that, in the event of total collapse, the Indians might feel again compelled to intervene in Bangladesh — even at the risk of additional strains on the already worn political fabric of that outsized country.

When excessive populations force the peoples of a country to go elsewhere for employment and necessities, migration can clearly be a disruptive factor. In Africa, for example, migration south from the drought-stricken Sahel countries is pressing people toward the coastal countries, which, suffering their own population growth, have tried to rebuff the migrants. While this has so far not resulted in serious conflict, an explosive situation could develop in the next two or three decades as the populations of both the inland and the coastal countries approximately double.

One must distinguish between the condition of overcrowding — simply too many people in relation to territorial space or resources — and the maintenance of an excessive rate of population growth. As the pace of population growth approaches the rate of economic growth, it slows the rate of increase in GNP per capita — or, in other words, retards the increase in goods available to improve the standard of living of the individual. For the development economist, that frustrates everything he is trying to do. For individual families, it represents continued misery and the loss of all hope in the possibility of progress. In addition, an excessive rate of population growth distorts a country's age structure. A nation with both low fertility and low mortality contains a relatively high proportion of people in economically productive age groups; but in a population with high fertility and low mortality, the lower age groups keep expanding. This can create major problems for a poor country. It means, among other things, heavy expenditures for rearing dependent children, which result in less funds for investment to increase national output. Since there are limits on the subdividing of farm plots, adolescents migrate from rural areas into swollen cities, where they cannot be accommodated in limited labor forces. Yet, by posing a threat to urban wage levels, their presence creates resentment and conflict. Detached from the tutelage of priest and family, they are an easy prey to left-wing or right-wing extremist movements; less reconciled than their elders to existing conditions, they are more politically activist. Thus it is not surprising that the steady lowering of the median age level in a rapidly growing population increases lawlessness. This is evident today in Sri Lanka (Ceylon), Guatemala, Ecuador, Colombia, and Peru, as well as in the Philippines, where adolescent unemployment has produced bands of armed outlaws terrorizing the countryside. In the Dominican Republic, there may well be serious social and economic dislocations as rapid population growth outpaces the development of food resources and public services.

To be sure, most of the countries mentioned in discussions of the population problem may seem to most of us Americans only tangentially related to our interests. Yet, the implicit danger will be brought sharply home when, by the year 2000, Latin America increases its present population of a little over three hundred million to well over six hundred million, for many millions of whom there will be little, if any, employment, shelter, food, or hope for the future.

Consider our neighbor Mexico. Her population is now growing at 3.5 percent per year and is thus destined to double in twenty years. By 1995, the present 57 million people in Mexico will have increased to some 115 million and, unless new and stringent measures are taken, will exceed 130 million by the year 2000. Already, a mounting number of adolescents is overwhelming the Mexican labor market, and the situation will get rapidly worse. In 1960, about 750,000 young Mexicans became fifteen years of age and began looking for employment. In 1970, the number was 1,200,000; in 1980 it will be 1,700,000; in 1990, 2,400,000, and in 2000, unless the growth rate is sharply reduced, it will be 3,400,000. Barring some extraordinary economic development in Mexico — or some horrendous natural calamity — the pressures of mounting unemployment will inevitably impel an increasing number of these young men and women to attempt to cross the border into the United States, where, according to the Bureau of

Immigration and Naturalization, several million of their brethren already reside illegally. Yet, one can be sure these uninvited guests will not be welcomed. Already, the southwestern states are filling up through internal United States migration; in fact, it is estimated that the 40,000,000 in the southwestern states will become more than 60,000,000 by 1995.

The problems one can predict between the United States and Mexico foreshadow those we will face with many other countries. They are problems for which we are not prepared — psychologically, intellectually, emotionally, or in terms of concrete plans and programs.

Obviously, the consequences of overcrowding and distortions in the age structure will be affected by their relation to other factors, such as technology, resources, territory, and trade. Nations with large and rapidly growing populations but inadequate technology and resources are — it has been said — more likely than not to become "the problem children of the world." Nations with growing populations which advance rapidly in technology but not in territory may feel pushed toward geographical expansion.

Even though densely populated, a rich advanced nation like Belgium can afford the luxury of democratic institutions. Yet a poor country, with backward technology, undeveloped resources, and an excessive population may well be forced toward a distasteful choice — either squalor and ultimate disorder or a repressive political system that dominates every aspect of life.

The comparison that comes most readily to mind is that between India and China, which are, in terms of population, the two largest nations in the world. Both are miserably overcrowded. Much of China's land area is mountainous or otherwise uninhabitable. Seven-eighths of the population, or roughly seven hundred million people, are crowded into the eastern one-third of the country and dependent for their food supply on the produce of less than 12 percent of the surface area of the country. India — with only one-third the land area of China, but with slightly more extensive agricultural lands — today contains nearly six hundred million people. But, although the basic economic and physical circumstances of the two countries are not far different, their social, economic, and political structures are poles apart. India developed what — until recently, at any rate — it proudly called the world's largest democracy. China is organized with the rigor of a beehive,

under an all-pervasive political control and with the people indoctrinated from childhood in a rigid code, their thinking directed on
a mass basis and their income and activity constrained within an
intricate bureaucratic command system. Yet, repulsive though the
Chinese system may be to anyone devoted to the values of the
West, the Chinese nation today seems capable of surviving and,
indeed, gradually beginning to move toward more efficient agriculture, industry, and higher standards of living. Although the extravagant claims of the Peking Government must be discounted, it
seems probable that the Chinese are approaching — or will within
a few years approach — a relatively stable demographic situation
that will insure a population with a diminishing, and ultimately a
zero, growth rate.

A realistic prognosis for India, on the other hand, must be
anything but sanguine. With an overblown bureaucratic structure
that impairs progress, and with great disparities of wealth between
a rich class and the vast mass of wretchedly poor, it is hard to
foresee how India will ever overcome, or even manage, its problems. The iron constraints of religion, cultures, and a cacophonous
babel of languages and dialects — these alone are a major impediment to material progress. With inefficient — and, for the most
part, primitive — agricultural methods and an even more imper-
fect system of distribution, with religious taboos that impose on
the food economy a parasitic cattle population almost one and a
half times that of the cattle raised for beef in the United States,
India is, even in the best years, a marginal food producer and, in
most years, a food deficit country, in spite of miracle rice and miracle wheat.

India's population is now swelling by over a million each
month.[13] If measures to reduce birthrates are not enormously intensified, it will considerably exceed a billion by the year 2000.
The so-called medium projection of the United Nations, made in
1973, sets the likely figure at 1059.4 million by that year, and even
this high figure assumes a far more effective birth control program
than the Indian Government is now conducting. It is difficult to
see how a population of that vast size can possibly be maintained
by the slow-growing Indian economy, or how it can ever be effectively governed by the inefficient bureaucracy in Delhi, even with
substantial decentralization.

It is possible, of course, that mounting pressures may lead to a breakdown in the health services and thus trigger at least a partial Malthusian solution. Death rates are already moving up in some parts of India, and a recent smallpox epidemic was a bad omen. But modern man cannot accept that kind of defeat.

What are the lessons to be drawn from this? Hardly that the Communist structure of China is good and Indian democracy bad, but, rather, that if population is permitted to outrun resources in any huge country with a low standard of living, the people may face the hard choice between ultimate collapse or authoritarian methods.

So far, I have mentioned the effect of excessive population growth only on the world's food supply. But the excessive consumption demands of advanced countries with high technology and wasteful industrial processes may also produce shortages of other critical resources. Energy in the form of oil comes immediately to mind, yet the problem it presents is not one of supply but of a price artificially maintained. Given a few years, we Americans can increase our coal production and can, at higher costs, convert our extensive coal supplies into gas or liquid form, thereby increasing portability. We can also develop more exotic fuels and nuclear energy. Yet that potential is by no means equally available for certain other key raw materials. Substitution is possible for many, but only at excessive cost.

The schoolbook case in which a lack of indigenous raw materials combined with rapid population growth to generate conflict was the Japanese military expansion that began in 1931 with the invasion of Manchuria and ended fourteen years later with surrender on the U.S.S. *Missouri*. In the Germany of the 1930s, the claustrophobia resulting from a sense of overcrowding provided an excuse for Hitler's aggression — although clearly not a rational justification, since *Lebensraum* was never as real as the Germans made out; after all, the population density of Germany was substantially less than that of some of its neighbors.[14]

If the efforts of raw-material-producing nations to restrict or withhold their product do not lead to conflict, wars can still arise between two would-be producing nations quarreling over raw material sources. Resort to the seabed for fossil fuels, or even for metals, may well prove a dangerous source of conflict. Thus, the oil under the China Sea could become a *casus belli* between China and her neighbors, just as the potential reservoir of offshore oil in the Aegean has already intensified the quarrel between Greece and Turkey over Cyprus.

To be sure, neither the raw material nor the energy problem is likely to remain static. New technological breakthroughs, new possibilities of substitution will continue to occur. Still, we are finding out that there are limits which mankind dares not transgress in employing certain extraction and manufacturing processes and techniques without so damaging the environment as to make life not merely uncomfortable or esthetically repulsive but even unsustainable. Although, so far, we know relatively little about the envelope of atmosphere in which we live and on which life depends, we have learned enough to know that it is fragile. None of this is news to any educated American. Books and magazines and television programs are filled with discussions of one aspect or another of our predicament; yet there is about the whole subject an aura of science fiction — an unreality because it has only been marginally expressed in political action. None of these problems will be assisted by delay; mankind has never before confronted a set of dangers calling for more urgent action.

It is quite obvious, on even the most optimistic assumption, that, if the world's surging population increase is to be kept within manageable bounds, the economically advanced countries will have to pursue intensive and costly projects over the next several decades; if they fail to do so, they may truly have to face the specter of a world outconsuming its resources. It is obvious, also, that leadership in mounting and sustaining such an effort must come largely from the United States. Not only are we the only large advanced nation capable of producing major agricultural surpluses (the only others being Canada, Australia, and Argentina), but we alone have the worldwide interests to support worldwide responsibilities.

That does not mean merely that we must increase foreign aid in the traditional pattern, with prime emphasis on industrial development; it will require a program skillfully designed to achieve certain quite specific objectives.[15] We must not only greatly expand agricultural production in poor countries, but, quite as important, we must accomplish that in such a way as to keep people on the land, provide them employment, and prevent the migration to the cities that can result only in disaster. At the same time, we must create the conditions conducive to family planning and provide the programs of information and facilities essential to accomplish a reduction in the birthrate.

Merely to follow the old pattern of trying to increase industrial production and, hence, the gross national products of developing countries is by no means adequate. Rapid industrialization will not solve the problems of disruption now being created by increasing urbanization and the unemployment that goes with it; it will tend, instead, to accelerate movement to the cities. Between 1920 and 1960 the urban population of the Third World countries rose at a rate of 4 percent — twice the rate of the developed countries. Nor is it correct to assume that the higher rates of economic growth produced by industrialization will mean adequate jobs for a growing population; an OECD study shows that, to absorb the annual increase in a labor force growing at 3 percent a year, industrial production would have to increase at 18 percent.

Nor does the solution lie in trying to increase agricultural production by expanding the size of farms and introducing labor-displacing machinery. That has been the pattern far too often. The best way to deal with the problem is to keep people in the countryside, and the best way to accomplish that is to provide farmers with land of their own, because the small peasant farmer is, in any country, a stable element. Studies made by both the World Bank and the FAO have shown that a smaller average size of holding and the diffusion of ownership in many hands results in an increase in output per hectare. Thus, land reforms produce two essential benefits: increased production and greater labor absorption. But to make programs effective, small farmers must be given access to credit and adequate supplies of fertilizer, while a substantial investment will normally be required for irrigation. In countries where there is not enough land to go around, developing countries might learn a lesson from the Chinese experience and systematically develop small-scale, labor-intensive, local industries throughout the countryside. Taiwan, for example, has followed a consistent policy of keeping as much of its industry in the villages and small towns as possible.

In agriculture, the Japanese, rather than the Chinese, provide the best model. Following General MacArthur's agrarian program,

Japan made a great surge forward in agricultural production. Eighty percent of the total cultivated land was transferred to the tenants, while the government invested heavily in agricultural research, created a well-designed extension service (with the extension agents actually living in the villages), made credit available, and assisted the establishment of marketing cooperatives. In addition, long strides were taken in education and literacy in rural areas as well as cities, for girls as well as boys; while agriculture was given a respected place in society. The last point is probably the most important; in many countries giving dignity to agricultural labor would require a drastic change in the emphasis of education and cultural attitudes. Through compulsion, the Chinese send their young to the countryside, but in India, where the favored subjects in the universities are law, philosophy, and the liberal arts, no student would consider going to live in a village. Yet in many countries, if urbanization continues at its present rate, urban unemployment will vault up, economic hardship will become intolerable, and political unrest will lead to revolution and chaos.

Along with economic assistance focused on the discouragement of urbanization and the development of employment in rural areas must go a far more concentrated frontal attack on population growth. Today, family planning activities are being carried out through several agencies: the World Bank, a United Nations fund for population activities (which by 1975 had achieved an annual budget of $80 million), and direct help by the United States and a few other countries. In considerable part as a result of American initiative and encouragement, a World Population Conference was held in Bucharest, Roumania, in August 1974. There a coalition of totalitarian countries, led by Algeria and Argentina (which included the Iron Curtain countries and was assisted by the Holy See), sought to frustrate the work of the conference with the customary Marxist contention that capitalist imperialism was at the heart of the predicament and that what was needed was not family planning but economic development. In spite of this attack, the conference adopted a world population plan of action by a consensus of 136 nations, with only the Holy See abstaining.

Although the plan of action was a typically windy United Nations document reflecting many compromises, it contained most of

the elements of a blueprint for worldwide action to bring population growth under control. Fundamental is the decision of the governments of underdeveloped countries to act decisively. If they
fail to do so, there is little the developed countries can do to spur
action, other than to advise them of the disasters they are bringing
on their peoples; direct sanctions in any form are likely to prove
self-defeating, although the industrialized countries should make
clear that, as they have demonstrated by the fact of their own
achievements, they have little patience with futility and will not
be eager to pour resources into hopeless situations. But to be effective — or even palatable — such advice must be backed up by
the demonstrated willingness of the developed countries to provide all possible assistance to make family planning programs effective for those developing countries that display the will to undertake them. That will require extensive assistance carefully
designed to help the poor countries keep their people on the land
and away from the swollen cities. Programs must be so tailored
and conditioned as to assure that the peasants are given plots of
ground, that heavy investments are made in rural education, that
health services with family planning are established in the villages, that small industry is scattered throughout rural areas, and
that the cities are assisted in meeting their most urgent problems
of housing and poverty.

All this will be difficult, costly, and frustrating, and the United
States, which must take the lead, has so far refused to face realities.[16] Yet we cannot let these problems drift without the most
urgent attention, since every week of delay makes them less and
less manageable. Although the effort required may be irksome, we
have no available option; the alternatives are unacceptable.

CHAPTER 14

Old Dangers
with a New Immediacy

THE PROSPECT THAT POPULATION PRESSURES WILL UNDERMINE
political structures in poor countries is made far more ominous by
the carelessness with which the means of violence are being proliferated. If we do not halt that proliferation, it is virtually certain
that an irresponsible government will, sooner or later, acquire a
nuclear weapon, just as one can predict that the conventional
weapons we are scattering about the world in vast and increasing
volume will intensify the destructive consequences of local quarrels, and even expand them into major wars. In several areas of the
world, marauding gangs are already equipped with sophisticated
light weapons, including hand-held rockets — and we should
brace ourselves against the shattering news that some group of terrorists somewhere has obtained, and is prepared to use, a nuclear
bomb to blackmail or overthrow a government. Sooner or later,
that will almost certainly happen; the only question is how soon
and under what circumstances.

With the spreading of the means of violence, overcrowded
countries, frantic for food and space and raw materials, may translate their anger and frustrations into widespread destruction. Nor
can one any longer assume that conventional wars will be narrowly contained, or rule out nuclear conflict because the major
powers are afraid of blowing one another up. The comforting,

though precarious, "balance of terror" resulting from the standoff between the superpowers will not deter nuclear wars by small nations.

We must, therefore, adjust our planning to a different and more complex world. So long as the nuclear club remained limited to four members, the United States felt menaced only by Moscow. On October 16, 1964, the alarm bells rang in the Pentagon when the Chinese first exploded their bomb, and there was somber talk of the need to "contain" China and speculation that Peking might someday lob a nuclear warhead into San Francisco. But, once China had recovered from the Saint Vitus's dance of the Cultural Revolution, few any longer regarded her as expansionist. Even if the Soviet Union and China were one fine morning to impose nuclear death on one another, we might escape direct involvement.

We came, therefore, to regard China, Great Britain, France, and the Soviet Union as "responsible" nuclear powers — using the term for nations that would stop short of a mutually destructive nuclear exchange. Nazi Germany taught — or should have taught — us that there could still be "irresponsible" governments — governments that might precipitate a *Götterdämmerung* on the lunatic impulse, as Hitler put it, to "slam the door of Europe until it brought the house down."

Beginning in the very first years after World War II, we thought it imperative to keep new members from joining the nuclear club so as to limit the bomb to nations that could be trusted — or, to put it another way, to maintain the existing nuclear oligopoly. Thus, for many months after a B-29 called the *Enola Gay* made its fateful run over Hiroshima, we concentrated on hiding the secrets of nuclear technology so they could not be sold or stolen. But, in 1953, under President Eisenhower, we totally reversed our course and initiated an aggressive program called "Atoms for Peace," through which we would share our nuclear technology.

It was in many ways an innocent period, when the American people — and that included the Government and the Congress — still regarded the prevention of nuclear proliferation as an exercise in counterespionage. The public had the vague impression that the key to making bombs was written down in a recondite formula on a piece of paper, and that if we could only keep foreigners from getting hold of it, we could live happily ever after.

Yet that, of course, was a trap and a fallacy, since science is a universal resource, as we should have known from those brilliant refugees — the Einsteins and Bethes and Fermis and Tellers — who had built us our bomb in the first place. The technology of how to make nuclear explosions was certain to spread or be discovered by others. The best means to discourage the spread of bombs was not to lock up secret formulas but, rather, to impose controls over nuclear materials.

Yet the full significance of material controls was largely overlooked at the time. All the Atomic Energy Act of 1954 explicitly required was that, before supplying nuclear fuel for the reactors we had furnished foreign governments, we must obtain a guarantee from those governments that the material or equipment and any resulting fissionable material they might produce would be used exclusively for peaceful purposes. In practice, the executive branch added a requirement that the United States be able to verify for itself that this limitation was being honored.

Such a safeguard was a considerable novelty, since it gave the United States far-reaching rights to enter the territory of recipient governments and carry out necessary inspections of both facilities and records. Moreover, the agreements stipulated that the United States could require the return of the nuclear material and equipment if the safeguard provisions were violated.

Yet bilateral agreements by themselves were clearly not enough as, one by one, other industrial nations became nuclear suppliers. So, on an American initiative, the International Atomic Energy Agency (IAEA) was set up in Vienna on October 26, 1956, with a mandate, among other things, to develop an international system of safeguards that could be generally applied. And on July 1, 1968, the Nuclear Non-Proliferation Treaty was opened for signature.

That treaty, reflecting a more mature view of the problem, was a forthright effort to mitigate an undeniable danger. It suffered, however, from an inherent asymmetry. In arrangements with Third World nations, the advanced countries customarily try to protect the advantages that derive from their economic dominance, while the underdeveloped nations join in the hope of some specific *quid pro quo*. But, in drafting the Non-Proliferation Treaty, the nuclear powers devised a cartel to protect their nuclear oligopoly. They agreed among themselves not to give nuclear weapons to outsiders and asked outsiders to agree not to join the nuclear club. In the world of American private enterprise, antitrust laws would have declared such a restrictive agreement illegal. Certainly no one could argue that the commitments of the two groups were in any way comparable or equal. It was a document hard to justify, except on the lofty assumption that the original five nuclear nations were the only ones that could be trusted to possess the bomb.

The principal considerations offered the non-nuclear powers — outside of the rather vaporous argument that they would be preventing a dangerous spread of lethal weapons — were threefold.

The first was that, if the non-nuclear powers would agree to halt "horizontal" proliferation — the spread of the bomb outside the club — the nuclear powers (which meant, for all practical purposes, the two superpowers) would try to reach an agreement to halt "vertical" proliferation — in other words, to stop, or at least to check, the expansion of their nuclear arsenals.

The second consideration was that all parties to the treaty would facilitate, and participate in, the fullest possible exchange of "equipment, materials and scientific and technological information for the peaceful uses of nuclear energy."

The third was that the nuclear powers would make available to the non-nuclear-weapon states who signed the treaty potential benefits from the peaceful use of nuclear explosions.

The non-nuclear nations were, of course, aware that the treaty was weighted against them. Their concern extended not merely to commercial but also security considerations. If they could not manufacture or acquire nuclear weapons, how could they safeguard their interests against the threat of nuclear attack? The sponsoring nations — the United States, the Soviet Union, and Great Britain — tried to meet that point by United Nations resolutions, in which each nation promised that it would act "immediately" through the Security Council in the event of a nuclear attack, or threat of attack, on a non-nuclear state. Although the declarations were given the blessing of the Security Council on

June 19, 1963, no one took them seriously, particularly since each of the declaring powers, as a permanent member of the United Nations Security Council, possessed a veto over any action the Council might propose to take.

I felt from the beginning that, although the treaty was inspired by the best of intentions, it was so patently discriminatory that it might generate resentment without achieving its purpose. In *The Discipline of Power*, a book published in 1968, I suggested that the non-nuclear nations would find it hard to accept the self-denying ordinances of the treaty.[1] And even the common interest of the superpowers, I pointed out, was illusory. The Soviet Union was primarily interested in obtaining an international sanction for keeping Germany away from nuclear weapons; the United States was anxious "to deflect such Asian nations as India and Japan from becoming nuclear powers."

Although subsequent events have largely validated these concerns of eight years ago, I admit, in retrospect, that my criticism of the treaty was probably not adequately balanced. Since, asymmetrical though the treaty may be, it has encouraged some nations to submit to more effective safeguards than might otherwise be the case, the world is obviously better off with it than without it. Our current problems arise largely because several key nations have never signed it and the nuclear powers have been lax in enforcing its provisions. Meanwhile, the action of the OPEC member nations in raising oil prices has greatly increased the demand for nuclear energy reactors.

Unfortunately, the dual function of the atom as a destructive force and a source of power renders any nuclear policy inherently contradictory. Although our country has sought to prevent nuclear proliferation, we Americans have spent hundreds of millions of dollars spreading nuclear equipment and technology around the world and earned a good profit in the bargain, while other industrial powers have strenuously competed in selling their nuclear products. As a result, many nations have acquired reactors capable of producing plutonium that — by a relatively simple chemical treatment — could be used to produce bombs. Although the United States has tried to insist on adequate safeguards, other nations that produce equipment — particularly West Germany and France — have not been so diligent. Not only have they been less careful to require adequate safeguards, but the West Germans have sold an entire fuel cycle — including a uranium enrichment plant — to the Brazilians, and the French have sold an isotopic separation plant to the South Koreans.[2] Although the French have refused to sign the Non-Proliferation Treaty (De Gaulle characterized all disarmament efforts as "vain and interminable"), they claim that, nonetheless, they are observing the spirit of it. But when they assert that they are free to sell separation plants because such sales are not expressly forbidden by the treaty, they are being hypocritical. They know there is no reason for the South Koreans to acquire such a plant except to make bombs.

In spite of the fact that we Americans have been liberal in extending the benefits of the atom, it is other industrial nations that have been the principal beneficiaries, and we have not made the non-nuclear nations happy. Their disenchantment came through loud and clear at a meeting held in Geneva in May 1975 to review the first five years of operations of the Nuclear Non-Proliferation Treaty. Only 57 of the 96 non-nuclear nations that had ratified the treaty even bothered to attend. Those who did promptly plunged the conference into the larger dispute between the Third World and the rich nations. They angrily complained that we nuclear powers had failed to live up to our treaty commitments; we had not reduced our nuclear arsenals, had taken no significant steps toward nuclear disarmament, had not ourselves accepted the safeguards we required of other nations, and had done nothing to make available the benefits of peaceful nuclear explosions (PNEs) to non-nuclear states.

But it was a dialogue of the deaf. While the non-nuclear powers were interested in little other than obtaining greater economic benefits from the atom, the United States and the other nuclear powers were preoccupied with the technical aspects of tightening and strengthening international controls, while at the same time pushing exports. No wonder the conference failed to provide a dialogue; it was merely an occasion for each group to deliver set speeches. Since the two groups could not agree enough to muster a two-thirds vote in favor of constructive measures, they fell back on the adoption of a bland compromise, which the non-nuclear nations grudgingly, and bitterly, accepted.

Except for a possible Japanese ratification in 1976, it will be difficult, if not impossible, to obtain further signatures and ratifications for the Non-Proliferation Treaty; indeed, we shall be fortunate if some nations do not begin to unravel it by exercising their right to withdraw on three months' notice. Present arrangements for preventing the spread of weapons are quite inadequate, and new ones are urgently required, some of which may necessitate a reconsideration of steps taken earlier.

Even though India had refused to sign the Non-Proliferation Treaty, the United States provided her with a reactor and Canada continued to supply nuclear material. Although Canada bore the brunt of the criticism when India announced that she had successfully tested a nuclear device "for peaceful uses," the American record was not much better.

Article III, Section 2, of the Non-Proliferation Treaty provides that a nuclear power is not to transfer "source or special fissionable material" or equipment for processing, using, or producing such "special fissionable material" to any non-nuclear state without subjecting that material to the special treaty safeguards. But immediately after the treaty was signed we let our desire to share the benefits of the atom — or to sell reactors — override our need to prevent proliferation; for we decided not to limit our nuclear transfers to nations that had signed and ratified the treaty. That obviously removed one lever by which we might have increased the number of treaty adherents, but we did not stop there; we went even farther in reducing the benefits for the signatories of the treaty when we interpreted Article III as not requiring the nonsignatory recipients of nuclear equipment to place under IAEA safeguards any materials or equipment other than those covered by the particular transfer. Since the treaty required non-nuclear signatories to accept safeguards on *all* their nuclear materials and equipment, and not merely on those received under the particular transfer, such interpretation obviously gave non-nuclear nations an incentive not to sign. A nonsignatory nation might be able to build up unsafeguarded stockpiles of plutonium; a signatory nation could not.

For the treaty to be fully effective, of course, we should have required that a non-nuclear state must become a party to the treaty before a nuclear signatory state could give it any nuclear help at all. To be sure, even had the Soviet Union gone along with this restriction, it would have created a two-class system, since France, China, and now India, nuclear powers not parties to the treaty, would not be bound by it. But, though such a restriction might have cost American industry some sales and even limited the flexibility with which our diplomats could use nuclear reactors as political bribes, it would certainly have helped check proliferation.

Even if we have made an irrevocable decision to provide reactors to nonsignatories, should we still give them to nations engaged in local quarrels in turbulent areas? It is a question raised by our government's decision in 1975 to offer reactors both to Egypt (which has signed but not ratified) and Israel (a nonsignatory), in spite of the fact that the Israeli Government will certainly not agree to apply safeguards on its existing reactors. Yet in intelligence circles, it is widely believed that Israel either has several bombs or could produce them quickly. It has almost certainly accumulated an adequate amount of unsafeguarded plutonium, and there is evidence that its brilliant physicists may have gone far with processes for the use of lasers in isotope separation to produce enriched uranium.

In 1961, the United States Government became suspicious of the contents of an odd-looking building at Dimona, south of Jerusalem, which, we discovered, housed a nuclear reactor. After protracted negotiations, we arranged for a series of increasingly unsatisfactory visits of inspection. These enabled our experts to make an educated guess that Israel would, after a brief period, be able to produce enough plutonium for at least one explosive device a year, of, as I recall, roughly the magnitude of the Nagasaki bomb (nineteen kilotons). But in recent years, to the best of my knowledge, no United States representative has ever been allowed another look at the Israeli installations.

To be sure, since the reactors now promised Israel will be adequately safeguarded, they will not contribute to any increased Israeli weapons capability. Yet, that is not the point. The question is how we can best use our leverage to discourage further nuclear proliferation, recognizing that, if the Israelis were to threaten to employ a bomb, the United States would — and with reason — be widely regarded as having condoned it. If, for example — and I do not believe it will happen, or that the United States would permit it to happen — the Israelis found themselves faced with possible defeat and extinction — or at least a protracted war requiring massive American resupplies — the Israelis might feel compelled to unveil their nuclear weapons and threaten to use them, which would certainly raise international emotions to the boiling point. If Egypt and Syria called on Moscow for help, the Soviets might either threaten to destroy Israel directly or at least to provide a matching nuclear capability for the Arabs. At that point, the scenario would move from the dangerous to the incalculable.

Thus it is pertinent to ask whether we should be providing reactors to either Israel or Egypt or, in fact, to any other nations engaged in local or regional quarrels. Should we not, instead, try to achieve an agreement among the supplier countries that certain turbulent areas are off-limits?

Unfortunately, our current avidity for short-term tactics gets in the way of prudence. In his statement before a Subcommittee on International Finance of the Senate Committee on Banking, Housing and Urban Affairs, Mr. Fred C. Ikle, the director of the United States Arms Control and Disarmament Agency, acknowledged that the export of nuclear technology to the Middle East violated one of the three standard criteria employed by the agency — that the region to which such technology is exported be "free of latent or actual hostilities." Yet, he said, "there is a countervailing consideration: the transfer of these power reactors can help strengthen United States influence in the area, and thus help this Administration and future administrations continue efforts to bring peace to the area." [3] That same comment can, of course, be made with regard to almost any turbulent area in the world — which means that, in practice, the criterion is nonsense.

Today several nations with the potential to build bombs are located in areas of political turbulence. South Korea is a case in point. Living under the constant threat of attack from the north, the South Koreans are under obvious pressure to reinforce their security by every possible means. Yet, if the South Koreans built a bomb, not only would it upset their Chinese neighbors, but it would put almost irresistible pressure on the Japanese Government to go down the nuclear road — a decision which, if made, would have catastrophic perturbations throughout Asia. Despite this, the French agreed to sell South Korea a pilot plant to reprocess spent nuclear fuel, which would enable it to extract weapons-grade plutonium. Certainly it was no excuse to contend, as the French Government did, that South Korea was presently a signatory to the Non-Proliferation Treaty; given the tensions between north and south, Seoul might, at any time, feel driven to exercise its right to withdraw from the treaty on ninety days' notice and build a bomb. Moreover, the French action, if finally taken, would have given South Korea a potential hold over the United States; whenever America might decide to withdraw her forces, the Seoul Government could have countered that action by threatening to become a nuclear power.

Even surpassing the irresponsibility of the French willingness to sell a processing plant to South Korea was the decision of the West German Government in 1975 to authorize the sale to Brazil of a four-billion-dollar nuclear package that would include the whole nuclear cycle — not only power plants but also the know-how and equipment for producing nuclear weapons material, either enriched uranium or plutonium. That transaction was even more reprehensible than the French deal with Korea, because Brazil is not even a signatory to the Non-Proliferation Treaty. But under no circumstances could the transaction be justified; for, even if strict controls were placed over the use of the German-supplied equipment, Brazil could build its own fuel-making equipment by reproducing the facilities it would be purchasing.

Unfortunately, neither President Ford nor Secretary Kissinger personally intervened to stop the Brazilian sale, nor have they yet been able to block a French sale of a plutonium plant to Pakistan, quite obviously for use in building bombs for defense against Pakistan's nuclear neighbor.

As with many international transactions where countries are influenced by commercial ambition or the desire for political advantage, the supplier country invariably justifies such nuclear transfers on the ground that if it did not make such equipment available, another country would. But a succession of such transactions will go far to assure the ultimate acquisition of nuclear weapons by some irresponsible power; since as less responsible nations become members of the nuclear club, they will be inclined, in disregard of any accepted standards of discipline, to confer membership on even less responsible nations — and so on down a declining curve of responsibility.

In dealing with the have-not nations, the nuclear powers have weakened their own position by failing to carry out the pledge in Article V of the Nuclear Non-Proliferation Treaty to create a special international regime to make the benefits of nuclear explosions available for peaceful uses. Many developing nations are entranced by the vision — shared initially by American scientists and engineers — that such explosions could provide a cheap means to construct harbors, dig canals, build highways, establish irrigation systems, and carry out other public works programs involving massive earth movements. From the positions they continue to assert in the threshold test ban negotiations in Moscow, it seems probable that the Soviets still have faith in the utility of the technique; yet our own experience with "Operation Plowshare" has been disillusioning. Not only does it require more nuclear explosions to accomplish a given task than we had originally thought necessary, but the movement of earth through such explosions could possibly trigger serious seismic disturbances. Moreover, because of fallout, those explosions must be restricted to points remote from human habitation and centrally positioned in large land areas so as to minimize the possibility of illegal fallout across national boundaries.

Since the "device" used for peaceful explosions is merely a bomb by another name, there is no way a country can achieve the competence to move earth by atomic means without, at the same time, developing the capability to produce nuclear weapons. But, so long as the nuclear nations fail even to establish the institutional mechanisms for putting peaceful explosions at the service of non-nuclear countries, some of those countries will (as India has done) try to justify the development of a nuclear capability on the ground it is needed for peaceful purposes. With this in mind, I proposed in the mid-1960s that we establish an entity (perhaps a multinational public corporation) in partnership with the Soviet Union and other nuclear powers that would contract with non-nuclear countries to conduct public works projects for them, either for a fee or — under the appropriate circumstances — as a grant.

Unhappily, the project suffered from the frictional drag of the bureaucracy; and — although substantial effort was invested in working through the problems it presented — the project lost momentum and stopped dead in its tracks after I resigned from the State Department in 1966.

Still, it would be worth doing something of the sort today, if only to show the non-nuclear nations our good-faith intention to carry out Article V. We would probably not be called on actually to use the techniques of Operation Plowshare, but by making case-by-case studies of specific projects we could demonstrate the practical limitations of the technique. At least, we could help show our honest intentions by undertaking a serious international study of the problem.

No matter how resolutely we strive to limit the nuclear club, it will almost certainly continue to grow during the years ahead. Yet the greatest danger is not additional members as such; it is that "irresponsible" governments may come to command fearsome weapons of destruction — a danger that gains reality from the prospect of Third World political disintegration described in the last chapter. The suffocation of political institutions under the stifling weight of huge populations is likely, in some countries, to bring to power reckless leaders who, armed with nuclear weapons, could turn local conflicts into large ones. (Imagine General Amin with his finger on the button!)

Nor is the danger confined merely to governments. Terrorism is the most dynamic growth industry in a number of overpopulated countries, and the chances are high that at some point a desperate gang (quite likely with student elements) will either steal a bomb or enough enriched uranium or weapons-grade plutonium to make one. After all, a crude explosive device can now be constructed by almost any bright Ph.D. in physics. What, then, will be the world's reaction if we awaken some morning to hear the eight o'clock news reporting an event that follows the plot line of the movie we saw the night before, with terrorists holding a whole city or country as hostage? Of course, we will take frantic measures to tighten nuclear procedures, but the world will never seem the same again, for, because of the suggestibility of the lunatic mind, events in the same pattern may occur with accelerating frequency. Think of the possibilities of collusion between governments and terrorist gangs, with the governments secretly assisting nationalist or irredentist organizations to obtain weapons and put forward demands which the governments themselves might find it inconvenient to urge. The basic assumptions underlying our theories of deterrence are made dubious by the obvious inappropriateness of retaliation in a situation such as that.

It is easy to conclude pessimistically that an America which lacks the political will to control the domestic sale of guns even to morons and murderers will prove quite as flabby and ineffective in keeping nuclear bombs out of the hands of terrorists or lunatic governments. (To echo the immortal wisdom of the National Rifle Association: "Nukes don't kill people, people do.") Yet the possibilities latent in the simultaneous spread of terrorism and nuclear weapons are the stuff of which nightmares are made.

Fortunately, there are at least faint signs of a new consciousness of this problem in United States governmental circles today. Perhaps the reckless proposals of the French and Germans to sell processing plants and other technology that facilitate the production of bombs by non-nuclear powers will stimulate more effective action. At least the principal supplying nations — the United States, the Soviet Union, Britain, France, Canada, West Germany, and Japan — met in London during July of 1975 and again in November and the American representatives tried hard to confront other nuclear powers with the enormity of the perils they were creating. Though the meeting apparently produced some strengthened guidelines, France and West Germany seem to have blocked essential American proposals to embargo the export of equipment and technology for the production of weapons-grade plutonium, the explosive material for nuclear bombs.[4] Ideally, of course, all nuclear problems should be discussed in the presence of the acquiring, as well as the supplying, nations. But the International Atomic Energy Agency in Vienna is not the best place for secret talks and the French in particular were fearful of leaks.

The time has come for the United States to take an extremely hard line to check the movement toward proliferation, which is rapidly gaining momentum. Above all, we must resist the virus of defeatism, encouraged by commercial greed and the specious rationalizations that go with it. The spokesmen for commercial interests are loudly heard. America, they contend, should stop trying to tighten down controls on the sale of nuclear equipment, since that results only in diverting the business to other nations with less sense of responsibility; if the United States is to influence proliferation, we must dominate the market. Moreover, it is argued, proliferation may be good for us, since, in the words of one writer, "a world in which every country possessed a few nuclear bombs might be a very peaceful world, since, as a last resort, any country could wreak intolerable damage upon any aggressor." [5]

In the environment that exists today — where the political legitimacy of governments is widely called into question and despots are not required to pass lunacy tests — we cannot afford to be put off by such seductive nonsense. Instead, the President should make it a prime objective of policy to explain the deteriorating situation to the American people, tighten even further the restrictions on nuclear sales by the United States, and utilize all available sanctions on the supplying governments to adhere strictly to agreed guidelines that will make proliferation increasingly difficult. We must, for example, continue to insist, even more strongly, that when and if it becomes economical to reprocess materials made available to the non-nuclear powers, such operation take place outside the recipient country. There is great merit in Secretary Kissinger's proposal for the construction of multinational regional nuclear fuel cycle centers, so long as it does not encourage governments to acquire national reprocessing facilities in addition to such centers, and we should make a strong drive, and spend whatever money is necessary, to give effect to that proposal.

Nor should the United States hesitate to use its full leverage to stop non-nuclear nations from acquiring processing plants that might move them substantially closer to building a nuclear weapon. We have clout and should use it more resolutely. In the case of Korea, not only do we have a defense relationship that the South Koreans regard as vital to their own security, but until sometime in the 1980s we will continue to be the "Arabs of enriched uranium," with a substantial monopoly over fuel supplies.

When the United States sells a reactor, it normally contracts to provide a continuing fuel supply and since, for the time being, practically all our production of enriched uranium is covered by long-term sales contracts, we would risk highly costly lawsuits if we sought to enforce new restrictions not contained in those contracts.[6] Nevertheless, the consequences of proliferation could be so grave that we should not hesitate to use what sanctions we have, no matter how financially expensive, to discourage non-nuclear nations from acquiring enrichment or plutonium separation facilities, or taking any other steps that might move them down the nuclear road. Certainly, in new contracts we should insist on explicitly reserving the power to withhold fuel if the recipient country should take any measures that might appear, in our judgment, as possibly pointing toward the acquisition of a nuclear capability. Moreover, we should carefully reexamine — preferably in consultation with other supplying countries — the dubious practice of transferring reactors to countries that have not first signed and ratified the Non-Proliferation Treaty. To be sure, that might inhibit us in providing political bribes in aid of tactical diplomatic maneuvers, but it would be a price well worth paying.

Only the United States can effectively mobilize the supplying powers to halt the proliferation of nuclear weapons, and there should be no more pressing item on our agenda. There is little point in talking about building a structure of world peace if that structure can be undermined by the spread of nuclear competence to governments of uncertain stability at a time when the world is entering a period of political unraveling. The importunings of commercial interests, the anxiety to improve the balance of payments, the temptation to use nuclear transfers as diplomatic bribes, and the blandishments and rationalizations of special pleaders — all such pressures must be sternly resisted if we are to avoid complicating an already intricate and increasingly crowded world by a new calculus of forces that could upset the fragile equilibria on which the peace now depends. So our leaders should take care that, by their careless actions, they do not validate President Eisenhower's forebodings about the military-industrial complex, just as they should be sharply on guard that, as a result of their weakness or cupidity, the capitalist system does not fulfill Karl Marx's dark prophecy by perishing from its own greed.

Nuclear bombs are not the only weapons capable of vast destruction, merely the most efficient. In assessing the consequences that may follow the increasing spread of the means of violence, we must also consider the current rapid buildup of sophisticated conventional weapons in the world's actual or potential trouble spots. Whenever the next war takes place in any of several overwrought parts of the world, the two sides will probably shoot at one another with American-made weapons procured by sale or gift through the agency of our own government. When Pakistanis fought Indians in 1965, and when Turks battled Greeks on Cyprus in 1964, both sides used American weapons. In fact, at a time when Secretary Kissinger and President Ford were making poorly veiled threats about the possible need for the United States to utilize military force to obtain oil from the Arab states, America was just concluding a sale of arms to Saudi Arabia, the largest Arab oil-producing country, amounting to over seven hundred million dollars.

Quite as much as the proliferation of nuclear weapons, America's aggressive promotion of arms sales adds a lunatic dimension to our military-industrial collaboration. Unlike the situation with any other product, the Government acts as an unabashed sales agent for American producers, who make the profits. Special military missions, as well as military attachés assigned to our embassies in foreign lands, try vigorously to persuade their local opposite numbers not merely to acquire American military equipment but to acquire the most sophisticated and costly items.

The Pentagon has a large vested interest in this system. Overseas sales of a weapon or piece of equipment lengthen the factory runs and help amortize research and development costs, thus reducing prices and enabling our military services to buy more for their money. The civilian side of the government also has reason to favor such sales. During the 1960s, when the White House was obsessed by America's chronic balance-of-payments deficits, it encouraged the Secretary of Defense to establish a high-pressure military sales office in the Pentagon that sent its drummers all over the world pushing American military products. Today, with the economy at a low ebb, Washington is under pressure to increase the sale of arms around the world so as to maintain the financial health of the defense — and particularly the aerospace — industry, which employs a tremendous labor force. Finally, to the special gratification of the United States Treasury, the sale of American military equipment to the oil-exporting countries is playing a useful role in recycling surplus oil money.

Our diplomats share the Pentagon's interest in arms sales because military equipment provides a ready currency for the acquisition of forward bases, as in Spain, and the right to establish intelligence installations, as in Turkey. Moreover, such military aid can be used to bribe military juntas or dictators in poor countries, as well as to help maintain in power governments dependent for their support on local military leaders.

Secretary of State Kissinger, in particular, has, from the beginning, profligately used the transfer of weapons to persuade nations to accept terms of settlement with their neighbors they would otherwise reject, as in negotiations involving Israel and South Vietnam.

Last, but by no means least, many American companies welcome government help in promoting exports that in 1974 amounted to well over eleven billion dollars, and something more than that in 1975.

The United States is not alone in this practice, merely the most successful. Other Western nations — particularly France, Britain, Italy, West Germany, Sweden, Switzerland, and Canada — are equally aggressive arms merchants for many of the same reasons that make the business attractive to the United States; while the Soviet Union is second only to America in pushing its arms on the world and Poland and Czechoslovakia also export large quantities.

In any situation where military and commercial motives so neatly converge, rationality is likely to be the first victim. Developing countries that cannot afford it are constantly increasing their share of total purchases. Far too often, our military missions encourage them to buy arms beyond their reasonable security requirements to gratify the whims of military leaders who control the levers of power. Since those nations are peculiarly vulnerable to the disintegrative forces I have described in earlier chapters, the process is likely to increase the means of violence in the hands of irresponsible governments and even outlaw groups (particularly since some of the arms we sell are transferred, with or without our permission, to other governments), while swelling magnitudes of sophisticated equipment (some from the vast supplies we left behind in South Vietnam) are finding their way into black market channels.

In defense of such arms sales, we hear the all-purpose answer that has been used to justify nonsense ever since the invention of bureaucracy: if we do not do it, other nations will. In other words, if America is to exercise any control over world stability, we must preempt the international arms trade. But, though the thesis has a seductive plausibility, it is not borne out by experience. The essence of the rationalization is that, if an acquiring nation acts in any way against American interests, we have the power to shut off the flow of spare parts and thus bring its military operations to a halt. In addition, it is argued, we gain a long-term hold over that nation's policies, since it would take years to reequip its forces with arms from other sources and even longer to retrain its forces in the use of different equipment. Yet when Turkey violated the restrictions, both of American law and the agreements under which we supplied it arms to meet its NATO obligations, by using those weapons to invade Cyprus, the Secretary of State tried hard to look the other way. Again, the fact that the Soviet Union had, for more than twenty years, supplied the principal weaponry for the Egyptian armed forces did not deter President Sadat in 1974 from expelling Soviet representatives when political relations deteriorated. Nor did the fact that we were the sole arms supplier for South Vietnam mean that President Thieu would ever take our advice to broaden the base of his government.

In practice, the leverage attributable to the supplier of arms is largely illusory. Nor is there much merit to the argument that, if we do not supply arms to unstable governments, or governments in unstable areas, other suppliers will. The United States today is supplying by far the largest share of all the arms sold or granted to foreign countries each year. If we dropped out of the arms-peddling business, the sale of arms would vastly decline. Not only would the other supplying nations lack the capacity to supply more than a fraction of the present total, but sales would no longer be stimulated either by America's military representatives or the itinerant peddlers of American munitions makers all competing against one another and, as recent revelations make clear, with their pockets full of baksheesh.

Still, I do not believe for a moment that we will ever stop all foreign arms sales, nor do I believe that we should. Not only are there far too many vested interests that would block a complete self-denying ordinance, but there are clear instances where our national interest would require us to make arms available to some threatened country, and I remember all too well the folly of the Neutrality Act of 1935.

But what the statistics vividly show is that the traffic is currently out of control. Particularly with mounting sales and grants of arms to the troubled Middle East, the curve of our arms transfers has mounted alarmingly — from $8.5 billion in 1973 to $11 billion in 1974, and almost $12.5 billion in 1975. To be sure, some of the increases in the dollar cost of sales and grants can be attributed either to inflation or to the augmentation of prices resulting from the increasing sophistication of the products. Yet that is by no means a complete answer, for any increase in the sophistication of weapons presumably adds to their destructive power, which, in the final analysis, should be the measure of our concern.

So far, that concern has found far greater expression in the Congress than in the Executive Department. In 1974, Congress approved the Nelson Amendment, requiring submission to Congress of all proposed arms sales above the level of $25 million, and in November 1975, Senator Hubert Humphrey introduced legislation that would subject the foreign arms traffic to Congressional restrictions.[7] Senator Humphrey noted that in the last three decades America had given away or sold some $110 billion in military equipment and supplies to foreign countries. Under his proposed bill, both grant military assistance programs and United States military missions abroad would be phased out over a two-year period; statutory controls over military exports would be strengthened and all government-to-government sales made a matter of public record. Finally, Congress would be given the power to revoke or suspend sales contracts or export licenses. Legislation of this kind is an essential first step in establishing some control over the current flow of arms exports. Yet it does not, as the Senator frankly recognizes, create a policy but merely provides a mechanism through which a policy can be carried out.

If we are to avoid the frightening confluence of forces generated by the developments outlined in the past three chapters, we will have to move promptly and incisively on several fronts. We must mobilize the political will and the physical resources to slow the world's demographic growth within the next two decades. We must check the proliferation of nuclear weapons — a trend that is gaining momentum every month. We must dam up the flow of conventional arms not merely by self-constraint but by organizing the major supplying powers to embargo the movement of weapons into turbulent areas. We must initiate cooperative efforts to suppress kidnapping and terrorism.

So far we have seen only the beginning of an era of turmoil

and destruction we are aggravating by our own carelessness with destructive weapons — and we must be careful not to get used to violence. The capacity of contemporary man to adapt to changing conditions, to become so accustomed to outrage as to regard it as normal, goes hand-in-hand with a moral relativism that rejects all absolute values. We witnessed the phenomenon in Nazi Germany, where apparently decent citizens yielded to the obscene madness of a poisonous society. I once asked Albert Speer, who headed war production for the Nazis, how he, an ostensibly civilized man, could have been intellectually and emotionally capable of spending his days and nights with the gross thugs and gangsters in the Hitler entourage. "When you live your life in the dim light of an aquarium, everything takes on a strange reality," he replied. "Once you get outside and look in, you wonder how you ever could have stood it." Well, the light of our world aquarium will quite likely grow dimmer over the years ahead, and already some of us are beginning to accept mindless violence as routine. A society that has lost its capacity for astonishment adjusts easily to murders and bomb outrages even in great cities such as London or New York.

Today the whole system of ambassadorial immunity established since the sixteenth century is threatened by desperate men and women moved by greed or anger or intemperate zeal. The medieval concept of hostages has been revived to increase the leverage of fanatics and felons; the airplane has become an instrument of extortion. Marauding bands roam the countryside in several Latin American countries, urban gangs flourish in cities of several continents. Machine guns chatter from the rooftops, bombs burst under automobiles on quiet streets — and still we have seen only the prelude.

Easy access to the means of violence will give terror a new dimension. Science has magnified the destructive power of the individual, while complex societies have become far more vulnerable to disruption by the nihilist. If the possession of increasingly lethal weapons will expand terrorists' ability to tear down governments and create political chaos, that chaos, in turn, will give the gangs access to even more powerful weapons. Terrorists with hand-held rockets have a meaning quite different from terrorists with pistols, for their extirpation becomes not the affair of police but of armies — and to use armies against citizens is the beginning of civil war.

The importance of terrorists as a political force is multiplied by another factor: the most militant of them are recruited from the frustrated idealists — the educated young, increasingly unable to find places for themselves in overcrowded societies. Ideologically driven, they pose a deadly menace to complex but vulnerable economies. Terrorism professionalized is no longer casual but operates with lunatic logic.

One of the central objectives of the terrorist is to invite repression, and governments beset by terrorists almost inevitably become repressive. Thus, terrorists have a unique ability to destroy liberal societies and create dictatorships and force the step from inhumane to irresponsible governments. The dictator who is indifferent to justice becomes the megalomaniac who is indifferent to suffering, to the destruction of whole populations. Yet it is the probability of an increasing number of irresponsible rulers that makes our careless handing out of conventional weapons so foolish and dangerous and our permissive attitude toward nuclear proliferation so reckless and stupid.

Since political instability is most likely to develop in the poor and overpopulated areas of the world, it may be well to turn our attention for a moment to the problems of poverty and the disparities of wealth among nations.

CHAPTER 15

The First, Third, Fourth, and Fifth Worlds

THROUGHOUT THE CENTURIES MILITARY COMMANDERS PRAC-
ticed economic warfare, imposing blockades and besieging cas-
tles, while wars were fought in a struggle for trade routes. But it is
only in the last half-century that economics has assumed a commanding place in international relations. No longer are economic
problems the exclusive concern of finance ministers and central
bankers; they are a major subject of foreign policy. Diplomats
shape rules to enhance the stability of economic relations; foreign
ministers give lectures on oil prices and world inflation; even
heads of state and chiefs of government assemble at economic
seminars, as occurred at Rambouillet in November 1975.

At no time has American leadership been more effective than
when we helped construct a framework for economic cooperation
among the nations of the West during the later days of the Second
World War and in the two decades that followed. The critical turning point was the Marshall Plan; had we not helped to rebuild
Europe, the whole history of the world since that time would have
been quite different. Soviet adventurism would have been encouraged, for there would have been no NATO. Nor would the
West have enjoyed the great period of economic growth that
began in the early 1950s. But, fortunately, we did carry out the
Marshall Plan; we helped construct the Bretton Woods institutions

and establish the GATT; the Organization for European Economic Cooperation (which we later joined as the OECD) evolved from the Marshall Plan; and we encouraged Europeans as they undertook first to create the European Coal and Steel Community and then the European Economic Community.

Many elements combined to make possible this succession of achievements, of which no doubt most important was the quality of the American leaders. A second factor was Adenauer's anxiety to end Franco-German rivalry and incorporate his people within the framework of a larger Europe to protect the German people against themselves. A third was the weakness of the French Fourth Republic, which made it clear to the people that they could not fulfill their aspirations through the instrument of a middle-sized nation-state in a world where not only economics but politics were affected by requirements of scale. Then came a period of retrogression that began when the Fourth Republic, whose very weakness had encouraged it to accept the broad concept of European unity, proved too irresolute to extricate France from Algeria without calling on a strong man.

Unhappily, De Gaulle's assault on European unity, which greatly chilled American hopes for Atlantic progress, occurred just at the time that Washington was becoming increasingly absorbed in the frustrations of Vietnam. The restrained but evident disapproval of United States policy by our European allies — who regarded that war as imprudent and irrelevant — turned a beleaguered American Government even more inward, thus removing its dominant voice from Western councils.

Adding to the distraction of Vietnam, the Nixon Administration's fascination with the Second World, as the Communist nations have been called, left it little time for the First World of Western democracies. The common economic problems that continued to pile up fell by default largely to the parochial whims of a narrowly focused Treasury Department, while the State Department, which had for years given a strong — and, for the most part, a wise — lead in international economic matters, effectively opted out.

Undoubtedly, if Western Europe and the United States continue to drift farther apart in their political preoccupations, while their economic structures undergo divergent change, cooperation in vital economic matters could become increasingly difficult and unsatisfactory. Undoubtedly, the differing impact of the high oil prices — and a potential oil embargo — on individual industrialized countries is a potential cause for abrasive friction. Moreover, although the potential strain on the Western banking structure from the excessive buildup of unused reserves in the Middle East has not materialized to the extent feared, that has been due in considerable part to massive arms purchases, which are anything but a healthy solution. Meanwhile, the whole industrialized world has been deeply troubled by the fact that "stagflation" has affected all of the major economies at roughly the same time. During most of the last three decades the fact that some economies expanded rapidly while others moved at a far slower pace served as a useful stabilizer, since mounting prosperity in one nation tended to assist the recovery of another. But with the trends running substantially all in the same direction, the advanced nations have experienced a pervasive stagflation, with economies ticking over at a reduced level while inflation and unemployment have persisted intractably.

American leadership during this period has been lamentably deficient, either in wisdom or sensitivity to the problems of other nations. Yet, even at its current unsatisfactory level, there is a strong commitment on the part of the major industralized powers not to let economic rivalries produce self-destructive actions of restrictionism and retaliation. The mechanisms of cooperation are in place, and governments know how to work them. Where the industrialized countries have been in far less agreement, however, is on how they should shape their relations with those nations that have not yet crossed the industrial threshold.

Historically, the external economic relations of the peoples in the poorer areas of the globe were internal matters of the great imperial systems. International economic affairs concerned little more than the ground rules and special arrangements by which one empire dealt with another. But, with the creation of almost one hundred new nations, economic relations became far more complex. That the nations emerging from the cocoons of colonial systems required special treatment was obvious. Their economies were far too weak to stand exposure to the liberal trading, investment, and monetary policies of the mature industrialized nations of the north.

Beginning with President Truman's inaugural address proposing the Point Four program in 1949, the advanced nations tried — with varying degrees of vigor — to respond to the plight of the poor nations. Inspired by the success of the Marshall Plan, which dealt with quite a different problem, the United States established an elaborate foreign aid organization to help the governments of poor countries finance their development, ranging from technical training to the building of vast infrastructure projects. But little attention was paid to the structure of trade between what Sir Oliver Franks perceptively described as the North and South — the economically advanced nations primarily in the Northern Hemisphere and the poor nations primarily in the Southern. Preferential trading relations had existed within the great colonial empires, with colonies producing raw materials for the industries of the colonial power. The various parts of the French empire had been permitted special trading privileges with the metropole on a reciprocal basis, while the British had also maintained a preferential system throughout the Commonwealth. Thus, the membership of France in the Common Market and the prospective membership of Britain brought into relief the far-reaching consequences of attaching their combined preferential systems to a trading unit as large as Europe.

This raised the central question as to how North-South relations and responsibilities should be organized. The world might be regarded as an apple cut into vertical slices, with lines of special privilege and responsibility running directly north and south. Thus, Europe would establish special reciprocal trading preferences with the Francophile states of Africa and the members of the British Commonwealth, which would inevitably trigger demands for the United States to establish a special trading regime with Latin America. Such a concept would almost certainly have implications beyond mere trading relations; it would be assumed that Europe would undertake primary responsibility for helping Africa develop, while America would undertake the same responsibility for Latin America. Not only would such a scheme result in an artificial and, hence, uneconomic use of world resources, but it would leave certain nations outside either the American or European preferential systems.

Since that seemed to me quite undesirable, I took the initiative during the Kennedy Administration of trying to persuade both

France and Britain to phase out their preference systems so as to bring about a world free from special trading regimes. I proposed that the major industrial nations should take generalized responsibility for helping the development of the less developed nations on a nondiscriminatory basis. Although these efforts did not then succeed, successive rounds of trade negotiations have since reduced the significance of industrial tariffs to the point where preferences no longer play the major role they once did. At the same time, progress has been made in putting many raw materials on free lists and in providing easier access to the major markets for some products of tropical agriculture.

A quite different proposal for generalized preferences was devised by Dr. Raoul Prebisch, an Argentinian economist, who, after impressive preliminary work, promoted a vast meeting that convened in Geneva in 1964. Attended by one hundred twenty-two nations, the meeting lasted three months and produced a number of resolutions, of which the most important was Dr. Prebisch's concept that the advanced countries should grant preferential access to their markets for the industrial products of underdeveloped countries.

Although sympathetic to the objectives of the developing countries, I felt compelled to tell the United Nations Conference on Trade and Development (UNCTAD, as it was called) that what they were seeking was not politically feasible. Labor-intensive industries in the United States were then pressing hard for restrictions on imports from the less developed countries, using the old argument about the unfair advantages of cheap labor. Refutable as it was by the rational answers we persistently gave, the "cheap labor" contention always found strong resonance in the Congress. Since we were, thus, hard-pressed to resist discriminatory restrictions against imports from the poor countries, it was quite impracticable to propose that we encourage those imports by preferential treatment. Although I disappointed the UNCTAD Conference and no doubt created the impression that I was indifferent to the predicament of the poor countries — which was far from the truth — it would have been a great disservice had we raised expectations we could not fulfill.

The Soviet representative, however, felt no such inhibitions, assuring the meeting, to enthusiastic applause, that his country would abolish all customs duties on the products from developing countries. Unfortunately, most of the delegates did not understand that, because the Soviet Union procured all its imports through state trading arrangements, tariffs had never been a factor in the first place.

For several years prior to the UNCTAD Conference, the industrialized countries had been steadily increasing the volume of their foreign aid. But, later, as the attention of the United States Government was focused first on Vietnam and then on cultivating the major Communist powers, the plight of the developing countries tended to receive less and less attention, while the economic slowdown in the advanced countries depressed world commodity prices. Finally, at the beginning of 1974, the action of the OPEC cartel in quadrupling the price of oil greatly aggravated the problems of those developing nations that were not oil producers. Possessing few other sources of energy, those nations faced mounting deficits in their balance of payments which they could finance only by adding to their already formidable external debts or by further reducing desperately low standards of living.

With the OPEC price action, the so-called Third World ceased to be an homogeneous group. The members of OPEC assumed a special position as the true Third World countries. A second group that had already achieved a considerable growth momentum, such as Taiwan, South Korea, Brazil, Israel, and Singapore, could properly be called the Fourth World countries, while at the bottom of the list was a Fifth World, consisting of nations such as Bangladesh, whose prospects for even holding their own are exceedingly dim.

During the first months of the oil crisis, abnormally warm winters and a worldwide recession cushioned the impact of exorbitant oil prices for the United States and the other industrialized countries. But that recession also reduced the earnings of the developing countries from their exports of commodities and other products, thus tending to aggravate, rather than mitigate, their hardship. It is not surprising that these events generated increasing agitation throughout the poor countries for a larger share of world income — especially since ferment had been at work for some time. The poor nations had tried to launch an organized drive to establish their claim for a larger share of the world's

wealth as early as two decades ago at the Bandung Afro-Asian
Conference in 1955. They renewed the effort at the first Non-
Aligned Nations Conference in Belgrade in 1961. Now, both encouraged and dismayed by OPEC's success, they began in 1974 to
restate their demands with such vehemence as to lead to predictions of a north-south Cold War. Formulated with increasingly
shrill rhetoric, those demands commanded impressive majorities
in the bloc-ridden General Assembly and other bodies under the
United Nations umbrella, even though the votes had only propaganda effect.

What was to be done by way of response? In a widely noted
article in *Commentary* magazine,[1] Daniel Patrick Moynihan, who
had just resigned as ambassador to India and was soon to be appointed United States Permanent Representative to the United
Nations, argued that the United States should "go into opposition"
against the Third World countries. As ambassador to India, Mr.
Moynihan had observed the influence of Fabian socialism on an
elite largely educated at British universities (and particularly the
London School of Economics, where he himself had studied). He
gave the Fabian socialists credit for the insistent theme of the
more radical nations that they were entitled to reparations for the
exploitation they had suffered at the hands of the colonial powers,
which had benefited from a vast store of "unethically accumulated
wealth." Although the Moynihan article made some valid points,
it generalized too much from the author's own limited exposure.
Two states that led the drive for an increased share of the world's
income were Algeria, which had emerged not from the British but
the French colonial system, and Mexico, which had not been a
colony since 1821.

For a substantial period, the United States largely ignored
these demands, leaving the debate in United Nations forums to
bureaucrats addicted to the soft answer. Kissinger took note of the
poor nations' campaign only by remarking that "we cannot accept
unrealistic proposals." Unsuccessful in trying to organize a
counter-cartel against the oil-producing states, he rebuffed every
suggestion that we might cooperate with the OPEC nations in
providing assistance to other developing countries. Even when he
felt compelled by European pressures to accept the idea of a
meeting with the OPEC states, he held out against expanding the

agenda to include commodities other than oil, thus, in the eyes of the developing countries, turning his back on their most pressing problem.

Meanwhile, the drive of the more radical countries picked up increasing momentum. The Sixth Special Session of the United Nations General Assembly, convened in May 1974 to study the problems of raw materials and development, adopted a declaration calling for the General Assembly to work urgently for the establishment of a "New International Economic Order."

The positions taken at that meeting and at the later General Assembly session in September 1974 posed disturbing problems, of both a legal and economic nature. Historically, the United States had always maintained that resolutions of the General Assembly were not international law. But the Group of Seventy-seven and the nonaligned states contended that, since they had not been states at the time international law was developed, they were not bound by any of the rules and that they could now rewrite international law through General Assembly resolutions.

Although the substantive grievances of the poor nations made a long list, they boiled down to a relatively few contentions.[2] Fundamental was the argument that the countries producing primary materials (excluding oil) were receiving too small a share of the final price paid for their products. While the exports of about twelve major primary commodities (excluding, again, oil) accounted for roughly 80 percent of the total export earnings of the developing countries, those countries received only about fifty billion dollars out of a total of more than two hundred billion dollars paid by the final consumer. Moreover, their export earnings fluctuated violently, while their purchasing power kept declining in terms of manufactured imports. Beyond that, the developing countries were far too dependent on primary commodities. Their exports of manufactures accounted for only 7 percent of the world total and were subject, in many cases, to discriminatory tariffs and quotas in the markets of the industrialized countries.

What the developing countries asked, therefore, was for a greater share of the final consumer price. That might be obtained by locating processing facilities in the primary producing countries, improving commodity markets, and by allocating a larger share of transfer prices (which, the poor nations contended, were often arbitrarily fixed by multinational corporations to their disadvantage), and so on. That was the first step; once measures had been taken to assure the producing countries higher returns from their primary commodities, those higher returns should be protected by price stabilization or indexing and by recognizing producers' cartels as legitimate units for international collective bargaining to offset the concentration of economic power in the hands of the consuming countries. Finally, they demanded that there be an end to discriminatory measures against the import of their manufactured products into markets of the industrialized countries and that their manufactures be accorded preferential tariff treatment in those markets.

Because a considerable part of foreign aid has been extended on a debt basis at something approaching commercial terms, the developing countries have accumulated over $120 billion in external obligations, which means that half of the fresh assistance every year has to be applied to servicing debt already outstanding. To gain some security of income, they demanded that at least a minimum of resources should automatically be transferred each year through some linkage with Special Drawing Rights (SDRs) in the International Monetary Fund or through royalties from oceanbed mining or a tax on nonrenewable resources.

With the pressure of these demands rapidly mounting, the United States could no longer afford to give evasive answers. The time had come for the Department of State to reassert its authority in foreign economic matters, to free United States policy from the parochial restrictions imposed by the Treasury and, by putting forward affirmative proposals, to show that America understood, and sympathized with, the predicament of the developing countries. Since the United States had demonstrated on past occasions that, once it made up its mind, it could produce results, the assembled nations listened with great attention when, on September 1, 1974, a statement was read by Ambassador Moynihan in the name of the Secretary of State (who was, as usual, shuttling about the Middle East).

It was a comprehensive statement. Unlike most of the Secretary's other speeches that were drafted within the small closed circle of his personal staff, it reflected the views of experts throughout the Department and, indeed, throughout the Government. Quite clearly, it was intended as a signal not that we were "going into opposition" but, rather, that we were ending a year and a half of confrontation between the United States and the "Group of Seventy-seven" (actually more than a hundred) developing nations, during which the United States had stood almost alone.

The Kissinger speech took account of most of the complaints of the developing countries. Instead of encouraging cartels of commodity producers, it proposed to approach the problem of fluctuating income of primary producing countries not so much by trying to stabilize commodity prices as by stabilizing earnings. Thus, America would support the creation of a special fund from which loans could be made to countries suffering commodity price fluctuations. Part of the financing of this proposal could come from a trust fund that might be raised by the sale of some of the gold held by the International Monetary Fund. Although commodity agreements were largely rejected in favor of measures to stabilize earnings, room was still left for an international food stock (in which the United States had great interest as a producer). In addition it was suggested that we might extend the buffer stock idea to certain commodities other than food.

The coolness of the speech to commodity agreements was well founded. During the early 1960s, I had put the State Department experts to work exploring the whole field with an open mind. We had then tried to develop such agreements in several commodity areas. The experience had not been reassuring. For agricultural products, the multiplicity of producers made discipline hard to maintain among suppliers, while the problem of storing perishable foodstuffs limited the utility of buffer stocks. In the case of metals and minerals, ease of substitution often limited the extent to which a competitive price structure could be maintained. The problem was further complicated because the developed countries, while principal consumers of the commodities, also produced a large percentage.

If the raw-material-producing countries wanted price stabilization, the consumer countries were equally interested in assured access to commodities. Thus the Kissinger speech proposed that, in the forthcoming trade negotiations, measures should be negotiated to prevent producing countries from abruptly restricting exports to the injury of traditional trading partners, as the United States had itself done in the case of soya beans in 1973.

Taking account of the extremely limited regime of generalized preferences possible under existing trade legislation, the Kissinger speech also suggested that we would try to eliminate some of the tariffs of the industrialized countries that operated to discourage the processing of raw materials in the developing countries. Although in theory the industrialized countries should relinquish an increasing share of the production of labor-intensive light manufactures to the Fourth World, that theory is not easy to translate into action against the resistance of vested labor and management in the West. The counterpressures of environmentalists, however, may facilitate the transfer of some processing operations that result in substantial pollution.

Mr. Kissinger tacitly acknowledged that, if the developing countries were to have a basis for long-range planning, they must be assured a minimum flow of revenue not dependent on annual appropriations by the developed countries. Thus, his speech suggested that, if other nations would cooperate, the United States might agree to the imposition of an international royalty on the value of oil and gas from the 200-meter depth mark out to the edge of the continental margin. This, it has been estimated, might provide at least two billion dollars in international revenue for aid purposes, starting in 1985, and moving up to about six billion dollars in the year 2000.

Finally, the speech attempted to meet the demands of the developing countries for the more effective transfer of technology, proposing both an international energy institute and an international industrialization institute. Whether anything concrete will come of these proposals remains to be seen.

This glittering Christmas basket of projects was useful as a palliative, yet it was largely a gathering together of measures under discussion for many years; the basket contained few new ideas and many appear more impressive than the benefits they are likely to produce. The test of American seriousness will come in the future. How far will the United States actually go in trying to press to fulfillment various proposals it has made?

Clearly, the rationale on which we maintained large aid programs in the early 1960s is no longer adequate. We justified those programs primarily as a weapon in the Cold War. Continued poverty without hope of improvement meant, as we then saw it, that nations would be vulnerable to subversion and infiltration by agents of the major Communist powers. To a considerable extent, our aid was, therefore, a kind of political bribe, designed to keep poor countries on our side. But we used it also as payment for the maintenance of forward bases and intelligence facilities and the support of alliances.

Today we are by no means as certain as we once were that instability will automatically enable the major Communist powers to extend their influence. It is quite as likely to produce local dictatorships of the right or indigenous forms of Communism that look more to Havana than to Moscow. Nor can we any longer take it for granted, as many did in the 1960s, that all areas of the world are of sufficient strategic importance to be worth the investment of American blood or even treasure; the Vietnam experience has taught us that lesson.

Thus, in seeking to justify major assistance to the developing countries, we should no longer think primarily in Cold War terms. At the same time, there is no logic in the contention of the more radical developing states that they are entitled to receive a large share of the world's wealth as compensation for their exploitation under colonialism. Can any country conclusively demonstrate that it is economically worse off as a result of its colonial experience? How fast would it have developed had it been left to itself? How would India have fared, for example, if the British had stayed home and it had continued to be governed by several hundred maharajahs, nizams, and other princely potentates? Certainly, we Americans should feel no obligation to compensate any country for our past activities. We were never a colonial power — except very briefly and expensively — and we left our colonial possessions far richer than we found them. As a former collection of colonies, the United States has, in theory, as much claim to receive compensation as does Mexico, one of the most vocal members of the Group of Seventy-seven, which broke free from colonial domination only fifty years after we did.

Nor can many developing countries demonstrate today that the aid we might provide — whether through special trading arrangements or commodity agreements or outright subsidies — would be distributed among their own people with any semblance of justice. There is no reason for taxing the poorer groups in America to reward a handful of rich who dominate the economic and political life of some wretchedly poor country where the disparities between income groups are far greater than in the West. Nevertheless, if, by our placing restrictions on our foreign assistance, we were to try to assure that funds would be used to narrow the disparities not only between rich and poor countries but between rich and poor classes within beneficiary countries, we would evoke outcries that we were trying to meddle in their internal affairs.

We should make clear, therefore, that America feels no obligation to pay anything that even remotely resembles compensation and that to the extent that we do try to ameliorate the lot of poor countries it is out of our concern for a stable world order and compassion for the peoples rather than any obligation to the governments. Yet we should not deceive ourselves; once we lift the problem out of the context of East-West rivalry, the contention that economic development promotes world order is difficult to sustain, for there is no automatic relation between economic improvement and stability. Indeed, an impoverished and underfed people is likely to be lethargic, rather than restless; revolt and uproar are more likely to be fomented when nations and peoples are moving up the economic scale than when they are stuck at a low level of poverty.

Yet, the feelings of most Americans are revolted by wide disparities between rich and poor. When that feeling is evoked by the disparities within our own country, we tend to attribute it to what we call a social conscience. Recently the idea has been put forward in some intellectual circles that the West may be developing something equivalent to a global social conscience — a "new political sensitivity" that will impel us to think seriously of a worldwide redistribution of wealth and income.[3] Yet, before accepting the idea that the wealth of the industrialized countries should be redistributed, we should be quite clear what we are talking about.

Within America, there is no doubt that we have within recent years been preoccupied — and quite properly so — with trying to improve the lot of the disadvantaged. Here members of our black minority particularly have an indisputable grievance, not merely for the years under slavery but for the discrimination practiced against them since Emancipation. Yet even in this instance we should not forget the distinction between equality under the law and equality of opportunity, which constitute a fundamental part of the American tradition, and the pressure to create equality of condition, which has never been an accepted part of our system.

The same distinction applies to foreign assistance. The most we should, under any circumstances, try to do for developing countries is to help them acquire the technology and equipment and capital and markets that will enable them effectively to utilize their resources — whether human or material — to improve their standard of life. Windy talk of a "new social contract" between north and south — or, stated in the most grandiloquent terms, a "planetary bargain" — does not add illumination to an intricate and troubling problem. It would be folly for us to try to share our own resources in an attempt to create equality of condition; the only result would be a poorer world for everyone.

The basic approach to follow, it seems to me, should be dictated largely by considerations of compassion and justice, and we should not try to conceal our benign motives by overlaying them with rationalizations of self-interest. To make available as genuine assistance to developing countries (untainted by considerations of political or economic advantage) something in the neighborhood of 1 percent of our gross national product seems a minimal effort. Our genuine development aid is, at the moment, running at the rate of only about .33 percent, which is shameful for a country of our wealth and moral pretensions.

Any discussion of north-south relations would be incomplete if it did not take account of the institutions by which we conduct our economic affairs with the developing countries, and particularly of the place in those relations of what has come to be called, with singular infelicity, the "multinational," or "transnational," corporation. Political leaders in the developing countries — aided by a few intellectuals in America — have converted the multinational corporation into a scapegoat through which poverty-stricken peoples can work off their frustrations. Since it represents the presence in a host country of valuable foreign property, it is a convenient target. Because that property is owned by private corporations and not by foreign governments, it can be taken over without major international incident. Expropriation accordingly tempts every local demagogue who finds that a golden egg is politically more useful than the goose that lays it. If the demagogue has Marxist inclinations, he can loudly denounce the world-striding company as a tangible symbol of capitalist exploitation within his country's grasp.

Ever since gunboat diplomacy went out of fashion forty years ago, the governments of the home countries of multinational corporations (principally the United States) have found the problem of expropriation singularly baffling. Few seriously challenge either the power or the right of nations to expropriate private properties within their jurisdiction; that is an indisputable attribute of sovereignty. But if an expropriating country does not pay reasonable compensation, the flow of capital to that country will dry up. Moreover, governments of developed countries will not be as eager to replace out of public funds a private capital flow that a developing country has deliberately shut off for temporary gain, or for political or ideological motives.

Concentration on the multinational company as a prime target has been aided by a great deal of irresponsible comment, primarily from the sages of the New Left. They have painted a picture of giant multinational companies ruthlessly exploiting less developed countries, while working hand in glove with the CIA to overthrow unobliging governments. Their documentation betrays a surprising reverence for the past, since they rely heavily on incidents from the 1920s when we did indeed practice gunboat diplomacy.[4] But they also cite the alleged activities of ITT in Chile as validating the thesis that the United States Government and the CIA have been obedient servants of the multinational companies, neglecting to mention that though the ITT did offer to help finance the overthrow of the Allende Government, the United States representatives rejected the offer. As the testimony has clearly shown, the motive of the White House for ordering the CIA to act in Chile was primarily political, reflecting the conviction that a Communist government would provide a center of infection for the entire area. Mr. Nixon was not prepared to "lose" Chile if he could help it. Contrary to the mythology of the New Left romantics, I never knew the CIA, or any other agency, to undertake to harass a left-wing government merely — or primarily — to help an American company. On the contrary, United States business constantly complains that the Department of State and the United States Government do little or nothing to protect their interests when they operate in foreign countries.

Sooner or later, we must strip the multinational corporation of the mythology that surrounds it. It is, after all, the best mechanism we have so far developed for spreading private capital and know-how around the world. So long as we continue to maintain a world environment in which the factors of production can move with reasonable freedom, the multinational company can provide an essential instrument for the flexible deployment of resources. By obtaining raw materials where they can be most efficiently procured, financing where money can be found most cheaply, transforming materials where there is the most favorable conjunction of labor and machinery, transporting them by the most efficient means, and selling the product freely wherever the best markets are available, the multinational company enables mankind to use the world's resources with reasonable efficiency. Indeed, if multinational corporations are permitted to pursue the logic of their evolution far enough, and the international trading environment is progressively freed from restriction, the managers of such enterprises should someday be able to consider the world economy as a whole and make their decisions in that broad framework.

That some kind of regulation must be placed on the activities of the improvised organism called the multinational company seems obvious in order to prevent a variety of possible abuses. Yet if each host state should try, without restraint, to place its own restrictions on the activities of multinational companies, it would destroy their unique capacity for flexibly using and deploying resources. Since such host-state decisions would be made in the narrow context of local advantage, and without regard to the interests of the enterprise as a whole or of other states, the result could be conflicting rules and ultimate strangulation. If we were to let that trend go far enough, the world economic map would be speckled with small autarkic states, each groveling in its own poverty, while our finite stock of natural resources was dissipated by inefficiency.

There is no doubt that some multinational companies are guilty of abuses, including arbitrary transfer pricing that ignores the interests of local governments. Nor are their decisions as to the location of processing or research facilities made primarily to benefit host states. Of course, there is need to regulate their activities, but the problem is how best to arrange it. Ideally, the multinational company should be regulated by an authority that makes its decisions not on the basis of the parochial interests of a single state but of the world economy as a whole.

That was the essence of a proposal I put forward eight years ago in London. It contemplated the negotiation of a multilateral treaty which would establish an international companies law administered by a supranational authority. Under that treaty, a multinational company might apply for an international charter that would give the company the right to operate in the territory of any signatory state, subject to the regulations imposed by the international companies law. The signatory states, for their part, would accept certain rules defining and limiting their right to interfere with the operations of the company, including the provision that, in the event of expropriation, compensation would be determined by some third-party tribunal.

I made it clear that this proposal was decades in advance of its time. Still, it seemed to me that it might be useful to put even a far-out idea in the public domain, so as to stimulate thought and discussion, recognizing that there are a number of other ways to approach the problem. Some would prefer, for example, not to try to move directly toward a supranational arrangement, but to concentrate on developing an informal code that would govern the relations of multinational companies and host states. There have been several private attempts to draw up such a code, and there has been created a United Nations Commission on Transnational Corporations. In the Kissinger speech, the United States Government agreed to participate in negotiating a code of fair treatment among multinationals, host governments, and home governments.

Whether or not anything will come of all this is by no means clear. The anti-enterprise views of many of the developing countries have been vehemently expressed. If they had their way they would render it uneconomic for multinational corporations to make investments and operate effectively. I doubt, in fact, that it is possible to draft guidelines today that would meet the minimum needs of multinational companies while still satisfying the nationalistic feelings of most Fourth and Fifth World countries. Thus it has seemed to me that we might do well to begin less ambitiously. A multilateral treaty along the line I proposed should, in the first instance, be drafted and signed only by developed countries generally hospitable to multinational companies. Later, after more experience had been gained, the provisions of the treaty could be progressively modified to accommodate the needs of a broader list of states. That, after all, has been the course of evolution of other successful multilateral institutions created to deal with international economic problems.

But while we continue to debate the best machinery for reconciling the interests of host states and preserving the useful values of the multinational company, we must not delay effective action to cope with the practices of bribery and corruption on the part of some major companies that have recently been revealed by investigations by the Securities and Exchange Commission and several Congressional committees.

Fully as disturbing as the corruption itself is the reported reaction of some leaders of American business in condoning these corrupt practices as a necessary feature of their operations in certain parts of the world. We hear again all the familiar excuses. Bribery, they contend, is an established part of the economic and social system in many countries, where underpaid bureaucrats are expected to achieve a living wage by supplementing their income through illegal exactions. Moreover, unless American business firms are prepared to pay such involuntary tribute they will lose business to foreign competitors. "When in Rome one must do as the Romans do."

Such hackneyed answers cannot stand analysis. That American business firms are compelled to engage in bribery is disproved by the example of a number of our most successful enterprises, which rigorously reject such practices yet still do enormous business all over the world. Nor can it always be argued that such corruption is a patriotic necessity to prevent the loss of business to foreign competitors to the detriment of the American balance of payments. Lockheed's only competitors for the sale of wide-bodied jets in Japan, for example, were two other American air frame manufacturers. It was a strictly intramural contest.

What all these excuses reflect is a slothful business habit and a fuzzy mentality — which amounts in some cases to gullibility, for the record is replete with bribes paid quite unnecessarily to individuals who in fact have no effective influence or who have pocketed the funds they promised to pass on to influential ministers. Thus I do not find it surprising that many of the same companies identified as practitioners of corruption in their international transactions have also been caught corrupting our domestic electoral process by illegal political contributions. Nor is it surprising that a high percentage of the companies paying bribes are engaged in the sale of military equipment. Although the problem of excessive arms sales by the United States, which I have touched on in Chapter 14, is separate from the question of bribes and kickbacks by multinational companies (since the question of excessive arms sales relates primarily to American Government policy and the role of Pentagon agents as salesmen for our military hardware), the issues are not totally unrelated. The prevalence of bribery merely emphasizes the irresponsibility of our current arms policies. Not only are defense ministers and military commanders in small countries often persuaded by our military representatives on the spot to buy weaponry more advanced than they need — or even, in many cases, more advanced than they can use effectively — but bribes are part of the process of persuasion. Yet it is against American interests for either Pentagon salesmen or American companies to contribute to the delinquency of small nations.

But if most Americans are repelled by the thought that major American enterprises are paying baksheesh to shady characters in far-off countries, what is the best way to stop the practice?

The automatic response in some business circles is that the remedy must be sought, if at all, through international action; otherwise, American companies may be placed under constraints to which their foreign competitors are not subject. In theory, of course, that is right; without doubt we should encourage host governments to enact harsh laws against such corruption, our government should be prepared at all times to cooperate in the apprehension and punishment of offenders, and we should take an active lead in the effort to develop international guidelines. But to rely on such actions alone would mean, in the present climate, avoiding and not facing the problem. Obviously, there is not yet a sufficient common approach among major trading countries to make effective international measures feasible. Measures now being considered by the OECD amount, for example, to little more than a pious expression of disapproval.

So let us be realistic, since this is far too serious a matter to dismiss with a procedural shrug. The only action that could materially reduce the practice — and mitigate its consequences — is for the United States Government to utilize its powers as the domiciliary state of most of the largest multinational companies by enacting and enforcing comprehensive laws imposing on American corporations a standard of conduct in their overseas dealings fully as strict as that required at home. Only when that is done will our government be able to speak with authority in shaping an international set of rules and sanctions. Having put our own house in order, we will be entitled to demand that foreign governments do likewise — and, in time, this procedure should gradually bring some solid results.

Perhaps the most efficacious means of policing such rules would be to entrust the task to the Securities and Exchange Commission, directing the commission to make public not only information as to the payment of bribes but also the details of those payments and the names of recipients. Although Mr. Kissinger might not like this procedure, it would not only deter corporate managements by exposing them to bad publicity and even shareholders' suits but it might also discourage assiduous middlemen in foreign countries and even impose new standards of discretion on foreign officials.

To be sure, for a limited time span some American companies might lose certain business opportunities, but that is an expense we should be able to tolerate for the good health of our political and economic system.

Thus I would suggest that American businessmen should not be guided by narrow, short-term considerations but ponder the full implications of the current predicament.

Excuses for collaborating in corruption reflect not only the counsels of moral bankruptcy but a disease of market economy countries that could in the end destroy them. As I pointed out in Chapter 14, it is no good to say: "We cannot impose too severe restraints on the purchasers of our nuclear equipment or other countries will get the business"; that argument will lose its persuasive quality when we come face to face with an irresponsible power with a nuclear bomb. Nor is it any more convincing when we are told that America should not prohibit its companies from paying bribes to foreign bureaucrats because that would give aid and comfort to foreign competitors.

America prides itself on proving by its example the benefits of free enterprise, but the vaunted machinery of the market mechanism is not impressive when competitive success depends not on market forces but on the debauching of government officials. To be sure, the correlative of bribery in many areas of the world is extortion, yet the managers of American corporations are not hired to give in to extortion. The vast volume of speeches, pamphlets, and advertising copy and propaganda leaflets extolling the virtues of free enterprise are canceled every night when managements demonstrate by their conduct that a sector of multinational business activity is not free; it is bought and paid for. This is a problem that, like so many others, has relevance in the struggle of antagonistic ideologies; for, when our enterprises stoop to bribery and kickbacks, they give substance to the Communist myth — already widely believed in Third World countries — that capitalism is fundamentally corrupt.

We cannot have it both ways. We cannot proclaim that competition is the lifeblood of our economic system, while slipping money under the table to foreign purchasers. That is asking too much of human credulity.

PART V

Foreign Policy
for
a Crowded World

CHAPTER 16

Checking the Compass and Correcting the Course

SO LONG AS THE NATION-STATE CONTINUES TO BE THE DOMINANT unit in the structure of world politics, the maintenance of peace must depend on some combination of three principles which might be roughly described as cooperation, balance, and domination.

By cooperation I mean, in essence, what has frequently been called the congress, concert, or council system, whereby the major powers agree to act together or in parallel, in pursuance of common principles, to resolve or suppress conflicts among smaller powers. During much of the nineteenth century the then great powers maintained peace in the West not merely by a shifting balance of power but also through the so-called Concert of Europe. In the twentieth century Woodrow Wilson sought to expand that conception into a concert of the world through the League of Nations.

The League differed from the Concert, of course, not merely in its more formal constitution but in the quite different principles to which it was pledged. For the Concert of Europe the initial operative principle was legitimacy — the preservation of the arrangements worked out by Metternich at the Congress of Vienna — although it later acquired a broader frame of reference. For the League of Nations — and the United Nations that rested on the same conceptual underpinning — the prime principle was self-determination as expressed in the League covenants and the United Nations Charter. But the underlying assumption was the same. If a concert system were to work, the major powers must not only agree on certain principles of action, but each must be prepared either to join together to resolve local conflicts that threatened the peace or at least to abstain from undermining the efforts of other great powers to resolve such conflicts.

Unhappily, and in spite of the bright hopes of the authors of the United Nations Charter, global politics ever since the Second World War have been complicated by much the same fundamental problem that troubled Europe during the year of the French Revolution and the Napoleonic Wars that followed; a major nation — in this case the Soviet Union — has refused to accept the status quo, behaving, in Professor Kissinger's terminology, like a "revolutionary" power. Because the Soviets have refused to cooperate in maintaining peace within the framework of the United Nations Charter, the Security Council has been disabled from dealing effectively with local conflicts.

That does not mean that the superpowers have not acted individually to suppress conflicts or impose their will within their own tacitly recognized spheres of influence. The Soviet Union disciplined Hungary in 1956 and Czechoslovakia in 1968, and the United States intervened in the Dominican Republic in 1965. But only in two exceptional situations — Korea in 1950 and the Congo in 1961 — has the Soviet Union stood aside — albeit accidentally in the former case — and thus made it possible for the Security Council to act effectively in areas outside great-power spheres of influence. So long as the United States and the Soviet Union not only continue to be committed to antipathetic systems but automatically take rival sides in every local quarrel, we will be unable to use concert diplomacy.

But if we write off concert diplomacy altogether and continue to place all our dependence on a bipolar balance of power to keep the peace, how shall we go about it? Shall we try to involve other countries in our strategic diplomacy or continue, as Secretary Kissinger has been doing, to play a lonely game of maneuver, utilizing our allies only when it seems convenient to do so and ignoring them otherwise?

Although there is no wholly apt name for our current policy, it exhibits a strong isolationist tinge. Primarily self-centered and unilateral, it is not only formulated without the advice of our allies, but executed without their consent and often against their better judgment. Professor Norman A. Graebner wrote twenty years ago that "the American isolationist tradition assumed that the United States was good enough and strong enough to do what it pleased." [1] America, the isolationists believed, did not need help from allies; it could go its own way without having to make concessions and accommodations.

But the so-called isolationism that marked American policy during the latter years of the nineteenth century, as well as between the two great European civil wars of the twentieth century (to borrow a phrase from Dean Acheson) was not so much a policy of nonintervention as of unilateralism. Prior to the Second World War, this meant in practice, according to Professor Robert W. Tucker, the high priest of the so-called New Isolationism, that, although America held aloof from Europe, it was interventionist in Asia. Professor Tucker points out that

> . . . Whereas America's intervention in Europe necessarily implied entangling alliances with nations that would be roughly our equals (Great Britain and France), intervention in Asia was based on the assumption that such relationships could be avoided, since our putative adversary (Japan) was the only major power in the region. Accordingly, it was in Asia that some isolationists were willing to engage the nation's interests and power, while refusing to do so in Europe. [2]

Mr. Kissinger today regards all other non-Communist nations as Americans in the nineteenth century regarded the nations of Asia; they are at best only regional powers. Thus he apparently feels, in Professor Tucker's words, that we can now freely "engage [our] interests and power," no longer fearing that "intervention in Europe necessarily [implies] entangling alliances." As the most powerful nation in the world, we can afford to act unilaterally.

All this is consistent with the thinking of earlier American isolationists who, so Professor Graebner pointed out, "confronted American thought with five clearly defined tendencies — a concern for the domestic economy, the overestimation of United

States power, the underestimation of the enemy, a belief in the nation's moral superiority, and unilateralism in diplomacy."

Such tendencies are as marked in the new isolationism as in the old. Kissinger's fondness for unilateralism is clearly shown by, among other things, his insistence on going it alone in the Middle East and by his persistence — against the judgment of our allies — in maintaining a posture of confrontation toward the OPEC countries, denying them the chance to contribute to the amelioration of the financial distortions created by higher oil prices. The only result of such confrontation has been to force OPEC into a greater unity against the interests of the consuming nations, while imposing on Americans an unnecessarily heavy potential burden of underwriting the balance of payments deficits of oil-consuming nations that result from high oil prices.

Thus, the result of our unilateralism — of what, in its historical context, we can call "isolationism" — is to alienate our friends without taming our adversaries. The result? Increasing signs of disintegration in the delicate fabric of Western unity, while our ties with Japan continue to wear thin.

It is dangerous for the United States to fall between the two stools — to pursue neither a policy based on seeking common action with the Soviet Union in resolving third-party quarrels (or, in other words, a concert policy) nor a balance-of-power policy based on the Western alliance. It is an illusion to think we can go it alone, yet still retain the ability to command support when we need it. It is time we adopted a more realistic course.

What that course implies, as I have repeatedly suggested, is that we should earnestly seek to develop our larger strategies through consultation and the formulation of a collective policy within a widening group of like-minded nations. Initially, at least, the core of such a group would be the principal Atlantic nations that are today members of the Western alliance. So far as possible, we should also try to bring Japan into our councils, particularly as concerns problems arising in Asia or the Pacific.

Obviously, I do not propose that we try to meld the NATO alliance and the Japanese-American Mutual Defense Treaty into a political coalition; nor do I wish in any way to delimit the nations with which we should consult and collaborate by applying any rigid criteria. Australia and New Zealand, for example, have special contributions to make in their area of the world and we should certainly work with them in any consideration of Asia and the Pacific; and, in dealing with problems of the Americas, we should work more closely with our Latin American neighbors on a hemispheric basis.

There are compelling reasons to form much closer working relations among the important non-Communist industrial nations. During the next decade or so, the most dangerous and difficult world crises are likely to arise outside Europe or Japan. To consign the nations of Europe to a strictly regional role, as Secretary Kissinger has done, is to deprive ourselves of their assistance, collaboration, and judgment, all of which we shall sorely need. After all, we have dramatically demonstrated within the past few years that we have no monopoly on wisdom; had we paid more attention to the advice of our friends during the late 1960s we would not have sent thousands of young men to kill and die in the paddy fields of Southeast Asia.

What I am suggesting is not that we try to create new, formal institutions for cooperation, although some may, in time, become necessary. To be effective, policy should not be announced in pompous declarations — or "doctrines," to misuse an overworked word — it should evolve from the give-and-take of conferring, working, and acting together. Since today the Secretary of State prefers to operate as a "lone cowboy," stealing every scene and upstaging every other actor, he would, no doubt, find irksome any limit on his freedom of maneuver. Yet that is the only prudent way for the United States to conduct its affairs in this curiously formless period as we prepare to face the problems of the new crowded world of the next decades. Forty years of active world involvement should have persuaded us of the fallacy of the isolationist assumption that the United States is "good enough and strong enough to do what it pleases" without help and assistance from other nations which see the larger issues in the same way as we do. Unilateralism is no longer an adequate policy for America — if, indeed, it ever was.

During the Vietnam War, the young put shrill emphasis on an abstract morality. The war in Vietnam was "immoral," and foreign policy was pasted with the same label. Yet American leaders preoccupied with the politics of the war felt an occupational com-

pulsion to appear tough-minded. In this they were paying deference to the myth cherished by retired diplomats that the successful diplomatic practitioner is an historical realist who doubts the
perfectibility of man and views the arena of international politics
as a jungle where only the fittest (or, in other words, the strongest
and most clever) nations can, or should, survive. In that tradition,
anyone who prattles of moral principles is dismissed as soft-
headed.

Most of our Secretaries of State in recent years have been of
that mind. Morality, they have asserted, is too subjective an abstraction to play the dominant role; actions which one nation
regards as highly moral may be repellent to others. Besides, it is
often impossible to translate moral precepts into day-to-day diplomatic business.

But at the same time, one should not confuse morality with
moralizing and ethics with sanctimony. All too many are misled by
a stereotype of the advocate of "morality" as a fuzzy-minded man
or woman who places undue trust in the benign purposes of other
nations, urges such dubious measures as unilateral disarmament,
and makes wishful, pious, but silly declarations that are frequently
utilized against America's interests. To avoid "morality" or "ethics" in this latter sense does not mean that our policies should be
designed on the basis of purely tactical and pragmatic considerations without reference to any body of recognized principles.

This is a central weakness of the Kissinger approach for,
though one of his favorite themes is the building of an "international system of order," he neglects the fact that a system of order
presupposes common adherence to a recognized set of ground
rules; since his addiction to the tactical opportunity so often di-
verts him from his ultimate destination, it is impossible to identify
the stars from which he takes his bearings. His guiding purpose is,
by constantly tinkering with the mechanism, to maintain a shifting
balance of power — an act which, unrelated to any body of basic
principles, becomes a tour de force with no meaning beyond the
virtuosity of the achievement.

That is not to say that Kissinger hesitates to participate in, or
even propose, the drafting of agreed rules. He was, for example,
involved in developing the "Principles Governing the Relations
between the United States and the Soviet Union" issued in Mos-

cow in 1972, and the "Agreement for the Prevention of Nuclear War" issued in Washington in 1973. He personally proposed a "New Atlantic Charter." But it is easier to draft principles than to follow them, and there is no evidence that, in conducting policy, he ever lets such formulations get in his way.

That is, perhaps, the basic flaw in Kissinger's foreign policy: he is, par excellence, a pragmatist who puts primary reliance on the managed play and counterplay of force. It is a policy strictly for the short term. It can work during periods when two powerful nations maintain a precarious power balance largely by their own exertions, or when a single strong nation manages briefly to impose its own version of order on the world. But even a world order enforced by the common support and action of major world powers — which is, in essence, the formula for peacekeeping contemplated by the United Nations Charter — can operate effectively only if it rests on a body of rules to which those nations agree.

That the lack of such a frame of reference constitutes the principal deficiency in Secretary Kissinger's foreign policy is demonstrated by his efforts to paint over the ugly lesions caused by the Arab-Israeli conflict. Choosing to pursue a tactical line designed to break the Arab common front, he ignored the one set of principles on which the major parties to the conflict had agreed. Those principles, embodied in Resolution 242 of the United Nations Security Council, adopted shortly after the Six-Day War in 1967, provided for "withdrawal of Israeli armed forces from territories occupied in recent conflict" * — which included not only the Sinai but the Gaza Strip, the Golan Heights, the West Bank of the Jordan, and Old Jerusalem. It provided also for the "termination of all claims or states of belligerency and respect for and acknowledgment of the sovereignty, territorial integrity and political independence of every State in the area and their right to live in peace within secure and recognized boundaries free from threats or acts of force."

It was a formulation agreed to not only by the major powers,

---

* Although the French equivalent of the word *the* was included in the French version to qualify *territories*, its omission in the English version of the resolution was a deliberate effort to allow for a future compromise on whether all or merely some territories would be returned.

including the Soviet Union, but by all the warring nations except Syria. Still, although efforts were thereafter made to carry out the resolution, none succeeded — even though experience in other situations had clearly shown that, so long as the Israelis continued to hold the occupied territories, there could be no lasting peace in the Middle East. Indeed, it is now clear from a recent book by a journalist close to Nasser that the Arabs, under Egyptian leadership, began immediately after the 1967 cease-fire to prepare the counteroffensive which finally culminated in the October 1973 War.[3]

Yet, instead of trying to secure the enforcement of that resolution or using it as the framework for a final settlement, the Secretary sought to exploit Egyptian anxiety for a period of respite by arranging a truce with only one of the front-line Arab states. It was a complex bargain with largesse for both sides. In effect, it bought off Egypt by providing for a sufficient withdrawal in the Sinai Desert to enable the Egyptians to reopen the Suez Canal and thus gain $500 million a year in canal fees. In addition, it returned to them the Abu Rudeis oil fields, which meant at least another $350 million a year in oil revenues. As compensation to Israel, Kissinger promised that the United States would underwrite its requirements for oil and would provide a massive amount of armaments and money over the next few years, which should enable it to withstand such Arab assaults as would almost certainly be provoked by the fact that the bulk of the territories taken in 1967 (87 percent of the Sinai, the Golan Heights, the Gaza Strip, the West Bank of the Jordan, and Old Jerusalem) still remained under Israeli occupation.

I doubt that we shall look back on this diplomatic episode either with pride or a sense of accomplishment. It will be noted in the history books as one more incident in the poignant chronicle of historic missed opportunities. Stripped of Kissinger's ritual chatter about maintaining the diplomatic momentum and the perfunctory insistence that the Sinai agreement is only the first step in a diplomatic process, the net result of our effort will have been: (1) to sidetrack any serious movement toward a final solution, and (2) to give one party to the conflict a massive arsenal to defend its continued occupation of territories taken by force without regard to accepted principles of international law or of the United Nations Charter as interpreted by one Security Council Resolution and reaffirmed by another. History will not mark this down as the finest hour for American diplomacy, which has on a number of past occasions produced results that were both moral and stable — and, very often, stable because they were moral.

Yet the Sinai negotiation is by no means the only example that could be cited to illustrate the absence of principle in the current direction of our foreign policy. One could mention, among many others, President Ford's willing participation in the mass gathering of heads of state at Helsinki, cynically called together to legitimate the Soviets' hold over Eastern Europe, the carpet-bombing of Hanoi to improve Mr. Kissinger's leverage in negotiating a face-saving and rickety peace, the secret promises made Thieu to induce him to sign the Paris accords, and the Administration's frantic insistence on waiving all sanctions against Turkey for NATO purposes. Nor is anything more immoral than the totally reckless way successive administrations have, from lack of vigilance and will, allowed the proliferation of nuclear weapons or have — as the present administration is doing with unprecedented profligacy — promoted the spread of sophisticated conventional weapons in order to buy temporary interludes of quiescence in turbulent areas.

In almost every one of these episodes we have tried to gloss over inherently unstable situations in order to show immediate results. Justifying our action or inaction is a cynicism mislabeled as realism, pragmatism, or hardheadedness. Suggestions for seeking solutions to central issues by incisive action in accord with fundamental principles of fairness are tagged as impractical or idealistic. Yet experience has repeatedly shown that diplomacy based merely on the manipulation of power without reference to any accepted body of rules or principles leaves no permanent monuments. Certainly it is no way to build a "system of international order" or a "structure of peace." An enduring structure must be founded on more than the transient friendship of mortal princes or the adroit manipulation of force and counterforce; it must have solid foundations based on conformity to a set of standards widely regarded as equitable.

This underlines the central deficiency in our current unilateralist policy: that it is not merely too narrow in its focus but too

niggardly in its objectives. Its declared purpose is to bring about a
"generation of peace," a phrase reminiscent of Neville Chamberlain's "peace in our time." Yet Americans have never been
content merely with peace; we have always seen liberty and the
dignity of the individual as higher values, and our current policy
is lamentably flawed by its indifference to those values. Although
no one can challenge the thesis that, because of the vast destructive power of nuclear weapons, the avoidance of nuclear war is a
condition precedent to all other policies, the emphasis on survival
as our single, consuming objective could rationalize tyranny. And
it is absurd to contend, as Secretary Kissinger implies, that because "the necessity of peace is itself a moral imperative," survival comprehends morality. In spite of the Secretary's insistent
but rather defensive avowals of moral purpose, it is hard to find
much trace of moral endeavor in what we have done or sought to
do. And it is a major omission.

Americans have regularly expected a moral content in their
foreign policy even though they have been repeatedly deceived
when ultimate accomplishments fell short of the expressed ideal.
We fought the First World War to "make the world safe for democracy." We fought the Second World War to save the world from an
obscene dictatorship. We helped rebuild Europe with the Marshall Plan not only — or even most important — because it was
good business but in a spirit of compassion and generosity. We
pursued a policy of containing Soviet power not just to protect our
own shores from invasion but because the Communists were enemies of other nations' freedom and individual liberty. We em-
barked on programs of foreign aid not only because the stimula-
tion of development was sound economics, but out of charity and a
sense of fair play. Finally, even our misbegotten venture in Vietnam — particularly in its conceptual stages — was touched by an
element of idealism.

A foreign policy that does not accord with the instinctive morality of Americans will not gain a constituency; and under our
democratic system a foreign policy cannot long endure without a
constituency. One can sustain such a policy for a while, as has
been done for the past few years, by concealing its emptiness with
contrived excitement — the drama and color and pageantry of
face-to-face meetings with Brezhnev and Chou En-lai, summit

conferences and negotiations staged as man-to-man contests with the breathlessness of tennis matches. Aided by television and the up-to-the-minute comments of "a senior official in the Kissinger party," the daily chronicle of shuttle adventures could be made, for a time, prime entertainment, and many were thrilled to have their affairs managed by "a miracle worker."

In fact — for a time — Americans loved all the excitement of to-ing and fro-ing. They were proud to watch their President flying off in his big airplane to Peking or Moscow; they loved to read of their Secretary of State spending fourteen hours with Chou En-lai. They felt reassured when Mr. Brezhnev patted the President on the back and behaved with the familiar bonhomie of the professional politician, a universal — though, unfortunately, not a vanishing — species.

Yet, inevitably, the effect of such theater began to wear off. People added up the results and wondered how much it all meant — especially when success failed to follow success; when the prestidigitator waved his wand to find the rabbit had hopped away. That, of course, was what happened when the Cyprus crisis was egregiously mishandled, when the second stage of Middle East shuttle negotiations broke down in March 1975, and when the highly touted Vietnamese settlement was followed by a nightmarish denouement. Entertainment can distract only so long; the drama may have a brilliant second act, but if it lacks a proper ending, Americans will grumble and ask hard questions.

Even summit meetings have lost their attraction as spectacles. Americans who had visited Madame Tussaud's gallery of wax figures in London inevitably felt a sense of *déjà vu* when the cameras displayed the futile gathering of "world statesmen" in Helsinki, where none but the Russians were sure why they were there, yet each uttered banalities for the hometown papers quite unrelated to the tawdry realities of the business at hand. Nor did Secretary Kissinger's shuttle trip to the Middle East in August 1975 do more than raise questions as to why it was necessary. The essential terms of the agreement had been reached with Jerusalem and Cairo before he took off, so the result seemed as fixed as a professional wrestling match. The Secretary's personal involvement served only to raise the stakes on both sides. Finally, President Ford's irrelevant trip to China in December 1975 was greeted by the American people with the boredom it deserved. This time there were not even panda bears to show for the effort.

Disenchantment has also been growing in the Congress, which is presumably closer to public sentiment than anyone in Foggy Bottom. It is not merely that the members of the legislative branch are no longer willing to remain shut out from the making or conduct of foreign policy — particularly since they have learned to mistrust what they are told about it — but also that the context of our policy satisfies neither them nor their constituents. It lacks an essential element. What is missing — as more and more Congressmen are beginning to realize — is a moral theme to give coherence to what we, as a nation, are trying to do. In the absence of such a theme, they feel unable to explain our policy to the home folks. America, after all, is not dynastic Europe but an open democracy where the people react effectively only to policies that engage their deeper emotions. And, at long last, they have grown tired of furtiveness and sudden surprises. *Realpolitik* — no matter how brilliantly performed with skillful maneuvers and tactical virtuosity — cannot permanently substitute for a sense of purpose; it is foreign to our instincts and experience — to coin a phrase, it is un-American.

Thus the changes urgently needed in our foreign policy relate both to substance and execution. Policy must be broadened and opened. Our angle of vision must be widened. We must design policies and actions related to some accepted body of rules and not merely to the tactical purposes of a moral relativist.

CHAPTER 17

The American Role

FOREIGN POLICY IS A CONTINUING CHALLENGE TO MAN'S ADAPT-
ability. Events move more quickly than foreign offices or even
foreign ministers; policies achieve a momentum that persists long
after they have served their purpose.

In 1945, a half-dozen large empires still bestrode the world,
and diplomacy largely consisted of adjusting interests among a
handful of capitals. Unscathed by the war, the United States was
the dominant power. But two developments reshaped the next
three decades of international politics. Almost a hundred new
countries with independent governments replaced disintegrating
empires, while Soviet nuclear power challenged America's
dominance.

From then on, the United States concentrated on preventing
Soviet expansion outside the encircling Iron Curtain that marked
the limits of its tacitly recognized sphere of influence. We sought
particularly to prevent the Kremlin from filling power vacuums
created by the progressive crumbling of colonial systems, which
was the perceived threat we tried to counter in Vietnam. That is
what Mr. Kissinger would still like to do in Angola at the time this
book is written.

But what was once a reasoned policy has now become a conditioned reflex. No longer does it reflect the evolving realities. Ab-

sorbed in checking Soviet expansionism, we have failed to note the shrinking dimensions of Soviet power other than in the military field or to take proper account of the evolving dynamics of the Third World. The menace Moscow posed in the 1950s — a nuclear struggle over the strategically vital areas of Western Europe — was ended with the Cuban missile crisis, when the two superpowers recognized that a nuclear exchange would be mutual suicide. Now, so long as America maintains at least nuclear equality with the Soviet Union, we keep NATO defenses in repair, and Western European governments remain committed to the same objectives of freedom, a direct challenge to major Western nations is improbable.

Yet because of the Soviets' military might we go out of our way to treat it as an equal world power, even though it has built its vast armies and its nuclear arsenal only by starving its other economic sectors. Doctrinally committed to a command economy that depends on a huge bureaucracy, it has fallen behind the West in industrial production — and its leaders know it. With 27 percent of its working force still on farms, it produces in a bad crop year less grain per capita than the Czarist regime did in 1913, a mediocre year when Russia was a net food exporter.

Its political influence is weakening all over the world. No longer is the Kremlin the unchallenged Vatican of the Communist church. The key Communist Parties of Western Europe have served notice that they will not take instruction from Moscow but will seek power within the framework of their own local political systems. Nor is the Soviet Union likely to gain significant influence in those vast third areas of the world outside the Iron Curtain, which, in the battle terms of the Cold War, have been regarded as a contested prize by both East and West. Most Third World states find the Maoist brand of peasant-based Communism a more relevant model than the industrial-based Soviet brand, while young revolutionaries pay homage to the legend of Ché Guevara, the most incompetent filibusterer since William Walker tried to seize Nicaragua in the 1850s. Enthralled by resurgent nationalism, the new people's republics look to Moscow less for instruction and guidance than for money and arms; and once their revolutions succeed, national pride overwhelms ideology. Disabled by an inability to conceal their compulsive arrogance and racial contempt, the Russians display a unique capacity for alienating the peoples whose revolutions they have assisted.

We now know that the superpowers are far less likely to clash over Western Europe, where the importance of the stakes would render a nuclear exchange almost inevitable, than over proxy wars in local situations, where because of the marginal stakes, each assumes that the other will not escalate beyond a certain point.

Yet we still appraise local quarrels not as affairs of tribal, national, or regional politics but as aspects of the Cold War — as new arenas for Soviet-American contention. Just as we helped the South Vietnamese to preempt a power vacuum left by the departure of the French in order — so we thought — to check the expansion of Russian and Chinese influence, the Ford Administration would now have us help one group of tribal leaders in Angola fill a vacuum of power left by the departure of the Portuguese against the opposition of another group supported by the Russians. Thus if Congress and the American people were to continue to write blank checks the current administration would repeat the pattern of Vietnam like a bad habit. And, as we did in South Vietnam, we would choose the beneficiaries of our aid not for their devotion to liberty or democracy — or even for their ability to fight or to administer a government — but primarily because the Soviet Union — or China — armed the other side.

Thus we fight the Cold War by proxy in remote outposts while we treat our allegedly improved relations with the Soviets as a resource to be hoarded, not a diplomatic lever to be used.

If we press the Soviets hard on any issue we are told that it may "jeopardize *détente*." Though Soviet intellectuals make it clear that the Kremlin can never be trusted internationally so long as it continues repression at home, we draw back from demanding that the Soviets pursue more liberal policies for fear of "interfering in their internal affairs." Yet that hardly justifies our winking at their continued disregard of the commitments they made at Helsinki.

For the purposes of our diplomacy, *détente* has become more a source of obfuscation than an aid to peace. Nor is it clear where *détente* leaves off and appeasement begins. Certainly we do not need *détente* as background music for arms control negotiations or efforts to crank down the nuclear weapons race through SALT, where the mutual benefits are manifest and the temperature of relations between the superpowers far from the controlling element. "Linkage" in that context is a spurious concept. A SALT agreement is self-contained; it is not a bargaining chip to barter away for some nebulous global deal. Both nations have an interest in reducing the danger of an ultimate nuclear collision. Both need to halt the waste of resources in building overkill capability; the Soviet Union, with limited technology and industrial plant, needs that relief even more than we do.

Thus, instead of letting ourselves be hypnotized by seductive but fuzzy concepts such as "linkage" or *détente*, we should be guided by four central considerations.

First, we should keep up our military guard and encourage our Western allies to work with us in maintaining the NATO defenses. Ever since the Kremlin achieved its most cherished objective at the Helsinki Conference — the legitimation of its Eastern European empire — the Soviets have been hardening their policies, probing for ways to exploit the "crisis of capitalism," as their ideologues perceive it. The new Soviet five-year plan assigns increased resources to heavy industry and the military sector rather than consumer production. Marshal Grechko and his colleagues appear to be getting their way.

Second, instead of talking about *détente*, we should put it to the test. We should not continue to bail out Soviet food deficits, or help improve their industrial competence, or supply capital to develop their natural resources unless they stop exploiting situations of local conflict — or, in their jargon, assisting "wars of national liberation." In addition, if we are to continue to act out the charade of *détente*, we must insist that they cooperate with us and the other industrialized nations to solve common world problems.

Third, we should stop automatically treating every local quarrel as the occasion for a proxy skirmish with Moscow, but instead try to localize local conflicts. If we intervene every time the Soviet Union undertakes an imperialistic foray against an African country, for example, Africa will be like a human body which, overprotected from exposure to foreign elements, develops no immunities. In the extraordinary situation where we must support one side or another in a local situation, we should heed the lessons of Vietnam and make sure the basic conditions exist that I outlined in Chapter 5.

Fourth, we should stop assessing all issues in terms of their effect on Soviet-American relations. By our obsessive attention to the Soviet Union, we have given it an illusory status of equality the facts do not support. What is now called for is a period of polite neglect — neither benign nor malign — while we urgently strengthen our relations with like-minded nations. This does not mean that we should reinstate the Cold War, but, rather, that we should downgrade it, ceasing to regard Soviet-American policy as the central pivot of our whole diplomacy.

Nor should we continue to pay China unbecoming deference — to the point where two American Presidents, to say nothing of the Secretary of State, make highly publicized pilgrimages to Peking (which appear to many Asians as the twentieth-century equivalent of the "kowtow"), with a conspicuous absence of reciprocity on the Chinese side. As Professor James MacGregor Burns has admonished: "We must not permit ourselves a new romanticism about China at the same time that we uproot romanticism about America." [1] Time and the inscrutable tidal movements of Chinese politics have now emphatically confirmed what I pointed out in 1972: that the attempt to build relations with China on the ephemeral foundation of personal diplomacy with an aging Chinese hierarchy was a foolish defiance of the actuarial tables. Today — only four years after "the days that changed the world" — we are not even sure of the names and principal players on Peking's side. On the substantive level as well, we urgently need to reexamine the inarticulate assumption which underpins our current China policy — that relations with Peking could provide us, in Secretary Kissinger's words, with a "self-regulating mechanism" — or, in a less elegant, less pretentious formulation, that we could make the Russians more tractable by ostentatiously cultivating the Mao Tse-tung regime, thus threatening the Kremlin that it might have to face a Peking-Washington axis — or, in other words, trouble on two fronts.

There is no solid evidence that our highly visible overtures to Peking have moderated Soviet policy in the slightest. In the one area where we are most eager to reach a sensible understanding — nuclear disarmament and a balanced force reduction — the thought that China and the United States were conniving against them might well encourage the Soviets to increase, rather than restrain, their military exertions.

That does not mean we should ignore China, but by our obsequious courtship, we have generated little effective pressure — except on ourselves. The Chinese leaders apparently made clear to Messrs. Ford and Kissinger during their chilly Peking visit in December 1975 that they disapproved of America's soft line toward the Kremlin, implying that they would view our actions in Angola as a test of our utility as a counterbalance to Moscow. Presumably that largely explains Kissinger's anxiety to escalate supplies to our client tribes, even at the risk of identifying us with South Africa and thus hopelessly compromising our relations with the whole of black Africa.

If we hold firm to our convictions, the Russians and Chinese may, over a long timespan, be forced by internal pressures to move toward a freer society. But if we try to force the pace by obsessive attention to their interests and activities, the West may move toward East-West convergence faster than the Soviets. In several Western European countries the public sector is expanding at the expense of personal freedom; in Italy and even France, local Communist Parties, advancing in voting strength and respectability, threaten to acquire political authority. Throughout Europe, the centrifugal forces encouraged by American unilateralism weaken Western unity.

Meanwhile, if we concentrate on working with like-minded nations to achieve common decisions and action, we should be able to sustain the present balance-of-power, sphere-of-influence system and thus preserve an essential equilibrium. But, at the same time, we must, in collaboration with our friends, make an all-out effort to deal with the pressing problems that threaten the well-being, and even the survival, of our world society. We dare not continue to ignore the rest of the world, where new dangers threaten while old problems grow more complex. It takes no weather expert to show that most of the clouds darkening the world's future are not generated by the relations between the United States and the Soviet Union — or China. Even had there never been a Cold War or a Soviet nuclear competition, most foreseeable, long-range developments would still menace the world's well-being.

No matter how hard we or any other nation may try to slow the world's vaulting population growth, most Americans now under forty-five will, within their lifetime, have to adjust to an unfamiliar and, in many ways, an unattractive global environment. Well before the end of the century there will be far too many people in the world. Although the United States will become only moderately more crowded, many poor nations will almost double in size. If the United Nations medium projection is realized, out of a world population of 6.25 billion by 2000, the people of America and the advanced nations will number only about 1.3 billion, with almost 5 billion very poor people as our neighbors.

Already we are beginning to feel our political isolation in a hostile world. In a few years that fact will obtrude on everything we think and do. Faster transport, instant communications, the inevitable increase in mobility — all that will make it impossible for us to turn our eyes away from what is happening even five thousand miles away, and certainly not from Latin America, which, by the end of the century will contain two and a half times as many people as the United States.

What gives the prospect a somber and menacing cast is not that Americans will be a small minority but that this teeming world will be far from tranquil. The Third World, as some imprecisely call it, will be nervous and discontented and turbulent and increasingly chaotic. The seething populations of nations such as India and Indonesia seem likely to expand beyond the capacity of central governments to provide a common direction to affairs, or even to furnish essential services, to the point where they may fragment into small quarreling units, some economically hopeless. Forced to choose between chaos and authority, an increasing number of countries are likely to opt for repressive governments, thus increasing the isolation of the Western nations as lonely exemplars of democratic principles. In many overcrowded countries a swelling flow of adolescents into overcrowded cities will swamp already overfilled labor forces.

With burgeoning populations, poor countries will require vast food imports that exceed their financial means. Unemployment and urbanization will threaten the continued authority of governments, drive more and more activist young into outlaw gangs, terrorism, and other illegal activity, and impel migrations that will threaten neighboring states. Because our government is now spreading conventional arms over the world in a wildly reckless manner, those menacing aggregations of desperate men and women will have within their reach increasingly sophisticated means of violence.

For Americans to live and flourish in this alien and hostile world, to avert the dangers it presents while utilizing the opportunities it offers, we must recognize hard realities. A world of such multiple and fluid forces is no setting for a Grand Design, nor is unilateralism good enough. Most of the tasks I have outlined in preceding pages will require a high degree of common action among the major world powers, and a willingness of the United States to concert its own policies and practices with other nations.

The maintenance of adequate defensive strength is the essential underpinning for all policies for the West. Not only must NATO be kept up to strength as a deterrent to Soviet expansionist ambitions, but we Americans must maintain a nuclear arsenal at least equal to that of the Soviet Union, while we continue efforts through SALT to achieve more rational controls. In proposing that we cease our obsessive preoccupation with the Soviet Union, I do not suggest for a moment that the maintenance of a proper power balance is anything but indispensable.

At the same time, the problem of keeping the peace will become increasingly complicated as nuclear weapons are proliferated. With such weapons no longer restricted to a tiny oligopoly of presumably responsible states, we cannot rule out the chance that some irresponsible leader may use them for threat or conflict within the Third World — or even that outlaw gangs may use an atomic device for terror or blackmail. Nor would the balance of terror deter smaller nations from utilizing nuclear weapons to terrorize their non-nuclear neighbors, since retaliation in kind by the nuclear powers would not be automatic. Thus it is imperative that we do everything possible to check nuclear proliferation, which will require on the part of all nuclear powers a far greater sense of urgency than now exists. Most difficult of all, it will mean a common agreement to resist the temptations of commercial gain in the interest of a safer world.

Conventional weapons present an even greater challenge to the containment of greed. To organize effective restrictions on the international arms trade, which world peace urgently demands, will require us to make drastic decisions of self-denial, since

America is, by far, the largest supplier. But even that will have little meaning unless we develop new means and a greater will to settle old regional quarrels. So long as we temporize with situations of conflict, leaving basic issues unresolved, a competitive arms flow will continue.

The effective cooperation required for these common tasks can never be achieved in an economically chaotic world. The days are long past when any large industrialized nation can indulge the luxury of national economic or financial policies not harmonized with the needs of the international industrial community. Inflation, deflation, even unemployment, are no longer truly domestic questions. Increasingly, a common, carefully coordinated approach will be imperative — particularly as we move into a period of increased raw material stringencies, environmental difficulties, and subtly altering relations between north and south.

If those relations are to evolve constructively and we are to minimize the polarization of positions that results from bloc politics, America must show more maturity in its dealings with the Third World, and, by returning to a more institutionalized foreign policy, develop a continuing dialogue at multiple levels in individual Third World capitals. That does not mean that we should refrain from stating our national positions plainly and frankly in international forums, but we should avoid unnecessary confrontations that consolidate opinion against us. Outrageous as are the charges and demands made by some Third World countries or political blocs, we cannot dissociate ourselves from the problems of the poor nations. It is their vast numbers that will surround us in the crowded world of the coming decades.

Agriculture in the poor countries must be rapidly expanded. We must greatly increase facilities and education to advance family planning, within the context of development programs that will make the slowing of population growth socially acceptable. As part of the same effort we must tailor our assistance to discourage the scourge of excessive urbanization by stimulating land reform, rural industry, and public works that will provide employment in the countryside.

We must avoid so far as possible the crystallization of attitudes between the developed and developing nations that could result in a kind of Cold War between north and south. That means the development of measures that will ameliorate the disruptive consequences of an unstable income flow for raw-material-producing nations and enable poor nations to utilize their great resource of manpower by increasing access for their goods to world markets. We must try to develop mechanisms for the overall supervision of multinational companies that will preserve their unique ability to use and distribute world resources efficiently, yet assure that they so conduct their affairs as to advance and protect the legitimate interests of host countries.

We can accomplish none of these tasks unilaterally. The world is far too complex. America must work collectively with other nations, benefiting from the interplay of ideas and not seeking merely to impose its own will.

To generate the internal strength as a nation that will enable us to play the essential role of leadership, we Americans must believe in the integrity of our institutions, understand what our diplomats are seeking to accomplish and why, and be satisfied that our foreign policy is directed at goals consistent with our national aspirations. To accomplish such a rebirth of confidence will not be easy. Before we can even begin the process, we must acknowledge the fissures and fault lines in our society — geological weaknesses that our recent ordeal of war and corruption has vividly revealed.

A major source of weakness is the preoccupation with governmental secrecy, the perversion of national security to conceal errors and duplicity and to prevent the questioning of judgment or authority. These reflect a distrust of the people, a sense that the people and the government are adversaries, a contempt for democratic processes, and an insistence that a leader — whether the President or Secretary of State — be given full authority to do what he pleases without accountability to the Congress or the public. Recall, for example, the secret commitments that President Nixon gave to President Thieu, as well as those commitments both to the Egyptians and Israelis that Mr. Kissinger sought to give in secret, but which the Congress made public. Recall the unconcealed outrage of the Secretary of State that Congress should seek to meddle in his proprietary domain.

In the prevailing atmosphere of distrust surrounding secret diplomacy, Secretary Kissinger feels compelled to shape and conduct all policies personally, without showing his hand even to his colleagues. Yet that has meant a retreat from diplomatic practices established as early as the sixteenth century; ambassadors have now become briefcase carriers, and the whole foreign policy apparatus as useless as a vermiform appendix. Diplomatic practice has been set back three hundred years.

We have as a people accepted this retrogression to a personalized diplomacy because it has been congenial with another facet of American life — the habituation to spectacle and the dramatized event as distinct from the process, which results largely from the fact that, as a people, we now watch rather than listen, listen rather than read. When one absorbs the news through television, events become a series of vignettes, and foreign policy a matter of unconnected visual images — the President at a summit conference signing a declaration with Mr. Brezhnev that has significance only because the President and Mr. Brezhnev sign an intrinsically meaningless piece of paper together. Or Mr. Ford's trip to Peking — the second Presidential pilgrimage to the Middle Kingdom and the ninth for Mr. Kissinger — a pilgrimage undertaken even though neither Mao Tse-tung nor Chou En-lai nor their Foreign Minister, nor even the Deputy Foreign Minister of the People's Republic of China, had ever condescended to visit us barbarians in Washington.

Unhappily, the way we live, including dependence on television and visual impressions, reinforces the short attention span of most Americans. Our current foreign policy practices focus public concern on only one problem at a time, because everything is handled personally by one individual, who can deal with only one problem at a time, yet in the episodic and visual comprehension of our foreign policy, there is serious danger that the larger significance of developments will be lost in a kaleidoscope of unrelated events. Continuities will be obscured, causal factors unidentified.

There is a provocative passage in Rebecca West's book *Black Lamb and Grey Falcon* where one character remarks to the other: "Gerda has no sense of process. That is what is wrong with Gerda." And that, to a considerable extent, is what is wrong with many of us Americans today. Because we do not have a sense of where things started or why they are leading where they are, we are surprised by events that should have been predictable. We are so often impressed by the symbols of policy — two political leaders shaking hands or drinking toasts together — that we fail to recognize those symbols as mere reflections that have meaning only as part of a process within a larger context.

It is this insensitivity to process that has disabled us from noting the diminished circumstances of the Soviet condition and has led us to follow a path that has lost its meaning. We can either be a rival of Moscow — although greatly superior in strength — or the two nations can cooperate in keeping the peace and resolving common world problems. But so long as the Kremlin continually opposes us and seeks to thwart our policies, we should not play the mood music of friendship, treating the Soviet Union as an equal, which, except in certain military areas, it certainly is not, and assisting it with technology, capital, and food to overcome the appalling inadequacies of its inefficient economic system.

Yet it would be unfair to blame our failure of perception purely on the methods by which foreign policy is conducted or the means by which problems and events are made known to the public. Underlying that failure is a substantive deficiency. Our aims are inadequate for a great country. Our policies seem tailored for a nation that, no longer believing in itself, has no higher ambition than to survive; they do not respond to the psychic and intellectual needs of a people capable of acting on a grand scale with strength, compassion, and nobility.

To evolve more spacious policies, we must come to terms with a paradoxical set of worldwide realities and imperatives. In some countries there is a recrudescence of nationalism, in others an evident loss of faith in national structures — what is known in current jargon as a "crisis of legitimacy." We should not be surprised that nationalism is tending to supplant more dogmatic ideologies just at the time that the nation-state is demonstrating its own inadequacy. Nor should we find it inexplicable that, when new magnitudes of scale and scope are more than ever imperative, men and women should be turning toward even smaller units than the nation in the search for some structure with sheltering walls to provide a sense of fulfillment. Those manifestations of the tribal instinct — what the London *Economist* has called "the new fragmentation politics of region, class and race" — result from three defects in the intellectual sustenance of the time: the loss of faith in established governments, the fading of a sense of community, and the absence of shared values to which people can look for guidance and reassurance.

The result is to cast many individuals adrift from their social moorings, sending them in quest of new islands of association. In America, that quest takes eccentric form — as, for example, the vogue for communes, a ritualistic addiction to drugs, street demonstrations, Oriental rites, and freak religions. To a large extent, such phenomena represent little more than the passing whims and quirks of a generation made excessively suggestible by visual communications that intensify the transient and faddish. Yet beneath the oddities of the day is a corrosive uncertainty eating away at our institutions.

Although psychologists and sociologists speculate endlessly as to why America is today so disunited, a basic cause is that we have lost faith in the shared values that gave our country its special distinction. Contributing to this is the fact that so many intellectuals have turned their backs on our national experience. A lamentable aspect of the degradation of American education is the short shrift now given history studies in our universities. A people that does not know its own history is incapable of understanding its institutions or of developing a sense of dedication to common national objectives. In short, a nation illiterate in its own history is incapable of unity.

Today sober historians are often outshouted by revisionists who twist events like pretzels to fit them into the Marxist mold, or systematically strip the American experience of any glory or heroism. Unquestionably stimulated by the Vietnam ordeal, such antipatriotism is part of the nihilism that mars the present age — nihilism with its emphasis on the antihero. It is manifest in our current literature, in the glorification of violence and the outlaw, in the taste for black humor and erotic books and films. It confuses exhibitionism with liberty and, in the current state of taste and literature, substitutes a puerile cynicism for loyalty to the community or any actions beyond self-interest.

Along with the denigration of our national institutions has come a factitious emphasis on ethnic differences. Students are not taught to be conscious that they are part of an American society with traditions of which they can be proud; instead, be-

cause their forebears came from some other country, they are told
to identify themselves with their ethnic past. It is nonsense to
argue that, because an individual's ancestors did not play a role in
the history of America, he cannot take pride in the national experience of the country where he has been brought up and intends to
live. The fact that my father was an immigrant, that my forebears on my father's side never saw the shores of America before
the 1880s, does not diminish my interest in the Battle of Concord
or the Civil War. It is enough that those events contributed to the
shaping of my country.

In spite of their diversity of origin, appearance, religion, race,
or habits of thought, Americans have had integrity as a people
because they have tacitly agreed on certain common values. Liberty, justice, compassion, respect for the rights of others, and an elemental sense of responsibility that does not require coercion
from the state are the chemicals in the glue that has united a great
but disparate people drawn together in common purpose from the
ends of the earth.[2]

Unfortunately, the "new fragmentation politics" is not limited
to America. Europe is teeming with romantic but illogical separatist movements such as those of the Celtic fringe — the Bretons in
France and the Scots, Welsh, and even the Cornishmen in England — as well as the Flemish and Walloons in Belgium and the
Basques and Catalonians in Spain. In North America, the rising
emphasis on the distinctive rights and attributes of the Quebecois
menaces the integrity of the Canadian nation.

In America where the word *revolution* is carelessly used to
describe every adolescent tantrum, the emphasis on ethnic differences has not yet shown itself in separatism but only in ethnic
voting and pressure blocs. Yet it still has relevance for our foreign
policy. For a country emerging from a season of discontent and
disillusion, it will be difficult to reach a national consensus on vital
issues if people are broken down into competing power blocs and
entangled in conflicts of loyalty that can interfere with the development of a foreign policy directed, as it should be, at the advancement of the American national interest as a totality.

It was the genius of the American republican idea that government should no longer be the enemy of the people, as had
been the case in so many countries, but rather an extension and

instrument of the citizen. The individual should have a sense that his government was accountable to him, that it worked to advance his interests, and that it protected and did not threaten his liberties. Stimulated no doubt by the exigencies of depression and then of war, as well as by the complexities of a large industrial society, we Americans came to look to our government for the solution of more and more of our problems. We extended the reach of government not merely to feed and clothe and house the less fortunate and to defend us against foreign foes as well as against one another, but even to protect us from our own defects and weaknesses by an increasing regulation of private conduct. The emphasis of state responsibility began to shift from a concern for personal liberty to a concern for equality not merely of opportunity but of condition or, as Daniel Bell puts it, "of entitlements." Yet equality of condition requires increased interference with individual liberties and the creation of an ever-swelling bureaucracy.[3]

It is the nature of bureaucracies that, beyond a certain critical size, they become increasingly unmanageable, exceeding the capacity of any elected official to control. The larger units tend to evolve into baronies, separate and apart from the mainstream of government and detached from the living corpus of democratic society. That is what happened to the CIA; it acquired not only a life of its own but also a whole set of principles and practices that deviated widely from the laws and traditions of our country.

Alongside this phenomenon is another — that if bureaucratic hypertrophy alienates people from their government they will yearn for a hero, which goes far to account for their fascination with a highly simplified concept of diplomacy in which the Master Player, the lone diplomatic manipulator, works miracles with the aid of a jet airplane. Yet today this whole process has become far from satisfying. Citizens now find their symbols of governmental authority in a few identifiable personalities primarily because the government itself is so huge and impersonal.

Traditional allegiances fade away. We find it hard to have pride in our country when our government seems more a ubiquitous presence led by a couple of TV performers than a body of familiar public servants accountable to us. By touching too intimately on our daily lives and our most private liberties, it has, paradoxically, become remote from us, no longer an extension of

ourselves and our neighbors, no longer our friend but our boss —
or even, to return full circle, our disciplinarian, our enemy.

But if we are to regain that devotion to our country and its institutions which I believe to be essential, if we are to prevent a
volatile world from blowing apart, we will have to do more than
merely recapture control of our governmental machinery and constrain bureaucratic excesses so that government becomes once
again the protector and not the transgressor of our liberties. We
will also have to reformulate for ourselves some absolute standards by which we can guide our affairs, for no society can prosper, or even avoid fragmentation, if moral relativism repudiates all
sense of obligation to the community or the state, and if we conduct our relations with the rest of the world on the exiguous basis
of day-to-day tactical advantage.

We saw the consequences of moral relativism in the squalid
Nixon White House, where hollow men debauched the democratic process, from cupidity and a mindless misuse of power. We
saw it again in disclosures of the excesses of our intelligence agencies. Finally, we have been — or should have been — shocked by
revelations of illegal campaign contributions by the managers of
corporations and equally repelled by mounting evidence that
some large American enterprises engaged in the unconscionable
bribery of officials of foreign governments. These disclosures, as I
have pointed out, are the product of the indispensable self-cleansing mechanism built into our democratic system. That mechanism
can produce wholesome results, however, only if we apply stern
sanctions to halt the practices now revealed and apply those sanctions relentlessly.

As I made clear in Chapter 15, we will never be able to persuade the peoples in the emerging nations, or even young
America, that a market economy serves the needs of mankind and
is essential to individual freedom unless we eradicate the chica-
nery that lends credence to the dogma of the Left that capitalism
is both corrupt and corrupting. Nor can we argue convincingly for
our form of democracy if, out of apathy and lack of explicit convictions, we tolerate hidden corruption as part of the system.

So far, our intellectual élite has failed us by treating with em-
barrassed silence any mention of absolute values. Yet there are, it
seems to me, signs that this attitude is losing its vogue. Honest

men who think deeply about America's problems are conceding a yearning for some agreed points of reference by which to fix the compass, something better than the mere manipulation of impersonal forces. I am not predicting an old-time revival — far from it — yet I think it likely that two or three years from now our intellectuals will not only feel no embarrassment in speaking of absolute values but may find such conversation actually in vogue. Thus, with luck, we may begin to move away from an uncertain period in American history, toward a more comprehending relationship with other men — and even with nature. That this must have its effect on our foreign policy seems inevitable. The current period of manipulative diplomacy is already becoming an anachronism, for it is essentially a Nixonian foreign policy in a post-Nixon era.

Some worried Americans today are now suggesting that, as a people, we have lost our sense of uniqueness — our belief in our country's "exceptionalism," as they call it.[4] That, some apparently believe, may be a good thing, a sign of our maturity. But if we had, indeed, lost our sense of "exceptionalism" — which I doubt — it would, in my view, be a disaster not only for this country but for the world, as many wise and well-disposed foreigners are quite ready to tell us.

The belief in America's exceptional qualities and unique mission is a theme that ran as a strong and shining thread throughout our formative years as a nation; undoubtedly, it served us well as we grew increasingly rich and powerful and found we could no longer hold aloof from the world predicament. The whole meaning of America's early experience was summed up in a few proud phrases. We were the "city . . . on a hill," free from memories of old conflicts that persisted as corrosive rivalries and led all too often to war and destruction; we were the nation free from the burden of an oppressive history and, as Hegel and Tocqueville and many others wrote, "the land of the future." Although during our early years we were too weak to do more than try to teach the world by our example, we came into our own during the middle years of the twentieth century, when we not only mobilized and inspired but led the nations committed to democracy.

Today the timid are proposing that we should abdicate that role; the masochists are proclaiming with glee that we are not worthy of it, that we are, after all, quite as venal and wicked as all the rest; the revisionists are insisting that the record does not justify a claim to uniqueness, and that we would be acting imperialistically to assert our leadership.

But there is a difference between leadership and arrogance. Certainly we should not announce policies tailored to American requirements and expect our friends to fall meekly in line — as we have done too often in the past few years. But, while displaying a decent respect for the opinions and requirements of others, we can and must lead. Otherwise, neither we nor other peoples committed to freedom will survive the troubled years ahead without the loss of their most cherished values.

To exercise effective leadership, we must once more come to believe in ourselves, in our uniqueness as a nation, and in our special mission; we must, in other words, recapture that faith in our own exceptionalism that assured us that we had something special to offer the world, that we were, as a nation, destined by history and geography and bountiful resources to show the way to others. At the heart of that uniqueness was a sense of space — a concept of vast plains, wide distances, where men and women could move at will. We were blessed with a continent to develop and the energy required for the task. Yet space meant more than physical distance. It meant an amplitude of resources and — related to it but even more important — a spaciousness of spirit. A cramped and poor environment engenders a defensive selfishness. Its influence finds reflection in an excessive willingness to temporize, the shying away from long-term solutions that require patience and that may, for the moment, seem costly and difficult.

Because America alone has possessed that spaciousness of land and resources and spirit, we alone could produce the Marshall Plan or mobilize the energies and capabilities of the West to resist the pressure of disunion and tyranny.

That is one reason why those who advocate a policy of zero growth offer no adequate prescription for the future. There is no possible way to raise the standard of living of the more wretched of the earth or even to feed them, unless the industrialized nations are able to apply a portion of an expanding income wisely and magnanimously to that task. Not only would an economically stagnant West mean a niggardly neglect of the urgent problems of the

Third World, but it would, by lowering consumption, reduce demand for the products of the poor nations, while at the same time stimulating self-protective devices to close world markets to countries that enjoy no comparative advantage other than the cheap labor that goes with a squalid standard of living.

To be sure, spaciousness, whether in physical terms, in terms of resources or even of spirit, is a relative matter. Statistically, we Americans are still less crowded today than were the men and women of Europe when our country was founded, before the population explosion that followed the Napoleonic Wars. Even leaving aside Alaska, our population density is today only twenty-seven people to the square kilometer, much less than the density in Europe in 1780 — forty-five for France and thirty-one for Britain.

Thus, particularly with the greater mobility of modern life, we can still be a free-striding people, while most of the rest of the world's peoples are increasingly huddled together in a poverty they have little hope of escaping. We are large and strong; we speak with a loud and — most of the time — with a clear and reasonable voice, and not only do others listen but they wait for us to speak.

And we still have a spaciousness of resources even though we may have moments of concern or even discouragement with a prolonged recession and what seems an intractable inflation. Compared with other peoples, we are fantastically well off, in spite of our dirty cities and high crime rates and a political disillusionment that reflects not a poverty of means but a poverty of civic will and of shared values.

One encounters today an odd misconception which serves as the inarticulate premise for a comforting self-delusion. It is that, if we only stopped trying to solve, or at least neutralize, problems arising in different parts of the world, those problems would, somehow, solve themselves. The world would muddle through, and America would be the better off for it.

But there would not long be a void of leadership. No family, no society, no nation, and no international community can long persist before a leader tries to emerge. If the United States, with manifestly greater resources than any other nation, does not continue to exercise leadership, we can be confident that other nations will try. Today the primary competitor for power is the Soviet Union; tomorrow others may enter the lists as well. But none of those now visible on the horizon would be likely to order the world's affairs in any manner compatible with the ideals and principles in which we ourselves believe.

Life will not be easy in the crowded world into which we are moving, where every problem will be compounded because it will impinge on the lives of more and more people. It will take all of our wisdom and the national cohesion that results from a sense of shared values to see us through complexities beyond those we have ever imagined. Yet we have no option but to try.

Notes on Sources and Other Comments

SINCE THIS BOOK DEPENDS MORE ON EXPERIENCE AND REFLECtion than on a study of other people's ideas, I have not burdened the text with elaborate notes other than to indicate the source of the factual material that forms the underpinning of certain more technical chapters. I am also including below some supplemental comments on occasional points made in the text.

CHAPTER ONE
Unilateralism and the Master Player

1. Dean Acheson, *Fragments of My Fleece*, New York: Norton, 1971.
2. Interview of November 4, 1927, reprinted in *The New Republic*, December 16, 1972.
3. *Newsweek*, December 30, 1974.
4. Since Kissinger has long held the view that the brilliant diplomat must personally conceive and conduct foreign policy, no one should have been surprised that he has failed to involve — or, in many situations, even failed to inform — his colleagues in the State Department. Thus he wrote almost twenty years ago: "There is an inherent tension between the mode of action of a bureaucracy and the pattern of statesmanship. . . . It is no accident that most great statesmen were opposed by their 'experts' in their foreign offices, for the very greatness of the statesman's conception tends to make it inaccessible to those whose primary concern is with safety and minimum risk." (Henry A. Kissinger, *Nuclear Weapons and Foreign Policy*, New York: Doubleday Anchor Books, 1957, p. 247.)

CHAPTER TWO
Tribute to the Middle Kingdom

1. Richard M. Nixon, "Asia after Viet Nam," *Foreign Affairs*, 46, no. 1 (October 1967): 111.
2. Marvin and Bernard Kalb, *Kissinger*, Boston: Little, Brown, 1974, p. 232.
3. David Caute, *The Fellow Travelers*, London: Macmillan, 1973.

CHAPTER THREE
The Anatomy of "Summitry"

1. Harold Nicolson, *Diplomacy*, London: Oxford University Press (second edition), 1958, p. 67. See also Charles W. Thayer, *Diplomat*, New York: Harper, 1959, p. 44.
2. Keith Eubank, *The Summit Conferences, 1919–1960*, Norman, Oklahoma: University of Oklahoma Press, 1966.
    After analyzing all of the summit conferences that took place between 1919 and 1960, Professor Eubank concluded (p. 196): "None of these summit conferences proved that the heads of government performed better, quicker, more accurately, or more efficiently than their foreign ministers or their professional diplomats. There is no proof that their presence made the agreement any better or any more durable; often the reverse was true. Although Wilson negotiated the Versailles Treaty, he could not convince the United States Senate to approve it. Chamberlain and Daladier had their parliaments approve the agreement, but they could never make Hitler observe it. Roosevelt, Churchill and Truman obtained paper agreements from Stalin, but they could not enforce these without another world war. Despite his great wartime reputation, Eisenhower failed with Khrushchev and suffered great humiliation. Neither Eden, Macmillan, nor de Gaulle could help him."
    Moreover, he points out (p. 203): "Reputations have been destroyed or harmed by these conferences. Wilson was condemned for being hoodwinked by Clemenceau and Lloyd George into accepting terms that brought a new world war. Chamberlain bore the burden of the Munich Conference to his grave. Roosevelt has been denounced for supposed giveaways to the Russians in secret deals at Teheran and Yalta. Churchill has been damned by the Poles in exile for his actions regarding Poland. Eisenhower ended his term in office with the failure of the Paris Conference. No other act of Hitler's so revealed his true character to the world as his destruction of the Munich Agreement in March, 1939. The political career of Edouard Daladier never recovered from the destruction of the Munich Agreement by Hitler. Orlando was never again to be prime minister because his opponents stopped him with his record at Paris."
3. Henry A. Kissinger, "Domestic Structure and Foreign Policy," reprinted in *American Foreign Policy*, New York: Norton, 1974, pp. 11–50.
4. The tragic failure of effective communication between the Japanese and United States Governments leading up to Pearl Harbor is vividly described in John Toland, *The Rising Sun*, New York: Random House, 1970, pp. 150–156.
5. *The New York Times*, October 27, 1974.
6. Arno J. Mayer, *Politics and Diplomacy of Peacemaking, 1918–1919*, New York: Knopf, 1967, p. 173.
7. Ibid., p. 212.
8. Nikita Khrushchev, *Khrushchev Remembers: The Last Testament*, translated and edited by Strobe Talbott, Boston: Little, Brown, 1974, p. 415.
9. Thayer, *Diplomat*, p. 44.

CHAPTER FOUR
How We Involved Ourselves in Vietnam

1. Edward M. Collins, introduction to a selection of writings of Karl von Clausewitz: *War, Politics and Power*, Chicago: Henry Regnery, 1962, p. 41.
2. Ibid., pp. 41, 42.
3. Ibid., p. 44.
4. Alexis de Tocqueville, *Democracy in America*, New York: Knopf, 1966, II, 263.
5. The *levée en masse* was first decreed by the Convention in 1793 by a stirring proclamation that placed the entire French nation on a footing of total war. The emergence of total war is recounted in Robert Leckie, *Warfare*, New York: Harper and Row, 1970.
6. The most persuasive exponent of this principle was Professor Richard Neustadt, on whom President Kennedy placed considerable reliance. Neustadt emphasized the irreversibility of decisions in the nuclear age and argued that relatively minor actions taken at low levels in the bureaucracy could lead to catastrophe. The theory is spelled out in Richard M. Neustadt, *Presidential Power: The Politics of Leadership*, New York: Wiley, 1960.

   Kissinger had begun even earlier to recognize the preservation of options as an essential part of the policy of maneuver he was later to practice. Thus, in summing up the diplomatic methods of Metternich, for whom he had a deep admiration, he wrote: "This was the basis of Metternich's diplomacy throughout his life. Freedom of action, the consciousness of having a greater range of choices than any possible opponent, was a better protection than an alliance because *it kept open all options for the hour of need* . . . since its achievements could not emerge until the last moment, while its risks were immediately apparent, *it was a policy that required for its execution the almost arrogant self-confidence which characterized Metternich.*" (*Underlining* added.) (Henry A. Kissinger, *A World Restored*, Boston: Houghton Mifflin, 1957, pp. 270–271.)

CHAPTER FIVE
The Failure to Develop a Doctrine of Extrication

1. Alexis de Tocqueville, *Democracy in America*, New York: Knopf, 1966, II, 268.
2. Eisenhower letter to Diem, October 24, 1954.
3. The exact figures for the period 1961–1968 are 30,614 dead and 99,787 wounded. (Supplied by the Southeast Asia Section, Public Affairs, Department of Defense.)
4. *Rebus sic stantibus*, defined as "at this point of affairs," "a name given to a tacit condition said to attach to all treaties that they shall cease to be obligatory as soon as the state of facts and conditions upon which they were founded has substantially changed." The definition notes, by way of example, that "as a result of the Wars of Napoleon, all treaties of the United States with European powers were considered as annulled excepting only one with Spain." (*Black's Law Dictionary* [fourth edition], Minneapolis: West Publishing Company, 1954.)
5. *The New York Times Magazine*, December 21, 1969.
6. The total bombs dropped from 1966 to 1968 amounted to 2,865,888 tons, and from 1969 to July 1973, 4,528,998 tons. (Supplied by Southeast Asia Section, Public Affairs, Department of Defense.)
7. Nixon speech of April 30, 1970, in announcing the United States invasion of Cambodia.
8. The exact casualty figures between 1969 and March 1973 were 15,345 dead and 53,526 wounded. (Supplied by Southeast Asia Section, Public Affairs, Department of Defense.)
9. See note 6, above.

10. Registered refugees by official Government of Vietnam/USAID count amounted, for the years 1965–1968, to 2,635,000 and for the years 1969–1972 to 2,456,000. During 1973 — the first year of "peace with honor" — we created another 818,700. (*Study Mission Report Prepared for the Use of the Subcommittee to Investigate Problems Connected with Refugees and Escapees, Committee on the Judiciary, U.S. Senate, January 27, 1975, Humanitarian Problems in South Vietnam and Cambodia Two Years After the Cease-fire*; Washington: Government Printing Office, 1975, pp. 6–10.)

11. Civilian casualty figures from *The New York Times*, January 25, 1972.

12. Henry A. Kissinger, "The Vietnamese Negotiations," *Foreign Affairs*, January 1969, pp. 211, 234.

13. Letter from Kissinger to Edward Kennedy dated April 1, 1974, cited in William Shawcross, "How Thieu Hangs On," *The New York Review of Books*, July 18, 1974, p. 7.

14. Kissinger press conference, April 29, 1975.

15. Text of two letters released at President Ford's press conference of April 29, 1975, after earlier release by South Vietnamese politician.

16. See note 10.

17. See note 10.

CHAPTER SIX
Détente — A French Word for What?

1. André Fontaine, *History of the Cold War*, vol. II, New York: Pantheon, 1968, 1969.

2. "Central Issues of American Foreign Policy," in *Agenda for the Nation*, Washington: The Brookings Institution, 1968, pp. 608–609.

3. Foy D. Kohler, *Hearings of the Subcommittee for Europe, House Committee on Foreign Affairs*, May 15, 1974, Washington: Government Printing Office, 1974, p. 4. I learned a great deal from Ambassador Kohler during the years we worked together in the State Department, and have drawn freely on his testimony in the comments that follow.

4. Ibid., p. 11. Secretary Kissinger now frequently uses the term "coexistence," apparently preferring it to "*détente.*"

5. Ibid., pp. 13–14.

6. Ibid., p. 15.

7. Ibid., p. 29.

8. That the Soviets were warned in advance of the Egyptian intention to attack Israel has now been made clear by Mohammed Heikal in *The Road to Ramadan*, London: Collins, 1975. Heikal asserts that on October 1, 1973, Sadat told the Soviet ambassador that an attack was imminent (p. 24). On October 4 Moscow sent word that the decision when to attack was up to the Egyptians and asked leave to withdraw Soviet personnel (p. 34). The attack began on October 6 (p. 38).

9. Nikolai Lenin, "The Imperialist War: The Struggle Against Social Chauvinism and Social Pacifism, 1914–1915," *Collected Works*, New York: International Publishers, 1930, XVIII, 224.

10. Edward M. Collins, introduction to Karl von Clausewitz, *War, Politics and Power*, Chicago: Henry Regnery, 1962, pp. 31–33.

11. Wolfgang Leonhard, "Domestic Politics and Soviet Policy," *Foreign Affairs*, October 1973, pp. 63–66. Western recalculations of Soviet growth and productivity statistics show the decline to have been from 6.4 percent in 1950–1958 to 5.3 percent in 1958–1967 to 3.7 percent in 1968–1973. *Detente: Hearings before the Committee on Foreign Relations, U.S. Senate, August–September 1974*, p. 32.

12. Leonhard, pp. 66–67.

13. Quoted in Gordon A. Craig, "Techniques of Negotiation," in *Russian Foreign*

Policy, edited by Ivo J. Lederer, New Haven: Yale University Press, 1962, pp. 351, 353.

14. During the nineteenth century Russian diplomats adopted the techniques and studied elegance of manner of their Western counterparts. Craig, p. 356.

15. N. N. Nekrasov, paper prepared for the Conference on New Initiatives in East-West Cooperation, held in Vienna, Austria, November 12–15, 1974.

16. The popularity of the Manchester Creed and the enthusiasm it evoked are described by Professor Geoffrey Blainey in *The Causes of War*, New York: The Free Press, 1973, on pages 18–23 and 26–28. The thesis that increased trade would diminish the prospects of war was extended to all forms of communication, including universal languages. The result was a transitory fervor for Volapük, Esperanto, and a whole outpouring of new synthetic languages.

17. Professor Gregory Grossman, in a statement to the *Joint Economic Committee — Hearings on the Soviet Economic Outlook, 93rd Congress, 1st Session,* July 17–19, 1973, Washington: Government Printing Office, 1973, p. 143.

CHAPTER SEVEN
Détente and Henry Kissinger

1. George W. Ball, "An American View of Ostpolitik," *Affari Esteri*, December 1970. It is curious that Kissinger has blamed so much of the current weakness of the West on Willy Brandt when incessant talk of *détente* has done far more to weaken Western will and solidarity than the *Ostpolitik*.

2. Theodore Draper, "Détente," *Commentary*, June 1974, p. 35.

3. Arthur M. Schlesinger, Jr., *A Thousand Days*, Boston: Houghton Mifflin, 1965, p. 904.

4. Lyndon B. Johnson, *The Vantage Point*, New York: Holt, Rinehart and Winston, 1971, p. 480.

5. Henry A. Kissinger, *Agenda for the Nation*, Washington: The Brookings Institution, 1968.

6. Marvin and Bernard Kalb, *Kissinger*, Boston: Little, Brown, 1974, pp. 106, 107.

7. *Hearings before the Committee on Foreign Relations, United States Senate, 93rd Congress, 2nd Session,* on United States relations with Communist countries. August 15, 20, and 21; September 10, 12, 18, 19, 24, and 25; and October 1 and 8, 1974, p. 249; Washington: Government Printing Office, 1975.

8. John Newhouse, *Cold Dawn*, New York: Holt, Rinehart and Winston, 1973, p. 5.

9. *Nomination of Henry A. Kissinger; Hearings before the Subcommittee on Foreign Relations, United States Senate, 93rd Congress, 1st Session,* September 7, 10, 11, and 14, 1973.

10. Interview quoted in *Arms Control and Disarmament Agreements*, Washington: U.S. Arms Control and Disarmament Agency, February 1975, p. 130.

11. George B. Kistiakowsky, *The Washington Post*, January 4, 1976.

12. Quoted in Theodore Draper, "Détente," *Commentary*, June 1974.

13. Henry A. Kissinger, *A World Restored*, Boston: Houghton Mifflin, 1957, pp. 1–15.

14. Quoted by Victor Zorza, *The Washington Post*, September 25, 1975, p. A-19.

CHAPTER EIGHT
Shuttle Diplomacy — The Preference for Tactics over Strategy

1. George W. Ball, "Slogans and Reality," *Foreign Affairs*, July 1969.

2. George W. Ball, "The Looming Mideast War and How to Avert It," *The Atlantic Monthly*, January 1975.

3. George W. Ball, article in *The Washington Post*, May 18, 1975.

4. The Soviets recognized from the beginning that the United Nations Security

Council would be effective only when the USSR agreed with the other permanent members. Thus at a time when some Americans were dreaming of the United Nations as a surrogate for a world state, Stalin is quoted as saying that the UN would be successful only "if the Great Powers that carried on their shoulders the main burden of war against Hitlerite Germany will act afterwards in a spirit of unity and collaboration. It will not be effective if this necessary condition is absent." Quoted in Adam B. Ulam, *Expansion and Coexistence — Soviet Foreign Policy 1917–73*, New York: Praeger, 1974.

CHAPTER NINE
Western Europe in Disarray

1. *Papers Related to the Foreign Relations of the United States, with the Annual Message of the President.* Transmitted to Congress, December 2, 1895, I, Washington: Government Printing Office, 1896, p. 558. (Olney to Bayard, July 20, 1895.) President Cleveland was favorably impressed with the note, describing it as Olney's "twenty-inch gun" blast.
2. Interview in *Time*, January 3, 1972.
3. Speech at Waldorf-Astoria to publishers and television executives, April 23, 1973.
4. Kissinger's pique and arrogance in referring to the European leaders during this period was a considerable departure from the traditional relations among allies. He was widely reported to have expressed "disgust," during a Congressional hearing on October 29, 1973, at the refusal of European countries to assist the American airlift and also to have commented on the "lack of legitimacy" of European governments in what he thought was a private talk to a women's group.
5. Nixon's television news conference, October 26, 1971.
6. Joseph A. Schumpeter, *Capitalism, Socialism and Democracy* (third edition), New York: Harper & Row, 1975.
7. Almost as important as the bureaucracy's steadily expanding size is its emerging trade union role. With the organizing of teachers, policemen, and other public sector employees, the public service unions could someday become the most powerful element in the trade union movement. Indeed, the time may come when the public bureaucracy will play such a key role in union affairs as to make the combined power of unions and the bureaucracy overwhelmingly dominant in the formation of national policies.
8. Tocqueville, *Democracy in America*, cited in chapter 5, note 1, above.
9. Robert A. Nisbet, *Twilight of Authority*, New York: Oxford University Press, 1975, pp. 194–229.
10. The state of the nation in the Bicentennial year is assayed and found wanting in *The Public Interest*, Fall 1975. In his introduction, "The American Experiment," on page 7, Ambassador Daniel Patrick Moynihan writes, "Increasingly democracy is seen as an arrangement peculiar to a handful of North Atlantic countries plus a few of their colonies as the Greeks would have understood that term."

The current Idea of the Month is that democracies may be ungovernable. See, for example, Michael J. Crozier, Samuel P. Huntington, and Joji Watanuki, *The Crisis of Democracy*, New York: New York University Press, 1975.
11. Quoted by Victor Zorza, *The Washington Post*, November 27, 1975.

CHAPTER TEN
Japan — The High Cost of Insensitivity

1. Based on private conversations with Japanese intellectuals.
2. The relation of population to the power of a nation in the international arena is discussed in A. F. K. Organski, Alan Lamborn, and Bruce Bueno de Mesquita, "The Effective Population in International Politics," *Governance and Population: The*

Governmental Implications of Population Change, vol. IV of Research Papers Published by the Commission on Population Growth and the American Future, 1972. The authors point out the obvious distinction between aggregate population and "effective" population. The subsistence farmer is classified as a "non-effective" just as are most housewives, whereas the farmer in commercial agriculture and the woman in paid employment are part of the effective population.

The power of a nation is affected by the level of skills and economic productivity of individuals within the population, as well as by the effectiveness of the political and social system in mobilizing individuals for national effort. The authors point out, for example, that China in 1949 was in a state of collapse, yet in Korea only two years later the Chinese were able to fight the United States to a draw, since, for the first time, China had a political party and a bureaucracy that could mobilize a large faction of the population. Similarly, the Viet Cong and North Vietnamese provided effective power to the forces fighting South Vietnam and the United States far in excess of their numerical numbers. They suggest that the danger of conflict is most likely to occur when the relative power of the nations in an area shifts, either because of an aggregate population increase, an increase in the effective population through better economic organization, or a changed political system that more efficiently mobilizes the exertions and talents of the people for national purposes.

CHAPTER ELEVEN
Overhauling Our Foreign Policy Machinery

1. Dulles had expressed the wish to play a major role in "planning" foreign policy without having to assume the burden of running the State Department. Eisenhower, who had really wanted John J. McCloy as his Secretary of State, asked Dulles to enter his administration on a basis where McCloy would move up to Secretary and Dulles would move to the White House as Personal Advisor to the President. McCloy, who understood the bureaucracy, refused the appointment on the basis that the Secretary of State must also be the chief advisor to the President on foreign affairs. Townsend Hoopes, *The Devil and John Foster Dulles*, Boston: Atlantic–Little, Brown, 1973, p. 136.
2. *Report of the Commission on the Organization of the Government for the Conduct of Foreign Policy*, Washington: Government Printing Office, June 1975, p. 33.
3. See note 1, this chapter.
4. During my years in the State Department I was constantly depressed by the quality of the prose in which department officers sought to express their views, particularly because the department's memoranda and draft statements and speeches were likely to be compared unfavorably with products of the White House staff, composed largely of professional economists and political scientists used to writing for publication. I told the Foreign Service Association that I had been taught that "the simple declarative sentence was one of the major architectural achievements of man" but that I found no sympathy for that view in the State Department. Finally, I resorted to the expedient of sending particularly inept memoranda back to their authors with the scrawled comment: "Please send this to the translation department and have it put into English." I would recommend today that Mr. Edwin Newman's book *Strictly Speaking* be required reading for every candidate to the foreign service.
5. Report by Flora Lewis, *The New York Times*, July 4, 1974.
6. Paul Nitze, "Vladivostok and Crisis Stability," in Donald G. Brenner, *Arms Treaties with Moscow: Unequal Terms Unevenly Applied*, Washington: National Strategy Information Center, Inc., 1975, pp. ix, xv.
7. Nixon letters to Thieu released at President Ford's press conference, April 29, 1975.

8. Testimony of Senator Sam Ervin, "Congressional Oversight of Executive Agreements," *Hearings of the Subcommittee on Separation of Powers of Senate Committee on the Judiciary, U.S. Senate, 92nd Congress, 2nd Session*, on S. 3475, p. 3.
9. *The U.S. Code, Abbreviated*, No. 1, Section 112b, August 22, 1972, p. 22.
10. Due to a disagreement on the interpretation of the words used in the Italian text and the Ethiopian (Amharic) text, the Italians believed they had secured a protectorate over Ethiopia, whereas the Ethiopians assumed that they had signed an equal treaty of alliance with Italy, in which the latter had pledged its support to protect Ethiopia against other powers. Efforts by the Italian Government to assert its alleged protectorate led to war and the Italian invasion of Ethiopia. At the Battle of Adowa, the Italians suffered the loss of 20,000 men, all of whom were either killed or mutilated.

CHAPTER TWELVE
The Right of Privacy of Nations

1. Nicholas de B. Katzenbach, "Foreign Policy, Public Opinion and Secrecy," *Foreign Affairs*, October 1973, pp. 1, 15, 16: "We should abandon publicly all covert operations designed to influence political results in foreign countries. Specifically, there should be no secret subsidies of police or counter-insurgency forces, no efforts to influence elections, no secret monetary subsidies of groups sympathetic to the United States, whether governmental, non-governmental or revolutionary. We should confine our covert activities overseas to the gathering of intelligence information."
    Because of his judgment and integrity, and his very considerable experience as Attorney General and Under Secretary of State, Mr. Katzenbach's views on this matter deserve thoughtful consideration.
2. The "just war" doctrine as applied to the CIA is discussed in Ernest W. Lefever, "The CIA and American Foreign Policy," *Lugano Review*, LR 4, 1974–1975.
3. Thomas A. Bailey, *A Diplomatic History of the American People* (eighth edition), New York: Appleton-Century-Crofts, 1969, p. 30.
4. According to estimates made by Senator Proxmire, intelligence funds and personnel are distributed as follows:

	Funds (millions of dollars)	Personnel
CIA	$ 750	15,000
NSA	$1,000	20,000
Army Intelligence	$ 775	38,500
Air Force Intelligence	$2,800 *	60,000
Navy Intelligence	$ 775	10,000
DIA	$ 100	5,000
State Department	$ 8	350
Total	$6,208	148,850

* Includes National Reconnaissance Office

5. *Congressional Record*, December 9, 1975, pp. H.12166–68.

6. Professor Arthur M. Schlesinger, Jr., testimony before the Select Committee on Intelligence, House of Representatives, December 11, 1975.

CHAPTER THIRTEEN
The Danger from Mankind's Second Enemy

1. Professor Robert L. Heilbroner has listed a number of natural disasters that may overtake us if we continue our present habits of wasting resources or if we generate excessive heat through the production of nonsolar energy. Heilbroner, *An Inquiry into the Human Prospect*, New York: Norton, 1974. Potential catastrophes are also described in Mihajlo Mesarovic and Eduard Pestel, *Mankind at the Turning Point*, London: Hutchinson & Co., 1975, a second report to the Club of Rome that substantially qualifies the doomsday tone of the original report (*The Limits of Growth*) and suggests the desirability of "organic" as against "undifferentiated" growth. Another critique of the original Club of Rome report is H. Cole et al., *Thinking About the Future: A Critique of the Limits to Growth*, London: Chatto & Windus, Sussex University Press, 1973.
2. The evolution of the concept of progress is still best told in that old standby, J. B. Bury, *The Idea of Progress*, New York: Macmillan, 1932; reprint, New York: Dover, 1955.
3. Myrdal expressed these concerns in his Godkin Lectures at Harvard in 1938. Gunnar Myrdal, *Population: A Problem for Democracy*, 1940; reprint, Gloucester, Mass.: Peter Smith, 1962, p. 9.
4. There are two kinds of population projections: those based on the assumption that current population growth rates and current mortality rates will continue indefinitely (which would manifestly be impossible, given the limited growth rate of the earth's carrying capacity), and projections that assume that any of a variety of factors will probably operate to influence the curves. In general, it seems prudent to use the "medium projection" made by the Population Division of the United Nations, as readjusted in 1973. ("World Population Prospects, 1970–2000, as Assessed in 1973," Population Division, Department of Economic Affairs of the United Nations Secretariat, March 10, 1975.) That publication also includes projections based on a low and high variant as well as a constant variant, but the medium variant projections are generally regarded as the most likely to be realized. In addition, projections of population growth are critically examined in Bernard Berelson et al., *World Population: Status Report 1974* (Population Council, 1974). Thomas Frejka, "The Prospects for a Stationary World Population," *Scientific American*, March 1973. *A Report on Bucharest, World Population Conference, August, 1974* (Population Council, 1974), and Michael S. Teitelbaum, "Population and Development: Is a Consensus Possible?" *Foreign Affairs*, July 1974.
5. Frejka, p. 3.
6. This chapter seeks in a very compressed way to consider some aspects of the relation of population, technology, and resources to violence and political and international instability. It is a subject which has so far been given little attention by scholars and largely ignored in the shaping of foreign policy. A few studies of the subject are particularly useful: Robert C. North and Nazli Choucri, "Population and the International System: Some Implications for United States Policy and Planning," in *Governance and Population: The Governmental Implications of Population Change* (vol. IV of Research Papers Published by the Commission on Population Growth and the American Future, 1972); Nazli Choucri, *Population Dynamics and International Violence*, Lexington, Mass.: Lexington Books, 1974; and Myron Weiner, "Political Demography: An Inquiry into the Political Consequences of Population Change" (reprint from *Rapid Population Growth*, edited by Roger Ravelle, Baltimore: Johns Hopkins Press, 1971). Professor Choucri's book is of particular interest since she considers the conflict implications not only of the

size of populations but of their composition, distribution, and change. In the course of her study she examines 45 conflicts in developing areas that have occurred since the Second World War.

7. Although the Malthusians feared that population growth and the limitation on resources would make war inevitable, the Marxists contend that, if the world's resources were properly utilized and distributed according to sound Marxist principles, there would be no limit to the population the earth could support. However, they argue, Malthusian pressures will operate on a capitalist society where distribution is unequal. On the basis of this glib analysis, the Soviet representatives do not hesitate to talk nonsense regarding international efforts to encourage the expansion of world agriculture and bring about essential constraints on population growth.

8. Books and articles that have posed the problem of population outpacing food supplies in the most alarmist terms are William and Paul Paddock, *Famine — 1975* (1967), Paul Ehrlich, *The Population Bomb* (1968), and a subsequent, more scholarly, and less polemical book, Paul Ehrlich and Ann H. Ehrlich, *Population, Resources, Environment: Issues in Human Ecology* (second edition), San Francisco: W. H. Freeman, 1972; Garrett Hardin, "Living on a Lifeboat," *Bioscience*, October 1974; and Wade Greene, "Triage," *The New York Times Magazine*, January 5, 1975.

9. Alan Berg, "The Trouble with Triage," *The New York Times Magazine*, June 15, 1975.

10. An additional concern which a number of serious scientists have expressed is that we may be facing changes in the weather that could profoundly affect the production of food in a number of major agricultural countries. On the whole these predictions would seem to favor an increase in food production in the United States and a decrease in the Soviet Union. Tom Alexander, "Ominous Changes in the World's Weather," *Fortune*, February 1974, p. 90.

11. Philip Handler in a speech at National Press Club, April 3, 1975.

12. Konrad Lorenz, *On Aggression*, New York: Harcourt, 1966, pp. 229–230, and Robert Ardrey, *The Social Contract*, New York: Atheneum, 1970, pp. 135–136 and 269–270.

13. Recently a panel of Indian social scientists reported that the country must try to stabilize its nearly 600 million population at 900 million, even if that should require such Draconian measures as coercive birth control. Certainly the attainment of that goal would require an enormously greater effort to constrain the rate of population growth than the Indian Government is now making. The recommendations of these social scientists should be taken with the utmost seriousness by the central government and the governments of the Indian states. It is at least theoretically possible that a campaign of hitherto undreamt-of dimensions could hold India's growth to around 900 million by the year 2000, although even then the built-in momentum of the youthful population would carry it far beyond that figure before it stabilizes.

14. Population pressures have long been assumed to have been a major factor impelling the expansion of the Greek city-states between 500 and 100 B.C., as well as the explosion of Islam between A.D. 700 and 1200 and the colonial adventures of the European powers in the nineteenth and twentieth centuries.

I have noted earlier in Chapter 8 that population pressure on the Egyptian economy was a major factor impelling President Sadat to try to buy time through the Sinai truce. Indeed, population pressures and induced migration are significant elements in the whole Middle East conflict, particularly because of the differentials in population, resources, and technology so clearly and abrasively evident.

Today attention is also focused on Lebanon, where demography obviously plays a central role because of the unspoken desire of much of the population to maintain an uneasy balance between the Marronite and Islamic populations. No census has been taken since 1935, even though it has been widely recognized that the Islamic population has been growing faster than the Christian.

Latin America is another area where population variables — density, migration, distribution — have played a political role. One example cited by Professor Choucri (p. 10) is the war between El Salvador and Honduras in July 1969.

15. In outlining the kind of program essential to keep people on the farms and away from cities, I have drawn heavily on Jonathan Power, "The Alternative to Starvation," *Encounter*, November 1975, pp. 11–35.

16. The bureaucratic play of forces that ultimately led the United States to undertake some responsibility for encouraging family planning in less developed countries is graphically described in Phyllis Tilson Piotrow, *World Population Crisis — The United States Response*, New York: Praeger, 1973. The chronicle is a study in bureaucratic frustration. In 1959, President Eisenhower categorically rebuffed proposals that the United States undertake an effort in that direction, stating: "This government, as long as I am here, will not have a positive political doctrine in its program that has to do with the problem of birth control. That's not our business."

Although a Catholic, President Kennedy showed greater flexibility, interposing no objections when the State Department, for the first time, appointed a full-time population officer, attached to my office at a time when I was Under Secretary of State for Economic Affairs. I had on my staff at that time a small group prepared to take heroic risks to move America toward what they conceived an essential role, including Robert Schaetzel, Henry Owen, and Robert A. Barnett, the new population officer, together with Richard Gardner, who was then Deputy Assistant Secretary for International Organization Affairs. They pursued shrewd bureaucratic strategy to induce top officials of departments to face up to the problem.

During the early 1960s — after foreign aid had been transferred into an independent agency (AID) — this small nucleus of skilled maneuverers hammered away with the argument that population increases were nullifying one-third of our aid effort. For a long while, the development economists, doctrinally committed to comprehensive country planning, refused to admit that long-term development loans would not provide the total answer. Besides, they were put off by an issue such as family planning that might complicate their relations with the Congress. Oddly enough, Congressional leaders were far ahead of AID. Senator Fulbright took a major initiative in trying to bring the problem to the point of Congressional action, and the situation dramatically changed when President Johnson announced in his State of the Union message on January 4, 1965, that he would "seek new ways to use our knowledge to help deal with the explosion in world population and the growing scarcity in world resources." Nevertheless, against the resistance of the AID economists, little serious action would have been taken had not the monsoon rains failed twice in India — once in 1965 and again in 1966 — while floods and droughts plagued other food-producing areas. Thus, it was clear that world food production would never suffice to feed the 35 million additional human beings added to the world population every year. Congress moved ahead of the bureaucracy to amend the food for peace program to provide resources to promote voluntary family planning activities and within a few months policy shifted toward a more active role.

A major new force was brought to bear when Philander P. Claxton, Jr., was appointed in April 1966 as Special Assistant to the Secretary of State for Population Matters. Claxton was quietly persuasive and thoroughly experienced in pursuing matters through the bureaucratic underbrush, and he had the full support of the President. In his 1967 State of the Union message, President Johnson said: "Next to the pursuit of peace, the really great challenge to the human family is the race between food supply and population increase. That race tonight is being lost, the time for rhetoric is clearly past. The time for concerted action is here, and we must get on with the job."

Meanwhile, Robert S. McNamara, as President of the World Bank, had turned the resources of the bank toward the problem of population growth as a major obstacle to economic development, while Richard Gardner was playing an extremely useful role in the United Nations. During the debate over the second United Nations development decade, he repeatedly focused the attention of governments on the relation of growth to per capita income. In 1969, the Secretary General recommended that a Third World Population Conference be held in 1974, and that 1974 be designated World Population Year.

CHAPTER FOURTEEN
Old Dangers with a New Immediacy

1. George W. Ball, *The Discipline of Power,* Boston: Atlantic–Little, Brown, 1968, pp. 198–220.
2. The issues involved in the Review Conference were well summarized by a report of a panel organized by the United Nations Association of the United States which served as the basis for a discussion with a parallel Soviet Panel. *NPT — The Review Conference and Beyond,* New York: The United Nations Association of the United States, 1975. Another useful reference is a volume of discussion papers prepared in advance of an unofficial international meeting held under the auspices of the Arms Control Association and the Carnegie Endowment for International Peace in Divonne, France, from September 9 to September 11, 1974, to examine the issues in advance of the Review Conference. *NPT: Paradoxes and Problems,* Washington, D.C.: The Arms Control Association, 1975. The work of the conference was reviewed by Thomas A. Halstead, *Non-Proliferation Today,* New York: Carnegie Endowment for International Peace, No. 6, May 29, 1975.
3. Fred C. Ikle, statement before the Subcommittee on International Finance of the Senate Committee on Banking, Housing and Urban Affairs, July 15, 1975.
4. *The New York Times,* June 18, 1975. A guarded indication as to the results of the discussion appeared in *The New York Times,* February 24, 1976, p. 1.
5. See, for example, views of unidentified military experts referred to in Tom Alexander, "Our Costly Losing Battle Against Nuclear Proliferation," *Fortune,* December 1975, pp. 143, 150.
6. The normal practice in the past has been for the United States to guarantee firm contracts for enrichment services for the life of the reactor. Although the vendors can make the sale without fuel guarantees, this has not been the case. Recently, however, some sales have been made to countries obtaining their uranium or enrichment services, or both, from other sources, such as the Soviet Union. But most of the operating United States reactors around the world have been accompanied by long-term contracts for enrichment services with the United States Government. Sometimes the Export-Import Bank financing has applied to both reactor and fuel as a package. The enrichment contracts have been made with AEC (now ERDA) and licensed by AEC (now Nuclear Regulatory Commission).

In the case of Iran, our consent to export reactors and fuels was conditioned on a mutual agreement between the two countries as to where the plutonium from the reactors was to be stored or processed. Much to the dismay of the United States vendors, the Iranians rejected this condition. Presumably they have in mind buying reactors from the French or Germans, in the hope that the fuel can come from the Eurodif diffusion plants (of which the Iranians own a 20 percent share) scheduled to come on line in 1985. Or from the Eurenco Gas Centrifuge. However, these sources are unlikely to provide enough fuel to supply all Western European needs, much less back up international sales.

CHAPTER FIFTEEN
The First, Third, Fourth, and Fifth Worlds

1. Daniel Patrick Moynihan, "The United States in Opposition," *Commentary,* March 1974, pp. 31–44.

2. I have relied heavily on a statement of the demands of the poor nations by Mr. Mahbub Ul Haq of the World Bank and on various speeches of Professor Richard Gardner.

3. Robert W. Tucker, "Egalitarianism and International Politics," *Commentary*, September 1975. The thesis has been elegantly refuted by Professor P. T. Bauer, "Western Guilt and Third World Poverty," *Commentary*, January 1976.

4. See, for example, Ronald Muller and Richard J. Barnet, *Global Reach — The Power of the Multinational Corporations*, New York: Simon and Schuster, 1975.

CHAPTER SIXTEEN
Checking the Compass and Correcting the Course

1. Norman A. Graebner, *The New Isolationism*, New York: The Ronald Press, 1955, p. 23.

2. Robert W. Tucker, *A New Isolationism, Threat or Promise?* New York: Universe Books, 1972. Professor Tucker writes on p. 33, "The belief in unilateralism, the insistence upon retaining complete independence of action . . . formed the essential base of the old isolationism. . . ."

3. Heikal, cited in note 8, Chapter 6.

CHAPTER SEVENTEEN
The American Role

1. James MacGregor Burns, *Uncommon Sense*, New York: Harper and Row, 1972, p. 53. So long as America maintains its commitments to Taiwan, *de jure* relations with Peking will continue to be ruled out. Nixon and Kissinger went far in the Shanghai Communiqué to deny the Taiwanese the right of self-determination by explicitly refusing to "challenge" the contention that "there is but one China and that Taiwan is a part of China," which had the effect of making Taiwan an "internal" matter in which the United States could not interfere. Yet, should we be party to letting Peking take over the people of Taiwan without providing the Taiwanese a free and honest opportunity for self-determination? To do so would make a total mockery of all our protestations during the Vietnam War that we were fighting to preserve the right of free choice for the South Vietnamese.

After all, as our former ambassador to Japan, Edwin Reischauer, has pointed out, Taiwan has a larger population and a greater GNP than two-thirds of the members of the United Nations. Of Taiwan's 14 million people, more than 12 million are Taiwanese, and the great majority of the Taiwanese seem to want a Taiwan separate from China and a government they themselves control.

2. Although it is trendy today to dismiss the whole idea of the "melting pot" as a conspiracy of white Anglo-Saxon Protestants to homogenize the citizenry, the phrase was, in fact, first used in 1908 as the title of a play by Israel Zangwill, one of the earliest Zionist leaders, who saw America as a crucible in which immigrants from all over Europe could be transformed into a new race. A new melting pot is now boiling away in Israel, another country taking shape out of an amalgam of immigrants from diverse lands, but there the government is wisely not going out of its way to emphasize Yemeni or Iraqi or Ukrainian or even American cultural differences — and with good reason. There is nothing more sterile than an expatriate culture shut off from its wellsprings and synthetically sustained.

3. The distinction between "equality of condition" and "equality of opportunity" or "equality before the law" is, of course, fundamental. The attempt to bring about "equality of condition" or, as one sociologist has called it, "equality of entitlements" is a substantial departure from American constitutional tradition. Today the most conspicuous example of this trend is represented by the so-called "affir-

mative action" programs designed to improve the lot of minority groups by suppressing discrimination in industrial hiring and in higher education. Its practical effect is to force educational institutions to practice racial and sexual discrimination in hiring, admissions, and other areas.

Programs of this kind necessarily require the building of all-encompassing bureaucracies that more and more interfere with the freedom of individual action and decision. The tradeoff between equality of condition and the loss of personal liberty is paralleled by the tradeoff between equality of condition and the loss of the efficiency necessary if the world is to produce enough goods to meet human requirements at substantially above the subsistence level. Arthur M. Okun, *Equality and Efficiency — The Big Tradeoff*, Washington, D.C.: The Brookings Institution, 1975. One of the most forceful statements of the problem has been made by Professor Robert Nisbet, *Twilight of Authority*, New York: Oxford University Press, 1975, pp. 194–229. He points out that equality of opportunity can be achieved only through the creation of an enormous political apparatus. He foresees the advance of this concept, along with the breaking down of the political community, the dislocation of the family and of voluntary association in our society. This can operate to create a political condition in which a strongly nationalized system of equality might come into being.

What Nisbet foresees is, of course, merely the realization of Tocqueville's prophecy that democracy would inevitably lead to equality and, hence, the erosion of individual liberty. The result could be uniformity and leveling and a degree of state intrusion into, and interference with, personal lives that Americans even a generation ago would have found appalling.

4. Daniel Bell, "The End of American Exceptionalism," *The Public Interest*, Fall 1975. The whole issue of the magazine is devoted to essays on "The American Commonwealth, 1976" and the general tone is one of considerable pessimism as to America's continued national effectiveness and preeminence.

Index